Tasty Trivia

A Collection of Interesting Food Facts

Nancy Slade

Copyright ©Nancy Slade
ISBN-13: 978-1979431859
ISBN-10: 197943185X

To family and friends near and far.

You add flavor to my life.

Acknowledgments

Trivia is defined as details or pieces of information of little importance or value. The information contained within this book won't change your life but it may entertain you and you might even find something useful. For me, the next best thing to eating food is talking about it, and I will add researching it too. I learned so much from the people I corresponded with and interviewed. I would especially like to thank Debby Duncan, Stephanie Van Coops, and Julie Hynson for sharing their insights. I would also like to thank the websites listed below for providing a lot of information. Sometimes I discovered conflicting facts that I had to sort through but, in the end, I included enough bits of trivia to make things interesting. To the many food blogs that I read for pure enjoyment, thank you for the chuckles (and recipes). A heartfelt thanks to the publishing company Createspace for the support it provides its authors, and to my husband, Steve, for all of his encouragement.

catholiccuisine.com	whfoods.com	authoritynutrition.com
herbinfosite.com	seriouseats.com	oldtimecandyshop.com
icecream.com	history.com	serving-ice-cream.com
organicfacts.net	nationalfooddays.com	thefoodtimes.org
healthdiaries.com	the kitchen.com	nutrition-and-you.com
spice-racks.com	encyclopedia.com	culinary arts.about.com
thefactsite.com	randomhistory.com	foods-healingpower.com
foodpyramid.com	dinerlingo.com	specialtyproduce.com
beef.org	hot-dog.org	smithsonian.com
amazingribs.com	pork.org	whoinventedit.net
foodreference.com	dairygoodness.ca	freshdaily.com
lifescript.com	fishchoice.com	delishably.com
cookingfishmonger.com	saltworks.us	thepoultryguide.com
answers.com	thenibble.com	wisegeek.com
popcorn.org	candyfavorites.com	sherlocks.com
beveragehistory.com	teaanswers.com	bestfoodfacts.org
foodtimeline.org	cooksinfo.com	seriouseats.com
candyhistory.net	candycrate.com	reference.com
nationalhistoriccheesemakingcenter.org		thefreedictionary.com
dailyhealthlifestyles.com	organicauthority.com	international dairy foods association

Cover photo ©monticellllo

Chapters

"Let food be thy medicine and medicine be thy food."
Hippocrates
Ancient Greek Physician
460-370 B.C.

**If you have food allergies or are on certain medications, consult your
health care provider before adding any new foods to your diet.**

CHAPTER 1

Sugar and Spice and Everything Nice

Spices and herbs, fresh or dried, are parts of plants that are used to enhance the flavor of foods. The difference between the two is where they are obtained from a plant. Herb refers to any green or leafy part of a plant used for seasoning and flavoring a recipe but not used as the main ingredient. Spice refers to bark, root, berry, seed, twig, or other plant matter other than the leaves, used for seasoning and flavoring. Spices are usually dried before being used to season foods. Herbs are grown in temperate areas; spices are grown in more tropical countries. Herbs have great medicinal value and are also used in cosmetic products. They've also been known to preserve foods. Spices start to lose their flavor when they are ground so, whenever possible, grind your own spices immediately before using them. Spices last longer when stored in a cool place and any that are older than six months should be replaced. The term 'seasoning' is used for items added during cooking and condiment refers to flavorings added at the table.

ALLSPICE

Allspice is mainly grown in Jamaica. It is the only spice whose production is confined to the New World because no one has been able to successfully cultivate it in other parts of the world. It is mostly used in pickling, in baking, in condiments like ketchup, and in chewing gum, ice cream, and soft drinks. Active principles in allspice have been found to have anti-inflammatory and anti-flatulent properties. It aids in digestion and is useful in dental treatment procedures. Allspice is enriched with a good amount of minerals as well as vitamins A, B6 and C, riboflavin, and niacin. The fruit and leaf oil are used in men's toiletries – any time you see the word 'spice' in the name of a product, the fragrance comes in part from allspice oil.

The Mayans used allspice to embalm the bodies of important leaders. The Arawak Indians of the Caribbean used allspice to cure and preserve meats – this was called *boucan*. Europeans who learned to cure meat with allspice were called *boucaniers* (buccaneers). In the nineteenth century, Russian soldiers put allspice in their boots to keep their feet warm, and it also helped with foot odor.

NOTE: Chapter 1's title is from the popular nursery rhyme dating from the early nineteenth century, "What Are Little Boys Made Of? "

ANISE

All above-ground parts of the young anise plant can be eaten as a vegetable but it is the seeds that are mainly used in cooking. Anise seeds, available in whole or ground form, as well as an essential oil, have a strong licorice-like taste and odor. They are used in soups, stews and curry, and sausage and pepperoni seasonings. They are added to cakes, cookies, pastries, sweet breads, and candy. The seeds are also the basis for alcoholic beverages like Absinthe, Anisette, Ouzo, and Sambuca. Anise seeds have many health benefits, mainly as a digestive aid, and are used for coughs in the form of lozenges. Anise oil destroys lice and other itch-inducing insect bites and is said to be a bait for mice. It is poisonous to pigeons.

Native of Egypt, Greece, Crete, and Asia Minor, anise was cultivated by the ancient Egyptians for at least four thousand years. It was often used for tithes, offerings, and payment of taxes. In first century Rome, anise was a flavoring in a spice cake eaten after a feast to prevent indigestion. The ancient Romans also hung anise plants near their pillows to prevent bad dreams and used it to ward off epileptic attacks. King Edward IV of England (1442-1483) was said to have slept on bed linens that had been perfumed with anise. Anise became so valued in England that its import was taxed and the tax helped pay for repairs to the London Bridge. During the 1800s, Germans believed in the medicinal value of anise and often flavored their household bread with whole aniseed.

NOTE: Anise is not botanically related to star anise.

ARROWROOT

The arrowroot plant belongs to the same family as ginger. The herb is obtained from the fleshy roots. Native to the West Indies and Central America, it was first used for religious and medicinal purposes. The indigenous individuals used it in wounds inflicted by poison arrows, hence its name. Today, it helps with urinary infections, digestion difficulties, nausea, colic, and as a calming cream for black spider bites and gangrene. It is also used in face powders, glue, paper, textiles, and confectionery items.

Arrowroot is also the name of the edible starch produced from the arrowroot plant. The fine white powder is used as a thickener in cooking because it is easily digestible and has about twice the thickening power as flour. It produces a clear sauce with a glossy finish so it is great for fruit glazes and light sauces.

"But in truth, should I meet with gold or spices in great quantity, I shall remain till I collect as much as possible, and for this purpose I am proceeding solely in quest of them."

Christopher Columbus   1451-1506

Italian explorer

ASAFETIDA

Asafetida, obtained from the gum of a giant fennel, is native to Iran and Afghanistan. Before it is cooked, this spice has an unpleasant smell and is known as Devil's Dung and Stinking Gum. It should be used in small quantities and stored in an airtight container as its sulfurous odor will affect other foods and spices. When lightly fried, the aroma is similar to onion and garlic. It adds flavor to pan-fried fish and is used on salted fish, grilled or roasted meats, and with vegetables like lentils. Alexander the Great carried the giant fennel west in 4 B.C. and it was used as a spice in ancient Rome. It has been used in Indian cooking and medicine for centuries. Asafetida was prescribed for respiratory conditions like asthma, bronchitis and whooping cough, and was believed to enhance a singer's voice. In some countries in olden times, a small piece of the resin was tied on a string and hung around children's necks – the strong odor was thought to protect them from disease. Asafetida was used to treat hysteria in the past and in the Wild West it was included in a mixture with other strong spices as a cure for alcoholism.

BASIL

Basil is Greek for royal or kingly – the Greeks believed only the sovereign himself should be allowed to cut the basil, armed with his golden sickle. Ancient Greek and Roman doctors thought basil would only grow if its cultivators sowed the seeds while shouting unintelligibly. In India, the basil plant is sacred to both Krishna and Vishnu and is cherished in every Hindu house. A good Hindu goes to his rest with a basil leaf on his breast, his passport to Paradise. Basil has always been a token of love in India. When a Romanian man accepts a sprig of basil from a woman, he is engaged.

Native to India and Asia where it has been cultivated for at least five thousand years, basil is now cultivated worldwide but Egypt is the principal source. It is a leafy, fragrant bush that only grows in the summer. There are many varieties of basil, different in appearance and taste. The most common type is Mediterranean sweet basil. Purple basil is less sweet. Other varieties offer flavors like lemon, anise, and cinnamon. Asian basil has a strong clove-like flavor and Thai basil has a licorice flavor. Basil leaves are used to flavor vegetables, poultry, or meat. The herb is also used in tomato and egg dishes, stews, soups, and salads. Italian large leaf basil is one of the main ingredients in pesto sauce.

Also called Saint-Joseph's-wort, basil has antioxidant and anti-inflammatory properties that improve cardiovascular health, digestive health, and boost the immune system. The essential oil enhances skin and hair health. Basil seeds resemble chia seeds and have the potential to help reduce appetite and food cravings. The seeds provide concentrated nutrition and fiber.

<h1 style="text-align:center">BAY LEAVES</h1>

Bay leaf, native to the Mediterranean region, is from the evergreen bay laurel tree. It can be used fresh or dry (fresh ones are rarely available) and dried ones have a stronger flavor. Bay leaves are usually simmered in a sauce and then removed before serving – but not because they are poisonous, which some people believe. (There are some types of bay leaf that are poisonous, such as the cherry laurel and mountain laurel, but these varieties aren't sold as herbs.) Bay leaves are a good source of vitamins A, B-complex and C, and minerals like copper, potassium, calcium, iron, selenium, zinc, manganese and magnesium. It has astringent, diuretic, and appetite stimulant properties. The lauric acid in the leaves have insect repellent properties. The components in the essential oil can be used in the treatment of arthritis, muscle pain, bronchitis, and flu symptoms. Bay leaf was highly praised by the ancient Greeks and the Romans who believed the herb symbolized wisdom, peace, and protection. Champions of the Olympic games wore garlands of bay leaves, and bay leaves and branchlets were used as wreaths to crown their victors. The word 'baccalaureate' means laurel berries and signifies the successful completion of one's studies, reminiscent of the bay leaf wreaths worn by poets and scholars when they received academic honors in ancient Greece.

Chamomile is a soothing, gentle relaxant with an apple-like aroma and flavor. The name chamomile is derived from the Greek *kamai* melon, meaning 'ground apple.' It is most often taken as a mild therapeutic tea. Concentrated extracts of chamomile are added to healing creams and lotions or packaged as pills and tinctures.

<h1 style="text-align:center">CARDAMOM</h1>

Cardamom, originating in India, Nepal, and Bhutan, is one of the oldest spices in the world and one of the world's most expensive spices. Cardamom is made from the seed pods of various plants in the ginger family. It is mainly used in Indian and Middle Eastern cuisine. Using whole cardamom pods is preferable because ground cardamom powder isn't as flavorful. Toast the pods in a dry skillet for a few minutes then remove the seeds from the pods and grind them before use. Cardamom is added to hot and spicy dishes as well as desserts and beverages. In the ancient Indian and Chinese science of medicine, it was believed to be a remedy for teeth and gum infections, throat problems, congestion of the lungs, gastrointestinal disorders, and gall bladder stones. It was also used as an antidote for poisons and venoms. Cardamom was traditionally believed to possess aphrodisiac properties and to cure impotency. It is rich in various vitamins and nutrients and the oil has antimicrobial and anti-inflammatory properties. Cardamom can lower cholesterol, relieve cardiovascular issues, and improve blood circulation. It is also useful for curing dental diseases and urinary tract infections. The seeds can be chewed as a breath freshener and are a popular ingredient in chewing gum.

CARAWAY

Caraway seeds, native to Asia and parts of Europe, are the small ripe fruit of the caraway plant, a member of the parsley family. The root can be eaten and the leaves can be used as an herb. The seeds were found in Switzerland dating back eight thousand years. Their use was first recorded in Egypt in 1552 B.C. The ancient Romans used the root as a vegetable (similar to a parsnip). Caraway seeds have a sharp aroma and are similar in flavor to aniseed. The seeds can be used in pickling and brining, and are found in most types of rye and brown breads. The seeds flavor curries, soups, stews, sausage, cheese, and liqueurs like the Scandinavian spirit aquavit. British seed cake is traditionally made with caraway seeds. Some people chew raw caraway seeds to aid in digestion, promote appetite, and sweeten breath. The seeds are a rich source of dietary fiber and have several health benefiting nutrients, minerals, vitamins and antioxidants.

CHERVIL

Chervil, from the parsley family of herbs, has a unique delicate scent and flavor, similar to but milder than tarragon and fennel. It resembles flat-leaf parsley but its leaves are paler green. It is also known as sweet cicily or gourmet's parsley. Originating in Eastern Europe and Western Asia, it is often used in French cooking, such as in béarnaise sauce. It complements mild dishes like sole and other white fish, chicken, eggs, zucchini, salads, sauces, and soups. Its flavor is best fresh so add it near the end of cooking. In ancient medical texts, the leaves soaked in vinegar were believed to cure hiccups. Chervil can be used to lower blood pressure or as a digestive aid. The leaves are helpful if you have eczema or acne. Chevril is beneficial for people who suffer from kidney or bladder disorders. It is a great source for minerals like potassium, manganese and calcium, vitamins B and C, and beta carotene. It is also a favored ingredient in lotions and cleansers. Dried chervil leaves added to dried flowers make fragrant potpourri.

CHIVE

Chives are an herb native to the northern parts of Europe, Siberia, and North America. They are the smallest member of the onion family and can be used as a substitute for chopped green onions. They have a delicate flavor and can be mixed into cream cheese, sour cream, cottage cheese, or butter. Freeze-dried chives are almost equal to fresh chives and can be substituted in equal amounts. Recipes that include chives date back at least 5,000 years in China. Rumanian Gypsies used chives as part of their fortune telling rituals. When dried bunches of chives were hung in a house it was believed to drive away disease and evil influences. Chives contain many flavonoid antioxidants, minerals like calcium and potassium, and vitamins A, B6, C and K. They are also an excellent source of folic acid and dietary fiber. They have antibiotic and anti-inflammatory qualities, lower high blood pressure, and may help the body digest food better and utilize more nutrients food provides.

"Part of the secret of success in life is to eat what you like and let the food fight it out inside."
Mark Twain   1835 - 1910
American humorist & writer

CILANTRO

Cilantro is often mistaken for flat-leaf parsley in appearance. Its flavor has a hint of pepper, mint and lemon. People either love it or hate it. Cilantro matches well with avocado, chicken, fish, lamb, lentils, mayonnaise, peppers, pork, rice, salads, salsas, shellfish, tomatoes, and yogurt. The cilantro herb is native to the Mediterranean and Asia Minor regions. It is mentioned in the Medical Papyrus of Thebes written in 1552 B.C. and is one of the plants that grew in the Hanging Gardens of Babylon. Ancient Greek and Roman physicians believed it had medicinal powers. The Hebrews added it to an herb mixture used at Passover. The herb is one of the earliest plantings in North America, dating back to 1670. Cilantro has many health-promoting properties. It is low in calories and contains no cholesterol. The deep-green leaves have good amounts of antioxidants, dietary fiber, essential oils, and vitamins like A, C, and K. (Vitamin K plays a role in the treatment of Alzheimer's disease). It is also a good source of minerals such as potassium, calcium, manganese, iron, and magnesium. The seed of the cilantro plant is known as coriander but their flavors are different and cannot be substituted for each other.

CINNAMON

Cinnamon is the dried inner bark of a species of evergreen tree. It is one of the first known spices and was used in ancient Egypt to flavor food and beverages, and also as an embalming agent. It is mentioned several times in the Old Testament as an ingredient in anointing oil (Noah used it to anoint the ark). The Romans used it as a love potion and also believed its fragrance was sacred. They burned it at funerals and in 65 A.D., Nero burned a year's supply of cinnamon at his second wife's funeral. In Chinese medicine, cinnamon has been used to treat colds, flatulence, nausea, and diarrhea. Medieval physicians used it to treat coughing, hoarseness, and sore throats. It has many health benefits today too, as in the treatment of diabetes, arthritis, high cholesterol, and memory function. Cinnamon can be used for the preservation of food because of its antimicrobial properties. It is also used in the cosmetic industry in various lotions and creams. Much of North America's cinnamon comes from Southeast Asia.

By the eleventh century, spices were used in place of currency in many instances.
In the Middle Ages, a person's social rank was determined by the number of spices
they could afford to buy.

CLOVES

Cloves are actually dried flower buds of the clove tree, a tropical evergreen that can live up to one hundred years. The buds are picked before the flower opens. The tree is indigenous to the Maluka Islands of Indonesia but cloves also grow naturally in India, the West Indies, Tanzania, Sri Lanka, Brazil, and Madagascar. Today, the leading producer of cloves is the island of Pemba, the smaller sister island of Zanzibar. The name 'clove' comes from the French word *clou*, which means nail (take a good look at one).

For over two thousand years, Indian and Chinese traditional medicine used cloves and clove oil. Arabic traders brought the buds to Europe in the fourth century, where they became popular as a food preservative during the seventh and eighth centuries. Cloves have been one of the major spices in European commerce. They were extremely costly and wars were fought to secure exclusive rights to the clove business. In the Moluccas, an archipelago within Indonesia, parents planted a clove tree when a child was born. They believed that the fate of the tree was linked to the fate of the child.

Cloves have a pungent aroma and a sweet and spicy flavor. Whole cloves can be used in pomander balls, as garnishes, to stud fruit, ham or onions, and for decorating gingerbread and other cookies. In manufacturing, clove is used in toothpaste, soaps, cosmetics, perfumes, and cigarettes. Cloves have many health benefits. They are used for upset stomach, diarrhea, hernia, nausea, toothache, bad breath, and as an expectorant.

CORIANDER

Coriander is the dried seed of the cilantro plant. (In North America, its leaves are more popular than its seed.) Native to the Mediterranean and Asia Minor regions, the seeds have been found in ruins in Southern Europe dating back to 5000 B.C. Coriander was mentioned in the Bible and found in tombs of pharaohs. It was introduced to Britain by the Romans, who used it for cooking and in medicine. The seeds are now produced in Russia, India, South America, Morocco, and Holland.

Coriander can refer to both an herb and a spice. It has a sweet taste with a touch of citrus. Ground coriander seed loses flavor quickly so it is best when freshly ground. The most common use of coriander seed is in curry powders and *garam masala*, an aromatic blend of spices from India. It is also used in stews, soups, Italian mortadella sausage, breads and baked goods, pickling spices, and with smoked meats. Sugared comfits made from coriander seeds, consisting of dried fruits, nuts, seeds or spices coated with sugar candy, are a traditional confectionery. Health benefits include its use in the treatment of skin disorders, high cholesterol, anemia, indigestion, smallpox, blood sugar disorders, and eye care. It has eleven components of essential oils, minerals, and vitamins. Coriander symbolizes hidden worth.

CREAM OF TARTAR

Cream of tartar is refined tartaric acid, the brownish-red powder that becomes a crust on the walls of wine casks. The French discovered that after it is refined into a white acidic powder it can be used to add an extra 'bite' to baked goods. It is also a leavening agent in baking powders and stabilizes delicate toppings like meringue. It gives a creamy texture to frostings, desserts, and candies. It is used as an ingredient in some soft drinks and gelatin desserts. When boiling vegetables, add a little cream of tartar to reduce discoloring. Cream of tartar is often used to clean brass or copper items, and stained bathtubs. It can brighten delicate whites and it will repel ants when combined with vinegar. It is also useful in photography products. Cream of tartar is used to naturally treat urinary tract infections and heartburn.

CUMIN

Cumin is native to the Nile valley and dates back over five thousand years. The ancient Egyptians used it as a spice in foods as well as in the mummification process. Ancient Greeks and Romans used cumin as a spice and for medicinal purposes. There is also a reference to it in the Bible. During the Middle Ages, cumin was thought to promote love and fidelity and to keep lovers and chickens from wandering. Married soldiers were sent off to battle with a fresh baked loaf of cumin bread. Cumin seeds are small dried fruits of the plant, with a strong, slightly spicy flavor. They are available freshly ground or as whole seeds. Roasting cumin seeds will bring out their flavor. Cumin is now cultivated in hot regions of India, the Mediterranean, and Northern Africa. Health benefits include its ability to aid in digestion, improve immunity, and help with insomnia, respiratory disorders, asthma, bronchitis, colds, anemia, morning sickness, skin disorders and carpal tunnel syndrome. The seeds are an excellent source of dietary fiber and minerals, vitamins, niacin, riboflavin, and antioxidants.

DILL

Dill is a green herb with feathery leaves. The oil is obtained from the fruits and leaves of the dill plant. The flat tan dill seed is the dried fruit of the herb. The seeds are very small and light so it takes more than ten thousand dill seeds to make one ounce. One tablespoon of dill seed contains more calcium than a cup of milk. When cooking with dill, add it at the end because the flavor is destroyed in heating. In medieval Europe it was believed that dill protected against curses and witchcraft, and made one drowsy. Today, dill is used in the treatment of digestion problems, colds, coughs, nerve pain, liver and gallbladder problems, and sleep disorders. Dill seed is sometimes applied to the mouth and throat for pain and inflammation. In manufacturing, its oil is used as a fragrance in cosmetics, soaps and perfumes.

The dill pickle is more than four hundred years old.

FENNEL

Fennel, a member of the carrot or parsley family, is sometimes incorrectly called anise because it tastes like anise or licorice and is thought to help with digestion. In ancient Greece, it was considered a symbol of success. The Puritans referred to Fennel as 'the meeting seed' because they often chewed the seeds during meetings. Flies are said to dislike fennel and powdered fennel has been used to keep flies away in kennels and stables. Its health benefits include relief from anemia, indigestion, constipation, colic and respiratory disorders, and eye care. Fennel can be found in desserts, mouth fresheners, toothpaste, and antacids. (For more information, see page 64).

FENUGREEK

Fenugreek, native to southern Europe and western Asia, is an herb similar to clover. It was one of the spices used in embalming by the ancient Egyptians. Today, the aromatic dried seeds are used as a flavoring. The seeds smell and taste similar to maple syrup. They are used in cooking and to make medicine or to hide the taste of other medicines. Fenugreek is included as an ingredient in spice blends and also used as a flavoring agent in tobacco, imitation maple syrup, and other foods and beverages. The leaves are eaten in India as a vegetable. Fenugreek can help with digestive problems, diabetes, and obesity. It is also used for conditions that affect heart health, kidney ailments, boils, bronchitis, tuberculosis, chronic coughs, chapped lips, baldness, cancer, and Parkinson's disease. Some men use it for erectile dysfunction and male infertility. Sometimes it is used as a warm poultice applied directly to the skin to treat local pain and swelling, muscle pain, gout, wounds, leg ulcers, and eczema. Fenugreek extracts are used in soaps and cosmetics.

GARLIC

Garlic, one of the oldest cultivated food plants, has a culinary, medicinal, and religious history dating back more than six thousand years. It is pictured on ancient Egyptian tombs and was found in the tomb of King Tutankhamen. In ancient Greece, it was believed to be one of the best ways to ward off evil. Garlic is mentioned in the Old Testament and is said to have grown in the left footprints of Satan when he left the Garden of Eden. Japanese monks believed that garlic could cause lust and anger and hinder their training so eating garlic was forbidden. Throughout history, garlic was strung into braids as a means of drying and storing it. The braids were hung in households and shops to ward off evil, ghosts, and disease. Garlic was one of the ingredients in mixtures used to attach gold leaf to early works of art.

In Chinese medicine, garlic has been used to treat bronchitis and respiratory problems, gastrointestinal problems, flatulence, boils, dysentery, high blood pressure, diabetes, arthritis, muscle pain, and sciatica. It has antibiotic, anti-inflammatory, and decongestant properties and has been used to treat diabetes, earaches, fatigue, fever, coughs, headaches, stomach aches, sinus congestion, gout, joint pain, hemorrhoids, asthma, bronchitis, and high blood pressure. Some people eat garlic to prevent different types of cancer and others apply garlic oil to their skin or nails to treat fungal infections, warts, and hair loss. Chicago got its name from the Native American word for wild garlic, *chicagaoua,* that grew around Lake Michigan. California is responsible for the bulk of growing and distribution in the United States. Gilroy, California, is The Garlic Capital of the World. Shakespeare disliked garlic but a few historical people who loved it are Moses, Aristotle, Hippocrates, Homer, Nero, Albert Schweitzer, and Eleanor Roosevelt.

Whole garlic has a very mild scent until the cloves are crushed or pressed; then it has a pungent aroma and flavor. All garlic cultivars are derived from ten specific varieties of garlic native to central Asia. There are hundreds of varieties that can be classified as hardneck or softneck types. Softneck varieties are either artichoke varieties, the most common, or silverskin. Inchelium garlic, an heirloom softneck variety, is the oldest strain of garlic grown in North America and is considered the benchmark variety. The cloves have a mild and savory aroma and their flavor is neither mellow nor too pungent. It has a rich and robust taste with a medium level of spiciness. Elephant garlic is closely related to the leek. The bulbs are very large and can weigh more than a pound. The flavor is milder and sweeter than regular garlic varieties and can be eaten raw in salads. Spanish Roja garlic is considered to be one of the most revered of all hardneck for its superior flavor. It is an heirloom variety of garlic and is believed to have originated in Spain and cultivated in northwest Oregon in the late 1800s. Bogatyr garlic is known for its fiery heat with a long lasting bite. It is known as one of the hottest hardneck garlic varieties. Green garlic is young garlic that is harvested prior to reaching maturity. It ranges in height from eight to eighteen inches producing thin, green stalks and small, white bulbs. It is entirely edible. Black garlic, produced in a curing process using specially designed machines and environmentally controlled temperatures, was first introduced in the early twenty-first century. It has a stronger antioxidant effect compared to raw garlic and its health benefits include improving arterial sclerosis, preventing heart disease and cancer, preventing Alzheimer disease, and inhibiting cholesterol build up.

Garlic flowers are the flowering seeds of the garlic plant, produced mostly on hardneck garlic varieties. They have a green stem or scape and are capped with a lime green, pink and white spherical bouquet of fresh miniature flowers and seeds. The blooms and scapes are milder than that of traditional garlic bulbs but still have a pungent fragrance and a fresh, green flavor reminiscent of chives. They can be sautéed, roasted, boiled, grilled, and added to salads.

When garlic is very close to maturity, Garlic Scapes occur. Also known as garlic shoots, they only form on hardneck varieties. The Scapes are miniature bulbs with pungent oil and peppery flavors when pressed. The flavor is similar to, but milder than, green garlic.

GINGER

Ginger is a Southeast Asian plant that resembles bamboo in appearance. Today, the top producers are India, China, and Indonesia. Fresh ginger is available in two forms: young and mature. Young roots require no peeling, are very tender and have a milder flavor. Mature roots have a tough skin that must be peeled to get to the fibrous flesh. The ginger root is pickled, preserved in syrup, candied, or chopped or ground for cooking. Ginger root is packed with vitamins, minerals, and compounds and is well-known for its use in treating nausea and indigestion. It also bolsters the immune system to combat colds and flu. Ginger can reduce muscle pain, ease osteoarthritis, and help lower cholesterol. The high levels of antioxidants in ginger have been found to be an effective natural treatment in the fight against Alzheimer's disease. In ancient India, ginger was believed to spiritually cleanse the body. During the Middle Ages, European ladies of the royal courts presented ginger to their knights prior to jousts, to bring them luck. In the 1800s, ginger was commonly sprinkled on top of beer or ale, then stirred into the drink with a hot poker (this was the first ginger ale).

Ground ginger is used primarily in sweets and curry mixes. Pickled ginger is usually colored bright red or pink and accompanies sushi. It is also eaten to freshen the breath. Preserved ginger is used as a confection or added to melons and desserts. Candied ginger has been cooked in a sugar syrup until tender and then coated with granulated sugar.

Wild ginger can be found throughout the United States and into Canada. The two species that are native to North America are the Eastern variety and the Western variety. They are not related to the commercial ginger found in grocery stores. Native Americans used it for seasoning food and to treat poor digestion, coughs and colds, sore throats, earaches, headaches, asthma, typhus, scarlet fever, urinary disorders, and venereal disease. **Caution: In extremely high doses, ginger may cause liver failure.**

HONEY

Honey is the only food that does not spoil. It was most likely the first sweet treat that humans discovered. In ancient Egypt, citizens paid their taxes with honey. It was also used as a medicine and the remedies are mentioned in Egyptian medical texts dating back to 2,500 B.C. The Greek physician Hippocrates recommended topical application of honey for infected wounds and ulcers of the lips. Roman physicians used honey as an oral medication for constipation, diarrhea, upset stomach, sore throat, and coughs. In the eleventh century A.D., German peasants paid their feudal lords in honey and beeswax. European settlers introduced honey bees to New England around 1638. Native Americans called them the white man's flies. A single hive of honeybees may contain eighty thousand bees. It takes about two million flower visits by honeybees to produce one pound of honey.

Honey was used in food and beverages, to preserve fruits, to make cement, furniture polish and varnish, and as medicine. Honey contains eighteen more calories per tablespoon than refined sugar. Legend has it that Cupid dipped his love arrows in honey before aiming at unsuspecting lovers. **Caution: Never give honey to infants under one year of age as honey may contain clostridium botulinum spores that babies have little resistance to.**

HYSSOP

Hyssop is an herb from the mint family. The plant, native to southern Europe and Central Asia, has a sweet scent and warm bitter taste. The highly aromatic and pungent dark green leaves can be used in fresh or dry form as a flavoring for foods and beverages. The flavor can overpower some dishes so it is used sparingly with meat, fish and vegetables, and in soups, stews and salads. It is also used in liqueurs like absinthe. The leaves contain oil of hyssop, used by perfumers. Tea made of the leaves and sweetened with honey was used for nose, throat and lung afflictions. It was also applied to bruises.

KETCHUP

The first record of the word 'ketchup' in English was in 1690 as 'catsup.' The spelling 'ketchup' appeared in 1711. In the eighteenth and nineteenth centuries, 'ketchup' was the word used for various sauces whose common ingredient was vinegar. Tomato ketchup appeared at the end of the eighteenth century. It was sold in the 1830s as medicine. Ketchup does not have to be refrigerated after opening – it has a high acid content due to the tomatoes and vinegar in it – and is safe to store at room temperature. But it tastes better if kept refrigerated. Ketchup is commonly used on hot dogs and hamburgers but other uses include adding it to soups, vegetable dips, barbecued dishes, and stews. Lycopene, which is a key component of ketchup, has powerful anti-cancer effects. It also lowers heart attack or stroke risk. Regular use of ketchup helps in reducing the onset of cataracts, gum disease, and osteoporosis, and enhances male fertility. But limit the amount you consume daily as it may cause an upset stomach.

LEMONGRASS

Lemongrass, a member of the sugar cane family, is a tall perennial grass native to Sri Lanka and South India. Today it is grown commercially within the United States in California and Florida. For centuries it was used for therapeutic treatments. It has numerous health benefiting essential oils, chemicals, minerals, and vitamins that are known to have antioxidant and disease preventing properties. It is also used in teas and herbal soups.

LAVENDER

A close cousin of mint, lavender grows as a small shrub that has violet flowers and green or pale grey leaves. It is native to northern Africa and the mountainous Mediterranean regions, although today it also grows throughout southern Europe, Australia, and some parts of the United States. Lavender has long been associated with royalty. Egyptian queen Cleopatra was said to have used a lavender-infused perfume to seduce Julius Caesar and Mark Anthony. The first Queen Elizabeth drank lavender tea daily to relieve migraines, and Queen Victoria commanded her servants to polish the furniture with a lavender-based solution. Lavender leaves and flowers, whether fresh or dried, are edible and have a mildly sweet but slightly bitter aftertaste. They can flavor salads, jellies, sorbets and ice cream, desserts and beverages, and can also be added to sauces and marinades. Low-calorie and free of fat and cholesterol, lavender is full of phytochemicals and antioxidants that have anxiety-relieving properties and potentially anti-cancer effects.

LEMON VERBENA

Lemon Verbena, native to Argentina and Chile, is a woody shrub with narrow, green, rough-textured leaves that are rich in essential oils. It has a lemony fragrance and a sweet and fruity flavor that is more potent than other lemon-scented herbs. The young leaves may be eaten raw but the larger leaves should be cooked. Its oil was initially used by the Victorians in their potpourri, perfume, and cosmetics but was later replaced by lemongrass. The oil is often used in herbal remedies for digestive ailments, fever and depression.

MAPLE SYRUP

Quebec is the leading producer of maple syrup, followed by Vermont, New York, and Ontario. It takes approximately forty gallons of sap to make one gallon of maple syrup. When the sap is boiled and thickens, then poured on fresh snow, it forms a sweet taffy. The process of making maple syrup is an age-old tradition of northern Native Americans, who used it both as a food and as a medicine. It was the main sweetener used by the colonists (sugar from the West Indies was highly taxed and very expensive). In the late 1700s and early 1800s, maple sap was produced into maple sugar, a granular, solid block of maple that had a long shelf-life and could be easily transported. The maple syrup industry began during the Civil War with the introduction of the tin can. Maple syrup has naturally occurring minerals, such as zinc, thiamine, and calcium. It contains antioxidants that quell inflammation. Darker grades have the highest levels of antioxidants. Pure maple syrup has the same beneficial antioxidant compounds found in berries, tomatoes, tea, red wine, whole wheat and flax seed. Calories in maple syrup are lower than in corn syrup and honey.

MAYONNAISE

Mayonnaise is a stable emulsion of oil, egg yolk, and either vinegar or lemon juice. It was created by a French chef for a victory banquet to celebrate the capture of Mahón, a city off the northeast coast of Spain, by French forces. Traditional sauces of the day were made of cream and eggs but the chef had no cream and substituted olive oil, naming the new sauce *Mahónnaise* in honor of the victory. Years later, French chef Marie-Antoine Carême lightened the original recipe by blending the vegetable oil and egg yolks into an emulsion. His recipe became famous throughout the world. In 1903, Richard Hellmann created a formula for bottled mayonnaise. Mayonnaise is a good source of vitamin E and contains small amounts of vitamins A. The eggs used in the recipe are rich in protein and some minerals. As part of a healthy diet, it can control sugar levels in the blood and help reduce the risk of sudden heart attack deaths. A tablespoon of mayonnaise has about one hundred calories, the same amount found in a tablespoon of butter or margarine.

MUSTARD

All parts of the mustard plant are edible, including the leaves, seeds, and flowers. (Mustard Greens are different.) There are about forty species of mustard plants. White mustard, which originated in the Mediterranean area, makes a bright yellow mustard. Brown mustard, which originated in the Himalayas, is the basis for most American and European mustards. Black mustard is popular in the Middle East and Asia Minor, where it originated. Canada produces about ninety percent of the world's supply of mustard seeds. Most of the mustard seeds used in Dijon, France are actually grown in the United States and Canada. Mustard seeds are high in antioxidants and anti-inflammatory properties. They have antiseptic and anti-fungal properties, making them useful for purging the digestive system and increasing the body's natural defense system. They have been found to be beneficial for reducing the frequency of migraines. Throughout history, mustard seeds were used around the home to ward off evil spirits, in tonics to reduce hair loss, sewn into garments to encourage feelings of security, and consumed as an aphrodisiac. Applied with a hot compress, they helped reduce strains and sprains in the body. They were also used in poultices and plasters massaged onto the chest to alleviate congestion.

In the ancient world, Egyptians added the seeds to their food and they were found in King Tut's tomb. Wealthy Romans mixed ground mustard seeds with wine at the dinner table. Cultivated for thousands of years, mustard was the primary spice known to Europeans before the Asian spice trade. The Mustard Museum in Middleton, Wisconsin has the world's largest mustard collection (more than 3,500 varieties). National Mustard Day and The Mustard Festival are held on the first Saturday of August each year. Pope John XXII was so fond of mustard that he created a new Vatican position, the *'grand moutardier du pape'* (mustard-maker to the pope) and appointed his nephew to the post. George J. French introduced French's® mustard in 1904, the same year the hot dog was introduced to America at the St. Louis World's Fair.

MINT

Mint, an aromatic plant native to the temperate regions of the Old World, was named by the Greeks after the mythical character, Menthe. They regarded it as a sign of hospitality. The Egyptians invented the first breath mint (a combination of myrrh, cinnamon, frankincense and honey that was boiled and shaped into pellets.) Ancient Romans and Greeks used it as an herb and condiment, and in perfumes and bath scents. Romans crowned themselves with mint leaves during feasts. It was used by the ancient Assyrians in rituals to their fire god. The ancient Hebrews scattered mint leaves on the synagogue floor so that each footstep would produce a fragrant scent. During the Middle Ages, powdered mint leaves were used to whiten teeth. Mint can soothe the digestive tract, help with asthma and allergies, and is good for dental hygiene. It is an expectorant that encourages the body to eliminate mucus from the airways, lungs, bronchi and trachea. Consuming mint causes your body to slightly lower its temperature so you feel cooler. Some people believe rubbing mint juice into your skin once or twice a day can remove pimples and reduce wrinkles. Fresh green mint leaves add a tangy flavor to fruit salads, ice cream, sherbet, brewed tea, and mint juleps. There are about seventeen types of mint, the most popular being spearmint, peppermint, and wintergreen. Peppermint can be an effective mouse deterrent.

NUTMEG

Used in Chinese and East Indian cultures as a curative and aphrodisiac, as well as a flavor enhancer, nutmeg was once a rare, costly spice prized by Byzantine traders who obtained it from Arabia. The earliest references to the nutmeg tree pinpoint its origin to Moluccas Island (Spice Islands) in the Indonesian rainforest. Around 1512, transported nutmeg trees began to proliferate in places like the Caribbean and Grenada, where they eventually became the main source. Nutmeg is actually a fruit with a single seed (which makes it a drupe), similar in size to an apricot. It is used for sweet dishes in India and savory ones in the Middle East. In Europe, potatoes, eggs, and meats are spiced with nutmeg, as well as soups, sauces, and baked goods. Nutmeg has many nutritional benefits and contains manganese, copper and magnesium, as well as antioxidants and volatile oils that can soothe and stimulate the brain, relieve tooth, joint and muscular pain, and provide antifungal, antidepressant and gas-inhibitive functions.

OIL

There are a wide variety of cooking oils. Avoid purchasing oils containing partially hydrogenated oil that are high in trans fats and solidify around your arteries and blood vessels. Healthier oils are more expensive but rich in nutrients that will nourish your body and decrease your risk of developing certain diseases like hypertension and coronary artery disease.

Canola oil, obtained from pressing canola seeds, has zero trans fats and the lowest level of saturated fat. Although high in calories, it is high in heart-healthy monounsaturated fat that can positively impact cholesterol levels, reduce cardiovascular disease and lower the risk of type-2 diabetes. It also has valuable amounts of antioxidant vitamin E. Canola oil has the highest smoke point so it is good for deep-frying. The name 'canola' means **Can**adian **o**ilseed - low **a**cid.

Coconut oil can help rid the body of bacteria and viruses. It is also rich in monounsaturated fat that helps to reduce cholesterol and triglyceride levels. Unrefined coconut oil smells and tastes like raw coconuts and adds tropical flavor to foods.

Corn oil is composed mainly of polyunsaturated fatty acids and low on saturated fat. When used sparingly, it can lower LDL blood cholesterol and blood pressure. It also contains Vitamin E, an antioxidant. Corn oil is used in skin moisturizers and hair conditioners.

Cotton seed oil, extracted from cotton seeds, is popular in cooking because it doesn't impart a flavor of its own. It is a good source of essential fatty acids and Vitamin E and is cholesterol free. The ancient Chinese used it as a medicine and a lamp oil.

Flaxseed oil is rich in nutrients. It is high in omega-3 fatty acids that enhance brain function and lower the risk of developing heart disease. It can improve joint mobility and enhance the function of the immune system.

Macademia oil, extracted from the nut meat of the macadamia tree, is rich in monounsaturated and polyunsaturated fatty acids while low in saturated fatty acids, making it heart-healthy. High in natural antioxidants, it contains more than four and a half times the amount of vitamin E as olive oil. It can be stored, unrefrigerated, for up to two years. Macademia oil is great for frying and baking but is more popular as a moisturizer for skin and hair.

Olive oil is high in monounsaturated fats that can help reduce the risk of developing heart disease, diabetes and certain cancers. Over ninety percent of the world's olive production is used to make oil and most of the acreage is in the Mediterranean region. Light olive oil refers to the light color and milder flavor (it is not lower in fat; it has the same calories as other olive oils, about one hundred twenty calories per tablespoon). It is used for high-heat cooking because it has a higher smoke point. Extra Virgin Olive Oil is from the first pressing of the best olives, with an acidity of less than one percent. Virgin Olive Oil is from the first pressing of top quality olives, with an acidity of less than two percent. Plain Olive Oil is a blend of virgin and refined olive oil with an acidity of less than one percent. Refined Oils use chemicals or heat to extract additional oil after the first cold pressing.

Peanut oil has a high smoke point, making it useful when deep-frying foods. It is low in saturated fats, free from cholesterol, has valuable amounts of antioxidant Vitamin E, and contains essential fatty acids making it one of the healthiest cooking oils, although it is high in calories.

Red palm oil is rich in essential fatty acids and contains a number of anti-inflammatory compounds and antioxidants including lycopene, beta-carotene, and vitamin E. It can lower cholesterol levels and protect against the buildup of plaque inside arteries. Alternative medicine praises it as a natural remedy for Alzheimer's, arthritis, asthma, high blood pressure, cataracts, and macular degeneration. It is also purported to have anti-aging benefits, support weight loss, stimulate the immune system, and enhance fertility.

Safflower oil is a colorless, flavorless, and odorless edible oil extracted from the safflower plant. It is used for preventing heart disease and stroke, to treat fever, coughs, breathing problems, chest pain, and traumatic injuries. While it lowers bad cholesterol levels (LDL), it also decreases good cholesterol levels (HDL). It is one of the few edible oils that does not contain vitamin E. Its history dates back to ancient times when it was used in fabric dyes. The plant's flower is still used for this purpose along with coloring cosmetics, and the seed oil is used as a paint solvent.

Sesame oil is used in Asian and Middle Eastern cuisines. It has a wide range of health benefits including its ability to improve hair and skin, stimulate strong bone growth, reduce blood pressure, increase heart health, manage anxiety, boost dental health, improve the digestive process, and lower inflammation.

Soybean oil, extracted from whole soybeans, is high in polyunsaturated and monounsaturated fats, low in saturated fats, trans fat-free, and has natural antioxidants. It is flavorless and has a high smoke point good for frying and stir-frying. Soybean oil is used in about seventy-five percent of all commercial U.S. food production. Most vegetable oil is soybean oil.

Truffle oil is top-quality olive oil that has been infused with either white or black truffles. It is not used in cooking but drizzled over foods after preparation to enhance flavor. It must be stored in the refrigerator. When purchasing truffle oil, look for "infused with truffles" on the label, otherwise you will be getting olive oil mixed with various chemical compounds that only create the aroma and taste of truffles.

An essential oil is a liquid that is distilled, by steam or water, from the leaves, stems, flowers, bark, roots or other elements of a plant. It contains the true essence of the plant it was derived from. Most essential oils are clear, but some are amber or yellow in color. They are not greasy and are highly concentrated, so use sparingly. They are also not used in aromatherapy. Essential oils, either inhaled or diluted and applied to the skin, provide psychological and physical therapeutic benefits. They may be used in making homemade lotions, shampoos, perfumes, soaps, and other natural products. Add a few drops of oil to a trash can, sink drain, or vacuum bag filter for a pleasant scent. Several essential oils act as a natural insect repellent. Essential oils are not the same as artificially created perfume or fragrance oils that do not offer therapeutic benefits.

Caution: First dilute essential oils before applying to the skin. Read all safety data before use. Essential oils are flammable.

Absolutes, like essential oils, are aromatic liquids extracted from plants. Chemical solvents are used in the process and, although later removed during the final stages of production, trace amounts can remain. They are used in holistic aromatherapy and natural fragrances but are not for internal use. Absolutes are more concentrated than essential oils.

Oils extracted by the carbon dioxide (CO2) method are called CO2 Extracts. They are thicker than their essential oil counterparts and none of the constituents of the oil are damaged by heat. CO2 Extracts have more of the aroma of the natural plant. Unlike Absolutes, no trace of harmful solvents remain in the final product.

According to Debby Duncan, "I'm not an expert by any means but I have tried some essential oils that I've really loved and some that I didn't feel did anything for me. There are several ways to purchase oils: join a group and become a distributor, from health food stores, or buy online stores. The important thing is to get pure, not commercial grade. I started as a Young Living distributor because my cousin loved it and it was a great way to get a variety of oils in one kit (not to sell, just for me to get a variety of oils, but people do make money if that's what they like to do). My favorite place to purchase is Bulkapothecary.com. Their prices are great and you get more for your money. There are a few oils that I can't get from there and so I order those from Young Living.

Essential oils are used for a wide variety of reasons, from health concerns including emotions and stress reduction, to non-chemical household cleaners, and more. Here's just a glimpse of oils that have worked for me, but the world of essential oils is one that can't be shown in one small conversation. For high cholesterol, my personal numbers went down almost twenty points just using lemongrass oil on my wrists. For common colds, Thieves dabbed on the back of your neck will lessen and shorten the duration. Peppermint works wonders for headaches, or in a spray bottle for getting rid of spiders. Purification is great for germs and or bacteria on your person or in a spray bottle around your home. I spray it on dog beds to kill odor and bacteria.

You can use multiple oils if you have multiple things going on. I use a diffuser daily in my home as an air freshener as well as other benefits. I would advise to try to find a diffuser that doesn't require distilled water because it's easier to not have to have distilled water available all the time. I also have a car diffuser with peppermint oil mostly, but if I start a cold I will put Thieves in it. You are not limited by oils; there is such a wide range of uses. It's up to you how far you want to venture with them. It's important to purchase a book that can help you navigate the proper uses for different oils. Essential Oils Pocket Reference is a great one. Oils can be used topically, internally, or diffused. Not all oils can be used in each of these manors so it's important to be able to know you are using them correctly."

OREGANO

Vitamins A, C, E and K, fiber, calcium, niacin, manganese, folate, magnesium, iron, and the carotenoids lutein, zeaxanthin and cryptoxanthin are all found in oregano. It has great antioxidant power and proven disease prevention. This fragrant Mediterranean herb can help the body detox, reduce fever, relieve diarrhea, prevent colds, flu and indigestion and regulate menstrual cycles. An oregano poultice can sooth sore muscles and improve eczema, and compounds in the leaves and flowers can aid digestion and prevent gas. Antiseptic and anti-inflammatory qualities are released in the oil, which also contains germ-fighting and bacteria-battling antibacterial agents. The Greeks called oregano the "delight of the mountains."

PAPRIKA

Paprika is a red powder made from grinding dried sweet red peppers. It is used as a garnish and seasoning. Ninety percent of the international spice trade is in whole spices, paprika being the only spice sold ground in significant quantities. Most commercial paprika comes from Spain, South America, California, and Hungary (Hungarian paprika is thought to be the finest). Paprika releases its color and flavor when heated so sprinkling it over colorless dishes adds to the appearance but does little to enhance the flavor. If a food item colored red, orange, or reddish brown says "Natural Color" it is likely from paprika. Paprika has a higher content of Vitamin C than citrus fruit. It also has vitamins A, B6 and E, iron, and beta-carotene. It can improve the appearance of your skin, prevent the occurrence of wrinkles, and has been found to be useful in the prevention and treatment of spider veins. It stimulates hair growth by improving circulation to the scalp. Paprika also has great anti-inflammatory properties, lowers blood pressure, assists digestion, and helps with sleep. It boosts your body's serotonin and norepinephrine levels, enabling you to stay happy and stress free.

PARSLEY

Parsley, native to the Mediterranean region, has been cultivated for more than two thousand years. It was first used medicinally and later used to flavor and garnish food. The name comes from the Greek word *petros,* which means stone (the plant was often found growing among rocks). The ancient Greeks regarded parsley as sacred and used it decorate the tombs of the deceased and to adorn victors of athletic contests. Wreaths made with parsley were worn to prevent intoxication. Parsley was brought to the New World by the colonists.

There are two basic parsley types: one with curly, crinkly leaves and the more familiar Italian parsley which is flat and has a more fragrant and less bitter taste. Parsley contains volatile oils and flavonoids, two types of unusual components that provide unique health benefits. It is also a good source of vitamins A, C and K, as well as folate and iron. The best way to keep parsley sprigs fresh is to wrap them in a damp paper towel, place them in a sealed zip-lock baggie, and keep them refrigerated. Dried parsley flakes are useful for several months when stored in a tightly sealed glass container. **Caution: People with already existing and untreated kidney or gallbladder problems may want to avoid eating parsley because it contains measurable amounts of oxalates that could become too concentrated in body fluids and crystallize.**

PEPPER

The pepper plant can grow up to thirty-three feet in hot and humid tropical climates. It forms small white clustered flowers that develop into berries known as peppercorns. Black and white pepper are obtained from the small berry. For white pepper, the berry is picked when fully ripe and soaked in brine to remove the dark outer shell. The dried, grayish-white kernel that remains has a milder flavor than black pepper. Black pepper is made by picking the pepper berries when they are half ripe. Black pepper was once presented to the gods as a sacred offering. In the Middle Ages, a man's wealth was often measured by the amount of pepper he had. It was weighed like gold and used as currency. Pepper added spice to bland foods and disguised a food's lack of freshness, an important quality in the times before efficient means of preservation. Black pepper can be stored for many years without losing its flavor and aroma. The first American millionaire, Elias Haskett Derby, made his fortune importing black pepper. He used his money to endow Yale University. The major commercial producers of pepper today are India and Indonesia.

ROSEMARY

Rosemary, a member of the mint family, is a perennial bush that grows in the Mediterranean area. It can reach a height of two to six feet and has pale blue flowers and spiky leathery leaves. According to one legend, when the Holy Family escaped into Egypt, Mary rested under a rosemary bush and spread her cloak on it to dry. The flowers miraculously changed from white to the blue of the Blessed Mother's cloak. A similar story has Mary washing the baby Jesus' clothes in a stream and placing them on a bush to dry. The bush was named 'rosemary' and God rewarded it with delicate blossoms of the same blue as Mary's robe.

In ancient Greece, people hailed rosemary for its supposed ability to strengthen the brain and memory. Students braided it into their hair to help them with exams. Rosemary was brought to England by the Romans in the eighth century. Its branches were placed on the floors of medieval homes to combat diseases during the black plague. Boughs of rosemary were carried at weddings as good luck for the new couple, and it is considered a symbol of fidelity. Early immigrants brought it to the New World. It was used to prevent balding and as a hair conditioner. Rosemary has been made into an ointment to treat rheumatism, sores, eczema and bruises. Its antioxidant properties make it good for preserving foods. Rosemary tea has been used as a digestive aid. As rosemary dries it loses its strength of flavor.

SAFFRON

The saffron plant is native to the Mediterranean region. Most saffron comes from Spain. The dried stigmas are used to make the spice, the most expensive spice in the world due to the amount of labor involved – it is largely cultivated and harvested by hand. It can take seventy-five thousand saffron blossoms to produce a single pound of saffron spice, used mainly as a seasoning and coloring agent in food. The Greeks and Romans used saffron to perfume their baths. The bright orange-yellow color also made it useful as a dye. Today, saffron extracts are used as fragrance in perfumes and as a dye for cloth. The ancient Assyrians used saffron for medicinal purposes. The stigmas are still used today to make medicines that help with asthma, cough, heartburn, dry skin, infertility, sleeplessness, and many other health issues like Alzheimer's disease. Saffron is also used as an aphrodisiac and some people apply it directly to the scalp for baldness.

SAGE

Sage, native to southern Europe and the Mediterranean, is an aromatic plant with grayish-green leaves that are used as an herb. Throughout history, sage has been used to preserve foods because it contains powerful antioxidants that slow spoilage. It was thought to cure snake bites, eye problems, infection, epilepsy, intoxication, worms and intestinal problems, and used as an aphrodisiac. It was believed that sage stimulated the brain and increased memory and reasoning (the word 'sage' took on the meaning of a wise person). Sage was rubbed on the teeth to make them whiter in nineteenth-century America. It is antibacterial in nature and effective in treating sore throats. It is also effective as an antiperspirant. Today, the leaf is used to make medicine for things like digestive problems, hot flashes, and gum disease. Some people inhale sage for asthma. It may even help chemical imbalances in the brain that cause Alzheimer's disease. Sage is also used as a fragrance component in soaps and cosmetics.

SAVORY

There are thirty types of savories but only two are used primarily for culinary purposes: summer and winter savory. Summer savory's smooth gray-green narrow leaves have an oregano and thyme-like fragrance and a flavor similar to a blend of thyme and marjoram. Winter savory's leaves are darker in color and have a less refined flavor with deep peppery undertones. The leaves contain scented oils that release a strong pine-like aroma. Native to southern Europe and the Mediterranean, savory has been naturalized in regions of North America since the colonists brought it with them as a medicinal herb in the eighteenth century. Its name is derived from a Roman mythology half-man, half-goat deity known as a satyr, and the plant's connection to love and nature was dedicated to this hedonistic creature.

SALT

Salt, also known as sodium chloride, has been an important part of the world's history, dating back to 6000 B.C. Its production was legally restricted in ancient times so salt was used as a method of trade and currency. About forty-seven hundred years ago, the Chinese made salt taxes a major revenue source. Salt was used in Egyptian religious offerings. Trade in ancient Greece involved exchanging salt for slaves which led to the expression, "not worth his salt." The early Romans salted their leafy greens and vegetables so the word 'salad' also originated from salt. Salt rations given to ancient Roman soldiers were known as *salarium argentum*, the English word for salary. Venice became a great economic center due to its salt monopoly. There are more than thirty references to salt in the Bible, including the expression, "salt of the earth."

Salting fish made long-range explorations possible in the age of sailing ships. In the late seventeenth century, salt was the leading cargo carried from the Caribbean to North America. In the early 1800s, salt was four times as expensive as beef on the Western frontier. The Erie Canal was known as "the ditch that salt built" because salt was originally its principal cargo. Syracuse, New York, is nicknamed Salt City.

The earliest method of salt production was the evaporation of seawater by the heat of the sun, followed by quarrying which exposed masses of rock salt. This soon developed into mining underground deposits of salt. Today, Salzburg, Austria has made its four salt mines major tourist attractions.

Iodized salt is a common source of dietary iodine, vital for the manufacturing of the thyroid hormone. Salt is also essential for sustaining hydration. Gargling with salt water can alleviate a sore throat. Salt water helps treat nasal and sinus problems. Soaking tired feet in warm salt water helps alleviate pain. Salt is good for skin exfoliation. A mixture of one-fourth teaspoon each of salt and baking soda in one quart of warm water helps to clean plaque, whitens teeth, and keeps gums healthy.

Cream will whip better if you add a pinch of salt.

Sea salt, obtained naturally from the sea, does not go through any processing that alters the natural make-up so it contains many essential trace minerals that the body needs to be healthy.

When a recipe calls for sour salt it is referring to citric acid, a white granulated powder that is extracted from the juice of citrus and other acidic fruits. The strong, tart taste is used in small quantities as a flavoring agent in food and beverages. It is a key ingredient in traditional borscht, a soup made with beets and usually served with sour cream, popular in several Eastern European cuisines.

SESAME

Sesame is thought to be one of the oldest spices known and most likely the first crop grown for its edible oil. Babylonians used the oil to make sesame cakes, wine, brandy, and toiletries. As early as 1500 B.C, Egyptians believed sesame to have medicinal powers. In Africa, the sesame seed is called *benne* and considered good luck. The seeds were brought to the United States from Africa during the late seventeenth century. Today, the largest commercial producers of sesame seeds include India, China, and Mexico.

The sesame plant is a tall annual herb that can reach five feet in height and bears pink-white flowers. The pods appear afterwards and contain white, brown, or black seeds. One pod may have one hundred or more seeds. Sesame seeds contains several health-benefiting nutrients, minerals like calcium and iron, antioxidants, and vitamins. They are a valuable source of dietary protein. The seeds have an abundant supply of niacin which helps reduce LDL-cholesterol levels. Sesame seeds are believed to enhance the immune system and decrease the risk of certain cancers.

When toasted, sesame seeds have a nutty flavor. They can be used in stir fry, salads, sandwiches, breads, bagels, cakes, and other desserts. They are highly valued for their oil which is exceptionally resistant to rancidity. The famous phrase, "Open Sesame" (the magical password that opened the entrance to the cave in Ali Baba and the Forty Thieves), reflects the sesame seed pod, which bursts open when it reaches maturity.

SORREL

Sorrel is a green, spinach-like herb. The name is derived from the word 'sour' and it is sometimes called sour grass. During the Middle Ages, before citrus fruit reached Europe, people used it in cooking to add a tangy flavor. It is usually paired with fish because, like lemon, the sourness brings out the sweetness of the fish. Sorrel is high in calcium, iron, magnesium, and vitamins A, C and B9. Sorrel is used for reducing sudden and ongoing pain and inflammation of the nasal passages and respiratory tract, for treating bacterial infections, and as a diuretic.

STAR ANISE

Star anise is a star-shaped, dark brown pod that contains a tiny seed in each of its eight segments. Native to China, it comes from a small evergreen tree and has a licorice taste similar to anise, only stronger. When purchasing star anise, look for whole pieces that aren't broken – it is usually added whole to slow cooked or simmered dishes and discarded before serving. Store it in a sealed container in a cool dark place so it will last for several months. In China, star anise is prescribed as a digestive aid and to help cure colic in babies.

NOTE: Star anise is not botanically related to anise.

SOY SAUCE

In ancient China, preserved foods and their seasonings were known as *jiang*. The process of making *jiang* eventually spread from China into Japan and other neighboring countries. Today's soy sauce – a salty, brown liquid made from fermented soy beans mixed with some type of roasted grain – originated from this seasoning. The sauce's consistency can range from very thin to very thick. Flavors vary by type. Light soy sauce from Japan has a thinner consistency and a saltier flavor than the darker varieties. Dark soy sauce is used throughout Asia and is richer and thicker than the lighter varieties and has a pungent flavor. Mushroom soy sauce (straw mushroom essence is added to the sauce's brew) is a dark soy sauce from China. It has a deep, rich flavor and can be used in place of other types of soy sauce in most recipes. Tamari is a deeply colored Japanese soy sauce with a rich texture and intense flavor. It is especially good to use as a table condiment and dipping sauce. Wheat-free varieties of soy sauce are available in some markets.

SUGAR

Sugar cane is a perennial grass that originated in Asia. People chewed the raw cane to extract its sweetness. The process of making sugar by evaporating juice from sugar cane developed in India around 500 BC. Crusaders were the first to introduce sugar to Europe. Sugar cane seeds were brought to the New World by Christopher Columbus in 1492. Prior to the 1500s, sugar was called "White Gold" and only used in small amounts as medicine and to sweeten wine, not food. European nobility used it to display their social standing. Around 1795 in France, Jean Etienne Bore developed the process for making granulated sugar from sugar cane. Henry Tate, an English sugar merchant, patented a method of cutting sugar into small cubes in 1872. Today, Brazil is the world's largest producer of sugar cane.

Refined sugar has no fat, but it also has no nutritional value. Generally, people consume five hundred extra calories a day from sugar. Sweet is the only taste humans are born craving. Sugar releases an opiate-like substance that activates the brain's reward system. Suddenly removing refined sugar from your diet can cause withdrawal symptoms. Sugar is used in leather tanning, printers' inks and dyes, and textile sizing and finishing. It prolongs the life of fresh cut flowers. Bottles and plate glass windows in movies are made of sugar. Add sugar water to a humming bird feeder to attract the small birds. Swallowing one teaspoon of sugar may cure hic-ups.

Brown sugar is brown because it contains molasses. Light brown sugar contains less molasses than dark brown and is the most common type used for baking. Recipes that call for brown sugar without specifying either light or dark generally require light brown sugar. You can make brown sugar by combining one tablespoon of molasses for every cup of granulated white sugar. Stir until an even color and texture are achieved. Some varieties of brown sugar are used to make rum and other alcoholic beverages. It is also a popular ingredient in body scrubs.

TARRAGON

Tarragon is thought to have originated in Central Asia and was used by the Greeks as early as 500 BC. French tarragon is an herb used as a flavoring agent, especially in Mediterranean foods. Russian tarragon is more robust and, although closely related to French tarragon, is less preferred in cooking. Fresh leaves provide better flavor and nutritional benefits than dried tarragon. Look for leaves that are fragrant and not shriveled or discolored. Tarragon is used in salads, to marinate fish, lamb and poultry, and is one of the main ingredients in béarnaise sauce. The herb is added in small amounts to recipes at the last moment in order to retain flavor. Tarragon is rich in nutrients and antioxidants that help promote health and prevent diseases. It has been used to stimulate appetite and alleviate anorexic symptoms, and lower blood-sugar levels. It is a rich source of vitamins A, C, and B-complex group, and also contains minerals like calcium, manganese, and iron. The essential oil in the herb has been used in dentistry as a local-anesthetic. Some people say Tarragon tea cures insomnia.

THYME

Thyme dates back to ancient Greece, where it symbolized courage and was burned as incense in sacred temples. Roman soldiers bathed in water infused with thyme to gain vigor, courage and strength. During the Middle Ages, a lady would give a knight a scarf with a sprig of thyme for bravery. It was placed under a pillow to induce sleep and prevent nightmares. Since the sixteenth century, thyme oil has been used as mouthwash and a topical antiseptic. Thyme is one of the herbs and spices used by the ancient Egyptians to preserve mummies. For centuries, thyme has been used in natural medicine to help with chest and respiratory problems. It also contains a variety of flavonoids that increase its antioxidant capacity. Thyme can prevent contamination and decontaminate previously contaminated foods, such as fresh produce, making them safe to eat. It is a good source of vitamins A and C, iron, manganese, copper, and dietary fiber. There are about sixty different varieties of thyme.

TURMERIC

Turmeric, the root of a tropical plant, is native to Indonesia and southern India and has been harvested for more than five thousand years. It has a peppery, bitter flavor with a mild fragrance similar to orange and ginger. It's been used in cooking (curry) and as a coloring agent for food (mustard) and fabric. Fresh turmeric will stain your hands and clothing so use gloves when handling it. Turmeric is a good source of iron and manganese, vitamin B6, dietary fiber, and potassium. It has long been used as an anti-inflammatory in China and India. It also has powerful antioxidant effects and may be able to prevent the oxidation of cholesterol in the body and protect against neurodegenerative diseases like Alzheimer's.

VANILLA

The vanilla bean is the fruit of a species of orchid that is native to the tropical rain forests of Central America. It is one of the few orchids that produce anything edible. The first use of vanilla dates back to Mexico, where the Aztecs used it to flavor chocolate. They introduced Spanish explorers to both items. Mayans believed that adding vanilla in drinks would give aphrodisiac effects (no modern research supports this, however). Initially, the vanilla bean has no flavor or aroma but as it ferments it develops a pleasant aroma and unique flavor. Real vanilla, although very expensive, is used as a flavoring agent in sweet drinks and confectionaries. Its extract contains small amounts of B-complex groups of vitamins that help in enzyme synthesis, nervous system function, and regulating body metabolism. It also contains small traces of calcium, magnesium, potassium, manganese, iron and zinc. Madagascar produces most of the world's vanilla.

VINEGAR

Vinegar was discovered when a cask of wine gone sour turned into a new item. The French origin of the word 'vinegar' is *vinagre,* which means 'sour wine'. Around 5,000 B.C., the Babylonians used it as a preservative and as a condiment, and flavored it with herbs and spices. Romans used it as a beverage. Supposedly, Cleopatra dissolved precious pearls in it to win a wager that she could consume a fortune in a single meal. The Greeks used vinegar to make pickled vegetables and meats. Vinegar was one of the earliest remedies and is mentioned in the Bible as being used for its soothing and healing properties. During the Civil War, it was used to treat scurvy and in World War I, it was used to treat wounds.

Vinegar can be made from almost any food that contains natural sugars. Yeast ferments these sugars into alcohol, and certain types of bacteria convert that alcohol a second time into vinegar. Through the centuries, vinegar has been produced from molasses, fruits and vegetables, honey, beer, maple syrup, and grains. Vinegar has a long shelf life and does not need refrigeration because of its acidic nature. Vinegar contains antioxidants that slow premature aging and reduce the risk of cancer. It has antibacterial properties that can help fight the infection that causes a sore throat.

The vinegars produced today come in a variety of flavors like distilled, wine, white, cider, malt, balsamic, and rice wine. Distilled vinegar is made by fermenting grain or ethyl alcohol, resulting in high levels of acetic acid (what gives vinegar its tart taste). White distilled vinegars are sometimes flavored with herbs, spices or other seasonings such as garlic, basil, cinnamon, and nutmeg. Wine vinegar is made from a blend of either red or white wines. White vinegar, the most common type of vinegar in the United States, is good for pickling and several nonedible uses such as removing stains on coffee cups, eliminating odors in plastic containers, eliminating germs in sinks and tubs, and removing light scorch marks on fabrics or antiperspirant stains.

There are two types of Balsamic vinegar: traditional and commercial (the type most often found in grocery stores). Production of the traditional type is regulated by a board in Modena, Italy (balsamic vinegar's birthplace). It is aged for a number of years (at least six) and some are aged for fifty to one hundred years and could cost over two hundred dollars an ounce. Balsamic vinegar was once considered so valuable it was included in the dowries of young ladies of nobility and was specifically mentioned in wills.

Fruit or fruit juice can be infused with white or wine vinegar to produce flavors like apple cider or raspberry vinegar. Apple cider vinegar, the second-most-common type of vinegar in the U.S., contains antioxidants called polyphenols that are good for your health. Here are some uses for Apple Cider Vinegar (ACV) that people have shared with me. I can't guarantee success, but it's worth a try.

- Soothe a sore throat by gently gargling some ACV with water every half hour.
- Help reduce the symptoms of many allergies and headaches, and reduce sinus congestion by drinking a quarter cup water, a half cup ACV, one tablespoon honey, and one squeezed lemon wedge.
- Drink ACV and water on a daily basis to help your body fight yeast infections.
- Take a teaspoon of ACV, then drink a glass of water to reduce heartburn.
- Drink two tablespoons of ACV in sixteen ounces of water throughout the day to help with weight loss.
- Dissolve a tablespoon of ACV in a glass of water, drink to detoxify the digestive system.
- Avoid red shaving rashes and dry skin by applying ACV to your face after shaving. You may then apply scented aftershave.
- Combine one pint ACV with two pints water and use to clean your face after removing makeup. Apply the solution with a cotton ball at night and again in the morning.
- To remove skin tags and warts, cover them with a cotton ball soaked in ACV; add a bandage. Continue for a few days until the wart or tag falls off.
- Add one cup ACV to bath water and soak for ten to twenty minutes to remove dead skin cells and regenerate new ones.
- ACV provides soothing relief when rubbed into your back or the bottom of your feet.
- Add a half tablespoon of ACV to one cup water; shake; use as a hair conditioner.
- Place one pint water and one pint ACV in a spray bottle and spray your pet; gently rub into its fur to remove and repel fleas.
- Mix a half cup ACV with one cup water to clean appliances, kitchen surfaces, and mirrors.
- Make salad dressing by mixing together two tablespoons honey, a half cup ACV, a quarter cup olive oil, salt and pepper to taste, and one squeezed lemon wedge.

Caution: ACV has been known to erode tooth enamel if consumed undiluted. If taken frequently, it could lead to low potassium levels. Potassium is needed by our muscles.

CHAPTER 2

Eat Your Veggies

A fruit is a part of a plant that develops from the end of a flower. Vegetables are any other part of the plant – stalks, roots and leaves. During the early 1800s in Europe, fruit was named for one of its characteristics (flavor or appearance) and its place of origin, or the name of the person who discovered the fruit. Heirloom fruits and vegetables are old, open-pollinated cultivars with a reputation for being high quality and easy to grow. Heirlooms can be traditional Native American crops that are pre-Columbian or old European crops, some of which have been in cultivation for hundreds of years. Other heirlooms trace their ancestries to Africa and Asia Modern. Select orchards throughout the United States specialize in heirloom varieties.

For thousands of years, new plant varieties have developed in nature through mutation as well as crosses between plants. With plant breeding, the fruit breeder collects pollen from one variety with desirable traits and applies it to the blossoms of another variety. If the cross is fruitful, the breeder keeps the seeds and plants them. Plant breeders introduced the first hybrids developed from inbred lines in the early 1950s. There are many varieties and each has its own unique appearance and flavor. For example, pluots are complex hybrid fruits that are part plum and part apricot. Apriums, another apricot and plum crossed fruit, have a high apricot to plum ratio and resemble an apricot without the fuzz. Plumcots have a higher plum to apricot ration and taste more like a plum. A peacotum, a cross of peach, apricot and plum, is the first three-in-one hybrid fruit.

Genetically modified plants, developed in the late twentieth century, are created in a laboratory. Genetic material from one plant or organism is inserted into the genes of another plant, creating species that would not occur in nature.

The types of fruits and vegetables that inhabit our world are too numerous to mention in one book but I have selected several that you may find interesting.

"A table, a chair, a bowl of fruit and a violin; what else does a man need to be happy?"
Albert Einstein   1879-1955
Physicist

APPLE

There are more than seven thousand varieties of apples. China is the world's largest apple producer, followed by the United States. There are twenty-five hundred known types of apples that grow in the U.S. but around one hundred varieties are grown commercially. Only eight varieties account for eighty percent of total production. Apples were planted in New England in 1623 and today they are grown all across the country. Washington State produces more apples than any other state. Many apple varieties, both historic and more modern, were discovered by accident in an orchard. In the last few years, over one hundred and thirty varieties of apples have been introduced through breeding programs around the world. Breeders in the United States are in search of new varieties that do not need as much chemical spraying as other varieties. Pristine apples are one such variety that has been bred to resist common diseases. Pearmains are a category of apple that are shaped like pears.

Apples, not caffeine, are more efficient at waking you up in the morning. Apples float because twenty-five percent of their volume is air. Eating flavonol-rich apples can help reduce the risk of developing pancreatic cancer. Apples are full of soluble fiber that binds with fats to lower cholesterol levels. Red apples contain an antioxidant that can help boost the immune system. Drinking apple juice could improve the effects of aging on the brain. Astronauts carried pureed applesauce in squeezable tubes on their space flights. **Caution: Do not eat apple seeds.**

The Crab apple is considered the parent of all apple varieties and has been growing wild for thousands of years throughout the Northern, Eastern and Western hemispheres. Crab Apple is a general name given to over a hundred different varieties of Crab apples. The color can be red, ruby, pink, and gold with apple stems as long as the length of the fruit itself. All crab apples are petite in size and have a high acid content. Hybridized crab apple varieties can be eaten fresh whereas original crab apple varieties were used for cooking and juicing. The Crimson Gold, solid red when mature, is a crab apple hybrid that is larger than most crab apple varieties and is a superior dessert and cider apple.

The Anna apple, a low-chill variety, was first developed in Israel in the 1950s and thrives in moderate regions of the Southern United States. It is light green to yellow in color with a red blush. It keeps its shape when cooked and is a good choice for pies and other baked goods. The Anna apple is a good source of both soluble and insoluble fiber.

The Arkansas Black apple originated in the 1870s in Arkansas and is also grown today in California, Washington, Oregon, and Ohio. It has red to dark purple waxy skin with a crisp texture and sweet-tart flavor. It is known as one of the best storage apples and becomes more palatable in cold storage. It contains both soluble fiber and insoluble fiber, vitamins A and C, potassium, and iron.

The Ashmead Kernel apple was developed from a seed planted in the early 1700s in England and later made its way to the New World. This green to yellow dessert apple has a sharp flavor and crisp texture with an aroma similar to orange blossoms.

The Black Twig apple, with light green or yellow skin and burgundy spots, is tart and juicy and the skin becomes darker and the flavor enriches when the apple is refrigerated. It was found as a seedling in Tennessee in the 1830s and was the favorite apple of former president and Tennessee native, Andrew Jackson.

The Braeburn apple was first discovered in 1952 in New Zealand. It is firm to the touch with a red/orange vertical streaky appearance on a yellow/green background. It is one of the most important commercial apple varieties.

The Calville Blanc apple, dating back to 1598 France, has a slightly misshapen shape with large ridges, and the color is yellow-green with red blush. It has been called the gourmet culinary apple of France and can also be found in Vermont and Oregon. It has more vitamin C than an orange. Claude Monet's 1879 still life painting "Apples and Grapes" depicts this apple.

The Cortland apple was developed in 1898 at Cornell University in New York. It is bright red with dark red streaks and a green blush. The crisp white flesh is juicy with a sweet-tart flavor. Slow to brown when cut, it is often used in fruit trays and salads. It contains vitamins A, B and C, dietary fiber, and trace amounts of boron that can help build strong bones.

The Divine apple tree has greater resistance to pests and disease. Its apples are red on a yellow background, low in calories, and high in healthy nutrients. The flavor is tastier after a few months of cold storage.

Empire apples were developed in the 1940s by Cornell University and named for the state they were created in (New York, the Empire State). They are bright red with faint white striation and capped with a light green blush. The flavor is sweet like a Red Delicious and tart like a McIntosh. They contain both soluble and insoluble fiber, and vitamins A and C.

The Flower of Kent is a large green skinned apple variety and is thought to have been the type that struck Sir Isaac Newton.

Fuji apples are a cross between two American varieties although they were first developed in Japan. Virginia Ralls Janet apples (first grown at Thomas Jefferson's Monticello home) and the Red Delicious, were taken to Japan in the 1930s. Their thick skin is light red with a yellow blush and the flavor is mild and very sweet. They are low in acid and contain vitamins A and C, and trace amounts of folate and potassium They are a good source of both soluble and insoluble fiber. Sun Fujis, that contain about ten percent more sugars than most apples, are much sweeter than regular Fujis since the sunlight that reaches them develops their sugars.

The Gala apple, one of the most extensively grown apples in the world, was developed in New Zealand in 1934 but commercial distribution didn't begin in Europe and the United States until the 1980s. The apple is covered in a thin yellow to orange skin with pink to red stripes. It has a sweet aroma and flavor that becomes milder when cooked. Royal Gala apples are yellow to orange with deep orange stripes and a blush of pink.

The Jazz apple is a cross between the Royal Gala and the Braeburn. The flavor is both sweet and tart with hints of pear and cinnamon. It is an excellent source of antioxidants that have been shown to help prevent Alzheimer's disease, lower cholesterol levels and prevent and slow the development of certain cancers. Jazz apples are also high in folic acid and the dietary fiber pectin.

The Golden Delicious apple that originated in West Virginia in 1890 is pale green to golden yellow in color. A good fresh eating variety, the flavor varies depending on where it is grown: in a cool climate, the amount of acid increases creating a sweeter flavor; in a warmer climate, the acid content is lower creating a milder flavor. The Golden Delicious is a parent apple to many well know varieties but is not related to the Red Delicious apple. A good source of soluble fiber, it contains vitamins A and C, and a trace amount of boron and potassium.

The Granny Smith apple was discovered in Australia in the 1860s and introduced to the United States in the 1970s. It has a thick bright green skin and a sweet-tart flavor. It is often used in baking because of its high acidity and ability to hold its shape when cooked. It ripens best in warmer climates and will often take on a yellow to pink blush when grown in colder climates.

Honeycrisp apples were first developed in the 1960s at the University of Minnesota. They have a yellow background covered with a red to pink blush and a sweet-tart flavor that is retained when cooked. They are rich in dietary fiber and contain vitamins A and C.

Kiku apples, discovered in 1990 by an Italian apple grower, are the sweetest apple. They are crisp and juicy with a firm flesh, like its Fuji apple parent. Ruby red with light colored stripes, they can grow up to five inches in diameter.

The tiny Lady apple was originally documented during early Rome in 700 B.C. It became naturalized in America during the 1800s. It has pale lime green skin blushed with crimson and a sweet-tart flavor. Grown more for its size than flavor, it is used to decorate Christmas trees, wreaths and garlands in England and America.

In 1811 in Canada, John McIntosh discovered several unidentified tree seedlings growing on his farm. One of the trees produced an apple that was given the family name. McIntosh apples are vivid red brushed with bright green. Early season apples have more green and later season ones may be almost all red. Later season apples have a slightly sweeter taste than those picked earlier in the season.

Developed in 1944 in California, Pink Pearl apples are one of the more popular red-fleshed varieties of apple. They have a balanced sweet-tart flavor with hints of raspberries and grapefruit. Today, they are grown mainly on the west coast at orchards that specialize in heirloom varieties.

The Pippin apple, originating in New York in 1730, is one of the oldest apple varieties in the United Sates. It was a favorite of Thomas Jefferson, George Washington and Ben Franklin. The green and yellow varieties have a sweet-tart flavor that mellows in cold storage. The Pippin is a good source of soluble fiber, contains vitamins A and C, and trace amount of boron and potassium. Ribston Pippin apples, yellow to green in color with red striations, have a higher content of vitamin C than most apples. Its flavor has subtle hints of pear. The Cox's Orange Pippin, often grown for hard ciders, is yellow with a red blush and brownish-red striping.

The Red Delicious apple is the most widely grown variety of apple in the world. It was discovered in 1872 in Iowa. It is higher in antioxidants than many other apple varieties and is better fresh than cooked. Criterion apples look similar to the Red Delicious variety in shape but their skin is yellow with a pink or red blush.

Rhode Island Greenings, discovered near Newport, Rhode Island, were a very popular apple in the first two hundred years of American history. The skin of these apples is bright green with a tart taste that sweetens with aging.

The Rome apple, one of the best cooking apples, was first planted in 1817 in Ohio and named after the township. It is solid bright to deep red in color with a mildly sweet and tangy flavor. It contains potassium, vitamins A and C, iron and boron, and is rich in soluble fiber.

The red skin Santana apple was first bred in the Netherlands in the 1970s. It is just one of two apples that people who are sensitive to apples can eat because it has reduced levels of certain proteins. The Dutch grown Elise apple is the second type that can be consumed safely by most people with a mild apple allergy.

Originating in France during the 1600s, the Snow apple was introduced to the Americas in the 1700s. It is a red apple that often has green or cream-colored spots. It is high in vitamins B6, C and K, and riboflavin, and it also contains potassium, copper, manganese, and magnesium. There is an old Snow apple tree that lives on the poet Robert Frost's farm in Vermont.

The Spitzenburg apple was first discovered in New York in the early 1700s and was another favorite apple of President Thomas Jefferson. It is vibrant red and capped with an orange to yellow blush. Highly aromatic, it has a rich and sweet taste with slight hints of nuts and spice.

The Twenty Ounce apple was introduced to the Pacific Northwest in 1914 and was considered to be the ultimate baking apple for more than one hundred years because of its size. It is green in color with red-orange striations, and a mildly sweet flavor with a tart finish.

The red Winesap apple has been popular since 1917 in cider production in New Jersey. A highly aromatic apple with a sweet-tart taste, it got its name from its spicy wine-like flavor.

"Eat an apple on going to bed, and you'll keep the doctor from earning his bread."
Old English proverb

APRICOT

Apricots originally came from China and then made their way into the Persian Empire and the Mediterranean. Spanish explorers introduced them to the New World and the apricot tree has been successfully cultivated in the United States. About ninety percent of apricots are grown in the U.S. and come from California. There are three different original types: Chinese apricot, Japanese apricot, and desert apricot, and there are dozens of different apricot cultivars. Apricot trees may be standard (growing up to twenty feet tall), semi-dwarf (up to fifteen feet tall), or dwarf (no more than eight feet tall). All trees produce full-sized fruit with smooth golden orange skin with a slight rosy blush, depending on the variety. Apricots are a good source of vitamin A and potassium and are especially high in soluble fiber. It takes three to four pounds of fresh fruit to produce one pound of dried apricots.

The apricot kernel is the soft part inside the seed of the apricot. It is said to be a good source of iron, potassium and phosphorus, and one of the best sources of vitamin B17. It is used as an ingredient in some apricot jams, Italian amaretto cookies, liqueur, and for adding a marzipan flavor to recipes. There are two types of apricot kernels: sweet, that are better for snacking, and bitter, that are known for their therapeutic values. The kernels have been used in Chinese medicine for respiratory problems, indigestion, high blood pressure and arthritis. In Russia, they have been used as a cancer remedy since 1845, and in the U.S. since the 1920s (although there is still some debate as to their effectiveness). Apricot kernel oil is a mild natural oil used in baby products, skin products, and massage oil.

Blenheim apricots, the most widely grown commercially, were found planted in the Spanish missions of California in the 1880s. They have a darker orange color flesh than other varieties and are most commonly used for drying and preserves.

The Hunza apricot that looks like a pale walnut comes from wild apricot trees in the Hunza valley in Kashmir, and from Afghanistan and Turkey. It is a small, round, hard dried apricot with a beige colour. The fruit is left on the trees to dry before being harvested. With an intense toffee-like flavour, it needs to be soaked and cooked before eating.

A few other types include the Autumn Royal, Earligold, Garden Annie, Fold Kist, Harcot, Harglow, Katie, Moorpark, Montrose, and King (a very large apricot).

<h1 style="text-align:center">ARTICHOKE</h1>

The artichoke was first developed in Sicily and was known to both the Greeks and the Romans. All artichokes commercially grown in the United States are grown in California but they were first grown in Louisiana, brought there by settlers in the nineteenth century. Artichokes are actually a flower bud and a close relative to the thistle. The phytonutrients in artichokes provide potent antioxidant benefits. They are a good source of dietary fiber to help improve digestive health and can reduce bad LDL cholesterol. They contain vitamin C, known for its immune-boosting properties, and vitamin K which can improve cognition in elderly people. Artichokes also contain cynarin that alters our taste buds so that the sweet flavor of foods and beverages, especially wine, is enhanced. The leaves produce an extract that was substituted for quinine and they have also been used as a substitute for hops in beer making.

The Green Globe artichoke has been the most popular since the 1920s. Its scale-like leaves produce short, tiny needle-like thorns that are inedible. The Globe has a buttery tasting heart with a dense layer of meaty flesh at the base of the petals and stem. Cocktail artichokes are smaller artichokes growing on the same plant as larger artichokes, such as the Globe artichoke and Desert Globe artichoke plants. Every part of the cocktail artichoke is edible and they are more tender but less meaty than larger ones. Baby purple artichokes are harvested on the stem. The stem has a flavor similar to the artichoke heart. The dark purple outer layer of leaves becomes lighter as you get closer to the heart and the flavor is sweeter than the green variety due to the darker pigmentation. The Fiesole baby artichoke is considered to be the most flavorful of all baby artichoke varieties. It is tulip-shaped and has a violet-wine colored exterior.

Castroville, California is known as the Artichoke Capital of the World. Norma Jean Dougherty (Marilyn Monroe) was crowned Artichoke Queen in 1947.

<h1 style="text-align:center">ARWEE</h1>

Arwee, or Indian Taro, is a root vegetable. The root (bulb) is consumed as well as the leaves. It looks much like a potato with a slimy consistency similar to okra. It is high in fiber and antioxidants and has a high level of vitamin B. Arwee can be mashed, boiled, cut into strips and baked like fries, fried or steamed. It is native to Southeast Asia and is said to be one of the earliest cultivated vegetables in eastern India. It is grown throughout the tropics.

Ancestral varieties of fruits and vegetables are those that were introduced into the human diet when the only foods eaten were whole, unprocessed, and easier to digest and metabolize. They usually predate the nineteenth century.

ASPARAGUS

Asparagus is a member of the Lily family and is related to onions and garlic. It takes two to three years for the plant to yield its first crop. Female asparagus stalks are plumper than male stalks. It is cultivated for its edible young stems, known as spears. The spears absorb moisture from the air which creates a swelling in size even after picked. The small scales at the tip of an asparagus spear are actually the leaves. California grows seventy percent of all the asparagus grown in the United States. It is an excellent source of vitamins A and K and contains more glutathione (antioxidant) than any other fruit or vegetable. Asparagus has no fat or cholesterol.

Jumbo asparagus are cultivated for their ability to maintain a succulent and firm texture when harvested at maturity. Large asparagus are harvested and sold in uniform sizes according to the diameter of the spears. Standard green asparagus is grown and marketed to be nine inches in length. Purple asparagus, originally developed in Italy by farmers, has violet hued stems with pale green to creamy white flesh. It is sweeter than other asparagus types and tender enough to be eaten raw (cooking will dull its color). White asparagus spears are pearly white because, while being cultivated, soil is mounded over the asparagus plants to prevent the sun's rays from producing chlorophyll as they grow, so they mature without color.

Native to most of Europe, northern Africa, and western Asia, asparagus has been cultivated for centuries. An Egyptian frieze (a broad horizontal band of sculpted or painted decoration on a wall near the ceiling) dating back to 3,000 B.C. depicts asparagus. Supposedly, Queen Nefertiti (1371-1330 B.C.) proclaimed asparagus to be the food of the gods and it was used in offering rituals to appease their gods. In ancient Rome, asparagus was grown in gardens where the stalks reached massive sizes. Rome became the first to preserve the vegetable by freezing it in the Alps in the first century B.C. King Louis XIV (1638-1715 A.D.) was the first to have asparagus cultivated in greenhouses in France.

ATEMOYA

The Atemoya looks like a pinecone with a pale bluish-green or pea-green skin that turns more yellow as it ripens. It can weigh up to five pounds. The first known Atemoya was bred in 1908 in Miami. It is now commercially grown in a few tropical areas throughout the world. Atemoya flowers are hermaphroditic (they turn from female to male over the course of a few hours) so any flower can pollinate any other. The atemoya is very high in Vitamin C, is a good source of dietary fiber, and contains some protein, calcium, and iron. The texture is similar to a firm custard and is best eaten fresh, chilled, and directly out of the shell with a spoon. **Caution: The large black seeds should not be eaten.**

"One cannot think well, love well, sleep well, if one has not dined well."
Virginia Woolf   1882-1941
Author

Fossils and artifacts have been found dating the avocado tree to 10,000 B.C. Avocados have been cultivated in Central America for more than seven thousand years. European sailors traveling to the New World used avocados as their form of butter. Spanish conquistadors discovered that avocado seeds yield a milky fluid that turns red when exposed to air. They used this indelible natural ink in documents that are preserved to this day. Mexico is the world's largest avocado producer. California is the leading producer of avocados in the United States, followed by Florida and Hawaii. Avocado trees were first planted in Florida in 1833 and it is the first state to cultivate them. Fallbrook, California is the Avocado Capital of the World.

A single mature avocado tree can produce more than four hundred pieces of fruit in a year. Unlike most fruits, the avocado is one of the very few that does not ripen on the tree. Few fruits contain fat but avocados, olives, and nuts have significant amounts. Avocados have the highest fiber content of any fruit and they contain vitamins C, E and K, and folate. The oil in avocados is known for being high in monounsaturated fatty acids which may help to reduce blood cholesterol levels. Until the mid-twentieth century, the avocado had a reputation as an aphrodisiac. The largest number of culinary dishes made with avocado is found in Israel.

There are more than eighty varieties of avocados. The Fuerte avocado is the original high quality California avocado – its green color, smooth texture, pear-like shape, weight (six to twelve ounces), and size are considered a standard for judging other varieties. The Reed is the largest of all known avocado varieties and can weigh a pound or more. It has a rich, nutty and buttery flavor considered by many to be the best tasting avocado. The Hass avocado is known for its leathery, fairly thick skin that turns near black when fully mature. The Bacon avocado is a hybrid of two Mexican avocado varieties, originally cultivated in 1954 in California. Sir Prize avocado, with the most flesh-to-seed ratio of any commercial avocado, is a great variety for use in guacamole because the flesh does not turn brown after it is cut. **Caution: Most avocado varieties have toxic foliage.**

Cocktail avocados, that were originally cultivated in Chile, are small elongated avocados with thin, edible skin, creamy pulp, and no central avocado pit. Mexicola Cocktail avocados originated in Pasadena, California in 1910 and have smooth, glossy and thin skin, which is nearly black in color. They have edible leaves, unlike most avocado varieties. The leaves of the Mexicola Cocktail avocado are thought to have many medicinal uses. Some people believe the leaves can treat arthritis, cold and flu symptoms, upset stomach, kidney disease, bacterial infections, and inflammatory diseases. When steeped in hot water, the tea can be rubbed directly on skin to sooth and treat the symptoms of acne, eczema and dry skin. When toasted, the leaves have a hazelnut aroma and anise-licorice flavor.

BAMBOO

There are over twelve hundred varieties of bamboo. Native to Asia, bamboo can be found on every continent except Europe and Antarctica. In the United States, they grow in Florida, California, and the Gulf States. Young, new bamboo canes are harvested for their tender inner core before they are a foot tall. Bamboo shoots, also called bamboo sprouts, are used mostly in Asian cuisine and salads. The two main varieties of bamboo shoots are winter shoots and spring shoots. Fresh bamboo shoots have a mild and sweet flavor, similar to baby corn, and must be cooked before eating. Evidence in Chinese literature dating back to 618 A.D. discusses the benefits of eating bamboo shoots. They contain protein, dietary fiber, and a good amount of vitamins and minerals. They have anti-inflammatory properties and can control bad cholesterol, strengthen the immune system, and are heart friendly. Bamboo shoots are rich in amino acids, carbohydrates, protein, sugar, fat, minerals, and fiber.

> Bamboo is one of the most utilized and versatile plants on earth. Every part of the plant is used by Asian cultures and various ethnic groups for a variety of purposes ranging from construction, furniture, musical instruments, and paper production.

BANANA

Bananas first appeared in written history in the sixth century B.C. The banana tree, the largest herbaceous plant in the world, is actually a giant herb, not a tree. Its fruit is actually a berry. Over one hundred countries grow bananas but the largest producer is India. There are more than five hundred different varieties of bananas. The most common banana commercially sold is the Cavendish banana, grown throughout the world. It is the identical twin to the first one discovered in South East Asia (all bananas are direct clones of one another). Bananas are full of potassium and vitamins B, B6 and C, fiber, and magnesium. In the early 1800s in Hawaii, most banana varieties were *kapu* – forbidden for women to eat under penalty of death. More songs have been written about the banana than any other fruit.

The Apple banana is native to Central and South America. It is stout and plump, with a thick taut peel and tart apple aroma. Baby bananas, native to Columbia, average only three to four inches in length and have a sweet flavor with hints of vanilla and caramel. The Brazilian Dwarf banana is a petite banana known for maximum sweetness and is regarded as one of the best tasting banana varieties sold. Burro bananas, mainly grown in Mexico, have a variety of culinary uses, both sweet and savory, and have also been used to stimulate hemoglobin in cases of anemia.

The small Ice Cream banana, the hardiest of the banana plants, has a silver-blue matte sheen when young and a canary yellow hue when ripe. The flesh has the texture of ice cream when ripe and its flavor is reminiscent of sweet honey and vanilla custard. Originally discovered growing within the Indo-Malaysian region, Ice Cream bananas grow wild in Fiji and are also found growing throughout the Hawaiian Islands. The Rajapuri banana, a dwarf banana plant, grows in large bunches that can reach forty pounds in weight. It is known for its dessert-like, extremely sweet flavor. The Red banana, native to India and Southeast Asia, is short and plump with a thick, brick-red peel. Its flavor has a hint of raspberry. The Red banana has more beta carotene and Vitamin C than yellow banana varieties.

All parts of the Banana plant are edible. Although the fruits are most commonly eaten, the leaves are used for a variety of culinary applications. White banana flowers are found at the large tapered cone at the tip end of a forming bunch of bananas. Younger blossoms are sweet and tender and a good source of vitamins A and C. The edible part of the stem, the inner portion of the fibrous stalk, is often seen in southern Indian cuisine. It has a crisp texture and a mild sweet-tart flavor. It is high in fiber, potassium, and vitamin B6, and can aid in the treatment of ulcers and help prevent kidney stones.

Plantains (cooking bananas) are native to Asia and West Africa. They are also grown commercially in the Caribbean and Florida. Plantains were first domesticated in Papua New Guinea around 8000 B.C. and are among the longest producing of banana plants. As they ripen, they develop a sweet taste and their color changes from green to yellow to black. Green plantains are the younger immature stage of the fruit and most often used for fried plantain chips. Yellow plantains are at the middle stage of the fruit's maturity and are often mashed, grilled, baked, or caramelized. Black plantains have a thick dark peel and a starchy pink to pale yellow-hued flesh with a strong vanilla aroma. Plantains have more than twenty times the amount of vitamin A, three times the vitamin C, double the magnesium, and almost twice the potassium as the common banana. They are often used in place of potatoes and rice in many Latin American dishes.

The Cassabanana, native to Brazil and cultivated in Central and South America, is not a banana. It resembles a cucumber and can be yellow-orange, orange-red, or maroon-black in color. It has a strong sweet, long-lasting fragrance and is often stored in linen closets as a moth repellant. The fruit is popular in jams and jellies.

BEAN SPROUT

Bean sprouts are classified as the edible shoots of germinated beans. They have a crispy texture and sweet taste and can be fresh, canned, or frozen (canned sprouts won't have the texture or flavor of fresh). They contain vitamins A, B, B1, B6, C and K, calcium and foliate, as well as iron, magnesium, phosphorus, calcium, potassium, manganese, and omega 3 fatty acids. Sprouts from mung beans, the most popular type, have been used for food since ancient times.

BEET

The Wild beet, the ancestor of all beets, is thought to have originated in prehistoric times in North Africa. It was also found growing wild along Asian and European seashores. The faster beets grow, the better the flavor. Beets have the highest sugar content of any vegetable and are an alternate source of sweetener that produce the same effect as sugar cane. Beet greens have a semi-bitter flavor similar to swiss chard. The greens are more nutritious than the beets and contain twice the potassium. They are also exceptionally high in beta carotene and folic acid. **Caution: The leaves contain concentrated amounts of oxalic acid that, when eaten in excess, can interfere with the body's ability to metabolize calcium.**

There are several varieties of Gold beets that have anti-inflammatory and antioxidant properties. The flesh of the Baby Gold beet is bright yellow and retains its color when cooked. Unlike Red beets, its coloring does not bleed. The Gold Forno beet is made up of both an edible root and edible leaves. These beets are a rare European heirloom variety. Gold beets can be used to replace Red beets in any given beet recipe.

Most White beet varieties originated in Germany, Holland, and Switzerland. Their flavor and texture is enhanced by roasting or streaming. Baby White beets can be used in place of any other beet recipe.

The Chioggia beet is an Italian heirloom variety. Baby Chioggia beets, roots, stems, and leaves are edible and contain the highest content of geosmin, an organic compound responsible for their deep earthy flavor and aroma. They can be processed into beet juice. The juice is used to color pasta.

Cylindra beets, from Denmark, are named for their long, cylindrical roots that sometimes grow up to six or eight inches in length. They are also called "Butter Slicer" beets because of their texture and ease of slicing.

Red Forno beets are made up of both an edible root and edible leaves.

Baby Bull's Blood beets, from the Netherlands, are the only beet variety featuring entirely red roots, stems, and leaves.

Aloe vera, a cactus-like plant, grows wild in tropical climates around the world and is cultivated for agricultural, medicinal, and decorative uses. It has serrated edges and a pliable texture. The medicinal aloe, with a jelly-like consistency, is found in the inner flesh of the leaf. Aloe vera has been consumed and applied topically for thousands of years.

Amla berries, native to the subtropical South Asian countries of India, Pakistan, and Bangladesh, are small round berries with light-green skin. The flesh is juicy and the taste is sour and bitter. Soak them in salt water to rid them of their bitter flavor. Amla berries contain phenols, flavonoids, tannins, and other antioxidants, and have twenty times the amount of vitamin C as an orange. They are revered by the Hindu and used in religious rites and ceremonies.

Blackberries (and raspberries) are not actually berries. They are an aggregate fruit with individual drupelets that are held together by very fine, nearly invisible hairs. Blackberries, originally known as bramble or brambleberries due to their heavy growth and thorns, are native to every continent except Antarctica. There are hundreds of varieties – they create new forms as they adjust to climate, soil, and other environmental factors. The name 'blackberry' is often used as a generic term that refers to a wide range of bush berries that are considered blackberries. These include loganberries, boysenberries, marionberries, and ollalieberries.

Loganberries are a natural cross between blackberries and red raspberries. They are long, dark red berries that are good for fresh eating, juicing, or making pies, jams and jellies. The berry is low in sodium, saturated fat and cholesterol, and high in vitamins C and K, dietary fiber, manganese, folate, and copper.

The Boysenberry is a hybrid fruit that was cultivated by cross pollinating the flowers of the raspberry, loganberry and blackberry. It is named after Boysen's farm in California, where it originated. It is a good source of vitamin C and potassium, as well as other essential vitamins and minerals. The Boysenberry's popularity made Knott's Berry Farm famous.

Marionberries are a cross between two Oregon blackberry hybrids and were named after the county in Oregon where they were developed. They are larger than blackberries, are high in antioxidants, vitamins and fiber, and are very low in calories. Marionberries are considered caneberries (blackberries and raspberries that grow on long canes and produce fruit in clusters). The Willamette Valley in Oregon is considered the Caneberry Capitol of the World.

The Olallieberry was developed in 1949 at Oregon State University and grows in the more temperate coastal regions of California. It is a cross between a blackberry, a loganberry and a youngberry (cross-pollinated with raspberries). It looks like an elongated blackberry with a sweet-tart taste and its coloring will stain when touched. The word 'Olalli' comes from the Northwestern Native American's word for berry.

Black chokeberries are very small (about a half inch in diameter) and are most often used to make jams, jellies, juice, and wine. Native to the Great Lakes region in the mid-western United States, they were used by the Native Americans in that area for multiple purposes. The berries are also widely grown in Europe. Black chokeberries have higher levels of antioxidants than any other berry. Supposedly, they got their name because birds are not too fond of the taste and choke on them. Their color is used as a natural food dye.

There are dozens of subspecies of Black Nightshade, each varying only slightly from each other. The berries and the leaves of the Black Nightshade plant were a crucial food source and an important natural medicine for early Native American tribes. They have a slightly sweet, yet tomato-like flavor. Most western cultures have long regarded Black Nightshade as inedible due to the myth of its toxicity even though it has been proven to be safe for consumption. The berries contain calcium, phosphorus and vitamin A.

NOTE: Belladonna, or Deadly Nightshade, is a very toxic plant in the same family.

Blueberries are native to North America and were first cultivated in the early twentieth century. Native Americans used the plant's leaves and roots for medicinal purposes. During Colonial times, colonists made grey paint by boiling blueberries in milk. The United States is the world's largest producer of blueberries. They are the second most important commercial berry crop in the U.S. Michigan is the leading producer of cultivated blueberries and Maine is the leading producer of wild or lowbush blueberries. The blue color is due to the concentration of anthocyanin present in their skin (this berry has the highest level of anthocyanins than any other fruit or vegetable). There are three types of blueberries: Highbush, Pink Lemonade, and Wild. The Highbush Blueberry is the most commercially important of the three types. Pink Lemonade blueberries, developed by the USDA, are pink and have a high sugar content. Wild blueberries are less sweet than cultivated blueberries but they have more antioxidants.

Cubeb berries, also known as Java Pepper, originated in Indonesia. They are sometimes also called Tailed Pepper because of the small stem that usually remains on each berry. Cubeb berries have a mild peppery flavor similar to black peppercorns, but the strongest flavor has a camphor or eucalyptus quality. They are best when used in soups and stews, or to flavor meat or vegetable dishes. **Remove the berries before serving the dish.** Cubeb berries are cultivated for their fruit and essential oil. They came to Europe with Venetian traders. The main use was in medicine but its similarity to pepper made it a good substitute. The berry is considered a diuretic, expectorant, stimulant, and antiseptic. It was used in the treatment of gonorrhea and was shown to be effective in easing the symptoms of chronic bronchitis. It is also used for digestive ailments and is effective in treating dysentery.

Curry berries are small, sweet, and shiny. The unripe fruit starts out white and speckled before turning green and then black when fully ripe. They are about half an inch long and contain a very large amount of vitamin C as well as minerals like iron and calcium. The edible products of the curry tree have been an important part of Indian cooking and medicine for hundreds of years. **Caution: Curry berries have toxic seeds that should not be consumed.**

Cranberries are native to North America. Wild cranberries grew on low-running vines in sandy bogs and marshes. Today, they are water cultivated in bogs so the buoyant berries float on the water's surface for easy harvest. Small pockets of air inside the berry cause it to float in water. Fresh cranberries are firm to the touch and will bounce because of their air pockets. Raw cranberries are glossy and scarlet red in appearance with a bitter and tart flavor. Once juiced, cooked and processed, the flavor becomes sweet-tart. The Cranberry was first called a Crane berry because the plant's flower resembled the head of the sand crane that frequented the bogs where these plants were found growing. Wisconsin is the number one cranberry producer in the United States, followed by Massachusetts.

Honeybees are often used to pollinate cranberry crops and are more valuable in the performance of this task than they are in the production of honey. Cranberries are one of the top antioxidant-rich foods and have been shown to have an anti-inflammatory effect. They've been used to prevent urinary tract infections and also benefit dental health by preventing bacteria from sticking to teeth. Cranberries, like olives, must be altered from their raw stage to become palatable for human consumption.

> Cranberry juice was first made by American settlers in 1683. The first cranberry sauce was marketed in 1912. It takes about two hundred cranberries to make one can of cranberry sauce.

The elderberry bush, a member of the honeysuckle family, is actually a small tree with delicate white flowers emerging as berry clusters. The blossoms have a sweet scent and sweet taste. Native Americans crafted items like arrow shafts, flutes, and pipes from the branches. The name 'elder' is from the Anglo-Saxon word *aeld,* meaning 'fire' (the hollow stems of this plant were used to gently blow on flames to intensify the fire). The flowers, leaves, berries, bark and roots have all been used in traditional folk medicine, such as to relax sore muscles and sooth burns and rashes. The dark berries contain many flavonoids and antioxidants, high amounts of vitamins A and C, vitamin B6, potassium, iron, fiber, and betacarotene. Elderberries add a unique tartness to various foods and are also used to make wine. **Caution: Green, unripe, or bright red elderberries are bitter and possibly toxic – the raw berries contain a cyanide-like chemical. Cook only the blue variety.**

Goji berries are native to China but The Himalayas, Mongolia, and Tibet produce most of the world's supply. They have a bright red-orange color and are similar in size and shape to currants, with a tangy yet sweet flavor. In ancient Eastern Asian medicine, these berries were said to help with insomnia, anxiety, and low energy. Goji berries contain the third highest amount of antioxidants of all the foods in the world, five-hundred times more vitamin C than oranges, more protein than whole wheat, more iron than spinach, and more beta-carotene than carrots. They also contain vitamin E.

The Golden berry, a small yellowish berry about the size of a marble, is native to South America. It has spread to other parts of the world, including South Africa and Europe and is known by more than a dozen different names. It is more closely related to tomatoes and eggplants than other berries. Considered to be a superfood that is loaded with nutrients and antioxidants, some of the health benefits include its ability to help with weight loss, detoxify the body, manage diabetes, optimize kidney function, reduce inflammation, prevent certain degenerative diseases, boost heart health, and maximize immune function.

Gooseberries are small and firm but sometimes ribbed and translucent, and grow on small, thorny bushes. Native to North America and Siberia, they were also cultivated in Asia and Africa. The British began developing new varieties around the sixteenth century, and competitive gooseberry growing was a popular pastime up to World War I. The two main gooseberry types are American and European and there are about two thousand cultivars. They come in varying shades of yellow, green, red or black, and can be round, oval, pear-shaped or elongated. Tart and sweet berries can be found on one bush, each with many tiny edible seeds. Gooseberries are rich in antioxidants, vitamins, and other beneficial nutrients, and they have twenty times more vitamin C than oranges. They are said to produce insulin, strengthen heart muscles, slow aging, protect the eyes, improve the skin, and prevent hair loss. The Indian gooseberry is light green and extremely bitter. The Cape gooseberry, sometimes called a Peruvian cherry, is yellow-orange and surrounded by a paper-thin husk that falls off as it dries. Gooseberries are banned from cultivation in some U.S. states because they can host a serious fungal disease that kills white pines.

The Huckleberry, native to North America, grows in the wild and its primary purpose is for wildlife. It resembles a tiny blueberry in appearance and taste although it is more sweet-tart. The Huckleberry is not a true berry, it is a drupe because it has a seed within. There are several species but the Black variety is most common. Huckleberries may be used fresh but are mostly found in frozen form, and can be cooked, baked in pies, and made into compotes and syrups.

The Juniper bush is native to the upper portion of the Northern Hemisphere. The small berry has a dark blue color with a silver bloom and a sharp flavor similar to rosemary. Use of the Juniper berry dates back to Ancient Egypt and the berries were found in the tomb of King Tut. Greek warriors ate them raw to boost stamina. Romans used them for medicinal purposes. The berry's oil is used as a diuretic, aids indigestion, and functions as a powerful detoxifier. The berries are the main ingredient in gin. Gin was originally known as *jenever* (juniper) in the Netherlands, where it was first produced.

Midgen berries, native to the Eastern Australian coast, have also been found growing in central Florida and Southern California. They are small, round white fruits with blue-gray spots and three to nine pale brown edible seeds. Often consumed raw, they have a mild, sweet-gingery taste. Native Australians use midgen berries to make a flavorful jam.

The Mulberry, native to China, became naturalized in Europe centuries ago. It is not actually a berry, but a collective fruit. It grows on a tree, unlike bramble berries that grow on bush-like plants. The tree was introduced to America during early colonial times. There are over one hundred fifty different species of mulberries that produce red, white, pink, and black fruits. Black mulberries are jet black in color with blushes of ruby. Their texture is fragile and syrupy and the color stains when touched. White mulberries have white, pink, or light purple flesh and a mild honey taste. They are very rich in vitamin C. Unlike black and white mulberries, Chinese Red mulberries are more rounded with a candy apple red flesh. They lack the tartness of the Black mulberry. In China, mulberries are used to treat fatigue, anemia, and insomnia. King White mulberries are longer than Black mulberries and are virtually seedless. The young berries start out dark green and gradually lighten into a soft white color. When mature, the taste is very sweet, with hints of honey. The Pakistan Mulberry has an elongated shape, usually three inches long, and is dark purple in color with a green stem. It has a unique sweet and spicy flavor.

Native to Turkey, the raspberry was cultivated by the ancient Greeks. Seeds were discovered at Roman forts in Britain. Raspberries were first used for medicinal purposes only. The fruit arrived in the United States by the late 1700s but there are also raspberry bushes that have origins within the New World. New York State began a breeding program for them in the late 1800s and by 1925 over four hundred varieties were available. Today, most varieties are cultivated in California.

The raspberry is composed of many connecting drupelets (individual sections of fruit, each with its own seed) surrounding a central core. There are three main varieties: black, golden, and red (the most known). They are distinguished by their size, shape, hollow core, and flavor (from sweet-tart to low acid). Black raspberries, indigenous only to North America, are smaller than other colored raspberries and more tart than sweet. Various hybrid berries developed from crosses between Red and Black raspberries. The Gold raspberry, another type of hybrid, is gold with pink hues and very sweet. There are several lesser known varieties, like the Purple raspberry, larger than the common red berry and sweeter due to a higher sugar content. Its plum color can stain lips and mouths.

Raspberries are an excellent source of vitamin C and rich in B vitamins. They contain fiber, folic acid, copper, and iron. They have the highest concentration of antioxidant strength amongst all fruits and they also have a phenolic compound that prevents cancer. Their oil has a sun protection factor. Loganberries and boysenberries are two hybrids of raspberries.

Though there are species of Strawberry native to temperate regions all around the world, the union of *fragaria virginiana*, native to North America, and *fragaria chiloensis*, native to Chile, gave us the garden variety strawberry. There are hundreds of varieties and all of them have seeds on the skin rather than skin around the seed, which distinguishes them from a berry and a true fruit. There are three types of modern strawberry cultivars: June-bearing strawberries are harvested in June; Everbearing strawberries thrive in hotter climates; and Day-neutral strawberries are not a berry but are the greatly enlarged stem end of the plant's flower. Strawberries were once avoided by pregnant women because it was believed that their children would be born with strawberry birth marks. Fresh strawberries were once used as a toothpaste, as the juice cleaned discolored teeth. The United States is the leading producer of strawberries. California grows about eighty-eight percent of the strawberries in the U.S. Plant City, Florida is the Winter Strawberry Capital of the World and holds a festival every year.

White strawberries are native to both the Old World and the New World and grow in wild and domesticated forms. There are two species: *fragaria vesca* (known as Alpine strawberries) is native to Europe; *fragaria chiloensis* (known as Beach strawberries) is a wild species native to Chile. The flesh is ivory white with pink blushes and red seeds on the skin. The flavor is characterized by notes of pineapple, caramel, and grape. The Puren White strawberry, also known as Pineberry, is the oldest known strawberry. It is now also grown in the United Kingdom in greenhouses. It has white to ivory skin with pale hues of blushing pink and studs of red seeds. The flavor is similar to pineapple.

Green strawberries are red strawberry varieties that have been plucked before maturity. They should not be used in place of ripe red strawberries but rather used as an acidic fruit replacement for other acidic fruits like citrus and tomatoes. They are also pickled.

Specific varieties are grown for Stem strawberry production and they all must be uniform in size, color, shape, and ripeness and maintain a two-inch stem. Each Stem strawberry is carefully cut by hand in order to leave a long stem on the strawberry. These large strawberries are served whole and intact.

Wild strawberries are indigenous to both the Old World and New World. They are petite and their flavor is more complex and tart than a cultivated strawberry. Red-fleshed wild strawberries are the most common but white and yellow wild strawberries have a higher sugar content and are less acidic. Native Americans used wild strawberry leaf as a disinfectant and a treatment for gastrointestinal, kidney, and liver problems. is a wild strawberry variety that is approximately the size of a raspberry and almost perfectly round. Its deep red color is richer than an ordinary strawberry and its exterior seeds are deeply inset into its surface. Its inner flesh is also deep red, sweet and mildly tart, with a rich juice content. The Strasberry strawberry originated in South America in the 1900s. This plant is not able to self-pollination so it must be planted within close proximity to ordinary strawberry plants.

Youngberries look similar to Boysenberries and are sweeter than Blackberries. They are a purplish-black color and lack many seeds. They were developed by a fruit grower in Louisiana in 1905 as a cross between a Blackberry variety called Phenomenal (a Blackberry-Raspberry cross) and a Mayes Dewberry. Dewberries, closely related to blackberries, are purple to black. Their leaves can be used for a tea and the sweet berries can be eaten raw, or used to make cobbler or jam.

BOK CHOY

Bok choy, or Chinese cabbage, belongs to the family of cruciferous vegetables that includes Brussels sprouts, broccoli, and cauliflower but it is not true cabbage. It is actually Chinese chard. Bok choy is rich in beta-carotene, an antioxidant. It is a great source of fiber and vitamin C that is effective in strengthening the immune system and preventing disease and infection. It contains potassium and calcium that help to lower blood pressure. Baby Bok choy, or Shanghai Bok Choy, is young, petite and more tender than mature Bok choy. Red Bok choy has deep violet oval shaped blades. The coloring gives the leaves a more pronounced mustard flavor.

BOTTLE GOURD

Bottle gourd is one of the first cultivated plants and was domesticated over ten thousand years ago in Africa. It can be short and round, curved, or long and thin and varies from light green to dark green. The interior flesh is creamy white with petite seeds that are tender and edible when young. The flavor is mild like summer squash and cucumber. In Africa, the dried gourd has been used as a vessel for water and rice, and as hats for sun protection. A soccer stadium was designed to model the shape and color of the dried bottle gourd. In India, dried gourds were used to make musical instruments. In Mexico, the dried gourd was used as a canteen for water. In South America, it is carved into a drinking vessel and in Hawaii, dried bottle gourds were used as a bowl. Rich in fiber, it is thought to help aid in healthy digestion. **Caution: The juice has vitamin C and zinc but never drink it if the taste is bitter as it may contain toxins.**

BREADFRUIT

A Breadfruit tree is a large evergreen that bears fruit that tastes as sweet as bread. A single tree can yield up to two hundred fruits per season making it one of the largest-yielding food plants. The breadfruit tree can be traced back thirty-five hundred years when it was found by ancestors of Polynesians in the northwestern area of New Guinea. Today, the trees are found in Micronesia, Hawaii, the Caribbean, Western Pacific islands, and Malay Peninsula. The large round starchy fruit is used as a vegetable and sometimes ground to make a substitute for flour. Rarely eaten raw, it can be steamed, boiled, roasted, fried, pickled, fermented, or frozen. There are more than two hundred types of breadfruits available in different colors, flavors, sizes, and with seeds or seedless. Breadfruit is a source of dietary fiber, vitamin C, and potassium. The tree's wood is used in canoe-making, and the latex produced by the trees can be used as boat caulk.

BROCCOLI

Twenty-five hundred years ago, broccoli was developed from wild cabbage on the island of Cyprus. The word 'broccoli' originates from the Italian word *broccolo*, which means 'the flowering crest of a cabbage.' Italian immigrants brought broccoli with them to the New World. The first commercially grown broccoli crop in the United States was grown and harvested in New York. Broccoli was planted in California in the 1920s and ninety percent of the fresh broccoli sold in the U.S. is grown in the Salinas Valley in California. Broccoli contains a high amount of potassium that helps maintain a healthy nervous system and optimal brain function, as well as promotes regular muscle growth. It also contains vitamins A and C, magnesium, and calcium. The B6 and folate in broccoli reduces the risk of heart attack and stroke. It bolsters the immune system and is high in fiber, which aids in digestion.

Broccoli flowers are commonly found among the still closed buds of the broccoli head. They may be removed and eaten raw by themselves or used with the stalks and florets as a salad or in a broccoli pesto. Broccoli leaves are a dark, blue-green with purple and grey highlights but color and shape vary slightly with each variety. Similar in appearance to collard greens, they have a mild broccoli flavor and are low in calories and high in vitamins A and C.

Broccoli sprouts have a mild flavor and contain a highly concentrated level of vitamins and compounds (often ten to one hundred times that of mature broccoli heads). Eating broccoli sprouts every day may reduce bad cholesterol levels and promote good cholesterol. They are a great source of protein and also contain highly concentrated levels of sulforaphane that may help the body fight cancer.

Baby broccoli's head is a petite cluster of florets with a mild, peppery and subtlety sweet flavor. The entire plant is edible.

Baby sprouting Calabrese broccoli has short thin stems and is much smaller and more tender than common commercial broccoli. It is named after its native location, the Italian province of Calabria.

Purple Baby broccoli has small loose clusters of florets sprouting from a slender stem that also produces side shoots and leaves. The clusters and leaves have a violet hue with light green undertones. It is more tender than common broccoli and cooks quickly under high heat. Purple baby broccoli is grown in Italy, the United Kingdom, and Southern California.

Broccoli raab (or rabe), also called rapini, looks similar to thin broccoli stalks with small clusters of buds and smooth leaves with sawtooth edges. It is a descendant from a wild herb and has a bitter taste and should be cooked to help mellow the taste. Originating in the Mediterranean and also China, it was brought to the United States in the 1920's by Italian farmers. Low in sodium and very low in calories, it is a good source of vitamins A and C, potassium, iron and calcium.

Spigarello broccoli, an heirloom variety considered to be the parent of broccoli rabe, are wavy edible greens with thin fibrous stems that produce edible flowers but never large floret heads like common broccoli. There are dozens of Spigarello varieties. Native to Southern Italy, they also grown in southern California.

Purple Peacock broccoli is a cross between green goliath broccoli and two different varieties of kale. It has wrinkled, serrated leaves, with a vibrant purple vein that runs down the center of the leaf, and loose heads of purple florets. The leaves and head will cook to a dark green color.

Broccoli Romanesco is a unique Italian variety of broccoli. It has a yellowish-green dense head that forms an unusual spiral pattern. It can be prepared like cauliflower or broccoli.

BROKALI

Brokali is a cross between broccoli and kale. It has long, tender stems, curly leaves, and its florets are smaller than those of conventional broccoli. It has a sweet and nutty flavor with the texture of baby broccoli. The plant also produces tiny yellow flowers from its florets that are edible.

BRUSSELS SPROUT

Brussels Sprouts are native to Belgium, in a region near its capital, Brussels. They have been cultivated throughout Europe and naturalized in the United States. They look like a small cabbage but the flavor is not similar. The leaves have a mild flavor similar to kale. Brussels Sprouts can be used in place of cabbage in any recipe and will have a sweeter flavor and more tender texture. The stalk is also edible but requires longer cooking.

There are many varieties. Baby Brussels sprouts are less than an inch in diameter in size. The younger the Brussels Sprout, the sweeter, more palatable the flavor. Micro Brussels sprouts are a smaller version of mature Brussels sprouts that have been picked at an earlier stage of growth. They are also milder and sweeter in flavor. The first purple variety of Brussels sprout was originally developed by breeding a red cabbage variety with a green Brussels Sprout in 1940. Baby Purple Brussels range from layers of deep purple to sea green with violet red tips and veins.

BULLOCK'S HEART

The Bullock's Heart, or Bull's Heart, is a tropical tree fruit native to the West Indies. It got its name for its resemblance to a bull's heart. Beneath its skin, it has a thick, cream-white layer of custard-like flesh surrounding the fruit's juicy segments. When ripe, the flavor is sweet and succulent. Bullock's Heart is low in calories, fat free, and sodium free. **Caution: Each segment has a hard, black seed that is toxic and should not be eaten.**

BURDOCK ROOT

Native to Northern Europe and northeast Asia, including northern India, Burdock root is similar in shape to a carrot or parsnip and the flavor closely resembles a Jerusalem artichoke or parsnip. Japan developed it as an edible vegetable when it was introduced there a thousand years ago. The roots, as well as the plant's young shoots, peeled stalks, and dried seeds, have numerous compounds that are known to have antioxidant, disease preventing, and health promoting properties. The root is very low in calories, loaded with fiber, contains a good amount of potassium, and smaller quantities of vitamins and minerals. Herbalists use it to treat snake bites and rabies. Burdock root oil extract, also called Bur oil, is used in Europe as a scalp treatment.

CABBAGE

Cabbage has been cultivated for more than four thousand years and domesticated for over twenty-five hundred years. Around 600 B.C. wild cabbage was brought from Asia to Europe where it was used mainly by peasant families as food for people and livestock. It was brought to the Americas in the 1500s. Early cabbage was not the head we know today but a more loose-leaf variety. The head variety was developed during the Middle Ages by northern European farmers. Spiced cabbage in vinegar was a staple food for sailors on long voyages. In the U.S. during World War I, Liberty cabbage was the name used to refer to the German word 'sauerkraut'.

There are hundreds of varieties of cabbage. The leaves can be wide-spread and waffled or smooth and tightly bunched. The colors are green, white, red, or purple. Smooth-leafed firm-headed green cabbage is the most common. All varieties have very short stems that are as edible and nutritious as the leaves. Cabbage has the highest amount of some of the most powerful antioxidants found in cruciferous vegetables. It is a good source of fiber, B vitamins, vitamins C and K, and contains healthy amounts of iron, calcium, and potassium.

Napa Cabbage, also known as White cabbage, is very popular. Native to China, it has barrel-shaped crisp, pale green, tightly-wrapped leaves with a more subtle flavor than European head cabbage. The water content is also higher so it has a crisper texture. There are dozens of varieties from heritage to hybrid.

Savoy cabbage has crinkly leaves and is considered the most tender and sweet. It is the better choice for stuffed cabbage leaves. The most famous award-winning variety of Savoy cabbage is known as Savoy King.

Sprouting cabbage has loosely packed leaves in small heads about the size of a golf ball. It resembles a cross between a small romaine lettuce head and a Brussels Sprout. The flavor is milder and sweeter than the main cabbage head.

Red cabbage is not as tender as green or white varieties and is most often pickled. It will turn pale blue when heated so add a few drops of vinegar or lemon juice, or cook it with apples or wine to keep its red color throughout cooking. The concentration of anthocyanin polyphenols in Red cabbage provide more health benefits than that of green cabbage varieties.

A Baby Red cabbage can range in size from a slightly large Brussels Sprout to a small fist. It is vibrant in color with deep purple leaves and a bright white core. Baby Red cabbages are slightly sweeter in flavor than their larger, more mature counterparts.

CACTUS

There are at least fifteen species of Barrel cactus. Many of the species are protected or endangered. Cactus develop yellow-green or red flowers that become small fruits with a golden pinkish exterior that resemble miniature pineapples. The fleshy yellow interior surrounds a cavity that is filled with small black seeds (like poppy seeds). The fruit is tart and lemony and the edible seeds have a nutty flavor. Cactus is rich in vitamins A and C and its pulp can be applied externally as an analgesic. Native American tribes across the American Southwest relied on this fruit as an important food. **Caution: They only used it as a drinking water source in extreme emergencies because it causes nausea, diarrhea, and temporary paralysis.**

The Agave Cactus plant is native to Mexico but has been naturalized to the American Southwest and other hot dry climates. The leaves were used by Mexican Indian tribes for basket weaving and building material. The plant has a central flower that produces hundreds of bright green oblong buds. The buds are crunchy with a firm texture, and sweet with a slight tang.

Cholla cactus are found in well drained rocky soils of the American Southwest. The tender thumb-sized buds of the cactus are the fresh growth of the plant. The interior soft flesh has a flavor similar to asparagus or artichoke, with a distinct lemony tang. Cholla cactus has more calcium in two tablespoons than a glass of milk. Their soluble fiber and pectin help to regulate blood-sugar levels. Cholla cactus that has died has a beautifully patterned skeleton that is often made into canes, souvenirs, and other pieces of art.

The Golden Torch Cactus is native to Bolivia and Western Argentina but is commonly found throughout the American Southwest and Mexico. Its fruit has a white inner flesh speckled with tiny black seeds. The texture is mushy and the flavor is sweet like strawberry and kiwi. Its name is derived from its glowing golden appearance due to the layer of fine, sandy-yellow spines that cover its surface. The spines turn a silvery gray and become almost reflective in the desert sunlight as the plant matures.

Cactus pads have been eaten by native Mexicans for centuries. The pads *(nopales)* are thick, oval, flat, edible stems of the cactus plant that contain fiber, antioxidants, vitamins and minerals that benefit health. The juice extracted from the pads may have immune-booster and anti-inflammatory properties. The pads can be eaten raw in salads or salsas, fried, or cooked in soups and stews. Purchase fresh, firm, pale green pads and avoid thick, mature leaves as they are out of flavor. Canned pads in brine are also available.

Blooms appear along the edge of cactus pads that develop into pear shaped cactus fruits known as Prickly Pear. It is eaten boiled or grilled and also made into juice and jams. Prickly pear cactus is used to treat diabetes, high cholesterol, obesity, and hangovers. It also has antiviral and anti-inflammatory properties.

CAIGUA

Caigua, native to Peru and Bolivia, is a small, spiky green fruit that grows along climbing vines. It is cultivated in Central and South America and the Caribbean. It is eaten in its immature state as well as when it is mature. An immature caigua is dark green, has fewer spikes, and edible seeds with a taste and texture similar to cucumbers. The mature fruit is light green and becomes hollow. It is known as the stuffing cucumber and the taste is similar to a bell pepper. In Peru, a tea is made of the fruit and used as a remedy for high cholesterol, diabetes, or gastrointestinal problems. The small fruits are boiled in milk and gargled for tonsillitis. It is also used as an anti-inflammatory, a diuretic, and analgesic.

CARDOON

A cardoon, a thistle-like plant with edible leaf stems, is in the sunflower family. The plant has grey-green downy leaves with yellow spines and violet-purple flowers. Wild and cultivated cardoons are very similar genetically. Native to the Mediterranean region where it was domesticated in ancient times, it was popular in Greek, Roman, and Persian cuisine. It was also a common vegetable in northern Africa. Only the innermost, white stalks are considered edible but the flower buds can be eaten like an artichoke. Various recipes using the stalks are part of traditional Christmas Eve festivities in Italy, Spain, Sardinia, Sicily, and France. The stems are also traditionally served battered and fried at Saint Joseph altars in New Orleans. Cardoon contains unique health benefiting plant nutrients such as antioxidants, fiber, vitamins, and minerals.

Vegetables will weigh less after boiling in water than they did before because they lose some of their water content.

Carrots originated over five thousand years ago and were first cultivated in Afghanistan in the seventh century. They started out as red, black yellow, white, and purple – but not orange. The Dutch developed the orange carrot, and in the seventeenth century the French developed the elongated carrot, ancestor of the type we eat today. The majority of these carrots are now cultivated in China. The carrot was brought by colonists to the New World, where it escaped into the wild and became Queen Anne's Lace. That name comes from its tiny flowers that grow in a flat-topped cluster that resembles lace.

The greens at the top of a carrot are edible. Orange carrots provide the highest source of vitamin A of all vegetables. Health benefits include reducing cholesterol, preventing heart attacks, warding off certain cancers, improving vision, reducing premature aging, increasing the health of your skin, boosting the immune system, improving digestion, increasing cardiovascular health, and boosting oral health.

Purple carrot varieties are one of the first originally cultivated varieties and were used as a clothing dye by Afghan royalty. Today, they are considered a potential natural food coloring. Purple carrots contain high levels of potent antioxidants. Yellow carrots are varieties that are grown to yield sweeter flavor at maturity. They were domesticated in Central Asia as early as the ninth century.

Nantes carrots, developed in the 1850s, are the Gold standard for medium sized carrots. Their near-red flesh is sweet and mild in flavor. Young Nantes carrots are extremely sweet and tender, entirely edible, and require no peeling. Imperator carrots are orange, eight to eleven inches long, and not as sweet as other carrots. They are one of the most common carrots sold fresh in North America. Many brands of pseudo baby carrots are cut from Imperators.

Chantenay carrots, an heirloom variety that was developed during the eighteenth century in France, are one of the sweetest fresh eating varieties of all carrots. They have a triangular-shaped stout and thick roots, and their orange flesh is crispy. Round carrots have a non-tapering globular shape and petite size. They grow faster than elongated varieties in poor soil conditions because they have a shallow root system. Their dill-like green foliage is also edible.

Orange Baby carrots and Baby Yellow carrots are tenderer and sweeter than mature carrots. Baby white carrots have a sweet, mild carrot flavor but lack the pigment found in other carrot varieties, giving it a lower nutritional value. Baby Red carrots, with burgundy skin and orange flesh, contain the antioxidant lycopene, known for its anti-cancer benefits. Young Black Knight carrots have ink stained skin with a light-yellow flesh and require no peeling.

"The day is coming when a single carrot, freshly observed, will set off a revolution."
Paul Cezanne   1839-1906
French Impressionist painter

CATTAIL

Cattails, native to both North America and Europe, date back thirty thousand years. Archaeologists found ten thousand-year-old mats made from cattails in a Nevada cave. People processed the roots of cattails and ferns into flour. Cattails are one of the most important and common of all the wild foods and can be found near wetlands, marshes, and ponds. There are two varieties of cattail that likely resulted from a hybridizing of the European variety. Peeling away the layers of leaves from the top down reveals the heart of the stalk that has a tender texture and mild flavor similar to cucumbers and zucchini. Cattails contain beta carotene, niacin, riboflavin, thiamin, potassium, phosphorus, and vitamin C. Native Americans used the jelly-like substance from between the leaves of the young Cattail shoots as a topical treatment for wounds, sores, and external inflammations to relieve pain. **Caution: Cattail flour should be avoided by people with Celiac disease.**

CAULIFLOWER

The white, crunchy stems and head of the cauliflower plant are actually the undeveloped stems and buds of a flower. Cauliflower is ninety-two percent water so it feels heavy for its size. Rich in vitamin C and dietary fiber, cauliflower is also a good source of vitamin B6 and folate. It, like other cruciferous vegetables, is rich in phytochemicals that have shown cancer-fighting potential. There are over one hundred varieties of cauliflower, most of which are white in color. The three main types are the common white cauliflower, the purple-headed cauliflower, and the broccoflower, a cross between broccoli and cauliflower. Baby cauliflower lacks some of the bitterness of larger cauliflower. Its leaves, trunk, stems, and florets are all edible. The heads of baby cauliflower are referred to as buttons.

Sprouting cauliflower develops from buds located in the bases of the older leaves. It shares similar characteristics to mature cauliflower but on a smaller scale. Green sprouting cauliflower has small stalks with green floret clusters at the very top. Its stalk and florets are edible. Orange sprouting cauliflower forms small stalks with orange floret clusters at the very top. The orange color is a result of a genetic mutation that allows the vegetable to hold more beta carotene (vitamin A). Purple sprouting cauliflower forms small stalks with small purple floret clusters at the very top. Its color is due to the presence of the antioxidant anthocyanin, which can also be found in red cabbage and red wine. White Sprouting cauliflowers are small long shoots with little white clusters on the very top. They have more stalk and less white florets than regular cauliflower.

CELERY

Celery is native to the Mediterranean and the Middle East. The wild form of celery is known as smallage. It has a bitter taste and the stalks are stringier than cultivated celery. Smallage was used by the ancient Chinese as a medicine, and the Greeks and Romans used it as a seasoning. Celery was developed by breeding the bitterness out of smallage. It was first recorded as a food plant in France in 1623. Pascal is the most common celery sold. It was first cultivated in 1874 in Michigan. Celery contains fiber, multiple vitamins, essential fatty acids, and nutrients. It lowers cholesterol, prevents cancer, reduces high blood pressure, and promotes overall health. It takes more calories to eat and digest celery than there is in the celery. Celery leaves are also edible. Celery seeds have the taste and smell of celery stalks but their flavor is more pronounced. In Chinese medicine, celery seeds are used to relieve stress, dizziness, and high blood pressure. Celeriac, also known as celery root, is one of the oldest root vegetables and was cultivated from wild celery. It is an excellent source of dietary fiber and potassium and also contains significant amounts of vitamins B6 and C. It can be a substitute for potatoes and be prepared in a similar way.

CHARD

Swiss chard, native to the Mediterranean region, is a leafy green vegetable related to beets although chard is grown for its leaves and not the root. The first documented use of chard in cooking was in Sicily. It is eaten raw in salads, cooked, or sautéed. The bitterness of the raw leaves dissipates when cooked. Health benefits include the ability to regulate blood sugar levels, prevent various types of cancer, improve digestion, boost the immune system, reduce fever and combat inflammation, lower blood pressure, prevent heart disease, increase bone strength and development, detoxify the body, and strengthen the functioning of the brain. Green Swiss chard has edible white stalks. Golden Swiss chard has yellow stems and crinkly green leaves. Rainbow Swiss chard has green and bronze leaves and the stems are gold, pink, orange, purple, red, and white. Red Swiss chard, cultivated in Greece around 400 B.C., has bronzed green leaves with red leaf stalks. Baby Red Swiss Chard is a young immature chard plant with delicate leaves that are sweeter than mature Red Swiss chard.

CHAYOTE

Chayote is a pear-shaped fruit with a large, soft edible seed in its white flesh. It is often used as a vegetable and can be eaten cooked or raw. There are many different varieties with different sizes and colored skins. It is a good source of vitamin C and amino acids but is high in carbohydrates and calories. Chayote is native to Central America and was cultivated by the Aztecs and Mayans. European explorers spread the plant to the Caribbean, South America, and Europe. Later, it was introduced to Africa, Asia, and Australia.

CHERIMOYA

Cherimoya, a subtropical fruit also known as Custard Apple, is egg-shaped, globe-shaped or heart-shaped, with a velvety, thin light green skin. The white pulp has a mild flavor and the texture is soft, smooth, and almost custard-like. Cherimoya trees are native to Peru, Ecuador, and Colombia. They are commercially grown in Australia, South America, Asia, Spain, Italy, and California. High in fiber, they are a good source of vitamin C and calcium, and contain niacin and phosphorus. A new hybrid, Atemoya, is a cross between the Cherimoya and the sugar apple.

CHERRY

Cherries are native to China. Cherry pits were found in Stone Age caves in Europe and the first documentation of cultivation dates back to 4000 B.C. Cherries were brought to America by early settlers in the 1600s. The health benefits of cherries include a boost to eye care, a stronger immune system, relief from infections, anti-aging properties, and improved digestion. They are fat-free, sodium-free and cholesterol-free, and a good source of vitamin C and potassium. They are rich in bioflavonoids and other antioxidants. Raw fresh cherries maintain many of their antioxidant qualities if frozen immediately after harvest. Freezing not only preserves but also concentrates and improves their taste.

The two main species of cherry are the sweet cherry and the sour cherry. Sour cherries, also referred to as tart or pie cherries, are distinguished by their acid content and crimson black coloring. They have high levels of melatonin and have been used as a natural sleep aid. There are dozens of sour cherry tree varieties. The most common is the English Morello but the Montmorency is considered the best cherry for making pies. It takes about two hundred and fifty cherries to make a cherry pie. The most cultivated sweet cherry variety is the Bing cherry that got its name from a Chinese worker at an orchard in western Oregon. The Rainier cherry, a genetic offspring of the Bing, was named after Mount Rainier and is famous for its creamy yellow flesh.

There are more than a thousand varieties of cherries in the United States but fewer than ten are produced commercially. Michigan grows almost seventy five percent of the tart cherries produced in the U.S. Eau Claire, Michigan is known as the Cherry Pit Spitting Capital of the World. Washington state grows more sweet cherries than any other state. Kane, Pennsylvania is known as the Black Cherry Capital of the World. Cherries Jubilee is a dessert created by Auguste Escoffier in honor of Queen Victoria's Diamond Jubilee. There are thousands of Japanese cherry trees that circle the Tidal Basin and the Jefferson Memorial in Washington D.C. The trees were originally planted as a gift from the people of Japan in 1912. Each spring, the two-week-long National Cherry Blossom Festival attracts tens of thousands of visitors from around the world.

Wild Cherry is also called Bird Cherry and a host of other names. Native to Mediterranean regions, by 800 B.C. it was cultivated in Turkey and later grown on all continents but Antarctica. It is high in vitamin A and C, folate, and other nutrients.

Cherums and Plerries are hybrid stone fruits of the cherry and the plum. Cherums have dominant cherry characteristics and plerries are a predominantly plum cross. Maraschino cherries are not a variety of cherry but named for the Italian cherry-flavored liqueur used to preserve them. The cherries were popular with aristocratic Europeans and were imported to the United States in the 1890s to be used in the finest restaurants and hotels. In 1896, U.S. cherry processors began experimenting with a domestic sweet cherry. Less liqueur was used and eventually the liqueur was eliminated. By 1920, the American maraschino cherry replaced the foreign variety in the United States.

CHICORY

Chicory has been cultivated in Egypt since 300 B.C. Ancient Romans used it as a medicinal herb to cleanse the blood. It was brought to the United States from Europe in the eighteenth century. Chicory root has a similar appearance to a parsnip, with a robust, bitter flavor. The root is dried, ground and roasted, and used as a coffee substitute. As a vegetable, it can be boiled and eaten. Chicory root is high in vitamin C and antioxidants and is a rich source of beta-carotene and fiber. It is said to have anti-inflammatory and antibacterial properties

CHIKOO

Chikoo trees are native to Southern Mexico and the Yucatan and have been grown throughout Central America since ancient times. The trees in Mexico are primarily grown for their chicle sap that is used to make gum. India is one of the largest producers of the Chikoo fruit. The brown fuzzy skin is inedible but the flesh has a soft and juicy texture and its sweet flavor is due to its high levels of fructose and sucrose. It is a good source of dietary fiber and the natural tannins in the flesh are antioxidants and have antiviral, anti-bacterial, and anti-parasitic effects.

COLLARD GREENS

Collard greens, native to Asia Minor, are the oldest known greens dating back to 5,000 B.C. Ancient Greeks and Romans grew collard greens in gardens. Around 400 B.C. they were brought to Britain and France, and then to America in the mid-1600s when collard greens had become globally cultivated. They are a good source of nutrients including vitamins A and K, folate, and the antioxidant beta-carotene. Fresh Collard green leaves are also used as a headache remedy and to ward off evil spirits. Sprouting Collard greens are the petite yellow flower of the plant. They have a slight crunch and taste like a young cabbage. Collard Green blossoms are used to infuse oils, vinegars, and marinades. According to folklore, eating collards with black-eyed peas on New Year's Day will promise a year of good luck.

CITRON

The first known citrons were grown in ancient Mesopotamia around 4000 B.C. Citron was the earliest of the citrus fruits introduced to Europe from Asia and the first to be cultivated. The Romans, Hebrews, and Greeks called it the Median or Persian apple. Citrons have a long association with the Jewish religion. One story from the Torah claims it was the forbidden fruit in the Garden of Eden. The citron's ancient nickname, Persian apple, may have led later generations to believe the forbidden fruit was an apple. Citron is commercially cultivated in the Mediterranean area and grown in California and Florida. There are many varieties, known for their fresh fragrance. The Dulcia citron is small with a thick, yellow to orange-yellow rind and a sour taste. The skin is used as a zest and also candies well for use in desserts. Buddha's Hand citron is used for its fragrant zest only. In China it symbolizes happiness and long life. The trees are sold as bonsai pot plants, and the dried peel of immature fruits is prescribed as a tonic in traditional medicine. The Etrog citron is related to Buddha's Hand and looks like a large, ribbed lemon. The oil and rind of this citron are the most commonly used portions of the fruit. Etrog is used to make marmalades, glazed citron, and infused vodka. In Japan, citron is a popular gift at New Year's as it is believed to bestow good fortune on a household.

COCONUT

The first mention of the coconut was in 545 A.D. Regarded as the world's largest nut, the coconut is native to either the East Indies and Melanesia or tropical America. Honduras, the Dominican Republic, and Puerto Rico are today's major growers. The islands of the Pacific regard the coconut as a sacred fertility symbol. Coconuts provide iron, potassium, protein, and saturated fat (unusual for fruits and vegetables). There are many varieties of coconut and three different stages of maturation: the young coconut, the white coconut, and the mature brown husked coconut. Young coconuts, harvested before they reach maturity, have a uniquely shaped ivory shell. Inside is a juice and a soft jelly-like sweet white meat that is soft enough to be eaten with a spoon. The white coconut is the best stage of coconut for cooking. It is pale cream to ivory in color and the inside is filled with a sweet milky liquid. The meat is moister than the meat of the brown husked coconut. The brown husked coconut is covered with hairy brown fibers. The thick fibrous husk of the coconut encases an inner shell and holds liquid called coconut water.

Young green coconuts have a smooth, green, and very hard outer shell. They are harvested for their high water content as they have not yet begun developing edible pulp. Fresh coconut water has a slightly sweet and refreshing taste and is drunk straight from the coconut or can be used in both cooked and raw recipes. Baby coconuts look like miniature coconuts but are no bigger than a marble. They have sweet, firm, white meat that has a coconut flavor and a crunchy texture. They grow on a Chilean palm tree in Mediterranean-type climates, like California.

CORN

Corn does not grow wild; it evolved from wild Mexican grass and was domesticated about ten thousand years ago by Native Americans. Christopher Columbus brought it to Europe in the 1400s. The word 'corn' was used to signify the most-used grain of a specific place. The corn mentioned in the Old Testament was most likely barley. In England, corn was wheat, and in Scotland and Ireland the word referred to oats. Corn is known as maize in most places of the world and is the highest produced crop worldwide. The United States is the largest producer of corn and most of it is consumed by domestic and overseas livestock, poultry, and fish production.

There are four types of corn: sweet, dent, flint, and popcorn. Sweet corn (corn on the cob) contains more sugar than other types of corn and will never pop. It is picked and eaten while the kernels are tender. Dent corn, also called field corn, is the most widely grown corn in the United States and is used primarily for livestock feed. Flint corn, also known as Indian corn, varies in size, husk, and color (ivory and purple are two of the most common husk colors). Ornamental Indian corn is used for fall decorating and crafts such as centerpieces, wreaths, and displays. Mini ornamental corn are approximately four inches long and can be yellow, black, brown, cream, and calico. Popcorn is a type of flint corn but has a thicker hull (see also POPCORN on page 246). Corn is considered to be either a vegetable or a grain but the kernels are classified as fruit. Sweet corn is a vegetable because it is grown for eating. Field corn is a grain because it is a dried grass seed.

Baby corn, a miniature version of corn on the cob, is about three to four inches in size. The ear is very flexible and is most often prepared whole. Thailand is the primary producer. Red corn is a type of sweet corn with brick red or creamy pink kernels, depending on the variety. It has twenty percent more protein and many more antioxidants than white corn or yellow corn. White corn is a sweet corn. The white kernels have a very high percentage of sugar and water in their composition. The less it is cooked, the better the flavor and texture. Yellow corn is an evolutionary mutation of white corn. The yellow kernels, packed in tight uniform rows, pop as you bite into them. It is being bred to have at least ten times higher the amount of beta carotene than average sweet corn varieties.

An average ear of corn has eight hundred kernels, arranged in sixteen rows. There is one piece of silk for each kernel. Corn is high in fiber and a rich source of vitamins A, B and E, and many minerals. Health benefits include controlling diabetes, preventing heart ailments, and lowering blood pressure. Corn is also used in fuel, ink, medicine, clothing, and cosmetics. Mitchell, South Dakota is home to the Corn Palace and Festival. Corn tortillas date back to 10,000 B.C.

Corn husks are the outer covering of an ear of corn. Dried Corn husks are used for wrapping food, like tamales, in Southwestern cooking. The Corn husks are not edible and are removed before eating.

CUCUMBER

Cucumbers, one of the oldest cultivated vegetables, are actually a fruit. They belong to the same family as melons and squash and are about ninety-five percent water. Native to India where they grew in the wild, they spread to other regions and made their way to North America by the mid-sixteenth century. First cultivated in ancient Egypt, they are the fourth most widely cultivated vegetable in the world. The ancient Romans were the first to grow them in a greenhouse-like controlled environment. China is the largest producer of cucumbers. In the United States, Florida and California grow the majority. Both cultivated and wild cucumbers were also used for medicinal purposes, such as helping ease headaches. Cucumbers contain multiple B vitamins (known to help ease anxiety) as well as vitamins C and K, copper, potassium, and manganese. They also contain numerous antioxidants and anti-inflammatories. Placing a cucumber slice on the roof of your mouth may help to rid your mouth of odor-causing bacteria.

There are hundreds of different varieties of cucumbers that can be divided into three main varieties: slicing, pickling, and burpless. Pickling cucumber varieties are known for their succulent, crispy and crunchy flesh that snaps upon bending or biting into even after canning and preserving. The Industrial Revolution brought about mass production of pickling cucumbers.

Hot house cucumbers distinguish themselves from common garden cucumbers by their crisp texture, underdeveloped and non-bitter seeds, sweeter taste, and thin edible skin. They can reach a length of two feet. Persian cucumbers originated in the Fertile Crescent where North Africa meets the Middle East. They have smooth and thin skin, are seedless, and are crisp and sweet. There are several different cultivars, both heirloom and hybrid, and they are the pinnacle variety of burpless cucumbers.

The seedless Japanese cucumber was developed from cultivated varieties from China. There are dozens of cultivars, heirloom and hybrid, short and long. The Lemon cucumber is small and round with a sweet and less acidic flavor than the common green cucumber. The Salt and Pepper cucumber, developed at Cornell University, is one of the first modern vegetables bred for organic production. It is white-skinned with black spikes that turn a pale yellow as it matures. Watermelon gherkin cucumbers, native to Central and South America, are oblong-shaped and have the appearance of a miniature watermelon.

To increase your intake of dietary fiber, potassium, iron and antioxidants, replace a few servings of fresh fruit a week with smaller portions of dried fruit like raisins, figs, plums and apricots.

CRESS

Cress is the name for a number of related peppery greens in the mustard family. Land cress grows on land in southwestern Europe and England. Garden cress is used as a leafy vegetable or garnish. The plant can grow two feet high and produces white or light-pink flowers and small seed pods. It is an important source of iron, folic acid, calcium, and vitamins A, C and E. The seeds contain fatty acids and are high in calories and protein. They have been used to treat sore throat, cough, asthma, and headache when chewed. **Caution: The seeds have been used as a laxative but if large quantities are consumed the oil it contains may cause digestive difficulties in some people.**

Watercress, an aquatic plant species, is the most popular of the cresses. It is related to collards and kale and is one of the oldest known leaf vegetables consumed by humans. The ancient Romans used it to prevent baldness and it was later used to treat scurvy. Also called Saint Patrick's cabbage in Ireland, it is thought to be the plant designated as the shamrock.

NOTE: Aquatic plants are plants that have adapted to living in saltwater or freshwater environments and require special adaptations for living in water or at the water's surface. These plants can only grow in water or in soil that is permanently saturated with water.

DANDELION

The dandelion is a member of the daisy family and is native to Europe and eastern Asia. The name comes from the French, *dent de lion* (lion's tooth, referring to the jagged leaves). All parts of the dandelion are edible raw or steamed, or dried, roasted and ground into a coffee substitute. The flowers are best known for their use in dandelion wine. Young greens that are harvested before the flower head appears will be less bitter. Dandelions contain anti-inflammatory properties which may be beneficial to those with asthma and other inflammatory diseases. The nutrients in dandelion greens may help reduce the risk of cancer, multiple sclerosis, cataracts, age-related macular degeneration, and stroke. The leaves are rich in potassium, antioxidants, and vitamins A and C. Dandelion greens have more protein per serving than spinach. The roots contain substances that may help balance blood sugar and stimulate digestion. During the tenth and eleventh centuries, Arabian physicians used the plant medicinally as a liver tonic and diuretic. Vineland, New Jersey is known as the Dandelion Capital of the World.

"So long as you have food in your mouth, you have solved all questions for the time being."

Franz Kafka   1883-1924

Author

DATE

The date palm tree is one of the oldest fruit trees in the world. Dates are among the earliest cultivated food. Date stones have been found in Egypt that date to 4500 B.C. and they are mentioned in the Old Testament. In these ancient cultures, the date palm tree was regarded as a sacred tree which was often used in religious rites and ceremonies. The name comes from the Latin word *dactylus*, meaning 'finger,' as the date was thought to resemble one. The male and female flowers of the date palm tree grow on separate trees and must be pollinated by hand. The dates are attached to a thin spindly vine.

There are hundreds of varieties of dates with hundreds of different names, with varying degrees of sweetness. The soft date has high moisture content, low sugar content, and a soft flesh. The semi-soft date has high sugar content, relatively low moisture content, and a firmer texture. Medjool dates, also known as the king of dates, are dried prior to consumption and sold already pitted. They are very large and extremely sweet in taste.

Dates are free of saturated fat, trans fat, sodium, and cholesterol and they may reduce the risk of some types of cancer. They contain dietary fiber, potassium, calcium, magnesium, manganese, zinc, copper, iron, and selenium. All of these minerals help lower blood pressure. The Middle East and North Africa are the top date producing regions. California grows ninety-nine percent of all dates grown in the United States. The Coachella Valley is known as the Date Capital of the world.

DOUM PALM

The doum palm is native to the Nile region in Africa. It is also called gingerbread palm, gingerbread tree, and Egyptian palm. The edible fruit tastes like gingerbread and has been used in folk medicine to treat high blood pressure. Doum palm was considered sacred by the ancient Egyptians and the seed was found in many pharaoh's tombs, such as King Tutankhamun.

DRAGON FRUIT

Dragon fruit, native to Central America and Mexico, is also grown and exported from some Southeast Asian countries. Obtained from several cactus species, its succulent stem provides a delicious fruit. It has a crunchy texture and the flavor is mildly sweet (a blend of kiwi and pear). The fruit may be red, peach-colored or yellow, with scales or spines and numerous tiny edible black seeds. **Caution: Eat only the white part with seeds.** Dragon fruit contains B vitamins, vitamin C, phosphorus, protein, calcium, fiber, and antioxidants. It's proven to lower blood sugar levels and blood pressure, strengthen bones and teeth, promote healthy blood and tissue formation, strengthen the immune system, and prevent respiratory problems. Like other red fruits, it contains lycopene that helps protect against cancer and heart disease.

DURIAN

Durian is native to Malaysia and Indonesia. The tree also grows in northern Australia, some South American countries, and Africa. This fruit has only been known to the western world for about six hundred years. It is shipped internationally only from Thailand and Indonesia where it is grown for commercial production. Durian is considered the King of Tropical Fruit throughout Southeast Asia and has the reputation of being an aphrodisiac. A large green fruit with a thorn-covered husk, it has a creamy, custard-like texture and delicious taste but a very offensive odor. Some countries ban the presence of durian in hotels and on public transportation due to its smell. Most airlines do not allow it on board. The flesh is pureed or blended and the flavor is a combination of savory, sweet and pungent. Its large seeds may be roasted or boiled and eaten as nuts.

The fruit is rich in vitamin C, tryptophan, potassium, carbohydrates, fats, and proteins. It has a number of health benefits and provides vitamins A, B complex and C, and magnesium, potassium, manganese and copper. It is high in calories and dietary fiber and low in sodium. **Caution: Wear protective gloves when slicing and removing the edible pods from the spiky skinned fruit.**

EDAMAME

Edamame, an edible young green soybean, is the only vegetable that contains all nine essential amino acids. It has many health benefits due to its high mineral and nutrient content. The word 'edamame' means 'beans on a branch.' It has its roots in China, dating back more than two thousand years. It was later introduced to Japan and, in 1902, was brought to the United States (although it did not become popular until the growth of the organic food movement in the 1970s). Edamame are soft, not hard and dry like the mature soybeans that are used to make soy milk and tofu.

EDIBLE FLOWERS

Edible flowers have been used in cooking since the earliest of times and can be traced back to Roman, Chinese, Middle Eastern, and Indian cultures. Edible flowers were especially popular in the Victorian era. A few edible flower varieties include apple blossoms, cloves, capers, rose petals, safflower, violets, chrysanthemum, nasturtium, marigold, jasmine, hibiscus, hyssop, orange blossoms, red poppy, honeysuckle, mimosa, lemon flowers, garlic flowers, forget-me-nots, lotus blossoms, primrose, pansies, daisies, fuchsias, carnations, hollyhock, gladiolus, tulips, yucca, mustard flowers, banana blossoms, day lilies, sunflower, fennel, and dandelions. **Caution: Not every flower is edible and some people have had strong allergic reactions to some.**

EGG FRUIT

The Egg Fruit is native to southern North America and northern Central America. The tree bears oblong fruits that can vary in shape and turn a golden-orange color when ripe. The interior is the color and texture of a hard-boiled egg yolk and it contains up to four hard black seeds. Its flavor is similar to roasted sweet potato. Egg fruit is rich in niacin, iron, calcium, beta-carotene and ascorbic acid.

EGGPLANT

Eggplant is a fruit classified as a berry. All eggplants can trace their ancestry to the wild eggplants of Africa but first cultivation was in India and China. The domestication, a centuries-long process that is documented in ancient Chinese literature, increased the fruit size and altered the flavor and peel color. Wild eggplant is prickly but the domesticated versions have few or no prickles. In various parts of old Europe, people thought eating eggplant caused madness, leprosy, cancer, and bad breath. Modern research disproved this but eggplants do contain an alkaloid that can cause flare-ups in those who have gout or arthritis. The fiber, potassium, vitamins B6 and C, and phytonutrient content in eggplant supports heart health. Eggplant skin is full of antioxidants. Thomas Jefferson is believed to have brought the first eggplants to the United States.

There are many different varieties of eggplant in a variety of shapes and colors. Common purple eggplant has glossy, black-purple skin, is oval and oblong in shape with a green stem, and often grows to ten inches long. Baby eggplants are petite eggplants that grow only two to three inches in length. They are an excellent source of dietary fiber. Chinese eggplants have a long, thin shape and violet color (there are also white and variegated varieties) and can grow up to eighteen inches long. They have the sweetest, mildest flavor of all eggplant varieties. African eggplants can be green, white or red. The leaves are eaten as a sautéed vegetable and are rich in beta-carotene, ascorbic acid, iron and calcium. This variety is firm and bitter and best stewed or pickled. Italian eggplant skin is glossy and smooth and can be varying hues of purple. The flesh is white with barely visible seeds and is known for its superior creamy texture and flavor when cooked. White eggplant has a bell shape with cream flesh. The peel tends to be thick and should be peeled prior to eating. It is much smaller than purple eggplant. The flavor is fruity and mild.

Wild eggplants grow in clusters on branched vines on all continents except Antarctica and can be found in a wide variety of habitats. Each fruit is round and the size of a large pea, with green coloring when young that matures to a yellow to orange hue. It has a jelly-like texture and bitter flavor. In folk medicine, wild eggplants are known for their healing properties and medicinal uses. They have anti-microbial, anti-bacterial, and anti-inflammatory properties.

EGUSI

Egusi gourd, native to West and Central Africa, is the biological ancestor of watermelon but the flesh is bitter and yellow or green instead of sweet and red. The fruit is not eaten – they are grown for their interior seeds that are similar in size to small pumpkin seeds. The seeds are ground into a paste with a small amount of water and used as a thickener for sauces, soups and stews (added towards the end of cooking to create a curdled, scrambled egg like texture). The seeds can also be roasted as a snack, made into a spread like peanut butter, or ground and formed into patties. The seeds are rich in vitamins A, B1, B2 and C, and phosphorous, potassium, magnesium, calcium, sodium, iron, zinc, manganese and copper.

FEIJOA

Feijoa, also known as pineapple guava, is of South American origin. The plant has golden-yellow flowers with white petals that become the fruit. Feijoa fruit is oval with a sweet fruity aroma similar to a blend of banana and pineapple. It is low fat, cholesterol-free, and full of vitamins and antioxidants. It is also a rich source of soluble dietary fiber. The fruit will perish within two days at room temperature if not eaten so refrigerate it (up to two days) or keep it frozen for two months.

FENNEL

Fennel, native to southern Europe and the Mediterranean region, has been used for centuries as a spice and for medicinal purposes. The plant, that grows three to ten feet tall, is entirely edible and has a sweet, licorice-like flavor. It has thick, ribbed, hollow stems that grow from its rooted bulb. Green branches and feathery foliage sprout off the stems. Baby fennel is immature fennel that produces licorice-flavored feathery leaves. (For more information, see page 9)

FIDDLEHEAD FERN

Fiddlehead ferns are the coiled fronds of a fern that have been harvested at the youthful stage of growth. The young shoots are tightly wound into a circular button-like shape. Fuzzy tawny brown scales cover the light green stems. The texture is crunchy, the flesh is slightly gelatinous, and the flavor has notes of artichoke and pine nuts. They are an excellent source of vitamins A and C, and are rich in niacin, magnesium, iron, potassium, phosphorus, antioxidants and bioflavonoids. Varieties include Lady fern, Ostrich fern, and Bracken fern. The Lady fern is a Western fern variety that grows from California to Alaska. The Ostrich fern grows wild throughout North America and in limited regions of Alaska. **Caution: The Bracken, one of the most common and widely distributed of all Fiddlehead types, contains high levels of carcinogens. Consume Bracken ferns carefully or avoid altogether.**

The fig appears to be the first domesticated plant. Dried figs, more than eleven thousand years old, were found in the Lower Jordan Valley in Israel. Figs were used by the ancient Egyptians and were a favorite of Cleopatra. They also grew in the Hanging Gardens of Babylon and were often mentioned in the Bible as a sign of peace and prosperity. Figs arrived in the United States with Spanish missionaries settling in Southern California in 1759. Although considered a fruit, the fig is actually a flower (the flower is inside the fruit so there are no blossoms on fig trees). Figs can be red, yellow, purple, or green-striped, each with their own unique flavor. There are more than one thousand fig species found in every major rainforest, tropical continent, and island around the world. Before figs are ripe, they are gummy with latex that contains skin irritants so protective measures for workers are sometimes mandated.

The fig is the sweetest of all fruits, with a fifty-five percent sugar content. It contains calcium, fiber, antioxidants, magnesium, manganese, calcium, copper, potassium, and vitamins B6 and K. These compounds have the capacity to regulate blood sugar levels, inhibit kidney and liver problems and cancer, prevent macular degeneration and high blood pressure, aid in weight loss, and protect the heart. Figs in dried form contain even greater nutritional value than fresh. Dried figs are sometimes roasted and ground as a coffee substitute, converted into alcohol as a liqueur, or used as a tobacco flavoring. Today, the primary producers of dried figs are the United States, Turkey, Greece and Spain. All dried figs harvested in the U.S. are grown in California's Central valley area.

The Black Mission fig received its name in honor of the missionary priests at Mission San Diego who originally planted figs in California.

The Brown Turkey fig is considered the best growing variety of figs. It has a variegated, rusted red to purple skin with slightly pale green shoulders. The fruit will often crack upon ripeness, exposing a rose-colored flesh with edible seeds.

Green figs are sweeter than both Brown Turkey and Black Mission figs. Larger and plumper than black figs, they are pale lime green with pink to brown variegation when ripe. The flesh contains a rusted strawberry colored jellied pulp with a lot of seeds. The pulp of this fruit has a candied syrup flavor that darker figs cannot achieve. The leaves are also edible.

The Celeste fig, also known as the Sugar fig, is a medium sized fruit with smooth, light brown to violet colored skin. The heavily seeded flesh has a pastel, strawberry-pink blush and a honey flavor. It is used to make preserves and jams.

White figs have thin tender skins and can range from beige to yellow or pale green. The interior flesh is soft and chewy and filled with tiny edible seeds that pop and crunch.

Tiger Stripe figs, also called Candy Stripe figs, have green and yellow stripes and a bottom-heavy tear-drop shape. The crimson-colored seeded pulp has a flavor similar to strawberry or raspberry jam. It is considered to be one of the best tasting of all figs.

The Strangler fig tree sprouts at the bottom of other trees, sending roots down to the ground and growing in strength until it eventually winds its way up the trunk, slowly squeezing the host tree until it dies. Strangler fig trees can grow as high as one hundred forty-eight feet.

GRAPEFRUIT

Grapefruit, the only known citrus to have originated in the Americas, is a hybrid between sweet orange and pomelo. It can be white, pink, and ruby, based on the flesh color. The flavor is tart and tangy but sweet. Grapefruits are grown commercially in Florida, California, Arizona, Texas, South Africa, Israel, and Brazil. They were first introduced to Florida in the 1820s by a Frenchman who planted the first grapefruit trees around Tampa Bay. Today, Florida produces more grapefruit than the rest of the world combined. Grapefruit got its name from the way it grows in clusters (like grapes) on the tree.

Grapefruits are very high in vitamin C. They also contain vitamin A, fiber, and beta carotene. Red and pink grapefruits additionally contain lycopene that fights free radicals and protects cells from damage. Grapefruit can increase the body's metabolic rate, lower insulin levels, and help fight various conditions like fatigue, fever, and indigestion.

The Star Ruby grapefruit, native to Texas, is the standard pink grapefruit regarding color, flavor and fragrance. Its flesh is a rich ruby color and the flavor is sweet-tart. The Oro Blanco grapefruit was developed in 1958. Its flesh is juicy, seedless, and sweet because it lacks acidity. Melo Gold grapefruit, also developed in 1958, is the sweetest of all varieties. It is a hybrid variety of the Oro Blanco. The Cocktail Grapefruit, developed in the 1950s, is about half the size of an average grapefruit. It is a premium juicing grapefruit.

Grapefruit are mostly eaten fresh but they can also be sautéed, grilled, barbecued, and served with vegetables, sandwiches, and sauces. For grilling, halve and cut a grapefruit into segments, leaving the flesh in the skin. Mix one tablespoon each of brown sugar, coconut, and flaked almonds. Sprinkle over fruit and grill until lightly browned.

Caution: grapefruit juice can affect the potency of various medications. It increases the concentration of many drugs in the bloodstream to three or four times the normal concentration and decreases the production of a certain enzyme in the intestines that is involved in the metabolizing of about one third of all drugs.

GRAPE

Grapes have grown wild since the dawn of time on every continent but Antarctica. The grape is one of the oldest fruits to be cultivated, as early as 6500 B.C. Under the influence of the Romans, grape production spread throughout Europe. Spanish explorers introduced the fruit to America about three hundred years ago. Grape growing is the largest food industry in the world. There are more than sixty species and eight thousand varieties of grapes that can all be used to make juice or wine. Health benefits include its ability to treat constipation, fatigue, indigestion, kidney disorders, macular degeneration and prevention of cataracts. Grapes are a rich source of vitamins A, B6 and C, as well as essential minerals like potassium, calcium, and iron. They contain flavonoids that are very powerful antioxidants. Grape seeds have a great concentration of vitamin E.

The three species of grapes are categorized as European, North American, and hybrids. White grapes are actually pale green. Wine grapes contain seeds and are small with relatively thick skins. Table grapes, usually seedless, are larger with thin skins. The first seedless grape was a natural occurring European grape strain, the ancestor to all seedless grapes. The color of Green Seedless grapes ranges from yellowish-green to bright green. The inner pulp is semi-translucent with a sweet and tart flavor. Red seedless grapes are sweet and crisp, juicy, and occasionally tart. Black seedless grapes may be round to slightly oval in shape with deep purple to near black color. They are juicy in texture with a sweet flavor. There are multiple species of Black seedless grapes. The blue-skinned Concord grape is one of the oldest domestically cultivated grapes in the United States. It is used to make Concord grape jelly. The Seedless Concord grape is used for making preserves, juice, wine, liqueur and vinegar.

The Muscat grape originated in Greece and has been a long time favorite for making fine wine. There are over two hundred varieties of Muscat grapes. The Pinot Noir grape has a sweet aroma and a slightly spicy flavor with cherry and strawberry tones. Sangiovese grapes, from the Tuscany region, are Italy's primary red wine grape. The Muscadine grape is another one of the first native grapes to be cultivated in the U.S. There are hundreds of cultivars that range in color and flavor. It is considered to be more of a berry than a grape because it resembles a small, round plum or black cherry tomato. Muscadine grapes are used to make jellies, jams, and wine. About fifty percent of the grapes grown in the United States are used to make wine. It takes about two and one-half pounds of grapes to produce a bottle of wine. Wine making was primarily associated with monasteries and later became a social custom. King Hammurabi of Babylon enacted the world's first liquor law when he established rules for wine trade in 1700 B.C.

Grape juice was first made by Thomas Welch, a prohibitionist who made juice as an alternative for communion wine. Grapes are also used to make raisins. It takes about four pounds of grapes to produce one pound of raisins (for more information see RAISIN on page 109).

Green beans, also known as string beans or snap beans, are classified as pole beans (the poles grow five or six feet high) or bush beans (the bushes grow one to two feet in height). There are several varieties in green, yellow, or purple and all common green beans can trace their origins to Central and South America. They have been cultivated in Mexico for at least seven thousand years. The first string-less green bean was developed in New York in 1894. Since the mid-twentieth century, the Blue Lake bean has been considered the benchmark standard of green beans. It is string-less and the plump pod contains tiny edible seeds. There are many hybrids and sub-varieties.

Green beans contain vitamins A, C and, K, niacin and thiamine, and are rich in fiber. They also contain protein, calcium, iron and several other essential nutrients. They have impressive amounts of antioxidants and provide cardiovascular and anti-inflammatory benefits. The green bean casserole recipe that uses cream of mushroom soup was developed by Campbell in 1955.

There are dozens of yellow wax bean varieties with either a matte or satin finish. Purple bean varieties have violet-hued skin that changes to green when cooked. The pale lime green peas inside the shell are the same as in green beans. Green Romano beans, also known as Italian Flat Pole beans, are native to Italy. They are broad and flat and can grow to five inches in length. They can be green, purple, or yellow and are rich in dietary fiber. Yard long beans grow to three feet long but are usually picked at about eighteen inches. They are related to black-eyed peas but taste and look like green beans.

NOTE: Within the bean group are those that are grown for dry use as a legume and those that are grown for the green bean. Shelling beans are grown for their edible seeds (beans) contained within the pods, unlike green beans which are consumed pod and all.

GUAVA

Guava is originally from tropical America. Seminole Indians were growing guava trees in Northern Florida in 1816. Guava has been easily naturalized in other tropical regions throughout the world. The skin is yellow and lemon-shaped but some may be brownish yellow. The inside of the fruit has pink or cream-colored pulp and a large number of small edible seeds. It can be eaten raw or cooked. Guavas are one of the few tropical fruits that can be grown in pots indoors although, if allowed to grow at will, can reach heights of thirty feet. Guava is used to produce jam, jelly, and juice. It is an excellent source of vitamin C and also contains iron, calcium, phosphorus, protein, fiber, antioxidants, and flavonoids. Its vitamin A content is five times that of an orange. There are many varieties throughout the world. The Strawberry guava is about the size of a cherry and has an edible red skin. The flesh is white with small round seeds that are swallowed whole. On some South Pacific Islands like Hawaii, it is illegal to plant new guava trees because they can be invasive.

HAWAIIAN MOUNTAIN APPLE

The Hawaiian Mountain apple is native to Malaysia but spread throughout the Pacific Islands. The tree grows only in tropical, humid climates. The wood of the tree was used by ancient Hawaiians to make idols and the bright magenta flowers are believed to be sacred to Pele, the volcano goddess. The bark of the tree was used to help ease symptoms of sore throats. The Hawaiian Mountain apple fruit has a bell-shaped body and the thin outer skin has a smooth waxy texture that becomes a darker shade of red as it ripens. The white pulp has a very crisp texture and is juicy with a sweet-tart flavor. It is not related to any apples.

HEARTS OF PALM

The heart of palm, the edible core of the stem of certain palm trees, has been eaten for thousands of years in Central and South America. Many wild species of palm, including coconut palms, Acai palms, and Cabal palms, serve as sources for hearts of palm. Unfortunately, the harvesting process kills the tree so several palms were domesticated and bred specifically for production of this vegetable. These trees have multiple stems, allowing farmers to harvest the hearts while allowing the rest of the tree to live. Palmetto and swamp cabbage are two alternate names for hearts of palm. This vegetable has a pale straw color and a tender, delicate flavor. It is high in fiber, vitamin C, and zinc. France is the largest importer and consumer of hearts of palm.

HORSERADISH

Horseradish is believed to have originated in Central Europe about three thousand years ago. The plant has been used as an aphrodisiac, a treatment for rheumatism, as a bitter herb for Passover seders, and as an accompaniment for beef, chicken and seafood. Early Greeks used it as a rub for lower back pain and as cough medicine. In Old England, inns and coach stations grew the root to make cordials to revive exhausted travelers. Colonists brought horseradish to North America. In some southern states, horseradish was rubbed on the forehead to relieve headaches.

Horseradish is a member of the mustard family and is cultivated for its thick, fleshy white roots. The bite and aroma of this root are almost absent until it is grated or ground. Horseradish contains a volatile compound that, when oxidized by air and saliva, generates the hot taste. Its name is a combination of the words 'horse' (to denote large size and coarseness) and 'radish' (the Latin word for root). Horseradish is low in sodium and provides dietary fiber. It is also trans-fat-free. Collinsville, Illinois hosts the International Horseradish Festival each May. Some Germans add it to their beer and horseradish schnapps is made in Germany.

The fruit of the South American Sandbox Tree explodes when it is ripe and scatters the seeds for fifty feet or more. The noise is loud enough to be mistaken for gunfire,

ICE CREAM BEAN

Often grown to provide natural shade for cacao, coffee, tea and vanilla plants because of its broad spreading canopy, Ice Cream Bean trees are grown in Mexico to the Amazon rainforest. Their bean pods have a sweet cottony pulp that tastes like vanilla ice cream. The large green or black seeds in the pulp are inedible unless roasted. The beans are a good source of dietary fiber, polyphenols, antioxidants, and anti-inflammatories. The tree improves soil fertility and is used as lumber for construction.

JACK FRUIT

Jackfruit, the largest of all tree-borne fruits, grows in most tropical areas including South Florida. It can weigh up to eighty or ninety pounds. Immature fruit is edible when boiled, fried, or roasted. When mature, the yellow-brown skin has a sweet fragrance and the pink, golden, or cream-colored juicy flesh is very sweet. The seeds can be boiled, roasted, or ground and used as a seasoning.

JERUSALEM ARTICHOKE

Also called Sunchoke, a Jerusalem Artichoke is not an artichoke. It is a North American sunflower with an edible, starchy, gnarled tuberous root that looks like ginger root and tastes like artichoke. It was cultivated by Native Americans long before the arrival of Europeans but is now cultivated more extensively in Europe than in America. Its name comes from the Italian word *girasole articiocco* which means sunflower artichoke (but sounds like Jerusalem artichoke).

For many years, the Sunchoke was shunned because the shape of the root looks like deformed fingers caused by leprosy. During World War II, sSnchokes (and rutabagas) were the most prevalent vegetables and were known as a poor man's vegetable. Over two hundred varieties are now available. They are high in potassium and protein and contain a good amount of iron, fiber, and magnesium. The Jerusalem artichoke can lower blood pressure, decrease bad cholesterol, and boost the immune system. It is used to create alcoholic beverages and also for the creation of biofuels.

JICAMA

Jicama is a round, bulbous root vegetable that grows on vines. Native to the Mexican peninsula, it is grown in Central America, the Caribbean, the Andes Mountain regions, and Southern Asia. Similar in texture to a turnip with a taste closer to an apple, it is also known as a Mexican water chestnut and Mexican yam bean. It has crisp, white, solid flesh. Slice off the top and bottom then remove the peel before eating. The inside can be eaten raw or cooked. It is an excellent source of vitamin C and contains potassium and fiber that is infused with inulin that promotes health. It also has copper, iron, magnesium, and a powerful antioxidant that protects against cancer, inflammation, viral cough, cold, and infections. **Caution: Eat only the root. The thick skin, vines, and leaves are toxic.**

JUJUBE

There are at least four hundred jujube varieties. They have a crispy texture, edible skin, sweet-tart apple-like flavor, and are red inside and out when mature. Legends in some Asian countries say that jujube trees were closely watched because their sweet smell had the reputation of making people fall in love. The tree was introduced to America at the beginning of the nineteenth century. The fruit has been used in Chinese medicine for more than four thousand years. Jujubes contain many nutrients and amino acids, and they have twenty times more vitamin C than any citrus fruit. They are also an excellent source of natural antioxidants and can help lower blood pressure, reverse liver disease, treat anemia, and inhibit the growth of tumor cells. Jujube extracts are used in skin care products and to treat sunburn. Their health benefits increase when boiled, baked, stewed or dried. In powder form, jujubes can lower anxiousness and improve strength. As a tea, it may help with a sore throat.

KALE

Kale was first cultivated from wild varieties by the Greeks and Romans. It spread throughout Europe and then to the United States in the seventeenth century. It is known as one of the healthiest foods grown. Loaded with vitamins A and C, and a good source of calcium and fiber, kale helps fight cancer, heart disease, autoimmune diseases, and macular degeneration. The blanched leaves can be applied topically to burns or irritated skin. Black kale leaves, with large palm tree-like fronds, are narrower than most other varieties and is one of the most delicious of all kale varieties. Purple kale has serrated and ruffled purple leaves that are variegated in shades of green. It has a robust cabbage flavor more intense than green or black kale. Redbor kale, with frilly, curled leaves and almost complete red coloring from rib to leaf tip, contains some of the highest antioxidant levels of many other fruits or vegetables. Sprouting Kale develops from buds located in the bases of the older kale leaves. They share similar characteristics to kale but on a smaller scale. Sprouting Black kale grows in loose bundles. The stems lack the fibrous texture of the mature plant and are tender and sweet. They may be eaten like asparagus or baby broccoli. Green sprouting kale is also known as kale sprouts and is produced right before the plant starts to produce seeds. Sprouting Red kale has deep purple to red stems and petite, deeply toothed leaves. Small clusters of chewy edible yellow flowers top the stems. It is similar in texture to baby broccoli and offers a sweet kale flavor.

KOHLRABI

Kohlrabi, a member of the cabbage family, is entirely edible and can be eaten raw or cooked. The taste and texture are similar to those of a broccoli stem. The small round central bulb is connected to stalks with white, light green, or bright purple leaves. The leaves can be cooked and the bulb is chopped raw into salads, boiled, stir-fried, sautéed or barbecued.

KEDONDONG

The Kedondong looks like a mango, but smaller. It is native to the Pacific regions of Melanesia and Polynesia and also grows well in other tropical and subtropical areas like Hawaii, Jamaica, and Central and South America. The fruits hang from tree limbs in bunches of twelve or more and fall to the ground while still unripe. When ripe, the yellow fruit has a floral aroma and a taste similar to pineapple. It is very high in vitamin C.

KIWI

Originating in China, Kiwi was introduced to New Zealand in the early twentieth century by missionaries, then to the United States in the late 1960s. California produces about ninety-nine percent of the kiwi grown in the U.S. Kiwi got its new name in honor of New Zealand's native bird. The two varieties of kiwi are green and gold. The Gold kiwi, with bronze, smooth, hairless paper-thin skin, is entirely edible. The golden flesh is dotted with black seeds and the flavor is sweet like pineapple and mango. Small and light brown in color with a fuzzy skin surface, green kiwi has a lime green interior studded with tiny black seeds. Its flavor is similar to a strawberry. Rich in vitamin C, it also has vitamins A and E, calcium, and iron. Green kiwi has more potassium than a banana and is high in fiber. It protects against several cancers, coronary heart disease and the risk of stroke, and provides relief from diverticulitis and irritable bowel syndrome. Baby kiwi fruit are about the size of a grape, with fuzz-free smooth green skin. Its lime green flesh studded with black micro seeds and a cream center tastes like regular kiwi.

KUMQUAT

Kumquats, native to China, were cultivated throughout Southeast Asia as an ornamental because of their gleaming leaves and fragile white flowers. China, Taiwan, and Japan preserve the fruit as jams and Taiwan also adds the fruit to teas. Kumquats arrived in the United States in the late 1880s and were planted primarily as decorative plants. Today, California and Florida grow them in the U.S. Kumquats were classified as a citrus prior to 1915 but were then given their own Genus, *Fortunella*. Unlike citrus, the entire orange Kumquat fruit is edible, except for the seeds. The peel has a sweet citrus aroma and flavor and the flesh is juicy and tart.

There are four varieties of Kumquats but Nagami and Meiwa are the most common. The Meiwa is more rounded and considered to be sweeter but the oval-shaped Nagami is most commonly grown. Nagami Nordmann kumquats are seedless and were first discovered in 1965 in Florida. Kumquats contain vitamin C as well as moderate amounts of vitamin A, riboflavin, and manganese. The rind contains liminoids that are phytochemicals that help safeguard from cancer. The kumquat leaves consist of an essential oil that has shown to act as an expectorant and may cure a sore throat.

Kelp is used to obtain alginic acid, used in the processed food industry for its thickening, emulsifying, and stabilizing properties (it prevents ice cream from crystallizing).
Kelp is also used in tire manufacturing and in paints.

LAMBSQUARTER

Lambsquarter is a leafy green vegetable that grows throughout much of North America. Although regarded as a weed, it is one of the most nutritious plant foods. Native Americans ate the leaves to treat stomachaches and prevent scurvy. They made it into a cold tea used for diarrhea, and a leaf poultice for burns and swellings. Lambsquarter is also a purifying plant that helps to restore healthy nutrients to the soil. The plant produces tiny green flowers that form in clusters on top of spikes, and the leaves resemble the shape of a goosefoot. There is a white powdery coating on the light green leaves. It tastes similar to chard and its nutritional value is greater than spinach. **Caution: The leaves, shoots, seeds, and flowers are edible but saponins in the seeds are potentially toxic and should not be consumed in excess.**

LEEK

The leek, one of the world's oldest known vegetables, has been part of the human diet for thousands of years. It has been the national symbol of Wales for at least seven hundred years. One Welsh legend about their patron saint, David, says that he and his soldiers wore leeks on their helmets in a battle against the Saxons, fought in a leek field. Native to eastern Mediterranean regions, leeks are hardy plants that can survive cold climates throughout the Northern hemisphere. It can be harvested at different stages of growth. The leek looks similar to a green-topped garden onion but is larger and cigar-shaped, with tiny hairs for roots rather than a bulb. It is more delicately flavored than the onion, garlic, or shallot. Leeks contain healthy amounts of folic acid, niacin, riboflavin, magnesium, thiamin, and powerful antioxidants. Baby leeks resemble scallions and are entirely edible, including the roots. They are mild enough to eat raw. Wild leeks, known as Wild Ramps, are also entirely edible. The plant's bulbs have a more intense onion and garlic flavor and may be used as a substitute for garlic cloves.

LEMONADE FRUIT

The Lemonade lemon tree, a hybrid between the common lemon and mandarin tree, was developed in Australia in the 1980s. The fruit looks and feels like a lemon with a sweeter flavor. Its flesh is similar to a mandarin. It is less acidic than other citruses.

LEMON

Lemons are native to Southeast Asia where they have been cultivated for over four thousand years. Lemonade was a favorite drink of the Chinese Emperors. Cultivation spread throughout the Middle East, Europe, and Africa. Third century Romans believed that the lemon was an antidote for all poisons. Lemons made their way to the Americas with Christopher Columbus. Catholic missionaries planted them in Arizona and California and they have been a major food crop in Florida since the sixteenth century. Lemons are high in vitamin C and contain thiamin, riboflavin, pantothenic acid, iron, magnesium, fiber, B vitamins, calcium, copper, folate, and potassium. When the peel is zested it releases a sweet citrus aroma. Lemon juice is highly acidic and tart but can be added to a wide variety of dishes and beverages. Lemons ripen after they are picked. They may have no seeds or numerous seeds, depending on the variety.

The Eureka lemon, developed in California in 1858 from seeds brought over from Sicily, is the standard commercial lemon variety. It has bright yellow skin with yellow flesh, few seeds, very tart juice, and a fragrant, oily peel. The blossom-end knob is characteristic of this lemon. Golden Eureka lemons look like oranges but taste like lemons. They have orange skin and flesh.

Meyer lemons are a natural hybrid of a lemon and a mandarin or a lemon and a sweet orange. Their rounded shape, bright yellow color, fragrant and oily smooth peel, low acidic flesh, and floral and sweet taste differentiate them from the common lemon. They were brought to the United States from China in 1908 by Frank Meyer, and named in his honor.

The Sorrento lemon, named for the town in southern Italy where it was cultivated, is the most widely used lemon for fresh consumption in Italy and the lemon used in making the Italian liqueur, Limoncello. It is one of the richest lemons in vitamin C.

True sweet lemons are acidless mutations of the sour lemon. Their flavor is sweetly tart but never bitter. Lemon pie and lemonade are better when made with this variety. Natural remedies use sweet lemons to relieve gastrointestinal problems, boosts liver function, and as an antiseptic. The juice may be used as a hair rinse.

LYCHEE

The lychee is a pale orange fruit, about the size of a walnut, with bumpy skin. It resembles a large raspberry but has a single, large, inedible seed which makes this fruit a drupe. The flesh's texture is jelly-like, chewy and juicy, with a fragrance and flavor similar to grapes. Native to Southern China and Malaysia, the lychee has been naturalized throughout Asia as well as in other regions in the Western and Southern Hemispheres. It is considered to be a super fruit because it contains the second highest amount of polyphenol antioxidants of all known fruits, as well as many other nutrients. Dried lychees are similar to raisins, only larger.

LETTUCE

Lettuce, a member of the sunflower family, is immune to any form of preservation. You can't freeze it, dry it, can it, or pickle it. Native to regions of Asia and Europe, Ancient Greeks and Romans believed that it induced sleep so they served it at the end of the meal. Christopher Columbus introduced lettuce to the new world. Today, lettuce grows in central and southern Europe and southern parts of the United States. Lettuce, of all types, is the second most popular fresh vegetable in the U.S. (potatoes are the first). Yuma County, Arizona, is the winter Lettuce Capital and hosts The Yuma Lettuce Days festival every year.

Lettuce is categorized into six different types: Crisphead, Romaine, Butter, Latin, Leaf, and Stem. All lettuce types are either red or green leaf. Green leaf lettuce is the most nutritious of all lettuce varieties, and the most commonly planted. It is the general name given to dozens of varieties that produce semi-frilled loose-leaf lettuces with varying green colors. The texture is crispy and the flavor is mild and slightly bitter. Red Leaf lettuces contain antioxidants, anti-cancer properties, and diabetes preventative qualities.

Iceberg, a mild, light green crunchy lettuce, got its name in the 1920s when California growers started shipping it covered with crushed ice. Loose leaf has large and curly leaves that are soft, tender, and mild in flavor. Arugula has large, dark green sturdy leaves with a peppery and nutty flavor. Chicory or Endive have jagged, crunchy leaves with a lightly bitter taste. Belgian Endive has white crunchy leaves tipped with pale yellow-green, and a bitter taste. Escarole has broad flat, dark-green leaves with a slight crunch. Some people prefer it cooked. Romaine has long crisp pale-green leaves. Asparagus Lettuce has a long thick stem. The mild-tasting leaves and stem are both edible but are prepared in different ways. When the stem is cooked it tastes like asparagus. It is high in vitamins A and C, with four times the vitamin C of regular lettuce.

Mache, also known as Lamb's Lettuce, is mildly sweet with small, round dark-green leaves. Boston, Bibb or Butter lettuces are small round heads with buttery-textured pale green leaves and a sweet flavor. Radicchio has a bitter and nutty flavor. There are three types named after towns in the Veneto region of Italy: Treviso has elongated red and white leaves; Rosso di Verona is a round, compact head of red leaves veined with white; Castelfranco has rosette-like heads with white and pale gold leaves, with small veins of red and pale green. Spring mix is made up of sixteen fresh greens and lettuces. Half are sweet and mild while others are slightly bitter.

Wild lettuce, a tall, leafy plant with small bright yellow flowers resembling dandelions, dates back to ancient Egypt where it was believed to be an aphrodisiac and psychoactive substance (its latex interior has narcotic effects). The Hopi smoked Wild lettuce resin before sleeping because they believed that it induced vision dream states. It grows wild in North America and, in the 1970s, was popular as both a recreational herb and an herbal remedy to treat insomnia, anxiety, asthma, headaches, sore muscles and coughs. The leaves and stems can be dried and prepared as a tea or smoked.

LIME

Limes originated in Southeast Asia and were transported to Egypt and Northern Africa by Arab traders in the tenth century. Three centuries later they were introduced to Spain and spread throughout Southern Europe during the Crusades. This small, green tropical fruit contains antioxidants and vitamin C and is known to improve digestion, help with respiratory and urinary disorders, relieve constipation, peptic ulcers and gout, and treat scurvy. In the eighteenth century, British naval ships on long journeys were required to carry limes to prevent scurvy (hence their nickname, 'limeys').

There are many varieties of limes but the two main sour lime varieties are Tahitian and Key. Tahitian limes are pale-yellow with smooth, thin, tightly clinging skin when ripe. The pulp is light greenish-yellow and mostly seedless. It lacks a distinctive lime aroma. Key limes resemble common limes but are smaller and more rounded. They have light green skin and a smooth thin peel filled with sweet aromatic oils. The flesh contains a sweet-tart juice.

Sweet limes look similar to more common limes but have yellow-green or yellow-orange rinds rather than green. Their flesh is very sweet because they have very little citric acid. They can be preserved as pickles or jam, and cooked. They are also high in Vitamin B and dietary fiber.

Limes are used in many different types of products, such as pie, sorbet, jams, and beverages. The oil extracted from the peel is used in cosmetic products, toothpastes, soaps, disinfectants, mouth wash, deodorants, and skin emollients.

LOQUAT

Native to China, the loquat was naturalized in Japan more than a thousand years ago. It spread throughout Asia, the Middle East, the Americas, and the Mediterranean. Japan is among the largest producers of loquats. In the United States, they grow in Hawaii, California, and Florida. Loquats are used in Mexico as offerings and ornaments on the altars to celebrate the Day of the Dead. Loquat tree wood has been used in place of pear tree wood in the making of rulers.

The fruit is round or pear-shaped and slightly larger than a plum. It can be smooth or fuzzy, with yellow to yellow-orange coloring. It is used to make jams, jellies, and plum wine. Loquat has a number of important health benefits, including the ability to prevent diabetes, lower cholesterol levels, lower the risk of cancer, protect bone mineral density, improve gastrointestinal health, aid vision, strengthen the immune system, soothe the respiratory tract, boost circulation, and decrease blood pressure. Poultices and salves can be made with the crushed leaves and then topically applied to wounds and aches. The leaves are beneficial when brewed into a tea.
Caution: The seeds contain toxic cyanide compounds. When some people consume too much loquat leaf extract they develop weakness and non-specific pain.

LIMEQUAT

Limequats are hybrids between varying limes and kumquats. Most have the juiciness of a key lime and the shape and tart qualities of a kumquat. There are three distinguished varieties: Eustis, Lakeland, and Tavares, named after towns in Florida where they were produced. The peel is thin, fragrant and sweet, and the flesh is tart. They are entirely edible but remove the seeds.

MAMEY SAPOTE

Mamey Sapote is native to Mexico and Central America and was brought to Florida in 1887. It is a medium to large-sized oval fruit with a hard, rough outer shell that protects the salmon colored flesh. Ripe fruits can be eaten fresh once the peel is removed. Its flavor has notes of vanilla, nutmeg, pumpkin, and apricot. A large central pit contains a seed that should be boiled before consumed. Mamey Sapote can be added raw to fresh salad, made into preserves and jams, used in baked goods, and also stewed and used for making wine. There are at least thirteen known varieties but only a few are popular.

MANGO

Mangos were first cultivated in India over five thousand years ago. Today they are produced in South and Central America, the Caribbean Islands, and other warm areas of the world. Hawaii, Florida, and Southern California grow them in the United States. Mangoes are in the same family of plants as pistachios and cashews. Oval in shape and around five inches long, they have a single, large seed or stone in the middle, which makes them a drupe. They are smooth-skinned and can be red, yellow, or green on the outside with yellow to bright orange flesh that is juicy and sweet, with a touch of tartness. There are hundreds of varieties but only thirty-five are currently cultivated. Mangos contain many minerals, vitamins, and dietary fiber. They are high in iron and folate and contain enzymes that aid in digestion. Their benefits include healthy immune function, normal blood pressure, good vision, strong bones, and protection from lung, mouth, colon, breast and prostate cancers, leukemia, and stroke.

The Alphonso Mango, known as the King of Mangos for its sharply sweet flavor and smooth texture, has multiple cultivars. This variety was shipped to London for Queen Elizabeth's coronation. Raw mangoes, also known as green mangoes, aren't fully developed so the seed is small and the crisp flesh has a sour and bitter taste. But they have more vitamin B and C than when fully ripe. Mangoes have been a part of Hindu and Buddhist practices for centuries. The paisley pattern, made popular in India, was an inspiration from the shape of a mango. In Thailand, it is believed that growing a mango tree on the south side of one's house will bring prosperity.

MANGOSTEEN

The mangosteen is found in the rainforest areas of Malaysia, the Philippines, Sri Lanka, and Indonesia. The round, glossy, purple fruit has a thick and rubbery outer rind and sweet white segments inside that contain one to four bitter-tasting seeds. Similar species (orange and yellow in color) grow in Southeast Asia, Africa, and South America. The mangosteen is high in fiber and contains vitamin C and B-complex vitamins, and powerful antioxidants. Studies have shown that it has the potential to slow the growth of cancer cells.

MAYHAW

The round petite mayhaw fruit, native to the United States, has grown for centuries in the southern states between Texas and Florida. There are three different varieties; big red, super spur, and heavy petite. The skin can be red, yellow, or orange with white pulp and a few tiny seeds. It is highly acidic and has a bitter to sweet-sour flavor depending upon variety. Although it is considered a nutritionally healthy food, most preparations involve sugar to offset the sour taste. It is commonly juiced and used to make jellies, jams, and syrups.

MELONS

Many melons originated in the Middle East and gradually spread throughout Europe and Africa. An Egyptian tomb painting from 2400 B.C. depicts melons, and China has cultivated them since 2000 B.C. Christopher Columbus brought melon seeds to the New World and they were eventually cultivated by Spanish explorers in California. Although there are many different botanical varieties, most melons are thick-walled with hollow centers containing a loose fibrous seed bank. The most common melons are winter, netted, cantaloupe, watermelon, and gourd. Melons maintain their sweet flavor well after harvest. The Ananas Melon, Native to Africa, is one of the more popular heirloom varieties of melon grown in the U.S.

The majority of Muskmelon production comes from China and the United States. In the U.S. muskmelons are often referred to as cantaloupe. Muskmelons are divided into eastern and western varieties. Eastern varieties have seams that run the length of the melon. They are known for their sweet and delicate taste. Western muskmelons lack seams and have a less sweet flavor. Muskmelons tend to weigh between five and eight pounds. Most are round with a light tan netting over the exterior skin. The flesh is thick, smooth, and bright salmon hued with a sweet aroma and flavor, and a high sugar content.

The Cantaloupe gets its name from the Italian village of Cantalupo, where it was cultivated. The cantaloupe is unique to other melons and is defined by two elements: its roughly netted and sandy hued skin (when ripe), and its aromatic orange-coral colored flesh. Most melons are not as dense as a cantaloupe (weight is determined by water content). Although there are dozens of cultivars of cantaloupe, there are two specific varieties: the true Cantaloupe and the North American cantaloupe. True Cantaloupes are not grown commercially outside of Europe. They are an excellent source of beta-carotene, folic acid, potassium, vitamin C, and dietary fiber.

Ambrosia melon is a petite variety of melon that resembles a small cantaloupe. Its exterior is covered in sandy hued skin and rough netting that becomes more pronounced as the melon reaches maturity. The rind is thin and the flesh is light orange with a small seed cavity. It has a sweeter flavor and a juicier consistency than the common cantaloupe.

The Minnesota Midget melon is named after the state where it was first bred in 1948. It is a petite variety about the size of a softball. It looks like a miniature cantaloupe, with a high sugar content.

Tigger melons also grow to about the size of a softball. They have a smooth rind with vertical variegations of rust-orange and yellow. The creamy, off-white flesh is juicy and sweet.

The Casaba melon has an oval to round shape that comes to a point at its stem end. Its skin is golden yellow with hints of green throughout when ripe. Its thick rind has irregular, shallow furrows running from end to end. The creamy pale green to white flesh is mild and sweet in flavor. Unlike other muskmelon varieties, its aroma is very subtle and its skin is void of the typical netting. It was introduced to the United States in the late nineteenth century from Turkey.

The Santa Claus melon is a casaba type, native to Turkey and cultivated in South America, Spain, Brazil, California, and Arizona. It resembles a small football-shaped watermelon. Its hard, wrinkled skin can be varying shades of green and yellow depending upon variety. Its flesh is pale green to white in color, with a mildly sweet flavor.

The Persian Melon grew wild in the area now known as Iran, made its way to England in 1824, and from there to the United States. It looks like a larger, rounder, heavily-netted, non-ridged cantaloupe. The light, pistachio-grey rind turns tan when ripe and its flesh is coral colored, aromatic, and sweet.

The Crenshaw is considered one of the sweetest varieties in the melon family. It is a hybrid cross between the Casaba melon and the Persian melon. There are two types: green and white. The white variety is the most common. It is full-flavored and sturdy enough to be cooked. The rough, firm rind is void of netting and has a slightly waxy feel when mature. Its dense, tender, peach-colored flesh is sweet and slightly spicy. It can weigh eight to ten pounds.

The Honeydew melon, a muskmelon variety, is the American name for the White Antibes variety that was cultivated in southern France and Algeria in the late fifteenth century. Its smooth, firm ivory rind encases sweet, pale green flesh. Round to oval and somewhat larger than a cantaloupe, it has a high sugar content.

The Sugar Cube melon, known as a breakfast type melon, has a petite size and will weigh no more than two pounds. Its seed cavity is smaller and more densely packed than the classic cantaloupe so it has more edible flesh. Its sweetness is known to last much longer than the average muskmelon.

The Watermelon, a member of the cucumber family, is not botanically classified as a melon but as a specialized type of large berry. It dates back thousands of years to ancient Africa where it grew wild. Originally it had yellow or white flesh, not red. Today, there are over twelve hundred known varieties that come in various shapes and sizes. Their thick, hard rinds range from pale to dark green, solid color or striped. The juicy flesh may be pink to dark red, white, yellow or orange, and seeds may be red, white, black, pink, spotted or brown. Often the deeper colored the flesh, the sweeter the taste. The flesh contains mostly water with about six percent sugar. Watermelons are rich in vitamins A, B1, B6 and C, as well as potassium. They contain lycopene which gives certain produce its red hue (lycopene is being studied for its potential ability to prevent certain types of cancer). Half of the watermelons grown in California are seedless although they may contain some white, edible seeds. When choosing a watermelon, select one that is heavy for its size with a symmetrical shape.

The Orange watermelon can be round to oblong in shape with a light green rind with darker green stripes running the length of the melon. It has bright orange-colored flesh with a crisp, juicy texture and a mildly sweet to very sweet flavor depending upon variety. Like red fleshed watermelons, it can be seedless or contain a combination of white, brown or black seeds. It ranges in size from ten and thirty pounds.

The Personal watermelon was developed in the early twenty-first century in California. The rind may be a solid dark green, or variegated dark green and lime green. Its dense flesh is ruby red, tender-crisp, and sweet. It was designed to be seedless but may contain a few small edible white seeds. It averages four to six pounds in weight. There are over fifty different Personal watermelon varieties being cultivated.

MICROGREENS

Microgreens, first grown in Southern California in the mid-1990s, can now be found throughout the world usually grown in greenhouses because of their short growing time – they can be ready to sell in about ten to twenty days. A study done in 2012 of the nutrients found in microgreens discovered that the first leaves of a seedling had anywhere between four to forty times higher concentration of nutrients than their mature counterparts. Micro Bull's Blood beet was one of the first microgreen varieties grown and is the most popular beet variety for microgreens. It has bright red stems with red and green leaves and is tender and sweet with a beet-like flavor. It contains vitamins A and C, antioxidants, and has anti-inflammatory and detox properties.

Micro Celery produces a flat fan-shaped green leaf with a tender stem that is completely edible. It has a slightly bitter and more concentrated flavor of celery. Its leaves contain large amounts of potassium, folic acid, carbohydrates, protein, dietary fiber, vitamins A, B-complex, C and E, iron, magnesium, phosphorus, and calcium. It is one of the slowest growing microgreens.

MIRACLE FRUIT

Miracle fruit, a tropical plant native to West Africa, was first noted by a French explorer in 1725. In 1852, a British doctor called the fruit a miraculous berry in a pharmaceutical journal. It has red berries that contain miraculin, a protein that adheres to the taste buds causing anything bitter or sour to taste sweet (only with fresh berries off the bush). The berry itself is not sweet. This fruit enhances the taste but never masks the essence of any food. Miracle berries have been given to patients undergoing radiation treatment, a side-effect of which is bitter, metallic tastes within the mouth.

MONK FRUIT

Native to the steep mountainsides of southern China, monks were the first to find and cultivate Monk Fruit in the thirteenth century. About the size of a small apple, it is green when picked but is generally sold dried, when the skin has turned brown. A chemical compound found in this fruit makes it about three hundred times sweeter than sugar. It is often used to make teas and other refreshing drinks, and Asian desserts. Chinese medicine has used it as a treatment for coughs, sore throats, and minor stomach ailments.

MONSTERA

Native to tropical American forests, Monstera now flourishes in California and Florida. It is a cylindrical fruit with hexagon-shaped tiles on its exterior that split away and fall when fully ripe. The kernels have a custard texture and a sweet and tart tropical flavor. It must be fully ripe before eating because sharp calcium oxalate crystals of unripened fruit can irritate the mouth. It is high in potassium and vitamin C. If the fruit is left on the plant it turns into a thistle-like flower that comes in various colors including white, pink, yellow, and purple and is used as an ornamental in gardens.

MOSAMBI

Mosambi citrus, a hybrid of a Mexican lime and a sweet lemon, looks like a lemon with a greenish hue. It is about the size of a tennis ball and a ripe fruit will be heavy for its size. The skin is full of essential oils and the taste is sweet. It can aid in ailments of the nervous system and to help reduce nausea or fever. Now grown in India and in some Asian countries, it can also be found in the United States in Florida and Southern California.

All mushrooms grow from microscopic spores, not seeds. Plants growing from spores are called fungi but they are placed in the vegetable category even though they have a protein profile similar to meat, beans, or grains. Unlike green plants, mushrooms are void of chlorophyll and need outside sources of food such as wood logs and other types of organic plant waste materials. Tiny threads spread from the mushrooms and collect nutrients from these sources, at the expense of the plant material. Refrigerating mushrooms can extend the life of the phytonutrients but don't store them in airtight containers because they'll collect moisture and spoil. Place them in a paper bag in the refrigerator. Some famous victims of mushroom poisoning are Buddha, the Roman Emperors Tiberius and Claudius, Alexander I of Russia, and Pope Clement II.

Mushrooms have grown wild since prehistoric times. Turf wars were waged over forage areas. The Ancient Egyptians believed the mushroom gave special powers or eternal life to whomever ate it. It was considered the "food of the gods" in Rome. In Russian and Mexican folklore, mushrooms gave people superhuman strength. In the seventeenth century, they were cultivated in the catacombs beneath Paris. The Netherlands is one of the world's major mushroom producers. In the United States, most mushroom are grown in Pennsylvania. Kennett Square, Pennsylvania is the Mushroom Capital of the World. The largest living organism ever found is a Honey mushroom. It covers over three-square miles of land in the Blue Mountains of eastern Oregon, and it is still growing.

Mushrooms are ninety percent water and rich in potassium, selenium, protein, and cancer preventing antioxidants. There are thousands of varieties of mushrooms but only a few types have produced some of the most powerful natural medicines in the world.

White Button mushrooms, the most common mushroom, have smooth rounded caps and short truncated stems and come in three sizes. The smallest is about the size of a button. The medium size has a slightly stronger flavor and is most often chopped. The larger size can be stuffed, baked, grilled, or roasted. The flavor is mild when raw and more fragrant and meaty when cooked. In the twentieth century, button mushrooms were grown in abandoned coal mines in Pennsylvania. In the right growing conditions, mushrooms can double in size in just one day.

Shiitake mushrooms are tastier than white button mushrooms. They contain iron, antioxidants, high amounts of protein, potassium, niacin, B vitamins, calcium, magnesium and phosphorus. They have lower cholesterol and support cardiovascular health. They also have natural antiviral and immunity-boosting qualities. Although they have been used in China for food and health for over two thousand years, they weren't commercially grown until the 1940s.

Cremini mushrooms are mature white Button mushrooms and slightly immature portobellos. They have a light to dark brown cap with a short white stem. Small brown gills are hidden beneath the cap. The flavor is mild with a meaty texture. They are entirely edible (the stem of a portobello is not). They account for ninety percent of the mushrooms cultivated in the U.S.

The Portobello is the largest mushroom and can measure six inches across the top. It has a rich and meaty texture and flavor that can be substituted for other proteins. The stem is not edible. One portabella mushroom has more potassium than a banana. Low in saturated fat and cholesterol and high in fiber, the portobello is an excellent source of copper (your body needs this to produce red blood cells and carry oxygen through your body) and a good source of vitamin B6 and niacin. It gets its namesake from Portobello, a town in Italy. The first documented cultivation was made by a French botanist in 1707. Different strains and growing times produce different variations in color, size and flavor.

Portobellini mushrooms are slightly smaller than a Portobello mushroom. The stem is white and slightly detached, yet still edible. Portobellinis have a firm texture. The flavor is richer than a Crimini and milder than a Portobello.

Porcini mushrooms have a large cap that is pale to rust brown and continues to darken as it matures. They have a nutty and slightly meaty flavor, with a smooth, creamy texture. Their yeasty aroma is similar to sourdough. Porcini mushrooms have a higher water content than other edible mushrooms. When dried, they have more protein than all other vegetables except soybeans. They can be found most commonly in Europe and North America but those harvested in Italy are considered true Porcini mushrooms. They have not been able to be cultivated.

The truffle is a rare, edible mushroom with an intense aroma and characteristic flavor found in a variety of regions around the world. Many are commonly known by their location and their value varies depending on their rarity and specific aromatic qualities. The rarest truffles are the most expensive food in the world and can cost up to fifteen hundred dollars per pound (one large gold truffle sold for one hundred thousand dollars at a charity auction). Though there are hundreds of different species, only some are considered delicacies. Found in France, Italy, and Spain, the summer truffle is the most common truffle. Truffles never show themselves above ground. Pigs and trained dogs are used to find them. The strong odor of the mature truffle allows animals to locate them. They are most often served raw and shaven on top of food before serving because cooking dissipates their flavor. They can also be used to infuse flavor into dishes. Truffles must be carefully handled to preserve their aroma and flavor. Most truffle oil does not contain truffles.

The dense Abalone mushroom is named for the abalone shellfish, whose shape it resembles. It is not edible raw but when cooked has a buttery flavor. It contains antioxidant properties, anti-inflammatory agents, and tumor inhibiting qualities. Native to China, modern commercial Abalone mushrooms are cultivated in an indoor controlled environment for year-round production. California, Oregon, and Washington produce them in the United States and they can also be found growing wild in Ohio.

Agitake mushrooms are medium to light brown with a thick broad cap of long tan gills on its underside and a bright white truncated stem. They are considered to be an excellent health food and contain niacin, vitamin B1, calcium, potassium, iron, and phosphorus. They can help lower blood glucose levels.

The Bear's Head mushroom is white with soft spines drooping downward from a thick, branched fruiting body. Often growing from hardwood trees, the mushroom grows in branched clusters that look like fungal icicles hanging from the trunk of the tree. Its texture is meaty and tender with a sweet and fragrant seafood-like taste. The Bear's Head mushroom, that grows east of the Rocky Mountains, is North America's only *Hericium* species. All *Hericium* species contain erinacine, a compound that is a potent anti-convulsant. Dried and powdered Bear's Head mushrooms were used by Native Americans to stop bleeding wounds and cuts.

The Black Trumpet mushroom is native to Europe. In the United States it grows in Northern California to Oregon and on the East Coast. It has a waxy charcoal-gray exterior and a deep brown, near black flesh. The cap blends into the edible stem. In Europe, it was called "the poor man's truffle" because it resembles the more expensive truffle when cut crossways into small squares. It is a wild mushroom that has resisted all attempts to be domestically cultivated.

Caesar's mushrooms have a smooth deep orange-red skin and a flavor and fragrance similar to hazelnuts or chestnuts. They have antimicrobial and antioxidant benefits and protect DNA from free radical damage. Native to southern Europe, they have been prized since ancient Roman times by the Caesars, which is what inspired their name. Legend says that the cruel Emperor Claudius's wife replaced some of his favorite Caesar mushrooms with the look-a-like Death Cap mushroom, causing his untimely death. (The world's deadliest mushroom is the Death Cap.)

Candy Cap mushrooms are native to the Pacific Northwest. They are round and very small with chocolate brown or burnt-orange caps that are slightly bumpy. Pale orange gills line the underside of the cap and run down into the stem. They have a burnt sugar or maple syrup-like taste. Fresh Candy Cap mushrooms produce a milky latex liquid when cut. They are most often used in sweet dishes, ground into a powder, or in dried form. Candy Cap mushrooms are foraged and cost more than most wild mushrooms. Its image was on Romanian and Polish postage stamps in the late 1950s.

The Golden Chanterelle mushroom is a dense and meaty, edible wild mushroom ranging in color from orange to gold. It has a nutty flavor and aroma of apricots or peaches. It is entirely edible but the stem is chewier and more fibrous than the cap. It contains high amounts of vitamin D2 that helps the body absorb calcium, and significant amounts of protein, vitamin A, potassium, iron, chromium and eight essential amino acids. It thrives in forested areas of the United States especially along the West Coast.

The White Chanterelle has a sweet aroma but the taste is not as fruity as a golden Chanterelle. It is best when cooked. The mushroom's stem runs up to the cap, lined with false-gills (similar-looking poisonous mushrooms have true gills that can be removed from the cap).

The Blue Chanterelle has a funnel-shaped cap with a velvety texture, and is dark bluish-purple to black in color. It can be found growing in clusters and has a fragrant sweet and woodsy aroma with a mild, nutty flavor. Compounds extracted from the Blue Chanterelle mushroom contain anti-angiogenesis compounds that are used to treat cancer.

The Chicken of the Woods mushroom has no apparent stem and a bright orange-yellow to deep salmon-colored cap that is shaped like a fan. The aroma is potent and the texture and taste is similar to cooked chicken. It can grow anywhere in the United States, up to two feet in width, in large clusters higher up on the trunk of its hardwood host. This characteristic helps differentiate the edible members of this species from the inedible ones growing on the ground. Chicken of the Woods mushrooms have antifungal, antibiotic, and tumor inhibiting properties.

Fried Chicken mushrooms, grown throughout Europe and the United States, are also successfully cultivated in Japan. They grow in clusters and can range from one to five inches in diameter. They have dome-shaped caps and range in color from light beige to darker brown and sometimes gray. The flavor is slightly sweet with a soft, chewy texture. Both the caps and stems are edible. They have an okra-like thickening effect that works well in soups, stews and sauces. Fried Chicken mushrooms have anti-inflammatory and tumor-inhibiting properties.

Cultivated Enoki mushrooms are almost pure white with long, thin delicate stems topped with petite, convex caps. Their texture is tender yet firm with a crunchy bite and mild flavor. They contain dietary fiber and protein as well as a significant amount of niacin, calcium, potassium, selenium and iron. They also provide antioxidants and have anti-inflammatory properties. Enoki mushrooms were one of the first mushrooms studied for cancer prevention. Wild Enoki mushrooms have larger caps and shorter stems and their coloring is orange to brown. They look similar to some highly poisonous varieties including the deadly Galerina mushroom.

The Wild Hedgehog mushroom contains properties that contribute to increased stamina and lessened fatigue. It also has anti-inflammatory and anti-bacterial properties. Its peppery flavor becomes milder as it cooks and it is ideal for canning. Some of the more brightly colored Hedgehog mushroom varieties are used for dying wool. Found predominantly growing in Europe and North America, and in some areas of Asia, a related paler species can be found in the Southwestern United States.

Lobster mushrooms have a color similar to that of cooked lobster shell, with an aroma and flavor similar to seafood or lobster. Grown under hemlock trees in North America and Europe, the Lobster mushroom is formed by attacking another mushroom. It contains a small amount of protein and fiber and can be used as dye for wool, fabrics and some paper.

The Milky mushroom is a very large variety with multiple stems often growing from a single base. It has a lower spore content and is less of an allergen. It is a rich source of protein and Vitamin B. The flavor is similar to a button mushroom. It requires much less water than most cultivated mushrooms.

Morel mushrooms can be found growing in the soil of forests throughout the Northern hemisphere. They are hollow from stem to crown and have honeycomb-shaped spores throughout their bodies. They have a hazelnut flavor with a smoky and woodsy aroma not found in other mushrooms. Although they are the most popular edible mushrooms in the United States, they can never be eaten raw. High in fiber and iron, they also contain significant amounts of manganese, more protein than most vegetables, and are rich in vitamins B, D, E and K. Morels are one of the first fungi to colonize forests that experienced fires the prior year. They are resistant to commercial cultivation.

China produces most of the world's Oyster mushrooms. They are one of the most cultivated mushrooms, next to button and shiitake. The fluted cap is shaped similarly to an oyster and can range in size from two to eight inches. Colors can vary from pale to dark gray, green, pink, or yellow. They have a chewy texture and are best eaten cooked. Wild Oyster mushrooms can develop a slight aroma of anise, while cultivated varieties are milder. The Oyster mushroom is one of the best sources of the antioxidant ergothioneine that decreases inflammation in the body. It is also a good source of protein, fiber, potassium, vitamin B6, and folate. There are three different species of Oyster Mushrooms: King Trumpet Oyster mushrooms (also known as Royal Trumpet); Pink Flamingo Oyster mushrooms (also known as Salmon Oyster or Strawberry Oyster) that taste like bacon or ham when cooked; and Yellow Oyster mushrooms. All varieties can be used for successful mycoremediation (the process of growing mushrooms to clean the earth).

Wood Ear mushrooms, native to China, are the first recorded cultivated mushroom, around 600 A.D. They got their common name from their odd shape, which is very similar to a human ear. They are gill-less and cup-shaped, with a thick, smooth, wavy cap and almost no stem. Ranging in size from two to eight inches, the texture is crisp and crunchy. The color of the skin often takes on the color of the tree that it grows on, and they tend to take on the flavors of other ingredients they are cooked with. Wood Ear mushrooms are a source of iron and protein, are high in fiber, and a good source of vitamins B1 and B2.

Wild mushrooms are generally meatier and stronger in flavor than cultivated mushrooms. Use caution when trying to identify wild mushrooms. Unless you can identify the type with one hundred percent certainty, do not eat or touch it.

MUSTARD GREENS

Mustard Greens, native to India, were cultivated in China and naturalized throughout the northern hemisphere. They have broad, wavy frilled leaves with a deep green color and crunchy texture. The flavor is reminiscent of pepper and horseradish. Mustard Greens require cooking but smaller leaves are more tender. There are many different varieties, including white, green and red. Mustard plants contain volatile oils that have strong antimicrobial properties.

NOTE: Mustard greens, also known as Chinese mustard, are not the same as a different genus of mustard plant that is responsible for seed production used in making the mustard condiment (see page 14).

NECTARINE

Nectarines are a smooth-skinned variety of the peach, the result of a natural occurring genetic mutation. There are two types: yellow-fleshed and white fleshed. White nectarines lack the acidity that yellow nectarines contain and yellow-fleshed nectarines are both sweet and tart. Their origin is unknown but peaches are native to central Asia so it is possible that the first nectarine was found growing on a peach tree within the same region. Trade routes brought it to Europe in the fifteenth century. Documentation in English of the first nectarine was recorded in 1616. Cultivation occurs in both the Northern and Southern hemispheres. A nectarine contains high levels of beta carotene, calcium and vitamin C. **Caution: A nectarine seed contains poisonous hydrogen and is not edible.**

There are dozens of varieties of nectarines. The Red Diamond nectarine is the standard in quality for yellow nectarines. It has blushed skin with juicy, firm, yellow flesh. Honey Kist nectarines, with hues of ruby, pink and gold throughout, have a high sugar content and a rich nectarine flavor. Honeydew nectarines are petite and somewhat heart-shaped. The flesh is aromatic but it lacks in both sugar content and acid value. It was developed in the late twentieth century by a fruit grower in California who also bred the Mango nectarine, similar in shape to a plum, with smooth, golden yellow skin with slight blushes of pale green. Donut nectarines are squat with a sunken center at the stem end. They have a high sugar content and are classified as a clingstone fruit, meaning the fruit's pit clings to its flesh (non-clinging varieties are known as freestone).

NONI FRUIT

Noni fruit is about the size of a russet potato with a lumpy texture. The skin is semi-transparent and can range in color between pale yellow and lime green. The flesh is off-white, semi gelatinous and contains many dark brown seeds around its center. It has a foul smell and is mostly mixed with other fruit juices to help mask its bitter, sharp flavor. It contains natural enzymes and is used fresh, in powdered form, juiced, in tea, and in pill form for a range of treatments from diabetes to fever, though its effectiveness is not supported. There are about eighty types that developed around the tropical islands surrounding New Guinea where its ability to thrive in new lava flows gave it a distinct advantage over all other native plants. For over two thousand years the Polynesian people have used Noni fruit and its tree for many survival needs.

OKRA

Okra, native to tropical areas of Africa, was cultivated in Egypt in the twelfth century. It spread throughout North Africa, the Middle East, and Europe, and was later cultivated in North America. Related to cotton, hibiscus, and hollyhock, it is widely used all over the world and is known by several names including lady's fingers because of its long shape. Okra contains vitamins A, B, C and K, folate, iron, calcium, manganese and magnesium, as well as beta-carotene. It is high in soluble and insoluble fiber. When cut, okra produces a liquid that is used to thicken stews and gumbos. Red okra tastes similar to eggplant and asparagus. When cooked, the red color disappears and the pods turn green.

Boil okra and apply the slimy juice on your hair to help moisturize and fight dandruff.

OLIVES

Olives have been a staple in the Mediterranean region for around eight thousand years. The average life span of an olive tree is about five hundred years but the oldest olive tree, five thousand years old, is on the island of Crete and is still producing fruit. The pit at the center of the olive makes it a drupe and places it in the fruit category. Green olives are picked before they're ripe and black olives are picked at peak ripeness. Fresh olives are not edible, green or ripe, and must be cured in brine or dry salt before being eaten. The texture and color depends on the length of time they're cured, and the taste depends on the ingredients, method, and variety. Olives are full of antioxidants like vitamin E, selenium and zinc. The fat in olives is a monounsaturated fatty acid linked to reduced blood pressure and cardiovascular disease risk. Spain is the largest producer, Italy is second, followed by Greece, Turkey, and Syria. Olives in the United States are mostly grown in California. Greek Kalamata olives are one of the best-known varieties worldwide. Over ninety percent of world olive production is used to make oil.

The onion has been cultivated for over five thousand years. It is easy to grow and adapts to a variety of soils and climates, and it is one of the few foods that does not spoil during the winter months. All onions can be categorized as either spring or summer varieties, or storage varieties, but they vary in shape, flavor, size, and color. The ancient Egyptians believed the onion's spherical shape and concentric rings symbolized eternity. King Ramses IV, who died in 1160 B.C., was found with onions inserted into his eye sockets. Egyptian, European, Asian, and Native American medicines used onion treatments.

Onions contain an antibiotic that fights infections, soothes burns, tames bee stings, and relieves the itch of athlete's foot. Onions are a good source of vitamins B6 and C, iron, folate, and potassium. Its manganese content provides cold and flu relief with its anti-inflammatory abilities. Its flavonoids are more concentrated in the outer layers. Once an onion is cut, sulfuric acid gas is released causing eyes to tear. Holding peeled onions under cold water for several seconds before slicing minimizes this effect. The caramelization that takes place when onions are sautéed is due to their high sugar content.

The Yellow onion is the most common cooking onion and one of the most pungent varieties of onions. The Red onion has a wine-colored paper sheath and ruby and white ringed flesh. Its flavor ranges from sweet to pungent depending on its age and variety. It has antioxidant properties that have preventative and curing properties related to cancer, heart, and digestive illnesses.

Green onions are any variety of onion that are harvested before they bulb. They have a slightly sharp flavor and succulent crunch and are most often used raw. This type of onion is the most widely used ingredient in Chinese and Japanese cuisine.

Sweet onions were cultivated beginning in the twentieth century. There are several varieties and they lack the sulfur that gives most other onions their sharp taste and tear-producing odor. The flesh has a high sugar and high moisture content. The Maui onion, known as a true raw-eating onion, is exceptionally sweet, crisp, and mild when ripe. Its sweetness cannot be duplicated if not grown in the red volcanic earth of Mt. Haleakala, where they were originally cultivated. Vidalia onions, by law, can only be grown in twenty Georgia counties where the sandy soil and mild growing climate give them their sweet taste.

Pearl onions resemble shallots and are small because they are planted tightly together and picked at their stunted size. Their flavor is savory, sweet, and slightly less pungent than full-sized onions. They are commonly pickled and used as a condiment in cocktails. There are multiple varieties, such as Gold Pearl onions (semi-round with a copper-gold dry, papery skin and a firm, juicy white flesh); Red Pearl onions (semi-variegated, dry, papery burgundy skin and pale purple and translucent flesh); and White Pearl onions (its skin encases a crisp, white flesh).

Boiling onions are picked at a size smaller than the common onion. They can be eaten raw, boiled, dry-roasted, grilled or braised, and flavors range from mild to savory to pungent. It is common to cook Boiling onions in milk. White globe onions are the most commonly used onion for boiling. The red boiling onion is similar in appearance to the common red onion.

Cipollini onions, an Italian heirloom variety cultivated in the 1400s, are petite with yellow and gold papery skin and translucent white flesh. They have a semi-sweet flavor and mild aroma. When cooked, they sweeten and soften and their high sugar content makes for easy caramelizing. They were brought to America with Italian immigrants. Red Cipollini onions have a ruby copper-toned, thin parchment skin. They can also be pickled.

Onion sprouts are the young shoots of onion seeds. They have long thin white and green stems. The more light the sprouts are exposed to in the sprouting process, the greener the stems will be. They have a crunchy texture and strong onion flavor and aroma, and are mostly used raw. They contain vitamins, A, B, C and E, as well as calcium, iron, potassium, amino acids and protein.

ORANGE

The orange does not grow in the wild – it is a hybrid of the pomelo and mandarin. It was first cultivated in Southeast Asia thousands of years ago. Oranges were brought to the Mediterranean region by traders in the 1400s. It is believed that Christopher Columbus brought them to North America, as well as Spanish and French explorers. In the United States, oranges were growing in Florida by 1565 and in California by 1769 (these states lead U.S. production). Today, oranges are grown commercially all over the world in subtropical areas. Brazil is a large producer.

There are about six hundred varieties of oranges that can be divided into sweet and bitter types. Taste varies from sweet to acidic, based on the variety. An orange can be seedless or contain a few seeds. It has ten to fourteen segments that are easy to separate. Oranges do not ripen after they are picked. Orange seeds contain volatile oils.

Oranges have a very high vitamin C content and contain almost two hundred nutrients such as potassium, calcium and fiber, most of which have shown to have anti-inflammatory, anti-tumor, and blood clot preventing qualities. They also have powerful antioxidants. The liminoid in oranges has been found to battle cancers in the mouth, kidney, skin, lung, breast, stomach and colon.

The orange was the first fresh fruit to bear a trademark. About ninety percent of the Florida orange crop is used to make orange juice. The process for making frozen concentrated orange juice was developed in Florida in 1945. Valencia oranges have thin skins, some seeds, and are very juicy. They are the classic orange juice orange but are delicious to eat as fruit. In Queen Victoria's day, oranges were given as Christmas gifts.

Mandarins are small and less spherical in shape. They are easy to peel and split into segments with antioxidant properties that increase good cholesterol and reduce bad cholesterol. They can also help fight wrinkles. The oil extracted from mandarins helps to grow new cells and tissues and speeds up the healing process. The Mandarin tree grew as long as three thousand years ago. It got its common name when it was introduced to England. In the 1840s, it was brought to New Orleans and later spread to California and Florida. In the nineteenth century, the varieties of mandarins that are deep orange in color got the name 'tangerine.'

The Temple orange, also known as the Royal Mandarin, is the largest of the Mandarin varieties. It is a hybrid of the Mandarin and Sweet orange and was first discovered in Jamaica in 1896. In 1915 it came to the attention of W.C. Temple, the fruits namesake. It is a deep orange-red color and has unusual aromatic and juicy qualities. In the U.S. they are grown in Florida and California.

Clementines and Tangerines are types of Mandarins. A Clementine is a very small seedless orange with a honey-like sweet flavor and easy to peel rind. They are grown around the world and often marketed in the U.S. as 'Cuties' or 'Sweeties.' Tangerines are smaller than oranges with slightly looser peels. Kishus are tiny tangerines, even smaller than Clementines, and are very sweet. Satsumas are seedless tangerines. They are easy to peel and usually sweet but can also be very bitter depending on when they are picked. Today, most of them come from California. In Japan they are known as *mikans* and can be traced back to the fifteenth century.

The most common eating variety of orange is the Navel orange, discovered growing as a mutation on a sweet orange tree in Brazil in 1820. There are over fifty varieties. The original seedlings were brought to California in 1873. The Navel orange is sweet and easy to peel and has a characteristic dimple on the not-stem end. The most popular fresh-eating variety is the Washington Navel orange. Cara Cara oranges, also referred to as the Pink Navel, are harvested in California. They have bright orange skins with pink seedless sweet and juicy flesh, similar to a ruby grapefruit. They were first found growing on a navel orange tree in 1976 at Hacienda Cara Cara in Venezuela and were later introduced to the United States.

Sour oranges come from northwest India and southeast China. They have been used in traditional Chinese medicine to treat nausea, indigestion and constipation. Sour oranges were brought to the Mediterranean region by Christian Crusaders and Arab traders. Cultivation of sour orange varieties led to the Spanish Seville orange. This type was the only orange variety in Europe for five hundred years. It has a rough, thick and bumpy deep orange colored peel that clings tightly to its pale orange translucent flesh full of seeds. When ripe it is extremely juicy.

Sour oranges are too sour to be eaten but are used in marmalade because of their high pectin content. They are also candied whole and their juice is good for cocktails and salad dressings. In the Mediterranean region and the Middle East, they are used like lemon zest to flavor dishes.

Sour orange peel contains fragrant essential oils used in perfumes, soaps, and aromatherapy. Its fruit leaves lather when crushed and mixed with water. In the Pacific Islands, this was used as soap.

Blood oranges are famous for their deep red flesh. Most varieties contain seeds. They are used for juicing and table-top decoration. Moro variety blood oranges, the most common, were grown in Sicily in nineteenth century. They are small, with a leathery and oily rind and a sweet-tart flavor. Arnold blood oranges, grown in Southern Australia, have an orange skin with a maroon flesh. Their juice has a reddish-purple hue. The Sanguinelli blood orange is from Spain and has a red-blushed peel and juicy and sweet flesh that is stained with a dark cherry color. The Tarocco blood orange flesh is ruby red and nearly seedless, and has a sweet flavor and aroma. It was first discovered growing in eastern Sicily in the nineteenth century and introduced to the United States in 1880. The Vanilla Blood orange, also known as the mango or strawberry orange, is medium-sized with a pinkish-orange rind and flesh. It is an acid-less sweet orange with a faint vanilla flavor and aroma.

The tiny Calamondin orange, a hybrid of a Kumquat and a Mandarin, is a little larger than a quarter and often grown in pots as an ornamental tree. The juicy flesh has a sour tangy flavor. The juice is used in beverages, marinades, and to flavor cakes. Native to China, it was introduced to the United States at the start of the twentieth century. It is grown in the Philippines and throughout Malaysia and used for various medicinal purposes.

The first documentation of the Bergamot orange, that looks similar to a lemon, can be traced back as far as 1708. A common orange cultivar in the Mediterranean, Italy produces more Bergamot oranges than anywhere else. Its bitter orange flavor is used for infusing.

ORNAMENTAL GOURDS

Native to northern Mexico and eastern North America, yellow-flowered gourds have been cultivated for a very long time. They were commonly used in Colonial America as a darning egg for mending socks. Today, ornamental gourds are primarily used in decorating (some are made into bird houses). They come in a variety of sizes, colors and color combinations, and may have stripes, spots, or splotches of color. They can be smooth or have warts or horns on the exterior. There are never two exactly alike. The Goose gourd produces a goose-like head and a long neck. Ornamental gourds are not edible.

> The Ancient Romans developed the first greenhouses. They were able to create additional growing seasons by replicating growing conditions in non-native growing regions and during months when plants are naturally unavailable as a field crop.

PAPAYA

Native to southern Mexico and Central America, the papaya dates back to prehistoric times. It is now cultivated in most tropical regions, including Hawaii, where it was introduced in the early 1800s. Hawaii is the only U.S. state where it is commercially grown – in the rich volcanic soil of the eastern end of the Big Island. There are two main papaya varieties: Mexican, which can weigh as much as twenty pounds, and the much smaller Hawaiian type. Hawaiian papayas are yellow when fully ripe, with sweet yellow flesh and dozens of small, black seeds at the center. They can weigh up to two pounds. The Mexican papaya turns greenish-yellow with shades of orange when ripe and has many round, shiny, inedible black seeds. It is not as sweet as the Hawaiian type. The papaya is known as 'the power fruit.' It has the most vitamins A and C, iron, niacin, calcium, folate, riboflavin, thiamine, potassium and fiber of all fruits. It is a natural remedy for heart disease and rheumatoid arthritis, and helps keep the digestive and immune systems healthy. It also contains beta carotene and other antioxidant properties. A papaya can be used as a meat tenderizer.

PARSNIP

Parsnips, native to the Mediterranean region, are sweet, succulent underground taproots closely related to the carrot. The stout roots are white or cream in color and sweeter than carrots because they contain more sugar than starch. They are rich in several health-benefiting nutrients, vitamins, minerals, and fiber. Their cultivation predates the potato in Europe by more than one hundred years. They were brought to America by English colonists. Parsnips are a popular ingredient in soups, stews, marmalade, beer and wine. They can be eaten raw or cooked. There are hundreds of parsnip cultivars. The All-American parsnip is a fast-growing variety with a sweet, nutty flavor. The Student, an American heirloom parsnip dating to the mid-1850s, is sweet and mild. Its root can grow up to thirty inches long. The Cobham Marrow parsnip is one of the sweetest parsnip varieties, used most often in desserts or glazed with brown sugar. People with an allergy to walnuts, figs, carrots, and parsley may develop sensitivity to parsnip. **Caution: Use protective gloves when handling parsnip plants as the shoots and leaves contain a chemical that can cause serious skin burns.**

PASSION FRUIT

The two main types of Passion Fruit are the Purple and Yellow. The Purple passionfruit, a subtropical fruit, is native to southern Brazil, Paraguay, and Northern Argentina. In the late 1800s it was growing in the coastal areas of Australia and then made its way to Hawaii. Today, it is also grown in Florida and California. The Purple passionfruit is a small, oval to round shaped fruit, about two to three inches in diameter when ripe. The skin color varies from dark purple to red, and below the skin is a cottony white peel. The interior is filled with edible highly aromatic yellow to green jelly and medium sized black seeds. It has a tropical sweet-tart flavor. Yellow passionfruit is a hybrid that will yield more fruit than the Purple variety and is higher in citric acid and carotene. It has a thick yellow skin tinged with spots of lime green. The yellow-orange pulp is very juicy and has many petite brown seeds. Its flavor is sweet and acidic, and its pulp can be used raw or cooked. In Hawaii, it is used as a flavoring for syrups and shaved ice.

Passion fruits are rich in vitamins A and C and the edible seeds are an excellent source of dietary fiber. The inner white rind is being studied for its ability to reduce asthma symptoms and alleviate osteoarthritis pain. The vines produce large white flowers with purple, green, black, and yellow detailing. The passionfruit got its name from Spanish missionaries who felt the flower resembled some of the symbolism found in the Passion of the Christ: the three stigmas as the three nails, the corona as the crown of thorns, the five stamens as the five wounds, and the purple petals as the purple robe. The flower has been used for centuries by many cultures to treat insomnia, asthma, anxiety, and menopause.

PAWPAW

The Pawpaw is one of the largest fruit trees native to America, originating in the southeastern United States. It is also known as Poor Man's banana, American custard apple, and the Kentucky banana. Native Americans brought the pawpaw across the country. Its leaves and fruit provided medicine and food. Pawpaw is chronicled in the journals of Lewis and Clark as a source of sustenance during their travels. Thomas Jefferson had pawpaw trees at his home in Virginia and shipped the seeds to friends in France. It was also enjoyed by George Washington, Daniel Boone, and Mark Twain. Albany, Ohio hosts an Annual Pawpaw Festival each year.

The pawpaw grows to about three to six inches in length and when ripe, its skin color ranges from green to yellow and dark spots may appear. The yellow flesh is custard-like in texture with dark brown to black seeds. It has a strong sweet aroma and its flavor has notes of banana, coconut, papaya, pineapple and mango. Pawpaw extracts are one of the most potent herbal products discovered and have a broad range of health benefits, but they can also cause allergic reactions. Kentucky State University has a full-time pawpaw research program.

PEACH

The peach is a member of the rose family. It was first cultivated in China in the tenth century B.C. The peach has been revered there as a symbol of longevity, and an image of the peach was placed on pottery. Travelers along caravan routes carried the peach seed to Persia before it was cultivated in Europe. The Romans called them Persian apples after the country that introduced them. In the early 1600s, Spanish explorers brought them to the New World and by the 1700s, missionaries were growing peaches in California. The United States is the world's largest producer of peaches. Johnston, South Carolina is known as the Peach Capital of the World. Peaches contain vitamins A, B-carotenes and C, fiber, potassium, niacin, lycopene, and several other nutrients. They provide many health benefits, such as free radical scavenging, improved eyesight, protection against infection, lowered blood pressure, a healthy heart rate, and protection from cancer and heart disease.

A peach is considered a drupe because it has a single, inedible pit at the center. There are hundreds of varieties of peaches, from heirloom to hybrid, but only two colors: yellow fleshed and white-fleshed. Peaches are also classified as clingstone (the pit hugs its flesh) or freestone (the pit is easily removed). Most yellow-fleshed peaches are clingstone varieties and white-fleshed peaches are freestone. Yellow-fleshed peaches are the quintessential peach. They have fuzzy thin skin with hues of red, pink and gold. When ripe, the flesh is juicy and has a classic peach flavor. They are firmer than white-fleshed peaches and better for cooking. White-fleshed peaches have fuzzy creamy white skin with blushes of red and pink. When ripe, they have a sweet aroma. They are also low in acid with a more delicate flavor and texture.

PEAR

There are more than four thousand varieties of pears but only about thirty types are edible. The majority are ornamental. Edible pears come in two varieties: Asian and European. Asian varieties have a crisp texture and vary slightly in shape and color. They are native to Japan and China where they have grown for over three thousand years. In China, pears signify justice, wisdom, and longevity. In Japan, pears were used to protect property from bad luck. Pear trees can produce fruit for over one hundred years. The fruit is cultivated in Australia and New Zealand.

Pears became popular in Europe in the early Middle Ages. European varieties are soft and juicy when ripe. (To slow the ripening process, refrigerate them for a few days.) At the end of the eighteenth century, pear trees were imported to Massachusetts. Today, almost one hundred percent of the pears sold in the United States are grown in Washington, Oregon, or Northern California. Pears contain copper, iron, potassium, manganese, magnesium, B vitamins and vitamins A, C and K, healthy acids, and powerful polyphenols. They can help the body fight infection, diabetes, cancer, colitis, arthritis, osteoporosis, gallbladder disorders, and gout. They are also very high in fiber.

Bartlett pears, the most popular variety of European pears, are the only pears that have a true pear shape and taste. Its fruit's color changes from vibrant green to yellow as it ripens, unlike other varieties. Discovered in England in 1765 by a school teacher, it was later sold it to a nursery that named it the Williams pear. It was then brought to Massachusetts in 1797 and grown at the estate of Enoch Bartlett, who renamed the pear after his own name. The Red Bartlett pear was discovered as a bud on a common Bartlett tree in Washington State in 1938. Its skin is bright red and aromatic, with an off-white flesh and sweet taste and smooth texture.

Anjou pears, another European variety, are the second most recognized pear in the U.S. They thrive in Washington and Oregon. Anjou pears are a medium-sized variety with green skin and a short, squat body. They have almost no neck typical of a pear. The soft flesh is juicy, white and dense, with a slightly sweet flavor. Red Anjou pears were discovered as a bud growing on a green Anjou pear tree in Oregon in the 1950s. Its skin color ranges from dark maroon to a lighter, crimson red.

Bosc pears are possibly native to France or Belgium. The tree was first planted in the Eastern part of the United States in the early 1830s and now thrives in Oregon and Washington. They have a rounded bottom and an elongated neck with a long, curved stem. The golden russet-colored skin covers a creamy, off-white flesh that is crisp yet tender. The flavor is sweet with a honeyed aroma. For centuries, artists have chosen the Bosc pear for their paintings and drawings because of its shape and skin color.

The Seckel pear, also referred to as Sugar Pear or Candy Pear for its sweet flavor, is the smallest of all the commercially produced pears. It was discovered growing as a wild sapling in an orchard outside of Philadelphia in the early 1800s. It may be the only true American pear. Today, it is grown in the Pacific Northwest.

Comice pears, also referred to as Christmas pears, are the sweetest and juiciest of all of the European pear varieties. They have yellow-green skin and a sweet aroma and flavor. They are grown in the Pacific Northwest and in some areas in France, where they were first cultivated in the mid-1800s. The Red Comice pear, with deep red and thin skin, has a sweet spice-like flavor.

The Warren pear is one of the most delicious American pear varieties. It is a cross between the Seckel pear and the Comice pear. It was discovered growing in an abandoned experimental orchard in Mississippi in 1976 by Thomas Warren. What is remarkable about this pear is that it survived the heat of the Deep South

Garber pears were developed in Pennsylvania in the mid-to-late nineteenth century by J.B. Garber. They are a cross between a European pear and a Japanese pear. They can be a standard pear-shape or a rounded apple-shape with a mild pear flavor and crisp texture similar to an apple. They are mostly used as a processing pear and are good for canning.

PERUVIAN APPLE CACTUS

Peruvian Apple Cactus are actually native to Brazil, Uruguay and Argentina. The fruit has magenta-red skin that splits open when ripe to reveal a white fleshy interior speckled with tiny black seeds (like a kiwi). The texture is similar to shaved ice with a sweet-tart flavor. They can be foraged in the wild or found commercially cultivated, especially in Israel.

Peas found by archaeologists on the Thai-Burmese border have been carbon-dated to 9750 B.C. They are native to Europe and parts of Asia. Cultivation of peas began in the seventeenth century in England and dried peas were brought to the New World with explorers. Peas are one of the first crops grown by early colonists. Today, only five per cent of the peas grown are sold fresh; the bulk of them are canned, frozen or dried. Gregor Mendel, an Austrian monk famous for plant breeding experiments in the second half of the nineteenth century, used pea plants as his basis. His work is considered to be the foundation of modern genetics.

The most commercially sold peas are of the English pea variety (also called Garden peas). They have a large bright green inedible pod that grows on vines. The pods must be shelled to reach the plump, round peas inside. Fresh English peas are sweet and tender enough to be eaten raw. They are rich in vitamins A and B, calcium, iron, zinc, and potassium. They contain protein, fiber, lutein (promotes healthy vision), and phytonutrients that have anti-inflammatory properties and can aid in the prevention of diabetes, heart disease and arthritis.

Snow peas, also known as Chinese pea pods because they are often used in stir-fries, have pale green, wide flat pods that contain petite flattened peas. The entire pod is edible, although the tough strings along the edges are usually removed before eating. Snow peas have a crisp-tender texture and are mildly flavored, and can be served raw or cooked. They contain protein, carbohydrates, dietary fiber, vitamins C and K, potassium, magnesium and iron. Snow peas are higher in vitamin C than other type of pea. Some varieties have antioxidants known to have anti-inflammatory properties that boost the immune system and can help aid in the prevention of certain cancers. The Golden Snow Pea, an heirloom that originated in India, has a pale-yellow skin that becomes more golden as the pea pod ripens. The Purple Snow Pea has a deep purple outer skin. Its flavor is slightly sweet and the texture is meaty.

Sugar snap peas, a hybrid variety developed in the late 1960s between snow peas and garden peas, are entirely edible. They have bright green thick walls with a row of petite green peas inside. The pea pod is crisp and juicy and the peas are tender with a sweet pea flavor. They are a good source of vitamins A and C, potassium, iron, riboflavin and thiamine. There are several varieties of Sugar Snap peas, many are string-less.

Pea shoots are the choice leaves and tendrils of pea plants and can be eaten raw or lightly cooked. They are full of strong antioxidants that protect cells from damage and help prevent certain diseases.

Pea vines are the thread, leaflet, and blossom of the snow pea and snap pea plants. The flavor is sweet like the pea pod. They can be eaten fresh or as a wilting green (cook them in olive oil, salt and pepper).

The term 'field pea' dates back to the American south where they were grown for their ability to produce nitrogen that enriched the soil in the fields where corn and rice were grown. The peas also provided nourishment for livestock.

PEPPER

All vegetable peppers, both sweet peppers and hot peppers, originated in the Americas. They were widely cultivated in both Central and South America as early as 5000 B.C. Columbus took pepper seeds back to Spain from the Caribbean in 1493A.D. He thought the hot chile peppers were related to the spice pepper since they were also hot and spicy, so they were called peppers. From Spain, different varieties were introduced to Europe, India, and Asia. There are now over a thousand varieties of peppers.

Each Chile Pepper (also spelled chilli, chillie, or chili depending on the region where they are grown) has a unique flavor, color, shape and heat factor. They are classified by shape and heat. The point where the seed is attached to the white membrane inside the chile pepper has the highest concentration of capsaicin (what gives it its hot taste). It is not water soluble so don't drink water to cool your mouth after eating one. It is, however, soluble in fat and alcohol so drink milk or beer. Some people wear plastic gloves when cutting, skinning, or seeding chiles. Chiles are cholesterol-free, saturated fat-free, low calorie, low sodium, and high in fiber. In the United States, they mainly grow in California, New Mexico, and Texas. Hatch, New Mexico is known as the Green Chile Capital of the World.

The Jalapeno is green, about four to six inches long, and cylindrical shaped with thick meaty walls. It is the most common chile in the United States. Its heat level differs from mild to hot depending on where it is grown and how it is prepared. A smoke-dried jalapeno is referred to as a chipolte. The process makes it hotter than the immature pepper and imparts a smoky flavor.

The Serrano Pepper is green when raw and ripens to red, brown, orange, or yellow. About one to two inches in length, it has thin walls and a crisp and biting taste that is about five times hotter than a Jalapeno pepper. It is mainly used in salsa and sauces.

The Habanero Chile is one of the hottest chilies. It is two and a half inches long with thin-walls and can be green, orange or red in color, and sometimes white, brown or pink. It has a unique floral flavor and is used as a seasoning for sauces, marinades and chutneys. A close relative is the Scotch Bonnet Pepper, almost indistinguishable from the habanero except it is slightly smaller.

The Poblano Chile is green, thick-walled, and heart-shaped, and generally stuffed. It turns from green to dark red and black when mature. The ripened poblano is significantly hotter and more flavorful than the less ripe, green poblano. Dried poblano chilies are called ancho chilies. Ancho chilies are about three inches wide and four inches long with a sweet hot flavor.

Thai chiles, also known as Bird Pepper, range in color from red to green when fully mature. They are often used in Asian curries. Thai peppers are extremely hot and should be used sparingly.

The Cayenne Chile Pepper is one of the most common chile peppers. It is long and curved, about two to three inches long and a half inch in diameter, with thick flesh. It is green to red in color, hot in taste, and used for sauces or in salsas. When dried and made into a powder, it is used as a spice.

An Anaheim pepper, also known as a California green chile or Magdalena, is named after Anaheim, California although it originated in New Mexico. It grows to eight inches in size and is the mildest variety of chili pepper. Varieties of the pepper grown in New Mexico tend to be hotter than those grown in California.

Chile de Arbol is also known as either Bird's Beak Chile or Rat's Tail Chile. It is a bright red color when mature and is often dried and used to decorate wreaths because it won't lose its red color when dried.

The Mirasol Pepper may be either small or large, smooth or wrinkled. It is a thin-skinned chile known for its distinct berry like, fruity flavor that adds spice to hot salsas, stews, and mole sauces.

The Cascabel Chile, also known as the Rattle Chili or Jingle Bell, is a Mirasol variety and gets its name from the loose seeds that rattle inside a dried cascabel when shaken. It is a medium-hot Mexican pepper that, when dried, is round like a cherry pepper with a translucent skin. When toasted, it develops a rich nutty flavor.

Cherry peppers are fleshy and heavily seeded. They mature from green to red. Their heat ranges from moderately mild to medium heat with traces of sweetness.

Yellow Wax Chile peppers are four to six inches in length and range from mildly hot to hot. They are served fresh in salads and salsas, or pickled. They are good peppers to stuff.

The Sweet Banana Pepper changes from pale to deep yellow or orange as it matures. It is long, tapered, and banana-shaped. It may be fried or sautéed, used raw in salads, or stuffed. It should not be confused with the hotter Yellow Wax Chile pepper.

Ghost Chile Peppers are one of the hottest peppers in the world and are best used very sparingly. They are two and a half to three and a half inches in length and about one and a half inches wide with a long, thin stem. They have a waxy shine on their thin and slightly wrinkled skin and can be green, orange or red at stages of ripeness. The dried chile pod is rusted red, shriveled and grooved.

The bell-shaped pod characteristic of the sweet Bell Pepper gave this pepper its name. Bell peppers date back to 5000 B.C. and are indigenous to tropical South America. Portuguese and Spanish explorers brought sweet peppers to Europe. The practice of cultivating peppers in hot houses under controlled temperature and light was pioneered in Holland. Sweet peppers contain large levels of carotenes and are an excellent source of Vitamin C. They are also low in calories, have no fat, and are sodium-free and cholesterol-free. When frozen, their crispness will be lost. A bell pepper's color is a reflection of its maturity. The most common colors are green (unripe), yellow, orange, and red. Red bell peppers are ripened green peppers.

Green Holland bell peppers are less sweet than other colored sweet peppers because they have not been allowed to ripen fully on the vine. Florida and California are the major producers of this pepper in the U.S.

Yellow Holland Bell Peppers are smooth-skinned with uniformly colored skin. Orange Holland bell peppers have a bright orange skin. The Red Holland bell pepper has a mild, sweet pepper flavor with a crisp-firm texture.

Brown Holland bell peppers, also known as Chocolate Beauty peppers, are a sweet pepper variety that are distinguished by their unique mahogany brown coloring.

White Holland Bell Peppers are a pale yellow-white color, with a sweet, mild flavor and crisp texture.

Purple Holland Bell Peppers are purple-skinned, with green flesh. They are slightly more bitter than other colors and most often used for display.

Green Tinker bell peppers, the size of a golf ball, have a sweeter flavor than mature green bell peppers and come in various colors.

Mini sweet peppers, available in red, yellow and orange, measure about three inches tall and have a crisp texture. They are sweet and have very few seeds.

PICKLED PEPPER

There are more than fifteen varieties of pickled peppers, ranging from mild to hot. Jalapenos are packed in brine and come whole or in rings. Yellow Banana Peppers are available whole or in rings. Cherry Peppers are available in red or green and are most popular whole. Pepperoncini pickled peppers are mild with a slight heat and a hint of bitterness.

Xylocarp refers to any fruit that has a hard, woody outer layer, like a coconut.

The Persimmon originated in northern China and has been cultivated for over a thousand years in Asian countries. China produces the most persimmons worldwide. Persimmons are one of a few foods associated with killing breast cancer cells without harming normal breast cells. They contain vitamins A, B-complex and C, along with copper and phosphorus. They also have phytonutrients, flavonoids, and antioxidants.

Persimmon seeds came to the United States from Japan in 1856. The large Japanese persimmon is cultivated in California and regions with moderate winters and mild summers. A smaller walnut-sized variety is a North American native. The name 'persimmon' was originally used by Native Americans to refer to the American persimmon that still grows wild today. The Latin word for persimmon means 'food of the gods.' There are three common persimmon varieties used as rootstock for grafting: Lotus, Virginiana, and Kaki. They provide the foundation for hundreds of heirloom and newer varieties.

The Fuyu Persimmon is the most highly cultivated and commercially successful variety. It has a squat and rounded tomato-like shape, pumpkin colored skin and flesh, and flavor similar to pear and brown sugar. It lacks a core and seeds, and, unlike most other persimmon types, has no astringency. It can be eaten fresh at various times during maturation.

The American persimmon is native to Kentucky. The small fruit is orange but also can be golden yellow to red in color. It is one to two inches in diameter and very soft, with sweet flesh when mature. It is most often eaten fresh or used in recipes for candies, baked goods and beverages.

The Gosho Persimmon, a Japanese variety, is non-astringent, large and globular shaped with a slightly flattened form. It has a thin reddish-orange skin that develops the deepest red color of any other persimmon variety. It may be twice as large as a Fuyu and is meant to be eaten crisp like an apple.

The Maru persimmon is native to Japan and prefers a subtropical to mild, temperate climate. It is petite, semi-squat and rounded, with orange thin skin and soft and juicy flesh containing up to eight large flat seeds patterned in the shape of a star when cut in half. Its sweet flavor has nuances of vanilla, pear, honey and dates.

The Tsuru Noko "Chocolate" persimmon, native to Japan, is petite, elongated, conical-shaped, and has orange colored thin skin. The brown flesh contains thin flat seeds and the flavor has notes of chocolate. It is a non-astringent variety.

Persimmons maintain their orange to yellow color when dried. They come in two different varieties, astringent (heart shaped) and non-astringent (shaped more like a tomato).

Pickling has been used to preserve food for almost five thousand years. Any food can be pickled, but a 'pickle' refers to a pickled cucumber. More than half the cucumbers grown in the United States are made into pickles. They provide essential vitamins and antioxidants, and contribute to improved digestion, liver protection, and the ability to heal ulcers. **Caution: Pickles are high in sodium so consuming pickles in excess may result in elevated blood pressure.**

NOTE: The recommended sodium amount consumed on a daily basis for the average person is fifteen hundred milligrams.

Amerigo Vespucci, for whom America is named, was a pickle merchant before becoming an explorer. In 1900, Heinz erected the first electric sign in New York, a forty-foot pickle. During World War II, the U.S. Government used forty percent of all pickle production for armed forces ration kits. Good luck or an extra present goes to the first person to find a glass pickle ornament hidden on a Christmas tree, an old German custom. Some famous people who loved pickles are Roman Emperor Tiberius, Aristotle, Cleopatra, Julius Caesar, Christopher Columbus, Queen Elizabeth, Napoleon, George Washington, Thomas Jefferson, John Adams, and Dolly Madison.

Most pickles are produced by one of three methods: refrigerated, fresh-pack, or cured. Each method creates distinct textures and flavors, achieved by adding different herbs, spices and seasonings to the pickle liquid. Each variety is packed whole, sliced lengthwise for sandwiches, cut into chips, or made into relish.

Dill is the most popular variety of cucumber pickle. Dill weed is added to the tanks during the last stage of fermentation. Kosher dill pickles have been manufactured and certified in accordance with Jewish dietary laws, and are made with dill and garlic added to the brine. Overnight dill pickles are placed fresh into brine and refrigerated for one to two days. They stay refrigerated when stored and shipped. There are also Polish and German varieties of dill pickle.

Sour/Halfsour pickles are placed into a seasoned brine that doesn't include vinegar and then refrigerated. The longer the cucumbers remain in the brine, the more sour they become. Half-sour pickles are extra crispy and keep their fresh cucumber color. The containers remain refrigerated when stored and shipped.

Sweet pickles are packed in a sweet mixture of vinegar, sugar and spices. Variations include Bread & Butter, available in smooth-cut or waffle-cut chips or chunks; Candied, packed in an extra-heavily sweetened liquid; and Sweet/Hot, made by adding hot spices and seasonings.

Oak bark is the tough, hard outer shield of the oak tree. It can be roasted and ground to make tea. In herbal medicines it is known to alleviate digestive issues.

PINEAPPLE

For thousands of years, pineapples found in the wild have been cultivated in the tropical Americas. Christopher Columbus introduced them to Europe where the pineapple motif showed up in wood carvings and other types of artwork. The pineapple got its name from the Spanish word *piña,* which means pinecone. It found its way to China by the end of the sixteenth century. The pineapple isn't one fruit, but one hundred to two hundred fruitlets fused together. There are hundreds of varieties, each displaying its own flavor and growth characteristics. Today, the bulk of the world's pineapples come from Southeast Asia.

The pineapple is covered in a hexagonal-patterned, rough and waxy rind with spiked protuberances. It is green to yellow in color and topped with a sprout of narrow, pointed, green leaves. The juicy flesh can vary from white to yellow depending on variety. A pineapple is ripe when it is slightly soft to the touch and gives off a sweet aroma.

Pineapples are divided into four classes: Smooth Cayenne, Abacaxi, Red Spanish, and Queen. The groups vary according to size, commercial availability, and sweetness. Smooth Cayenne, the largest pineapple type, can weigh from four to ten pounds. It is known for its juiciness and accounts for ninety percent of the world's canned fruit. The Abacaxi pineapple is considered to be the most delicious and is the major pineapple grown in the Caribbean. The Red Spanish variety weighs from three to six pounds. The Queen pineapple is grown mostly in South Africa and Australia. The Baby Queen Victoria pineapple, smaller than the common pineapple at only four to five inches tall, is sweeter and more aromatic than its larger counterpart.

A pineapple contains dietary fiber, vitamin C, some iron and calcium, and bromelain which possesses powerful anti-cancer compounds and anti-inflammatory capabilities. Most of the nutrients aren't lost when pineapple is canned, except for vitamin C. To grow your own pineapple plant at home, twist the crown off and dry it for two to three days, then plant it. It can take two years to yield one fruit.

PRUNE

Some plum varieties are specifically bred so that they can be dried and still retain their sweetness. These are used for prunes. The prune plum has a higher sugar content, firmer flesh, smaller pit, and a higher acid content. Today, about seventy percent of the world's dried plum supply, and almost one hundred percent of domestic dried plums, come from California. The most common variety of plum used for drying is California French, also known as d'Agen. It is a descendant of the first prune plums brought to the United States in the 1850s from France.

Prunes can relieve constipation, provide antioxidant protection, prevent pre-mature aging, promote cardiovascular health, and reduce the risk of cancer and osteoporosis. Prune juice retains a higher proportion of the plum's nutrients than any other juice made from other fruits. Prune butter is a thick paste made of pureed dried prune plums. It is used in baby foods, as a pastry filling, and as a spread.

The first plum trees are thought to have originated in China. Some plum trees are fruit-bearing and some are not. Ornamental trees have pink flower clusters while the fruit-bearers develop little white flowers. Alexander the Great cultivated plum trees in Mediterranean regions as early as 65 B.C. Today, they are grown on every continent except Antarctica. Plum tree cultivation began in the United States in the mid-nineteenth century and more than one hundred forty varieties are sold in the U.S. There are three species of plums: Japanese, European, and American. Japanese plums originated in China but were first domesticated in Japan. European plums are a hybrid of the wild plums of Europe and western Asia. American plums are native to North America. Each species is responsible for the hybridization of thousands of plum subspecies and varieties. Plums contain many free radical-scavenging antioxidants, vitamins A and C, potassium, and fiber. They have numerous health benefits such as helping maintain vision health and protecting against stroke, asthma, and rheumatoid arthritis.

All plums have thin skin, a single central pit, and a succulent flesh when ripe. The smooth skin can be yellow, green, purple, or red (the sweetest). The benchmark plum variety is the Santa Rosa plum, a Japanese plum developed in the U.S. in 1906. It has a thin speckled ruby red skin and strawberry and orange colored flesh that is very juicy when ripe. It is low acid and has a sweet flavor. The Lemon plum, first bred in Israel, is heart-shaped with yellow or greenish-yellow skin that changes to a rosy red blush when ripe. It is nicknamed 'chameleon' and can be eaten when it is still yellow but will have a slightly acidic taste. When the plum has fully ripened it will be very juicy, with a mild, sweet flavor.

The Cherry plum is native to Asia. There are dozens of varieties that produce edible fruit although many are grown for ornamental purposes. Almost perfectly round in shape, it is the size of a ping pong ball. Its skin is very thin and flushed with cherry tones and peach speckles. The flesh has tones of peach and cherry and the flavor is sweet, spicy, and slightly tart. The Cherry plum is considered a benchmark cooking plum, used in jams, pies, and other baked goods. Wild plums are native to North America and grow on prairies, woodlands, and riverbanks. They were widely used by Native Americans as food and medicine. Small and round, they range in color from yellow-orange to purple and have a tart taste. They contain vitamin A, beta carotene, and potassium.

Sugar plum is the name given to a variety of Italian plums. Its name is an indicator of its high sugar content. Most Sugar plums are dried and eaten as prunes. They are also used for making brandy and wine. The Sugar Plum is small, egg-shaped, with a deep purple, powdery dark blue smooth thin skin. The flesh is firm, amber lime green in color, and the flavor intensifies as the fruit ripens.

NOTE: The sugarplums mentioned in the 1822 story *A visit from St. Nicholas* by Clement C. Moore were originally sugar-coated coriander seeds. Eventually the recipe included small pieces of fruit.

POMEGRANATE

Ancient Egyptians were the first to cultivate the pomegranate and used the juice to fight intestinal worms. They crushed the blossoms to make a red dye and the peel was used for dyeing leather. Pomegranate symbols were found on Egyptian wall paintings in tombs, symbolizing life after death. In India, the pomegranate is thought to bring health and is a Hindu symbol of prosperity and fertility. Pomegranates are mentioned several times in the Bible. In 1769, Spanish settlers brought them to California. They are one of the world's most popular and cultivated fruits. Its name comes from two French words, *pome* and *granate*, which means 'apple with many seeds.'

A pomegranate is about the size of an apple and has an inedible thin, tough, leathery, reddish-purple skin. The inside of the fruit is filled with an average of six hundred ruby-red arils (edible seeds) enclosed in a translucent, bright red pulp separated by thin, bitter white membranes. To remove the arils, immerse in a bowl of cool water. The arils have a sweet-tart taste.

The outer skin of the White pomegranate is light yellow with a pinkish blush and contains a white inner flesh. It has a higher sugar content than the red type and its arils are sweeter. Pomegranates are a rich source of antioxidants and contain vitamins B5, C and K, and fiber. They are low in saturated fat and cholesterol and offer cancer protection. The juice may improve blood flow to the heart and help stop plaque from building up in blood vessels.

POMELO

The Pomelo, native to China, is related to the grapefruit but has a sweeter taste. It is the largest of all citrus fruits. It has an abundance of vitamin C, beta-carotene, and B vitamins, and is a source of folic acid and potassium. Collagen, that helps skin development and creates healthy and balanced gums and teeth, is found on the pomelo.

POTATO

The potato, a relative of tobacco and the tomato, is the fourth most important crop in the world after wheat, rice and corn. Native to Peru, archaeological evidence suggests that people were eating potatoes thirteen thousand years ago. The tuber of wild potatoes contains poisonous alkaloids so one of the first steps made by ancient Andean farmers toward domestication was to select and replant a variety with low alkaloid contents. The potato arrived in Spain in the sixteenth century and made its way to Italy and northern Europe, then to Bermuda and the Virginia colonies. The first potato planted in the United States was planted in New Hampshire in 1719. Today, the potato is cultivated worldwide. Idaho is one of the largest producers.

During the Alaskan Klondike gold rush (1897-1898) potatoes were worth their weight in gold. They were valued for their vitamin C content and miners traded gold for potatoes. In 1952, Mr. Potato Head® was created and it was the first toy to be advertised on television. The toy came with parts but consumers had to supply an actual potato. Mrs. Potato Head® appeared in 1953 and in 1964, plastic bodies were included with the parts. Instant mashed potatoes (dehydrated potatoes) were introduced commercially in 1955. Clark, South Dakota, is home to the world famous Mashed Potato Wrestling contest. The white potato became the first crop to be grown in outer space.

Potatoes are rich in vitamins A, B and C, as well as certain types of minerals. Some varieties have phytonutrients that have antioxidant properties. There are thousands of types of potatoes, each varying in shape, size, color, flavor, and nutritional content. Varieties fit into one of seven categories: russet, red, white, yellow, blue/purple, fingerling, and petite. Most potatoes have a white or pale yellow flesh with brown, red, or yellow skins that are either smooth or rough.

Russet Potatoes, the most popular type in the United States, are medium to large in size, oblong, and have a light to medium russet-brown skin color. Red Potatoes are small to medium in size, round, with smooth, waxy, thin red skin. They have a subtly sweet flavor. White Potatoes are small to medium, round or long shape, and have a delicate white or tan skin. They hold their shape well after cooking. Yellow Potatoes are large, round or oblong shape, with light tan to golden waxy skin. Grilling gives them a crispy skin and they can also be roasted or mashed.

Fingerling Potatoes are two to four inches long, finger-shaped or oblong, and can have red, orange, purple, or white waxy skin with red, orange, purple, yellow, or white flesh sometimes streaked with veins of color. Purple Potatoes are small to medium-in size, oblong to fingerling in shape, with a deep purple, blue or slightly red skin. The inside is blue, lavender, pink or white. They have a low sugar content and are usually roasted, grilled or baked. Petite Potatoes are bite-sized and have the same features as their larger-sized counterparts but their flavor is more concentrated.

"What I say is that, if a man really likes potatoes, he must be a pretty decent sort of fellow."
A.A. Milne
Author   1882-1956

The Sweet Potato has provided food and nourishment to multiple regions of the world. It is the sixth principal world food crop and about ninety percent of the world's crop is grown in Asia. Its skin color can be cream, yellow, orange, pink or purple and its dry flesh can be white, orange, yellow, or orange-red. Its shape is usually oval with tapered ends and the texture can be either firm or soft. The sweet potato is distantly related to the potato but has higher amounts of fiber and higher levels of vitamins A and C, potassium, and beta carotene. Regular potatoes are higher in starches. The leaves of the Sweet potato plant provide nutrients comparable to spinach. George Washington grew sweet potatoes on his farm at Mount Vernon, Virginia. George Washington Carver developed over one hundred different products from sweet potatoes, including a mucilage for postal stamps, an economic method for sizing cotton fabrics, dehydrated food, and an alternative to corn syrup. In 1896, he showed the value of soil regeneration by planting sweet potatoes as the rotation crop for cotton. During World War I, the U.S. Department of Agriculture used sweet potato flour to stretch wheat flour. Vardaman, Mississippi, is the Sweet Potato Capital of the World and hosts an annual Sweet Potato Festival. The numerous varieties of sweet potatoes are sweet tasting and often confused with yams (see YAM on page 122).

PUMPKIN

Pumpkins, native to Central America, are large, vining plants with a hard, orange shell that can be smooth, bumpy or vertically lined with ridges. The thick edible orange flesh contains numerous small white seeds that can be roasted and eaten. Native Americans often grew pumpkin and squash with corn and beans, a process called "the three sisters." This method was used so that each plant could support the other, producing a better yield. The name 'pumpkin' is from the medieval French word *pompom*, meaning 'cooked by the sun.' Pumpkins were once recommended for removing freckles and curing snake bites. Pumpkin halves may have been used as guides for haircuts in colonial times, giving rise to the nickname 'pumpkinhead.' One of the first published recipes for pumpkin pie was in Amelia Simmons' 1796 book, *American Cookery*, the first cookbook to be written by an American and published in the United States. Illinois produces the most pumpkins in the U.S.

There are many varieties of pumpkins that come in different shapes, colors, and sizes. The orange, smooth-skinned Pam pumpkin is mostly found in the United States and is considered the standard pie pumpkin because of its uniform round size and extremely sweet, string-less flesh. The Cinderella pumpkin owes its name to its resemblance to the pumpkin carriage in the fairy tale *Cinderella*. It is a French heirloom variety with a bright red-orange, hard exterior with deep ridges, and a slightly squat shape. Its flesh has a sweet flavor and creamy texture. Blue pumpkins, grown in Australia, New Zealand and the United States, tend to have deep, rounded ridges running from top to bottom. The skin ranges in color from dusky blue-gray to blue-green, with a dark orange flesh. Many varieties of blue pumpkin are known for their exceptionally sweet flavor.

Pink pumpkins, a new hybrid variety grown in the United States and Canada, have large ridges on their light pink to salmon colored skin, and a sweet, orange flesh. Growers that sell them agree to donate twenty-five cents per pumpkin to the Pink Pumpkin Patch Foundation for breast cancer research. Mini pumpkins are a petite, ribbed version of the common large, orange pumpkin and are actually a type of gourd. Mostly used for ornamental and decorative purposes, they can also be hollowed out, stuffed, and baked. Mini white pumpkins have a white shell and bright orange flesh. Mini Tiger pumpkins have orange and green stripes on their white skin.

Pumpkins contain lycopene, beta-carotene, lutein, magnesium, potassium, vitamin A, and antioxidant carotenoids. The seeds are a great source of vitamins, minerals, proteins, and omega-

3 fatty acids. About ninety-nine percent of pumpkins sold are for decorative purposes. In the 1970s, a new strain of pumpkin was developed specifically for carving. These types are bland in flavor and more fibrous. The tradition of pumpkin carving dates back to centuries ago in Ireland where the people carved turnips and potatoes with scary faces, then added a candle and placed them in windowsills to ward off evil spirits, creating a jack-o-lantern. American colonists found pumpkins in the New World and it soon became the vegetable of choice for carving.

PURSLANE

Native to Indian and the Middle East, purslane is now also grown elsewhere and varies in leaf size, thickness, and pigment. Its leaves and tender roots have a slightly sour and salty taste. The yellow flower buds are also edible and the seeds are used to make herbal drinks. Rich in dietary fiber, it is an excellent source of vitamins A and C, and some B-complex vitamins, and iron, magnesium, calcium, potassium, and manganese. The dark green leaves have more omega-3 fatty acids than some fish oils. **Caution: Purslane contains oxalic acid which may crystallize as stones in the urinary tract in some people.**

QUINCE

Quince, native to the Middle East, is one of the earliest known fruits. It is thought to be the 'apple' mentioned in the Bible. Ancient Romans used the flowers and fruit of the quince tree for perfume, honey, and many other things. Quince was a symbol of love and happiness and in the Middle Ages it was used at wedding feasts. The small, twisted quince tree is grown in the United States but the Asian variety produces fruit that is softer and much juicier. Quince belongs to the same family as apples and pears but is not edible when raw and must be cooked before eating. It has yellow skin and hard, dry, yellow-white flesh with a tart flavor. It has a high pectin content and is used to make jams, jellies and preserves. Quince paste has a very firm texture and is a classic accompaniment for cheese. Rich in dietary fiber, quince aids in digestion and contains potassium that helps lower blood pressure. Vitamin C present in quince helps reduce the risk of heart disease. It also helps lower cholesterol and its antioxidant properties help fight against free radicals and reduce the risk of cancer.

"Learn to do common things uncommonly well.
We must always keep in mind that anything that helps fill the dinner pail is valuable."
George Washington Carver
Botanist
1861-1943

RADISH

The radish, native to China, is the root of a plant in the mustard family. It got its name from the Latin word *radix,* meaning 'root.' Radishes come in a huge number of varieties, in several different colors, shapes, and sizes. They are classified by their shape or by their preferred growing season. The black radish, a relative of the wild radish, was first cultivated in the eastern Mediterranean. Other varieties come in pink, purple, yellow, and two-tone green and white. All types produce edible roots, leaves, flowers and seeds. They are eaten raw, cooked, or pickled. The ancient Egyptians grew radishes and used radish seed oil before olive oil was known. Radishes were highly regarded in Greece and gold replicas were made. They were also used as a means of payment. Greeks and Romans liked them large and served them with honey and vinegar. In Britain, radishes had medicinal as well as culinary uses, usually for kidney stones, bad skin, and intestinal worms. Radishes were commonly served for breakfast in colonial America.

Round pink radishes (and some of the long carrot-shaped slender varieties) are known as table radishes. They can be the size of a small cherry to a small orange, and their flavor ranges from mild to peppery. Asian radishes, rounder, elongated and plump, grow larger than table radishes and may weigh up to a pound. In the United States, the average large radish is round, red with a white interior, and about the size of a ping pong or golf ball. Radishes contain fiber and are a good source of vitamin C. They can regulate blood pressure, relieve congestion, and prevent respiratory problems such as asthma or bronchitis. They have antibacterial, antifungal and detoxifying properties, and can soothe rashes, dryness, and other skin disorders. Radishes also contain sulforaphane, a proven inhibitor of prostate, colon, breast, ovarian and other cancers.

The rat-tailed radish, native to South Asia, is grown solely for its crunchy seed pods. It grows in most temperate climates across Europe, Russia, Australia, and the United States. It varies in length and color (from green to purple) but all pods have a tapered end and contain one to two seeds when mature. They have the same peppery flavor as the root. Although mostly pickled, they may also be eaten fresh or lightly sautéed.

RUTABAGA

The Rutabega, a root vegetable that resembles a large turnip, is thought to have originated in Bohemia in the seventeenth century as a hybrid between the turnip and wild cabbage. The name comes from the Swedish word *rotabagge,* and it is called a Swede in other parts of the world. Northern Europe, Ireland, Scotland, and Scandinavia are the main areas where the rutabaga is most used. In Ireland, the rutabaga was the first Jack-O-Lantern. Canola is a variant of this plant.

The rutabaga has a thin pale yellow skin and sweet, firm light yellow flesh. It has a nutty and sweet, mild turnip-like flavor that is enhanced by light frost. The rutabaga is rich in vitamin C, beta-carotene, dietary fiber and potassium, and high in antioxidant and anti-cancer compounds. **Caution: Rutabega may cause bloating, abdominal pain, and flatulence in some people.**

RAISIN

Raisins were sun-dried from grapes as long ago as 1490 B.C. Today, grapes are either sun-dried or dehydrated mechanically. In ancient Rome, physicians prescribed raisins to cure anything from mushroom poisoning to old age. Until medieval times, raisins were the second natural sweetener because of their high sugar content (honey was the first choice). Raisins contain a variety of vitamins and minerals and are especially rich in iron. Their health benefits include relief from constipation, acidosis, anemia and fever. They also have a positive impact on eye health, dental care, and bone quality. Raisins can be stored tightly wrapped at room temperature for several months, or refrigerated in a tightly sealed plastic bag for up to a year. When adding raisins to batters, first coat the raisins with flour so they stay suspended within the batter being prepared. California is the world's leading producer of raisins. Fresno, California is the Raisin Capital of the World. It takes four and a half pounds of fresh grapes to make one pound of raisins.

The most common grape used for raisins is the Thompson Seedless grape, the most popular green grape for eating fresh. Dark and golden seedless raisins can be made from this type of grape. Dark raisins are sun-dried for several weeks until they appear shriveled and a dark color. Flame Seedless raisins come from the Flame Seedless red grape and are large, dark red, and extra sweet. Monukka raisins, that come from black Monukka grapes, are very large and dark with an apricot-color and distinctive flavor. Big Muscat grapes have their seeds removed mechanically before processing and create a dark, intensely sweet fruity-tasting raisin. Sultanas are from large, yellow-green Sultana grapes. They are much plumper, sweeter, and juicier than other raisins. Turkey is the main producer of sultanas. In the United States, sultanas are referred to as Golden raisins. Golden raisins are treated with sulphur dioxide to prevent their color from darkening, and dried with artificial heat. This produces a moister, plumper raisin.

Currants, one of the oldest known raisin, are made from small black seedless Corinth grapes. In the United States they are known as Zante Currants (from the island of Zante in Greece where they were originally cultivated). These raisins are seedless, tart, and dark in color, and about one-fourth the size of Thompson Seedless raisins.

NOTE: Dried currants are not the same thing as fresh currants. Fresh currants are the fruits of plants in the gooseberry family. Red currant berries are known as superfruits because they have naturally high antioxidants. They are used mainly for jelly or jam. Black currants are used in juice, jam, jelly, pies and other desserts. Black currant juice was used to treat bladder stones, liver disorders, coughs, and lung ailments. White currants are not as popular as black and red currants but the leaves and young shoots of their plant are also edible.

The Japanese Raisin Tree is native to China, Korea and Japan. There are several in the United States that date back to the 1930s. The small, thick, greyish-brown stalk is the edible portion of the tree, not the fruit. The taste and texture are similar to a dry raisin, with a hint of cinnamon.

RHUBARB

Rhubarb, the stalk of the Rhubarb plant, has been used for medicinal purposes since 2700 B.C. in China and neighboring areas. It thrives in cold climates. In the mid-1500s, it sold for ten times the price of cinnamon in France. In the eighteenth century, it began to be consumed in foods and was introduced to the United States. Though rhubarb is eaten as a fruit, it is botanically a vegetable. The thick stalks can reach up to two feet long and range in color from light pink to deep ruby red. The texture is often compared to celery but the flavor is tart and requires sweetening to be edible. The stalks are the only edible portion of the plant. **Caution: The leaves contain oxalic acid and are fatally toxic and should never be eaten.**

There are over one hundred different species of rhubarb, most of which are hybrids and some are strictly ornamental. They fall into two basic types: hothouse and field grown. Hothouse rhubarb is distinguished by its pink to pale red stalks and yellow-green leaves. Field-grown plants have cherry red stalks and green leaves and are more flavorful. In 1815, it was discovered that "forcing" rhubarb (keeping it in the dark) caused the plant to produce rapidly elongated leaves and stalks and suppressed chlorophyll production, creating a sweeter stalk. Rhubarb contains vitamins A and K and is rich in multiple B-complex vitamins. Vitamin K has a role in the treatment of Alzheimer's disease.

SALSIFY

Salsify, native to Spain, is a brown root that looks like a skinny parsnip and can grow as long as a carrot. The fleshy interior can be boiled, mashed, or fried like a potato. The leaves are also edible and were a popular vegetable with the Victorians. Salsify was first cultivated in Italy and France where it was known as 'goat's beard' for its hairy appearance. It was brought to North America in the eighteenth century where it earned the name 'oyster plant.' Salsify is low in sodium and has a good amount of protein, modest amounts of vitamin C and B, and is a good source of iron, potassium, calcium, and copper. Its health benefits include its ability to lower blood pressure, boost the immune system, stimulate hair growth, increase circulation, improve digestive health, increase metabolism, and positively affect bone mineral density. There are different varieties. The White is long and often hairy when harvested. It was cultivated before the smoother black variety that has a more uniform shape and is mild and subtly-flavored. White salsify contains as much potassium as bananas. Up until the 1500s, Black salsify was thought to have been effective in treating the plague.

"A man seldom thinks with more earnestness of anything, than he does of his dinner."
Samuel Johnson
British author
1709 - 1784

SCALLION

Scallions, also called spring onions, Welsh onions, or Japanese Bunching onions, are young immature plants harvested before the plant grows bigger. Native to Central Asia, where they were a popular remedy in folk medicine for thousands of years, they are now widely cultivated for their top crispy greens in many parts of Europe, the Americas, and Asia. They contain many vitamins, copper, iron, manganese, and calcium. They have more plant-derived antioxidants and dietary fiber than onions and shallots, and have antibacterial, anti-viral, and anti-fungal activities. **Caution: Their volatile oils may cause skin irritation. Scallions can also increase sweating.**

SHALLOT

Shallots have been grown for hundreds of years. Native to Southeast Asia, they were brought to India and traveled to the Mediterranean region through trade. The shallot belonged to the onion family but in 1963 was given its own category. There are more than five hundred different types. Its head has multiple cloves, each covered with a thin, papery skin that range in color from golden brown to rose-red. The inner flesh is grey-white. The flavor is similar to garlic and onions and becomes more delicate and sweet when cooked. Its health advantages consist of its ability to reduce bad cholesterol levels, prevent certain kinds of cancer, offer anti-fungal, anti-bacterial, and antiviral protection, lower blood pressure, help manage diabetes, calm nerves, boost circulation, and aid digestion. To substitute shallots for onions, use half the amount of shallot that you would onion.

Shallot shoots, also known as Spring Shallots, are immature fresh shallots. They have bright green shoots with thin purple skin bulbs and white roots. The bulb has a higher moisture content than mature shallots and their flavor is milder and sweeter.

SHEA FRUIT

The Shea tree, both farmed and wild, grows in the savannah belt of sub-Saharan Africa. Europeans discovered the benefits of shea and began importing it. The thin, mildly sweet fruit resembles a small green plum and has an oil-rich nut inside. Both the fruit and the nut have been consumed for centuries. When ripe, the fruit can be eaten raw or cooked. The nuts are dried, cracked, cooked, and processed into shea butter, used as a cooking oil and as a skin product that can keep up to a year. The oil has a mild, nutty flavor. The blossoms and fruit are processed into local medicines treating a variety of ailments including arthritis, congestion, and gastric pain.

SPINACH

Spinach is an edible flowering plant from Persia (now Iran). It was brought to China in 647 B.C. where it was first cultivated. By the twelfth century it had spread across Europe and was known for good health. It has four times the beta carotene of broccoli and is rich in iron. It is an excellent source of vitamins A, C and K, and folic acid, and also contains manganese, magnesium, iron and vitamin B2. It has dark green, spoon-shaped leaves with the bitterness of beet greens and the slightly salty flavor of chard. There are three different types: savoy, semi-savoy, and flat leaf. Savoy spinach has crinkled leaves and is the most common commercially. It is ideal for sautéing and wilting. Semi-savoy has partially crinkled leaves and is mainly processed, along with flat-leafed.

Baby spinach, the immature leaves of flat leaf spinach, is more delicate than mature spinach and is most often eaten raw. There are several varieties of Water Spinach, an aquatic leafy plant found in subtropical and tropical regions. It flourishes in water and moist soil, is rich in nutrition, and has many health benefits. The presence of selenium and zinc in water spinach helps to relax nerves and can make people sleepy.

During the Renaissance, Catherine de Medici of Florence, Italy brought spinach, her favorite vegetable, to France when she married the king. She popularized the dish style that became known as Florentine. Today, Florentine is used to describe dishes containing spinach. Spinach was the first frozen vegetable to be sold (1930). In 1937, spinach growers in the United States erected a statue in honor of Popeye, the comic strip sailor who was strong because he always ate spinach. Alma, Arkansas is the Spinach Capital of the World.

SPROUTS

There are as many types of sprouts as there are edible plants. Vegetables, grains, and legumes can all be sprouted. Sprouts are the first edible shoots, and they vary in texture and taste. They contain ten to one hundred times the glucoraphanin of the mature vegetable, which helps protect against chemical cancer-causing agents. They are also an excellent source of fiber, manganese, riboflavin and copper, along with smaller amounts of protein, thiamin, niacin, vitamin B6, pantothenic acid, iron, magnesium, phosphorus and potassium.

Alfalfa Sprouts, one of the most common sprouts, have threadlike shoots with petite leaves in various colors of yellow, brown, and light to dark-green. They have a subtle nutty flavor. Broccoli sprouts have petite green leaves attached to a thin white stem. They have a crunchy texture similar to alfalfa sprouts, with a peppery flavor. Sunflower Sprouts are similar to alfalfa sprouts and have a mild, sweet flavor with notes of lemon and almond. They have long white to yellow shoots capped with two petite bright green leaves. Sunflower Sprouts are unique in that they cannot be sprouted in water alone and require soil to grow.

Bean sprouts, the young shoots of the mung bean, have small light yellow leaves and a silvery white shoot. They have a subtle nutty flavor and lots of crunch. They are added to stir-fry, soup, and salad. Green-Leaf Sprouts, often used in salads and sandwiches, have two tiny green leaves at the tip of a slender shoot. China Rose Sprouts are the young shoots of the China Rose radish. They have thin white and rose hued roots capped with petite green leaves and a crisp texture. Their flavor is spicy, like a radish.

Pea sprouts are grown in water and can be harvested within five days. Pea shoots, grown in soil, are the bright green young leaves of a pea plant. Pea plants take months to produce peas but pea shoots are ready to eat in two weeks. They taste like fresh peas and are very high in vitamin K and also contain Vitamins A and C, and folic acid. Yellow pea shoots are grown in darkness.

Wheatgrass, the young grass sprouted from wheat seed, dates back over five thousand years to Egypt and Mesopotamia. The bright green blades of grass are long, thin and delicate, and naturally sweet. It is most commonly served juiced.

SQUASH

Squash, a gourd, is one of the oldest known crops. Archeological sites in Mexico estimate them at ten thousand years old. They were used as containers or utensils because of their hard shells. The seeds and flesh later became an important part of the pre-Columbian Indian diet in both South and North America. Squash later made its way to Europe and Asia and has a long culinary history in southern Italy and Sicily. *Goo-gootz*, Italian slang for Cucuzza squash, is a name used to describe a zucchini-type squash and is also used as a term of endearment. Squash and gourds are divided into four species: Cucurbita Pepo, Cucurbita Maxima, Cucurbita Moschata, and Cucurbita Mixta.

Cucurbita Pepo includes all varieties of summer squash, a few winter squash, and pumpkin. Styrian pumpkin, small and round with yellow-orange and green stripes, are processed for pumpkin seed oil. Yellow summer squash is slender and bright yellow. Baby Yellow squash blossoms are the female fruit-bearing flower of squash plants and can be eaten raw or cooked. Baby Gold Bar squash is known for its soft, edible skin but contains less nutrients than mature squash. Crookneck squash is similar to Yellow squash but has a hook end and darker yellow coloring. Yellow crookneck squash is a bush type squash whose fruit can be picked at various stages of maturity. Baby Yellow crookneck is the most preferred stage.

Gem squash is a small, round squash with solid, dark-green coloring. Pattypan squash is mint green in color, resembling a flattened circle with scalloped edges. Baby Yellow patty pan squash is bright yellow with a green tipped stem and is known for its high water content. Scallopini squash is a summer variety and zucchini-type squash. Baby Scallopini squash is petit and saucer-shaped, with deep green skin and cream flesh. Spaghetti squash features an oblong shape with yellow to orange rind and yellow or orange flesh that is stringy like spaghetti noodles when cooked. Delicata squash, also called Peanut squash or Sweet Potato squash, is yellow with thin green stripes.

Acorn squash is acorn-shaped and dark green, and may have a touch of orange coloring. The Golden Acorn squash, with a thin orange hued skin, has a high protein content and three times the beta carotene of traditional acorn squash. The White Acorn squash is ideal for use in sweet preparations. Zephyr squash is easily distinguished by its slender crooked shape and its signature two-toned appearance. Its stem end is yellow and its blossom end is a pale lime green. It has a sweet and nutty flavor and is tender enough to eat raw like other petite summer squash.

Cucurbita Maxima includes the Banana squash, with an elongated shape and yellow-orange flesh. Its rind color can be light orange, pink, and light blue and can weigh up to thirty pounds. Hubbard squash has a rounded teardrop shape, yellow-orange flesh, and the rind can be dark orange and blue-gray. Green Buttercup squash is spotted and flecked with light green to gray markings, and has a mildly sweet flavor similar to a sweet potato. It is one of the most popular varieties of winter squash. There are also several different varieties of Orange Buttercup squash. The Cupcake squash has thick dark green skin, white flesh with small edible seeds, and a mildly sweet flavor. Its squat round shape makes it ideal for hollowing and filling with meat, cheese, and grains. Zucchini squash, the most popularly grown and consumed of all summer squash, is oblong and dark green, sometimes with white striping. There are numerous varieties such as Golden zucchini with golden yellow outer skin. One zucchini is called zucchina.

Cucurbita Moschata includes the Butternut squash with a long neck and bell-shape. Its bright orange flesh has a nutty flavor and the color of the rind varies from yellow-tan to orange. Dickinson field pumpkin, used for canned pumpkin puree, is tan in color with a slightly elongated sphere shape. Kentucky field pumpkin, ranging in shape from a flattened sphere to tear-drop, has light orange skin and dark orange flesh. Long Island cheese pumpkin, shaped like a cheese wheel, has soft yellow flesh. It is one of the oldest varieties of squash cultivated in America. Orange Neck pumpkins are bulbous at the base with a narrow, curved neck and can be tan to pale in color. The Calabaza squash, also known as West Indian pumpkin, Cuban pumpkin, and Green pumpkin, has a rounded to pear-like shape with a mottled green to yellow-orange rind that may be striped or splotched with varying shades of green. It ranges in size from as small as a cantaloupe to as large as a watermelon, and the taste is similar to Butternut squash.

Cucurbita mixta includes varieties of cushaw pumpkin with a vase shape and straight or crooked, elongated neck. Green-striped cushaw has dark green and white stripes. White cushaw is bright white to ivory white in color. Golden cushaw is golden orange in color and can be solid or striped with ivory white. Seminole pumpkin, native to Florida, is a small, spherical or teardrop-shaped pumpkin with fruit that is mottled with white over a dark green to yellow-tan base color.

Squash seeds offer many benefits along with their distinct flavor. They are high in nutritional value and an excellent source of vitamins B1, C and E, and beta carotene, and are a god source of zinc. They are anti-inflammatory and filled with fiber and protein. They lower bad cholesterol and increase good cholesterol. The seeds contain the amino acid tryptophan which gets converted into serotonin and niacin, helpful with sleep. Squash seed extracts and oil have anti-microbial, anti-fungal and anti-viral benefits and the oil has positive effects on prostate health. Native American tribes used squash seeds to get rid of parasites like tapeworm and roundworm.

STAR APPLE

The Star Apple was found growing in Peru in the 1500s. The tree thrives in warm to hot tropical climates. In the late 1800s, the United States began growing the fruit in Florida, where commercial production is done on a small scale today. The star apple is round and two to four inches in diameter when mature. Its skin is either purple to red or yellow to green in color, depending on variety. When the fruit is cut in half it forms a star shape. The inner rind of the purple variety is dark purple, and white in green fruits. The rind surrounds a soft, creamy, white pulp with six to eleven gelatinous cells. Some of the cells have small, pointed, flat black seeds. It has a tropical sweet flavor with notes of apple. Star fruit contains vitamin C, calcium and phosphorous and is rich in antioxidants. The pulp has been used to treat sore throats, laryngitis, and pneumonia. When ground, the seeds can be used as a diuretic. **Caution: Star Apple can cause constipation if eaten in excess.**

STAR FRUIT

Star fruit, a star-shaped tropical fruit native to the Malayan peninsula, is cultivated in many parts of Southeast Asia, Pacific islands, and China. The small, bushy evergreen tree grows well in hot, humid tropical conditions. It bears small lilac colored, bell-shaped flowers in clusters that develop into yellow-orange oblong shaped waxy fruits with five angled sides that resemble a starfish when sliced in cross sections. Star fruit contains many nutrients, antioxidants and vitamins, and provides a good amount of dietary fiber. Only the sweet variety can be eaten fresh. Sour type fruits are used in cooking.

SUGAR APPLE

The Sugar Apple, also called a Sweetsop or Custard Apple, has a thick scaly rind with a creamy, sweet segmented pulp containing shiny black seeds. It is most often green in color but there is also a dark red variety. The pulp has a minty or custardy flavor. The leaves and leaf extracts can be used for medicinal purposes. **Caution: Remove the toxic seeds.**

TARO

The Taro plant has very large, broad leaves shaped like a huge heart. Native to Southeast Asia, it spread across the tropical regions of the world. More than ten percent of the world's population use some variety of taro as a food. The most known is poi, a creamy, slightly purple staple food served at luaus. Taro stems, the young leaf stalks, must be cooked to remove the calcium oxalate that can cause irritation to the mouth and throat. The leaf stalks are high in fiber and contain beta carotene, calcium and iron, and are a good source of vitamins A and C. In Hawaii, the plant is considered sacred and is central to the Native Hawaiian creation story.

NOTE: Luau originally referred to only the leaves of the taro plant that are eaten as a vegetable. It then came to refer to dishes prepared with the leaves, and finally to the feasts where the dishes were served.

TINDA

Native to India, Tinda is a small vegetable that looks like a cross between a green apple and a pumpkin. It is three inches in diameter, short and squat like a pumpkin, with a dark green stem. It's also known as the Indian Apple gourd. The white flesh is tender and tastes similar to a cucumber. The seeds are edible but can be removed for cooking. It should be eaten when it is immature, while the skin is still thin and not tough. High in vitamin A, it can help soothe and relieve stomach acidity.

TOMATILLO

Tomatillo, a relative of the tomato, is native to Mexico and Central America. The Aztecs first cultivated it as early as 800 B.C. It is one to two inches in size, with a papery outer skin and slightly sticky husk. The firm, green flesh fades to light brown as the fruit matures. It has a very tart flavor. The tomatillo is packed with antioxidants and flavonoids, is rich in dietary fiber, and contains Vitamins A, C and K, and niacin, potassium, manganese and magnesium. The Purple Tomatillo's interior flesh is deep violet color and has a tangy-sweet taste, much sweeter than the green ones. The Milpero Tomatillo is about half the size of a tomatillo with a slightly sweeter taste. Most varieties are green, though some can have a purple hue.

TOMATO

The tomato, that originated in South America, is actually a fruit and a berry. It was domesticated in Mexico and the first cultivated tomatoes were yellow in color and cherry-sized. Spanish colonists introduced tomatoes to Europe in the early 1500s. The word 'tomato' is derived from the Aztec word *xitomatl* (plump thing with a navel). The name was shortened to *tomatl* in Europe. The Spanish and Italians were the first Europeans to use it in cooking. The tomato became popular in Naples, where marinara sauce originated. In France, people thought the tomato was an aphrodisiac and began calling it *pomme d'amour* (love apple). In North America, tomatoes were thought to be toxic, although they were grown by colonists for ornamentation. The notion that they were poisonous was disproved in 1820 and the tomato was finally embraced. Today, the tomato is the second most-grown fruit in the world. China is the largest producer. Florida and California produce the most tomatoes in the United States.

There are at least ten thousand varieties of tomatoes. They are classified based on how they grow and produce: determinate varieties grow on bush-like plants with short vines and bear just one crop per season; indeterminate varieties are long, sprawling vine plants that bear fruit continuously throughout the season. Tomatoes should not be refrigerated – cold causes the fruit to stop producing compounds that create the tomato flavor and aroma.

Tomatoes are rich in vitamins A and C and are full of fiber. Fresh tomatoes have more vitamin C than cooked or canned tomatoes. Field or vine-ripened summer tomatoes are higher in vitamin C than greenhouse tomatoes. Tomatoes also contain the antioxidant compound lycopene, which protects against prostate cancer and heart disease. More lycopene is absorbed by the body from cooked tomatoes than from fresh. Yellow tomatoes do not contain lycopene, although they are milder in taste and less acidic than red varieties. Eating tomatoes or drinking tomato juice can help prevent airline passengers from developing deep vein thrombosis (DVT) on long flights.

Heirloom tomatoes vary in size, shape, color and taste. Most are fragile, with meaty flesh, a thin skin, and few seeds. The thin skin is what gives them a higher sugar content and excellent flavor. An heirloom variety is one that has been around more than fifty years, can reproduce from seed, and has a unique history.

On-the-vine tomatoes, with four or five tomatoes to each vine, are sold with the stem still attached. They are allowed to ripen to a later stage of maturity so they have a higher sugar content. Also, the vine contains nutrients and continues to feed the fruit while they are ripening, even after they have been picked. Other varieties are picked green and ripened with a poly ethylene gas that reduces the natural sugar content.

Beefsteak tomatoes are large and heavy (some can be four pounds), with a meaty texture. They have a classic tomato flavor but can also be sweet, depending upon the variety. They range in color from pink, to vibrant red, to orange. Most are smooth in shape.

Firm and smooth-skinned Cherry tomatoes are miniature versions of beefsteak tomatoes, but equally nutritious. They are much sweeter than large tomatoes. There are hundreds of varieties and the size and color varies. They are the first tomato species to be domesticated. The very first recipe for salsa, by the Aztec's, contained cherry tomatoes, hot chili peppers, and salt.

Grape tomatoes, a hybrid from Taiwan, were first gown in North America in Florida in 1996. They were given this name in order to distinguish the variety from cherry tomatoes. They have a firm, smooth skin and the shape is similar to an olive or grape. They have a high sugar content which gives them a sweet flavor. Their colors can be red, yellow, or green (seedless).

A Green tomato is the unripe fruit of any tomato cultivar. Its skin is very firm with an olive green color and bright chartreuse flesh. It has a sharp and astringent flavor. It contains antioxidants, vitamins A, B-complex, C and K, and iron, phosphorous, and other minerals. Tomaintine, an alkaloid being researched for its cancer fighting properties, is also present. Fried green tomatoes are a popular food.

Roma tomatoes, a hybrid variety developed around 1955, have an elongated egg-like shape and bright red, smooth and thick skin. The meaty flesh has few seeds, high sugar and acid levels, and a low moisture content compared to other varieties. They grow to about three inches long and, unlike a slicing tomato, are not juicy. They are better for making thick tomato sauce or paste.

The Green Zebra tomato is considered a classic among striped and bi-color tomatoes. It is perfectly round with dark green and yellow stripes and grows to about two inches in diameter. Its green flesh is juicy and has a classic tomato flavor. Red Zebra tomatoes have a cherry-red outer skin with light yellow-orange streaks. The dark red inner flesh is very juicy and has a sweet-tart flavor. The Black Zebra tomato resembles the Green Zebra in size and shape but its exterior color is purple and mahogany with vertical deep-green streaks. The flavor of the mahogany interior flesh has hints of smoke and sweetness.

Red Currant tomatoes are the smallest edible tomato, measuring half an inch in diameter. The round, red fruits have a strong, sweet-tart flavor and firm, juicy texture. They are thin-skinned and glossy and tend to be seedy. There are many types, both red and yellow. They are closely related to one of the original wild species of tomato and are an exceptional source of lycopene.

Sun-dried tomatoes are dehydrated slices of vine-ripened tomatoes. They are bright red to reddish-brown, tart and chewy, and require soaking in a liquid before use. It takes twenty pounds of fresh tomatoes to make one pound of sun-dried tomatoes. Sun-drying can be traced back to ancient Egypt and Mesopotamia. Native Americans used sun-drying techniques.

TURNIP

The wild turnip is native to Europe and was domesticated in Greece in 300 B.C. For hundreds of years it was grown primarily as livestock fodder. In sixteenth century Europe, it was often found displayed on the coat of arms of several royal families. Turnips were used in Celtic festivals as lanterns (like the jack-o-lantern). During World War I in Germany, the winter of 1916-1917 was named 'the turnip winter' because soldiers survived on them when meat and potatoes were scarce. The turnip became an important vegetable as food for both humans and animals. It was also used as a substitute for coffee and flour.

There are over thirty domesticated varieties of turnips that vary in size, color, flavor and usage. They can be white, gold, pink, and purple topped. Common turnips are made up of edible bulbous roots, stems, and broad green leaves. The white flesh is firm, crunchy, sweet and peppery, similar to radishes. Turnips are a great source of vitamin C. Their leafy greens are also nutritious and contain vitamins A, C and K, folate, and calcium. They are best eaten cooked.

The Japanese turnip, a newer variety, can be eaten raw, unlike other turnips. When cooked, it produces a buttery sweet flavor. Baby turnips are smaller turnip varieties. Most are heirloom varieties with European origins but there are also hybrid varieties and Asian varieties.

WASABI

Wasabi, a relative of the watercress family, is a Japanese plant with a thick green root that tastes like horseradish. The root releases a series of hot vapors when grated. It can be found in powder or paste form, usually as an accompaniment to raw fish. It may also be used to flavor mustard or mayonnaise, as a meat sauce, or in salad dressings. Genuine wasabi root is very expensive (a pound can cost up to one hundred dollars). Most often, the hot, green paste served with sushi or sashimi is actually extra hot horseradish mixed with hot Chinese mustard and green food coloring. Wasabi peas are crunchy fried peas coated with wasabi and sugar.

WATER CHESTNUT

Chinese water chestnuts are an aquatic vegetable with a mildly sweet apple-coconut flavor. They were used in traditional Asian and aboriginal medicine to heal wounds. The outside of the bulb, when crushed, releases antimicrobial properties. Water chestnuts contain vitamin B6, potassium, copper, riboflavin, manganese, and small amounts of other vitamins and minerals. They are high in fiber and contain flavonoid antioxidants. They are used for making salt in Zimbabwe. Fresh water chestnuts are sweeter and more firm than the canned variety.

NOTE: The Chinese water chestnut is not the same as the European water chestnut, or horned chestnut, that is often **toxic**.

WILD RICE SHOOT

The Wild Rice plant, also known as Water Bamboo, was cultivated in Asia in ancient times for its shoot instead of its grains. The large edible shoot has husk-like wrapper leaves that are removed. The thick, pale white shoots have a crunchy texture similar to bamboo shoot, and are slightly sweet, depending on when they are harvested. The shoot is most often prepared by stir-frying. It is an excellent source of vitamins A and C, calcium, iron, and other minerals. It is also a diuretic. The Wild Rice plant is related to the Wild Rice of North America, an aquatic plant that grows in shallow water in small lakes and streams.

WATERMELON

Native to Africa, the watermelon was cultivated in Egypt and India as far back as 2500 B.C. Pictures of the fruit were found in paintings on the walls of ancient buildings. It was a valuable and portable source of water for when natural water supplies were contaminated. Early explorers used the watermelon as a canteen. It is over ninety percent water and full of important electrolytes that contribute to hydration. The watermelon is a nutrient dense food that provides a high amount of vitamins, minerals and antioxidants. An excellent source of vitamin C, it is also great for your skin and hair because it contains vitamin A. The U.S. Watermelon Seed-Spitting and Speed-Eating Championships are held every September in Wisconsin. Cordele, Georgia is known as the Watermelon Capital of the world. Watermelon rind can be pickled.

   Hundreds of watermelon cultivars have been developed. They vary in taste, texture, shape, size, and color. Some types have a higher sugar content and are sweeter. The most common watermelon is sweet, juicy, red fleshed and has a hard, green rind but others may be light pink, yellow and orange. There are four basic types of watermelon: seedless, picnic, icebox, and yellow/orange fleshed.

Seedless watermelons, created in the 1990s, have tiny underdeveloped seeds that are easily consumed. They can weigh from ten to twenty pounds.

The Picnic watermelon is larger and can weigh forty-five pounds or more. It is oblong or round with a green rind and sweet, red flesh.

Icebox watermelons, weighing between five to fifteen pounds, are much smaller which allows them to easily fit in a refrigerator (hence the name). The Sugar Baby watermelon, nine to thirteen pounds, is often referred to as an icebox watermelon. It was developed in 1955 and has soft, sweet fruit and a dark green rind.

Yellow/orange fleshed watermelon are round and can be seedless or seeded. The rind of the Golden Midget, weighing only three pounds, turns yellow when ripe.

WOOD APPLE

Wood apples, native to India and Sri Lanka, look like small coconuts. They have a hard, brown shell and a rough exterior. The brown pulp, which contains numerous small, crunchy, white edible seeds, will taste acidic or sweet, depending on the variety. Its aroma is similar to raisins. There are two varieties; the larger, more common variety and a small variety known for more acidic fruit. The wood apple has antioxidant properties and is a natural antimicrobial agent. The unripe fruit is used to treat gum disease, hiccups and sore throat, and promote healthy digestion. It is mentioned in Buddhist writings that date back to six hundred A.D.

WILD ROSE HIPS

Wild Rose hips are the berry-like buds left after the bloom falls from the wild rose plant. The hip (fruit) has a sweet, citrusy, cranberry-like flavor. With a deep red color and an oblong shape, the hip is filled with small, hard seeds covered with small hairs. **Caution: The hairs on the seeds can cause irritation in the mouth and digestive tract if not properly ripe.** The shape, color, and size varies depending on the variety of the rose plant they are foraged from. Wild rose hips has twenty times more Vitamin C than oranges. It also contains bioflavonoids and increases the effectiveness of all other vitamins. Most commonly found in teas, they may also be candied, made into juice, jelly or jam, or even wine. Native to many regions around the globe, they can be found growing along the eastern and western coasts of the United States.

Wild Rose hips have been eaten since ancient times by both humans and animals. In Medieval Europe, they were grown in monasteries for medicinal purposes. In the eighteenth century, large containers of Wild Rose hips were stored on ships to prevent scurvy. During World War II, it was used by the military in the winter when citrus fruit was scarce.

YACON

The Yacon plant, native to South America, belongs to the same family as sunflowers. Because it is drought resistant, it can be grown almost any place where there is no frost. It is known for its crunchy, sweet-tasting root. The plant produces two types of underground tubers: The Red variety, although edible, are mostly used for planting more yacon. The Brown variety are larger in size and used for food. When eaten in its raw state, remove the outer dark skin and inner white skin to get to the tasty pulp. The root can also be boiled, steamed, or baked. Health benefits include controlling blood sugar levels and cholesterol levels, boosting the immune system, and helping with weight loss. Thick, dark brown Yacon syrup, extracted from the root, is an ideal alternative to sugar.

YAM

Yams and sweet potatoes are not related; they are in two different botanical families. Yams are actually related to grasses and lilies. They are large, starchy roots grown in Africa and Asia. True yams may have been cultivated as early as 8,000 B.C. in Asia. The Water Yam, cultivated in Southeast Asia, grows up to eight feet long and can weigh over one hundred pounds. On the Pacific Island of Ponape, yams are referred to as two man, four man, or six man yams, depending on how many men it takes to lift it. There are about six hundred species of yam but only one hundred fifty are cultivated for food. **Caution: Many wild species of yam contain poisonous dioscorines, but when peeled and boiled or roasted they may be safe to eat**.

NOTE: Yam also refers to sweet potatoes that are grown in Louisiana.

The Zapote, native to the tropical rainforests of Central America, was highly regarded by the Mayans. Today, it can be found throughout Central America, Mexico, India and parts of southern Florida. It is a small fruit (one to three inches in diameter) with a smooth brown exterior. Once the tough rind is peeled it reveals a bright orange, stringy flesh that tastes sweet, similar to a fig. There are two to five hard, inedible black seeds in the center of the fruit. When ripe, the Zapote is soft to the touch and emits a sweet aroma. **Caution: When unripe, it contains high amounts of saponin, an astringent that can dry out the mouth.**

The Zapote tree's wood has been used for lumber, cabinetry and furniture. A byproduct is a gummy latex known as chicle, which has been used as the main ingredient in chewing gum.

CHAPTER 3

Nuts!

Nuts, Grains, Seeds & Beans

Nuts are botanically a specific type of fruit but that term is also applied to many edible seeds that are not nuts. Most nuts contain similar nutrients but vary in health benefits. They also have different fat content and calories. Aarcheologists found evidence of nuts being a major part of the human diet as far back as 750,000 years ago. Seven varieties of nuts, and the stone tools to crack open the nuts, were found buried deep in a bog.

ALMOND

The almond tree is native to western Asia and North Africa but California produces eighty percent of the world's supply of almonds. It takes more than one million bee hives to pollinate an almond crop. Chocolate manufacturers currently use forty percent of the world's almonds. Almonds are one of only two nuts mentioned in the Bible (*Genesis 43:11*) – the other is the pistachio nut. The protein in almonds is similar to the protein in human breast milk. The nuts are high in fiber, a good source of zinc, and are very rich in vitamin E. Almonds have many antioxidants and can lower cholesterol and heart disease. They may also help fight different types of cancer.

BRAZIL NUT

Brazil nuts, native to the Amazon, are actually large seeds with fifteen to thirty arranged in a pod. They have an edible white meat kernel with a sweet nutty flavor. The first reference to the Brazil nut dates to 1569 when a Spanish colonial officer collected thousands of them to feed his troops. They were introduced to Europe by Dutch traders in the late seventeenth century. Brazil nuts are loaded with healthy polyunsaturated fatty acids and are the richest and most reliable food source of selenium, a powerful antioxidant. They have been shown to lower the risk of heart disease and cancer, and play a role in reducing allergies and inflammation. They are also a great source of magnesium which is vital for healthy nerves and muscles. Brazil nut oil, extracted from the nuts and used in cooking, has a sweet smell and taste. It has also been used in traditional medicine and as massage oil that helps protect skin from dryness. It is a base oil in aromatherapy and cosmetics.

CASHEW

Cashew nuts are native to the Amazon and were introduced to India by the Portuguese in the sixteenth century. Today, India and East Africa are the world's largest producers. Cashews are lower in fat and have a higher protein and carbohydrate content than other types of nuts. They also contain a large amount of zinc and potassium. Between the outer and inner shells covering the cashew nut is an extremely caustic oil so they are never for sale in the shell. The outer shell must first be roasted or burned off with the oil (the smoke is also an irritant). The kernels are then boiled or roasted again, and a second shell is removed. Oil from cashew nut shells is used in insecticides, brake linings, and rubber and plastic manufacture. The milky sap from the tree is used to make a varnish.

CHESTNUT

Chestnuts have been cultivated in the Mediterranean for at least three thousand years. They have also been popular in China for over two thousand years and in Japan since the eleventh century. They are the only low-fat nut, with a fraction of the calories of other types of nuts. They are also the only nut that contains vitamin C. Chestnuts have a sweet and nutty flavor and must be peeled and cooked before using. Cooking methods include roasting in their shells, boiled, braised or puréed. Dried chestnuts are most like fresh chestnuts in flavor and texture. Canned chestnuts are cooked and ready to use. Vacuum-packed chestnuts are softer than fresh ones but taste better than dried or canned. Chestnut spreads are sold sweetened and unsweetened.

NOTE: A conker is the seed of the Horse Chestnut tree and not for human consumption. Though eaten by animals, Horse chestnuts are semi-poisonous.

COLA NUT

The cola tree is a tropical evergreen tree native to West Africa. The nuts within the star-shaped woody fruit contain caffeinated seeds (cola nuts) that are about the size of a walnut. They have a rose-like smell and bitter taste that decreases with chewing. The seeds, important in West African culture and medicine, are eaten at social events and at the beginnings of political and spiritual meetings. Cola nuts are used as a stimulant, an antidepressant, a painkiller, and to treat fever, wounds and swellings. They are also used as an aphrodisiac. Cola nuts are found in the wild and grown commercially. Cola extract is used in energy drinks, dietary supplements, and performance enhancers. It is also used in soft drinks but may be replaced with a synthetic caffeine ingredient. **Caution: Caffeine can be a health stimulant in moderate doses but it increases heart rate which can potentially be dangerous for people who suffer from pre-existing heart conditions.**

COCONUT

The coconut, native to the tropics and subtropics, is a drupe fruit, not a nut. Because it is light and water resistant it floats, enabling it to be transported by water currents. Today, it is grown in more than seventy countries throughout the world. The three indentations on the bottom are the key for opening the coconut successfully. First, insert a screwdriver into the softest hole to drain the liquid into a bowl. Then use a knife to circumvent the coconut's seam and give it a sharp thwack on a hard surface to break it into two pieces.

Coconuts have been used as food, fuel, and in the cosmetic industry. For centuries, they were used as a traditional Asian and Pacific Island folk cure for nausea, rash, fever, earache, sore throat, bronchitis, kidney stones, ulcers, asthma, syphilis, bruises, toothache, and lice. Today, the fruit is used to treat a wide range of health issues. Once thought to be a high-fat food, coconut is now a powerhouse of nutrition and healing. Coconuts are high in manganese, potassium, phosphorus and fiber, and are rich in lauric acid (which converts to monolaurin, the compound found in breast milk that strengthens a baby's immunity). Coconut oil is good for thyroid gland function, strengthens hair follicles, and can control dandruff. Coconut water, inside young coconuts, can be used as a substitute for blood plasma.

NOTE: Ripe coconuts contain much less coconut water than immature ones. Coconut milk is the white liquid obtained from grated coconut processed with water.

HAZELNUT

Hazelnuts were gathered in prehistoric Britain and were known in China over five thousand years ago. They are referenced in ancient Greek and Roman writings, and in the Bible, for their nutritional and healing power. Throughout history, they have been considered a symbol of wisdom and knowledge. European hazelnut trees arrived in the Pacific Northwest in the seventeenth century. Today, ninety-nine percent of all hazelnuts in the United States are grown in Oregon. Turkey is the largest producer of these nuts worldwide. Hazelnuts are a great source of vitamin E and have an exceptional concentration of copper. They are also a very good source of the B vitamin biotin which promotes healthy skin and hair. Like other types of nuts, they can lower high cholesterol. Hazelnuts are also known as filberts because in European folklore they are ready for harvest on Saint Philbert's Day.

NOTE: Wild, Native American Hazelnuts can be found throughout the Midwest, East, and Southeast of the United States and Canada. They are rarely cultivated and sold because they are smaller than commercially produced European hazelnuts.

MACADAMIA

Macadamia nuts, native to Australia, are named for John Macadam, a Scottish physician and chemist. The trees were introduced to Hawaii around 1881 but were only used as an ornamental. The first commercial orchards were not planted there until 1921. Today, most of the world's macadamia nuts come from the Big Island of Hawaii. After harvesting, the husks are removed and the nuts are fried. The shells are cracked and the kernels are removed to be oil-roasted or dry-roasted. The kernels are the delicious edible part but the shell and husk also have uses. Shells can be used as a mulch, fuel, and a substitute for sand in the sand-blasting process. Husks are used as mulch or composted for fertilizer. The oil extracted from the nuts is used in the cosmetic industry for soap, sunscreen, and shampoo. Macadamia nuts contain manganese, magnesium, vitamin B1 and thiamin. They are one of the heathiest nuts and can lower high cholesterol and triglycerides, fight heart disease, and lower your risk of stroke.

PEANUT

The peanut is not really a nut but a legume or bean, and a member of the pea family. It originated in South America where it was cultivated. As early as 1500 B.C., the Incans used them as sacrificial offerings and placed them with the dead to aid in the spirit life. Spaniards and Portuguese slave traders introduced them to Africa and Europe. At first, the peanut was regarded as a food for poor people but by the turn of the twentieth century there was a great demand for peanut oil and roasted and salted peanuts. The first peanuts grown in the United States were grown in Virginia. Today, Georgia produces almost half of the total U.S. peanut crop. More than fifty percent of the crop is used to make peanut butter. It takes about five hundred and fifty peanuts to make a twelve-ounce jar. Peanut butter was developed in 1890 by a doctor in St. Louis who gave it to his patients with bad teeth. Peanut butter's high protein content draws moisture from your mouth and that's why it sticks to the roof of your mouth. (Arachibutyrophobia is the fear of peanut butter sticking to the roof of your mouth.)

Peanuts are high in protein, monounsaturated fat, and resveratrol which protects the heart and blood vessels. The term 'Peanut Gallery' became popular in the late nineteenth century and referred to the cheaper balcony seats in a theater. People seated there were able to throw peanuts, a common food at theaters, at those seated below them. (People sitting in the first row of seats could throw peanuts at the stage, stating their displeasure with the performance.) Dr. George Washington Carver researched and developed more than three hundred uses for peanuts in the early 1900s. When Rudolf Diesel introduced his diesel engine in 1900, it ran on peanut oil. Mr. Peanut® was created by thirteen-year-old Antonio Gentile in a logo contest held by Planters in 1916. He won the grand prize of five dollars and his drawing of a peanut person was later refined to include the top hat, monocle, white gloves and cane. Two peanut farmers have been elected President of the United States: Thomas Jefferson and Jimmy Carter.

PECAN

Pecans are native to the Mississippi valley area of the United States. Archeologists found remains of pecans dating back to 6100 B.C. in Texas. The U.S. produces about ninety percent of the world's pecans. Georgia has been the top pecan-producing state since the late 1800s. There are about one thousand varieties of pecans, many of them named after Native American tribes. Pecans were an important food staple for them and they taught early colonists how to harvest, utilize, and store them. Pecans contain healthy fats and can significantly lower LDL cholesterol. They have a high percentage of manganese, copper, magnesium, and zinc. They are also high in fiber and antioxidants and contain vitamin E, betacarotenes, lutein, and zeaxanthin which neutralizes free radicals and protects the body from infections and diseases. It takes about seventy-eight pecans for one pecan pie. Astronauts took pecans to the moon in two Apollo space missions. Albany, Georgia is the Pecan Capital of the U.S. The pecan is the official nut of Alabama, which hosts a Pecan Festival every fall. April is National Pecan Month.

PILI NUT

Pili nuts are a rich buttery tasting nut grown in the volcanic soil of the Philippine peninsula. They are high in calcium, phosphorus, potassium, and rich in protein. In the South Pacific, the pili nut is a major source of fat and protein in the diet. The tropical tree grows to sixty-five feet in height and produces up to seventy pounds of nuts each year. The roasted nut is similar in shape and taste to an almond. The uncooked nuts are used as a laxative. The sweet oil is used in confectionary.

PINE NUT

Also called piñon or pignoli nuts, pine nuts are small and teardrop-shaped and harvested from pine cones. They are expensive because the process is labor-intensive. Their delicate, piney flavor is used in pesto and cookies. Pine nuts are higher in fat and calories than other types of nuts but they are a good source of potassium, iron, copper and zinc. They contain more protein than any other nut or seed. Pine nuts can lower blood pressure and improve blood flow. They are classified as a gymnosperm – they produce nut-like seeds but no flowers or fruits.

Bedda nuts, native to India, have been revered throughout history for their healing benefits: pain relief, throat ailments, conjunctivitis, high blood pressure and immune health. Oils derived from the Bedda nut are used as a hair dye. **Caution: Bedda nuts should not be eaten without adequate instruction as they have narcotic effects that may prove toxic in large doses.**

Acorns aren't edible raw but can be consumed after the preparation of removing the tannins (a reddish acid that comes from plants). Tannin is used in making wine – it makes wine taste dry.

PISTACHIO

The Pistachio nut originated in Central Asia and the Middle East. It has been cultivated for over seven thousand years. Iran is the largest producer. Pistachios are one of only two nuts mentioned in the Bible (*Genesis 43:11*); the other is the almond. Legend has it that pistachios were a favorite of the Queen of Sheba. The nut reached Greece and Rome and was later introduced to Italy and Spain. The first commercial crop in the United States was in 1976. Today, California comprises ninety-nine percent of the U.S. commercial pistachio production. Pistachios provide valuable amounts of calcium, iron, magnesium and zinc, and are the richest source of potassium of all nuts. They also contain an excellent source of protein and fiber and can reduce LDL cholesterol and increase HDL cholesterol.

SOY NUT

Soy nuts are made from dried soybeans that have been processed to taste like nuts. Since ancient times, dry roasted soy nuts were popular throughout East Asia and most likely originated in China. Soybeans and soy products are among the only plant proteins that provide a source of all the essential amino acids. However, the roasting process may destroy as much as fifty percent of these amino acids. Soy nuts contain high concentrations of protein, fiber, vitamins and minerals. They have a high caloric and fat content but they do not contain cholesterol, and they are low in saturated fats to help raise good cholesterol and lower bad levels. Soy nut butter is made like peanut butter. **Caution: People with iodine deficiency should avoid soy products because they cause enlargement of the thyroid gland.** (For more information, see SOYBEAN on page 140)

TIGER NUT

Tiger Nuts are one of the oldest cultivated crops. Traces of tiger nuts were found on prehistoric tools dating back nine thousand years. They have been cultivated in the United States, Africa, the Middle East, South and Central America, Europe, and Asia. Tiger Nuts are rich in protein and high in vitamins C and E, phosphorus, and potassium. Their oil is similar to the fat composition of olives. Tiger Nuts grow from an herbaceous evergreen plant that can produce up to twenty-five hundred nuts. Each one is fibrous, nutty, slightly juicy, and slightly sweet.

WALNUT

The walnut is one of the most popular edible nuts, second only to the almond. Walnuts date back to seven thousand B.C. and grew in the Hanging Gardens of Babylon. The Persians reserved them for royalty. They were traded along the Silk Road route between Asia and the Middle East. The Greeks enlarged the Persian walnut to resemble the size of the walnuts we eat today. Walnuts were considered 'food for gods' by early Romans. They were used for oil and were powdered to thicken foods (like cornstarch is used today). English merchant marines transported them for trade around the world and they became known as English Walnuts but England never grew them commercially. The walnut was first cultivated in California by the Franciscan Fathers in the late 1700s. Today, California is the world's largest producer of English walnuts. They have thinner shells and a milder taste than black walnuts, a native American species mainly used as rootstock for English walnuts. Walnuts contain omega-3 and omega-6 polyunsaturated fatty acids, as well as monounsaturated fats, but no cholesterol. They are rich in antioxidants and contain high levels of serotonin and pain-relieving compounds.

SEEDS & GRAINS

Some seeds are edible as is, some are used in cooking, some need to be roasted before eating, and others are ground into powder form before use. Cereals, grass-like crops harvested for their dry seeds, are the most important source of human calories and protein. They include barley, corn, oats, rice, spelt, and wheat. They are often ground to make flour. Pseudo-cereals like buckwheat, flax, amaranth, and quinoa can also be ground into flour. A pseudo-cereal is a broadleaf non-legume that is grown for grain.

ANNATTO SEED

The annatto tree, native to Central and South America, has white or bright pink flowers. The fruit is made up of spiky brown and red pods that grow in clusters. When the pods dry and crack open, they expose red seeds (a red pigment can be extracted from them that has been used as a dye for fabrics and body paint since pre-Columbian times). The small and triangular-shaped seeds have a peppermint scent and taste peppery and slightly bitter. Once ground, they can be added to soups and stews or made into a paste. Annatto seeds are used in cosmetics and to color cheese, margarine, butter, rice and smoked fish. They can be substituted for saffron, a more expensive spice. Some health benefits include its ability to promote healthy digestion, strengthen bones, promote healing, lower fevers, boost eye health, eliminate headaches, reduce nausea, and protect respiratory distress. The correct term for the seeds is achiote seeds.

Sunflower seeds are a good source of vitamin E and magnesium that helps reduce asthma, lowers high blood pressure, prevents migraine headaches, and reduces the risk of heart attack and stroke.

CHIA

Chia seeds, native to the southwestern United States and Mexico, are obtained from a plant in the mint family with edible seed-like fruits. This unprocessed whole grain dates back to the Mayan and Aztec civilizations. Chia means 'strength,' and these cultures used the tiny black and white seeds as an energy booster. They have a mild, nutty flavor. Whole seeds can be added to foods such as oatmeal, rice, couscous, vegetables, baked goods and desserts. The seeds can be soaked in water to create a gel used in dressings, dips, sauces, soups, spreads and a host of other foods. The seeds can also be ground into flour. Chia seeds contain healthful protein, calcium, fiber, antioxidants, omega-3 fatty acids, vitamins and minerals. Some people believe the seeds help with weight loss because they supposedly expand in the stomach to help you feel full and eat less but studies showed no effect on weight loss. One study did show some beneficial heart effects when used as an alternative to processed grains.

NIGELA

Small, black nigella seeds are hard and crunchy. Their aroma is similar to onions but they have a mild peppery flavor which intensifies when cooked. They are mistakenly called black onion seeds, black cumin, and black caraway but they have no relationship to these spices. Nigela seeds are dry roasted in India and used on flatbreads. They also complement potatoes and root vegetables. Some people use the oil from nigella seeds as an antioxidant, for upset stomach, to stop rheumatoid arthritis, and treat kidney problems. Their odor is said to repel some insects.

POPPY SEED

The poppy seed has been cultivated for over three thousand years. It was used as a condiment as early as the first century A.D. The tiny seed comes from the plant that produces opium but is safe to use as food. The botanical name for the poppy flower means 'sleep bearing' (poppies were used in *The Wizard of Oz* to put Dorothy to sleep) but the seed does not have this effect. The poppy plant is a biennial herb of East Mediterranean and Asia Minor origin. Today, the seeds are a commercial crop in many parts of the world. They add a nutty flavor to recipes. Poppy seeds contain many plant derived chemical compounds that have antioxidant, disease preventing, and health promoting properties. The plant's lilac, blue, red, or white flowers appear during spring on long stalks then turn into oval shaped fruits. Poppy seeds are harvested from the fruit head. The red poppy flower has been the symbol of fallen warriors throughout history and was adopted as the emblem to commemorate Veterans Day in the United States.

AMARANTH

A staple of the Incas and Aztecs, this pseudo-grain has been grown for thousands of years. Amaranth kernels are tiny (about four thousand per teaspoon) but their nutritional impact is big. They contain more protein, iron, potassium, phosphorous and magnesium than other grains. It is a great source of the amino acid lysine (a constituent of most proteins). People who are allergic to gluten can eat amaranth with no side effects. Amaranth has a pleasant, nut-like flavor. Toasting them before grinding them adds to their flavor.

BARLEY

Barley is one of the oldest domesticated grain crops. It has been cultivated for over eight thousand years. It was a special food of the gladiators. Until the sixteenth century, it was the most important grain on the European continent. Barley was also used as currency and as a measuring standard. Around 1305, Edward I of England decreed that one inch should be the measure of three barleycorns, and English shoe sizing began (a child's shoe that measured thirteen barleycorns became a size 13). Almost half of the United States crop of barley is used for brewing beer and most of the rest is used for feeding livestock.

BUCKWHEAT

Buckwheat, an ancient grain, is actually a fruit seed that is related to rhubarb and sorrel, making it a suitable substitute for grains. Consumed in Asian countries for centuries, it has many health benefits. The seeds (also called groats) are a high source of amino acids, vitamins, minerals, and antioxidants. They can lower your risk of developing high cholesterol and high blood pressure. Buckwheat seeds have few calories and practically no fat, and don't contain any wheat or the protein gluten. The plant's flowers are very fragrant – bees are attracted to them and use them to produce a strongly flavored, dark honey.

CORN

Corn is considered to be either a vegetable or a grain but the kernels are classified as fruit.
(For more information, see CORN on page 58)

EINKORN

Einkorn may have been the first domesticated grain, as far back as 12,000 B.C. It originated in the fertile crescent of the Tigris-Euphrates regions. Einkorn is a variety of coarse grained wheat and is believed to be the ancestor of all modern wheat. It is still grown in France, Italy, Turkey, and Yugoslavia. Einkorn is a rich source of the beta carotene lutein, a powerful antioxidant. It has the highest amounts of lutein than any other variety of wheat. Einkorn is also a rich source of powerful antioxidants and Vitamin E. Compared to modern wheat varieties, einkorn has higher levels of protein, phosphorous, and potassium.

EMMER WHEAT

Emmer wheat, domesticated around 10,000 B.C. in Egypt, is an early hybrid of wild einkorn that was more suitable for a wider range of climates and geographical areas. It is most likely the main grain recorded in the Old Testament (although in the Bible, the word 'emmer' was often translated as spelt, a relative of emmer wheat that was eaten much later in history). Emmer was originally consumed as a porridge before bread making was developed. Over time, emmer wheat was replaced by other forms of wheat that were free threshing (grains that can be removed from their husks without pounding or grinding). Emmer wheat is high in protein, fiber and minerals. People with gluten allergies can eat it. Also called 'two grained spelt' or 'starch wheat,' emmer wheat is still grown as a cereal grain in Europe. It is used in a number of ways in Italian cooking such as boiled whole and served like a risotto, or used to make pastas.

SPELT

Spelt, a hybrid of emmer wheat, has been cultivated since 5000 B.C. It was an important staple in parts of Europe through medieval times. Spelt was introduced to the United States in the 1890s but was replaced in the twentieth century by bread wheat. Spelt is similar to wheat in appearance but has a tougher husk that helps protect the nutrients inside the grain. Flour made from spelt has a sweet, nutty chewiness and contains more protein than wheat. It is high in fiber. Spelt is most commonly used as a feed grain for animals.

FLAX

The Babylonians cultivated flaxseed as early as 3,000 B.C. Hippocrates used flaxseed for relief of intestinal discomfort. The French Emperor Charlemagne passed laws requiring flax seed consumption. Its main health benefits are due to the rich content of Alpha-Linolenic Acid (ALA), an essential fatty acid that is a powerful anti-inflammatory, as well as soluble fibers that can lower blood cholesterol levels. Flax also contains lignans (antioxidants that are excellent at helping to balance hormone levels in the body and may help reduce cancer risk). Ground flax seed provides more nutritional benefits than the whole seed.

Farro is an Italian word that encompasses three varieties of heirloom grains: einkorn, spelt, and emmer wheat. The term 'farro' can refer to any of these three grains. Ancient grains and heirloom wheat are lower in gluten, higher in protein, and higher in minerals and antioxidants.

OATS

Oats were not cultivated as early as wheat or barley. The oldest known oat grains were found among remains in Egypt around 2,000 B.C. The oldest cultivated oats were found in caves in Switzerland from the Bronze Age. Oats were brought to North America with other grains in 1600. They are a hardy cereal grain able to withstand poor soil where other crops are unable to thrive. Oats gain part of their distinctive flavor from the roasting process they undergo. Once hulled, they retain a concentrated source of fiber and nutrients. Oats can lower cholesterol levels and reduce the risk of cardiovascular disease, and there are antioxidant compounds unique to oats. They have also been shown to stabilize blood sugar and enhance immune response to infection. There are many different species and subspecies of oats.

QUINOA

Native to the Andes, quinoa (pronounced kēnwä) has been cultivated for five thousand years. It was a sacred staple of the ancient Incan empire. Natchez Indians along the lower Mississippi River also cultivated the seeds. Archeologists discovered a cave in Alabama in 1961 with remnants of a charred basket that contained quinoa seeds dating back to 2,000 B.C. Today, quinoa is grown in the Canadian prairies and the Colorado Rockies, but most quinoa sold in the United States is imported from South America. The seed is white and the leaves are also eaten. Quinoa is a highly nutritious food – one cup of quinoa has more calcium and protein than a quart of milk. Ounce for ounce, it has as much protein as meat, contains all of the essential amino acids, and has high amounts of iron and calcium. Quinoa is used to make flour, cereal, and alcohol. Chichi is a beer made from fermented quinoa.

RICE

Rice has been cultivated for over five thousand years. It is the highest yielding cereal grain and can grow in many kinds of environments and soils. It is grown on every continent except Antarctica and it is the main dietary staple for more than half the world's population. Rice was first cultivated in the United States in 1685 in South Carolina. Today, Arkansas is the largest producer of rice in the U.S. Stuttgart, Arkansas is known as America's Rice Capital. It takes two thousand to five thousand tons of water to produce a ton of rice. One seed of rice yields more than three thousand grains. After World War II, a rice company began selling high quality rice and named it Uncle Ben's®, after an African American Texas rice grower who had a reputation for the quality of his harvested rice. Over a billion people throughout the world are involved in rice production. September is National Rice Month.

There are thousands of different varieties of rice that can be divided into long, medium, and short grain. They are all equal nutritionally; the only difference is their cooking characteristics. Long grain rice is separate and fluffy when cooked. Medium grain rice is more moist and tender when cooked and cling together. Short grain rice is soft and cling together. Regular-milled white rice is the most common form of rice. Aromatic and specialty varieties are produced as well. Arborio rice is an Italian short grain rice with a high starch content. It is used to make Risotto. Aromatic rice has a flavor and aroma similar to roasted nuts or popcorn. Basmati rice is a long grain fragrant rice that is dry, separate, and fluffy when cooked. Jasmine rice is a long grain Thai rice with a unique aroma and flavor. Its cooked grains are soft, moist and cling together. Black rice is a black whole grain, aromatic rice used in desserts. It takes longer to cook and is slightly chewy, and has a subtle sweet spiciness. Brown rice has kernels from which only the hull has been removed. It may be eaten as is or milled into white rice. Cooked brown rice has a chewy texture and a nut-like flavor. Its bran layers are rich in minerals and vitamins. Sweet rice becomes glutinous when cooked. It is used in frozen products as a binder for gravies, sauces and fillings because it is resistant to breakdown during freezing and thawing.

SORGHUM

Sorghum, native to North Africa, was cultivated as early as 2000 B.C. It spread to the Middle East and India and from there to China and throughout Asia. It was brought to the Americas and later to Australia. Sorghum is the fifth most important cereal crop in the world and is grown for grain, fodder for animals, use in syrup and alcoholic beverages, as a colorant, and as a medicinal plant. It has been used as a folk remedy for cancer, epilepsy and stomach ache, and as a tonic for anemia. The deep red color extracted from the leaves is used to dye baskets, textiles, grass mats, wool, mud houses, and as a body paint. It can also be used in the production of biofuels. There are more than thirty different species of sorghum but only Sorghum Bicolor is harvested for human consumption. People with wheat (gluten) allergies can eat it.

WHEAT

Wheat originated in southwestern Asia. Primitive relatives of present day wheat have been discovered in some of the oldest excavations in the Tigris and Euphrates river valley, near what is now Iraq, dating back nine thousand years. Its common name, cereal, is from the Roman goddess Ceres who was the protector of the grain. Wheat is grown on more land area worldwide than any other crop and is a close third to rice and corn in total world production. Leaders in production are China, India, the United States, France, and Russia. Wheat was introduced to the U.S. in 1600. Today, it is grown in forty-two of the fifty states, and Kansas is the largest producer. (Kansas is also the number one state in flour production). Sumner County, Kansas, is known as The Wheat Capital of the World.

There are various classes of wheat used for different purposes. The major classes used for bread in the United States are hard-red spring and hard-red winter (there is also some production of hard-white wheat, a higher quality than red wheats). Extensive crop breeding efforts have created many modern cultivars. Macaroni and spaghetti are produced from durum wheat. Soft wheats are softer in texture and lower in protein than hard wheats. They are used in pastry flours and shredded and puffed breakfast foods.

One bushel of wheat yields forty-two loaves of white bread or forty-two pounds of pasta. Much of the wheat used for livestock and poultry feed is a by-product of the flour milling industry. Industrial uses of wheat include starch for paste, alcohol, and oil. Wheat straw can be used for newsprint, paperboard, and other products. Wheat contains gluten (protein that enables leavened dough to rise). Gluten is also found in other grains like rye and barley. Often, people who experience digestion difficulties will not eat foods containing gluten. **Caution: Those with celiac disease, non-celiac gluten sensitivity, and wheat allergies should not consume gluten.**

Wheat germ, bran, and malt are additional types of wheat products. Wheat germ is an edible section of the wheat kernel often removed during wheat processing to prevent rancidity. It is valued for its rich nutritional content. Bran is the hard, outer layer of cereal grain, often produced as a byproduct of milling. It is very high in dietary fiber and provides digestive regularity. Bran tends to absorb water and expand in the digestive system resulting in a feeling of fullness. Malt is left over after a cereal grain has been dried, allowed to sprout, air dried again, then heated in an oven. It is often used in beverages like beer. Malt Whiskey goes through a process that is similar to beer, until the distillation starts.

Alfalfa is supposedly the oldest know plant used for livestock feed, dating back to 1,000 B.C. in the Middle East. It is the primary hay crop grown in the United States. Alfalfa is an excellent honey crop for bees.

LEGUMES

The term 'legume' refers to plants whose fruit is enclosed in a pod. There are more than thirteen thousand species. Common legumes are beans, lentils, lupins, peas and peanuts. Alfalfa, clover, mesquite, carob, soybeans and tamarind are also legumes. They are a significant source of protein, dietary fiber, and minerals. The seeds are used for human and animal consumption or for the production of oils. Remains of beans have been found in ancient Egyptian tombs. The United States is the world leader in dry bean production. Forty percent are shipped to international markets around the globe.

ANASAZI BEAN

The Anasazi were Native Americans who lived in Colorado, Utah, Arizona and New Mexico, dating back to 130 A.D. The name 'Anasazi' is a Navajo word meaning 'the ancient ones.' Anasazi Beans where one of the few cultivated crops grown by the Anasazi. They were found by settlers in the ruins in the early 1900s. This bean is a very tasty baking bean. It contains less than twenty-five percent of the carbohydrates that are the primary source of flatulence in dry beans.

BLACK BEAN

Black shelling beans have an inedible, green pod that contains plump seeds (beans) that are black and glossy. As the beans dry, they harden and shrink. They are most commonly sold in dried form or canned. Black beans have a high protein content and are rich in carbohydrates, fiber, iron, B vitamins, potassium, and antioxidants.

BLACK-EYED PEA

Originally from Northern Africa, black-eyed peas are not really a pea but a shelling bean. They are found in long green and black mottled pods. The black circle at the center of the bean, which is located at the exact point where the bean attaches to the pod, became known as the eye. They are one of the most widely dispersed beans in the world. They were brought to America during colonial times and became a staple food across the Deep South, where eating black-eyed peas and greens on New Year's Day is considered good luck.

CACOA BEAN

The Aztecs used cacoa beans as currency. Today, about seventy percent of the world's cacao beans are grown in West Africa. The beans are found within pods that grow directly out of the trunk of Cacoa tree. It takes seven to fourteen pods to produce one pound of beans and about four hundred beans to make one pound of chocolate. The spelling 'cacoa' was later changed to cocoa, a mistake on a ship's manifest. Hawaii is the only state in the U.S. that grows cacao beans to produce chocolate. (For more information, see CHOCOLATE on page 235)

CALYPSO BEAN

There are several different varieties of Calypso shelling beans in shades of red and white, tan and white, or black and white, in a yin-yang pattern. They are high in protein and are believed to be one of the beans grown by the Native American tribe, the Abenaki. The beans were grown along with corn and squash in a process known as the 'three sisters' (the crops provide natural support for one another).

CANNELLINI BEAN

Cannellini beans, also referred to as white kidney beans, are white in their raw state and maintain their creamy color when dried and cooked. Originally cultivated in Argentina, they are known as an Italian heirloom bush type bean. There are different varieties sold in dried or canned form. Cannellini beans are high in protein and offer some fiber, calcium, and iron.

CAROB BEAN

The Carob bean, native to the Mediterranean region for over four thousand years, has a thick pod with multiple small, very hard, brown seeds. The ancient Egyptians extracted a honey-like substance from the pods and used it to make syrups and preserve fruits. Today, the beans are used for a variety of things such as a stabilizer in food products, to cure tobacco, and as a substitute for chocolate. Fresh Carob beans are lower in fat and higher in sugar than chocolate, have no caffeine, and are non-toxic to animals. They are also used for tea, processed into a form of molasses, and as animal feed. The beans are high in fiber, protein, and vitamins A and B. They contain four times the amount of potassium as bananas. All of the Carob bean may be eaten, including the outer pod.

Carob beans are believed to have been the original carat weight used to measure fine jewels and metals. They are also called St. John's bread – the passage in the Bible that refers to John the Baptist in the wilderness eating locusts may have meant carob beans. They were introduced to the United States in the mid-1800s by Spanish missionaries.

CROWDER BEAN

The Crowder shelling bean is an heirloom legume variety that has a bright green shell when fresh and then turns a pink and rose hue when dried. It got its name from the pea's tendency to crowd into its shell (the pods contain anywhere from twelve to eighteen small globular brown beans). The beans take on the flavor profile of what they are being cooked with. Crowder beans made their way to the southern United States from Africa during early colonial times.

FAVA BEAN

Fava beans are one of the oldest crops known. Remains found in Israel date back to 6500 B.C. They are now cultivated in over fifty countries. The pods are inedible but they have two to seven large lemon lime-colored beans inside that are rich in insoluble fiber that promotes digestive health. Pythagoras, a sixth century B.C. philosopher, condemned the fava bean and would not let his followers eat it. It was thought that they contained the souls of the dead.

GARBANZO BEAN

First domesticated in the Middle East, garbanzo beans spread to the Mediterranean in 4000 B.C., to India in 2000 B.C., and to the New World in the sixteenth century. They are the most widely consumed legume in the world. The beans, also known as chickpeas, are encased in a paper-like, light green shell when fresh and each shell contains one or two light green beans. There are two predominant types: small seeded known as desi, grown mainly in Southeast Asia and the Middle East; and the more commonly grown larger seeded, known as kabuli. Garbanzo beans have less protein than other beans but their higher fat content helps support healthy digestion. They are commonly used in dried or canned form. Garbanzo beans are pureed into hummus.

LENTIL

The Lentil, native to southwestern Asia, was cultivated as early as 6,000 B.C. Seeds have been found in Egyptian tombs dating to 2400 B.C. They are mentioned in the Old Testament (*Genesis 25:21-34* – Esau sold his birthright as the eldest son to his younger brother Jacob for a "mess of pottage," a lentil soup or stew). Lentils can help reduce bad cholesterol levels and the risk of heart disease. They are a great source of magnesium, dietary fiber and vitamins, and they contain the third highest level of protein of all legumes and nuts.

LIMA BEAN

The lima bean is native to the Americas and was named after the city of Lima, Peru although the pronunciation of these two words is different. They were used as a protein source by native Mayans, Aztecs, and Inca tribes. The large-seed variety of lima beans was cultivated around 6000 B.C. A small-seed variety was domesticated around 800 B.C. Domestication spread to Europe during the sixteenth century. Fresh beans have flattened semi-circle pods with two to three oval squat seeds (beans). The leaves and pods are also used as food. Fresh lima beans are difficult to find in the United States – most are dried, canned, or frozen. Fresh beans contain cyanide compounds and many countries (including the U.S.) restrict commercially grown varieties. Lima beans also contain fiber, folate, vitamins B1 and B6, and numerous minerals. They have been shown to lower diabetes and cancer rates. There are dozens of lima bean varieties varying in shape, size and color (white, cream, red, purple, mottled, brown and black). Dixie Butter shelling beans, a lima bean variety, produce a pod with three to four beans that, when mature, are speckled with pink streaks or dots. They've been a staple in the southern United States since the 1700s where many lima beans are commonly referred to as butter beans.

NAVY BEAN

The Navy Bean, a type of kidney bean native to the Americas, is also known as the Boston bean or Yankee bean. It got its name after serving as an important source of nutrition for the Navy during the second half of the nineteenth century. This small, dry white bean is a nutrient-dense food that is considered to be both a vegetable and a protein food that can serve as an alternative to meat. Navy beans can help lower blood cholesterol levels and improve heart health. They are high in fiber and are a good source of vitamins and minerals.

PINTO BEAN

Pinto Beans, native to Peru, are the most widely produced bean in the United States. They contain the most fiber of all beans. They also have protein, vitamins B1 and B6, and assorted minerals. The beans look like painted splashes of color and are named pinto, which means 'painted' in Spanish. They turn pink when cooked and the color splashes disappear. They are also named cowboy beans, after the Mexican cowboys employed in Texas. Dove Creek, Colorado is the Pinto Bean Capital of the world.

RATTLESNAKE BEAN

Some sources say Rattlesnake beans are called by that name because the pods twist and coil and climb like a rattlesnake as they grow. Others say it is from the way the beans make a rattling sound within their pods when dried. Their flavor is similar to pinto beans and they are rich in protein, fiber, folates, and vitamins A and B.

SOYBEAN

Soybeans were first domesticated in China in the eleventh century B.C. The Chinese have been using moldy soybean curds to treat skin infections for over three thousand years. The world's largest producer of soybeans is the United States. Soybeans are the largest cash crop in Missouri and the majority are used for livestock feed. Soybean oil is the most widely used vegetable oil. There are even soy crayons that are brighter in color and less expensive to produce than petroleum wax crayons. (For more information, see SOY NUT on page 129)

TIGER'S EYE BEAN

Tiger's Eye shelling beans, native to Chile or Argentina, are known for their tan hue and beautiful tiger-like dark brown/maroon swirls. They are rich in protein, carbohydrates, fiber and antioxidants.

VELVET BEAN

Velvet Beans come in a variety of colors and dappled patterns. Their flavor is similar to peanuts. They have high amounts of protein and dietary fiber and are also used medicinally. Ancient texts describe the beans being used to treat a disease similar to Parkinson's (today, Parkinson's patients use Velvet Beans to alleviate their symptoms). **Caution: Velvet Beans can be toxic if prepared and used improperly.**

WHITE CAP BEAN

The White Cap shelling bean, originally known as the Snow Cap shelling bean, has an ivory base with cranberry colored speckles throughout the curved lower half. Its name was given due to its pinkish purple markings with a snow-white cap.

In 1876, B&M baked beans were the first baked beans to be sold in cans.
Heinz came out with their version in 1895.

COFFEE BEAN

Coffee trees produce highly aromatic flower blossoms and the cranberry-sized coffee beans are the pits. The first coffee plant was found in Yemen. Turkey began to roast and grind coffee beans in the thirteenth century. Cultivation began in the fourteenth century and soon coffee was exported to the rest of the world. In London in the 1600s, it was thought that coffee was a cure for scurvy, gout, and other ills. The first Parisian cafe opened in 1689, to serve coffee. Before there were cafes, coffee was sold by street vendors, as it was done in the Arab fashion (the forerunner of today's sidewalk espresso carts). Beethoven always counted sixty beans for each cup when he brewed his coffee. The French philosopher Voltaire reportedly drank fifty cups of coffee a day.

Coffee plants were introduced to the Americas in the late 1600s. In 1773, the Boston Tea Party caused colonists to switch from tea to coffee and drinking coffee was an expression of freedom. During the Civil War, soldiers were given coffee beans as a primary ration. In 1900, coffee was often delivered door-to-door in the U.S. by horse-pulled wagons. Hawaii is the only U.S. state that grows coffee beans.

Coffee is the most popular beverage worldwide with over four hundred billion cups consumed each year. As a world commodity, it is second only to oil. Coffee is grown commercially in over fifty countries and all of them lie along the equator. Brazil is the world's largest producer. The two most important varieties of coffee plant are the Arabica and the Robusta. Eighty percent of the coffee produced worldwide is Arabica. It takes around four thousand Arabica beans to make a pound of roasted coffee. Coffee beans, like grapes, are affected by the temperature, soil conditions, altitude, rainfall, drainage, and degree of ripeness when picked. Coffee is graded according to three criteria: bean size, bean quality, and type of preparation. The longer coffee beans are roasted, the darker the roast. Dark roasted coffees have less caffeine than medium roasts. The majority of coffee available to consumers are blends of different beans. Flavored coffees are created after the roasting process by applying flavored oils specially created to use on coffee beans. Irish cream and hazelnut are the most popular whole bean coffee flavorings. A cup of coffee contains one hundred to one hundred and fifty milligrams of caffeine (an average chocolate bar contains only thirty milligrams).

Europeans first added chocolate to their coffee in the 1600s. Adding milk to coffee became popular in the 1680s when a French physician recommended that *cafe au lait* be used for medicinal purposes. Adding sugar to coffee is believed to have started in 1715, in the court of King Louis XIV. The drip pot was invented by a Frenchman around 1800. The first commercial espresso machine was manufactured in Italy in 1906. Espresso is so essential to daily life in Italy that the price is regulated by the government. In Italy, a barista is a respected job title.

Hills Brothers Ground Vacuum Packed Coffee® was introduced in 1900. The coffee filter was invented in 1908 by a German homemaker – she lined a tin cup with blotter paper to filter the coffee grinds. Kopi Luwak, the most expensive coffee at over one hundred dollars a pound, is made from the droppings of a marsupial that eats only the very best coffee beans. Supposedly, regular coffee drinkers have about one-third less asthma symptoms than non-coffee drinkers. Coffee, along with beer and peanut butter, is on the national list of the ten most recognizable odors. The steam rising from a cup of coffee contains the same amounts of antioxidants as three oranges. Raw coffee beans, soaked in water and spices, are chewed like candy in many parts of Africa. (For more information, see COFFEE on page 268)

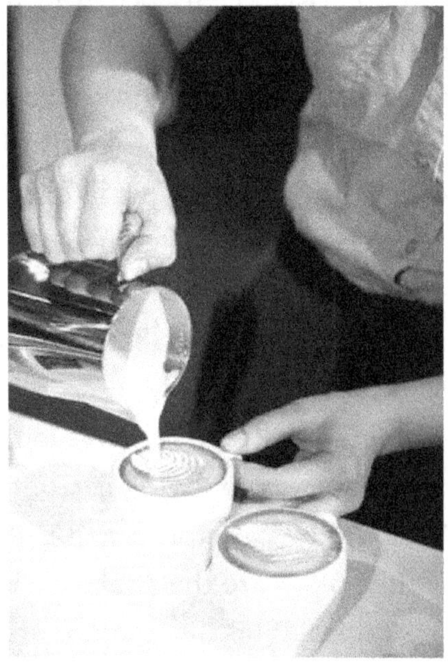

CHAPTER 4

Got Meat?
Meat, Poultry, Dairy & Eggs

Archaeological excavations at a thirty-one thousand year-old site discovered a cooking pit with the remains of two mammoths and other animal remains (the ancestors of cattle, deer, and boar). Additional evidence suggests that cattle were domesticated over eight thousand years ago. Prior to the fourteenth century, the word 'meat' referred to any solid food (that's why the inside of a nut is called nut meat) and the word 'drink' meant liquid food. Around the year 1300 A.D. 'meat' began to be used to refer to the flesh of animals.

BEEF

Beef is the culinary name for meat from cattle. It is one of the most nutrient-rich foods and it has one of the highest concentrations of these nutrients compared to many other proteins. It is the number one food source for protein, vitamin B12 and zinc, and the number three food source for iron, behind fortified cereal and grains. It also contains special fats that have potential anti-carcinogenic properties. There are several cuts of beef that are leaner than a skinless chicken thigh. With lean beef, you get the nutritional benefits while avoiding much of the saturated fat known to increase the risk for heart disease. Eighty to ninety percent lean is the most popular type of ground beef purchased. The diet of the cattle determines the nutrients and fats you get from eating different types of beef. Grass-fed beef comes from cattle that eat only grass and other foraged foods throughout their lives. Conventional beef cattle eat a diet that includes grains and other feed. Grass-fed beef may have less fat, more heart-healthy omega-3 fatty acids, and more antioxidant vitamins (however, limited long-term research has not definitively proved that grass-fed beef is better).

The different grades of beef indicate the amount, regularity, and quality of marbling (fat interlaced within the beef). Prime is the best, most abundantly marbled beef, mostly found in restaurants. Choice is an excellent beef and is available in grocery stores. Select is leaner and has less flavor and juiciness. Standard and Commercial grade beef is much leaner and often sold without a specific label. Unless labeled Choice or Select, store-brand beef is often Standard or Commercial grade.

When beef is labeled Certified it verifies that the USDA's Food Safety and Inspection Service and the Agriculture Marketing Service evaluated the beef for class, grade, or other characteristics.

USDA-certification for organic beef forbids the use of growth hormones, antibiotics, genetically modified feed, or animal by-products in raising the livestock. Labels that read "100% grass-fed" verify that the beef has only been fed grass and hay. Kosher beef is prepared under rabbinical supervision according to Jewish customs and laws. The beef comes only from the front of the cow. Aging develops flavor and tenderizes the beef. Dry-aging takes place in a chilled environment so moisture can evaporate, resulting in a more concentrated beef flavor. Wet-aging involves vacuum-packing the meat (and may result in less flavor).

There has been a great deal of discussion about how antibiotics are used in raising livestock. Farmers and ranchers evaluate the way they use antibiotics based on the best possible science. For nearly thirty years, there have been quality assurance programs in place to help make sure farmers and ranchers are continuously improving the way they raise beef, including the way they use antibiotics, in order to protect human health, as well as animal health. The most common types of beef are:

- Chuck roast and flat iron steak are types of chuck best cooked slowly over time.
- The shank is one of the toughest meats and is best used in soups, stews, or to make beef stock.
- Brisket, also known as brisket flat cut and brisket point cut, can also be tough unless cooked properly. It is best cooked smoked or braised.
- The rib is known for its juiciness, tenderness, marbling, and flavor. Types includes prime rib, short rib, rib-eye steak, and rib-eye roasts. They are best cooked over dry heat and for long periods of time.
- The short plate is fatty and tough and includes short ribs, hangar steak and skirt steak, and is best braised.
- The flank, one of the toughest cuts of meat, is usually used for stir-fry, fajitas, or as London broil.
- The loin is one of the most tender cuts of beef. Types include filet mignon, porterhouse steak, T-bone, KC strip, tenderloin roast, and shell steak. They are best when grilled.
- Sirloin is not as tender as the loin cuts and is best when grilled, pan fried, or broiled.
- The round, also known as the rump, has very little fat. Types include rump roast, top round, bottom round, eye of round, and the sirloin tip center roast. They are best braised or roasted with low levels of moisture.

Angus beef is from Angus cattle and is prized for its intense marbling that contributes to flavor and texture. Wagyu cattle is a breed with even more intense marbling than Angus. Kobe beef comes from Wagyu cattle raised in Japan in a specific way involving sake and massage. The term 'corned' (as in corned beef) refers to the very coarse salt originally used in the curing process. In the U.S., corned beef is a whole piece of beef brisket that has been cured in a brine solution. In Britain, corned beef is beef that has been brined, chopped and pressed, and is sold in cans.

Hernando Cortez brought the first cattle to North America in 1519. The first cattle ranch in the United States was started in 1747 on Long Island, New York. The Texas Longhorn breed of cattle developed naturally from the first cattle that were brought to the U.S.

In the early nineteenth century, a porter house was a coach stop where travelers could dine on steak and ale. A porter house keeper served the steak. In 1814 in New York City, it became very popular (hence the name).

The Philly Cheesesteak made its debut in 1930 in Philadelphia when Pat Olivieri, a hot dog vendor, cooked some beef on his grill and put it on bread. Eventually, Pat's King of Steaks opened and the cheesesteak became very popular.

Salisbury steak was named after a nineteenth century English physician, Dr. James H. Salisbury. Believing that bread and vegetables poisoned the body and caused disease and mental derangement, he proposed that people eat broiled, lean ground beef three times a day.

The hamburger is over one hundred years old. Hamburg, Germany exported high-quality beef and restaurants in the United States began offering a Hamburg-style chopped steak. A bun was added in the last decades of the nineteenth century. People at the 1904 St. Louis World's Fair enjoyed this new way of eating ground meat. Today, hamburgers account for forty percent of all sandwiches sold. White Castle® was founded in Wichita, Kansas in 1921 and is the oldest hamburger chain. Their system included on-premise meat grinding and was the inspiration for other hamburger chains founded after World War II. Louis E. Ballast, a drive-in owner, trademarked the cheeseburger in 1935 but he never enforced his trademark. McDonald's was founded in 1948, Burger King in 1954, and Wendy's in 1969. When the Big Mac® was introduced in 1968, the price was forty-nine cents. The popularity of the hamburger soon spread globally. The Hamburger Hall of Fame is located in Seymour, Wisconsin

Barbecue is not an American invention. Around one million years ago, man first tasted cooked meat. The first cooking implements were a wooden fork or spit to hold the meat over the fire. Eventually, wooden frames were built to hold the food above the flames, which resulted in the meat cooking slowly and absorbing smoke. Early cooks learned quickly that flavor, tenderness, and juiciness were related to how foods were cooked and how long. Smoked foods tasted better and kept longer. The wood used to hold the meat over the open pits was replaced by metal gridirons and later the pits were built with stones or bricks above ground. Spit roasting is common around the world and for many years was the major barbecue cooking method.

In India, food has been cooked for centuries over coals in ceramic urns called *tandoors*. In Japan, the *kamado* ceramic cooking urn has been around for about three thousand years. Barbecue grills were not commonly used in the 1800s. They were only for special occasions and events. In 1897, Ellsworth Zwoyer patented the charcoal briquette which became popular when Henry Ford, in collaboration with Thomas Edison and EB Kingsford, began to commercially manufacture them in the 1920s. They were made from sawdust and wood scraps from Ford's auto plants in Detroit. Ford also began selling small portable grills. Early barbecue restaurants cooked in dirt pits out back. The first commercial indoor pits were brick.

In 1968, inventor Herbert Oyler built wood-fired smokers with shelves that revolved around an axle like a Ferris wheel. This allowed all the meat to get even heat and smoke, and increased capacity. Over the years it was improved upon by other inventors and eventually evolved into a high-tech device that can be run by a computer. Lexington, North Carolina is known as the Barbecue Capital of the World. It has over twenty barbecue restaurants. The first one opened in 1919.

Rocky mountain oysters (or mountain oysters) refer to sheep's, bull's, boar's or prairie dog's testicles used for food. They are usually served breaded and deep fried but can also be sautéed, braised or poached. Clinton, Montana, has an annual Testicle Festival each year.

PORK

Pork is a good source of protein and an excellent source of thiamin, selenium, niacin, vitamin B6, and phosphorus. It is also a good source of riboflavin, zinc and potassium. Today's pork is sixteen percent leaner and twenty-seven percent lower in saturated fat compared to twenty years ago. Many cuts of pork are as lean or leaner than chicken (pork tenderloin is just as lean as skinless chicken breast). Pork, although not graded by the USDA, is categorized by size and gender of the animal.

The word 'roast' refers to a large cut of pork. Center cut rib roast is the most desirable and expensive portion. A pork loin roast can be brined or rubbed with a spice mixture and barbecued over indirect heat. It has a tendency to lose tenderness and fall apart when cooked using moist heat so it should not be braised or stewed. The tenderloin is a smaller cut of pork, usually weighing about a pound, that comes from the full pork loin. It is one of the most tender cuts of pork and has a mild flavor. It is best prepared when marinated or rubbed with spices for grilling. Pork chops are the most popular cut from the pork loin. They can be boneless or with the bone attached. Length of cooking depends on the thickness of the chop. Center Cut Chops are boneless. Butt, or shoulder blade roast, is best for pulled pork because of the slow-roasting process. Pork Brisket, an ideal cut to roast or braise, has flavor-filled fatty areas that break down while cooking to result in a juicy piece of meat.

Pork ribs are commonly prepared with either wet or dry rub. Dry rub consists of a mixture of herbs and spices and is applied just before barbecuing or grilling. Ribs basted with sauce during the grilling process are called wet ribs. Brush ribs generously during the last thirty minutes of cooking to prevent burning. Spareribs are large and heavy and known for their flavor. Baby Back Ribs are shorter than spareribs and weigh less, hence the name 'baby.' St. Louis style ribs are often the best type of ribs for recipes that require browning in a frying pan because the ribs are straight and flat. Country-style ribs are not really ribs, they are pork chops because they are meatier and less fatty than ribs. They should be cooked like chops.

Bacon is one of the oldest processed meats. The Chinese salted pork belly over three thousand years ago. Until well into the sixteenth century, *bacoun* was a Middle English term used to refer to all pork in general. In the twelfth century, a church in England promised a side of bacon to any married man who had not quarreled with his wife for a year and a day. A husband who brought home the bacon was held in high esteem by the community, and the phrase "bring home the bacon" began. In England, a side of bacon is called a gammon, and a slice of bacon is known as a rasher.

There are breeds of pigs particularly grown for bacon. An abundance of fat gives bacon its sweet flavor and tender crispiness. It may be packaged in thin slices, regular slices or thick slices, and is also available in slab form (one solid piece). Slab bacon usually comes with a rind that is meant to be removed before slicing. Fried, diced bacon rind is known as crackling. Pancetta, unlike bacon, is cured and unsmoked. It is eaten thinly sliced as a cold cut or used to enhance flavor. Canadian bacon, a name for cured loin meat in the United States, is more like ham than traditional bacon. It is a fully-cooked, smoked pork loin.

You can cook bacon in advance and store it in a refrigerator in a plastic bag. To reheat, roll it in a paper towel and cook in the microwave for about thirty to forty-five seconds. There is bacon-flavored chocolate, bacon-flavored toothpaste, bacon-flavored dental floss, bacon mayonnaise, bacon soap, and bacon-scented cologne. September third is International Bacon Day.

The USDA Dietary Guidelines for Americans recommends consuming twenty to thirty-five percent of calories as fat and less than ten percent of calories as saturated fat. The guidelines for cholesterol are no more than three hundred milligrams per day.

There are many different kinds of ham: raw, cooked, brined, and cured. Fresh ham is a raw uncured rear leg with the skin still on that can be roasted, skin on or off. Cooked hams can be served cold or warmed. Most hams are fully cooked but check the label. All varieties of cured ham are either boneless or bone-in. Wet-cured ham is soaked in a brine or injected with a cure. A cure is a salt and water solution with other ingredients like sugar, sodium nitrite, sodium nitrate, sodium phosphate, potassium chloride, or liquid smoke. These hams are available in three varieties: ham with natural juices has had little water added during the curing process; ham with water added retains more water during the curing process than ham with natural juices (it is ideal for steaks, thin-slicing, and shaving); and a ham and water product that has the most water added and is often found at the deli counter. Smoked Ham has usually been wet-cured and then smoked, or smoked without the cure. A Spiral-Cut ham is wet-cured and pre-cooked, and is usually coated with a sweet glaze and vacuum packed in plastic wrap. It doesn't have to be cooked but if you warm it, wrap it in foil and heat for only ten minutes per pound so it won't dry out.

Dry-cured ham is rubbed with salt mixed with sugar, black pepper, garlic, or other spices. Sodium nitrate and sodium nitrite may also be added. It is then hung to air-dry for six to eighteen months at cool temperatures. As it dehydrates, the flavor becomes more concentrated. Often it is smoked at low temperatures. Dry-cured hams are usually served uncooked and sliced thin because they are very salty. Country-style, or Southern-style ham, is dry-cured. Black Forest Ham is a German dry-cured and smoked ham. Prosciutto is an Italian dry-cured ham preserved with salt, lard, and other spices. It is usually sliced paper thin and eaten uncooked. Prosciutto is often wrapped around sliced cantaloupe, chopped in salads, added to a sandwich, or featured in an antipasto. Prosciutto di Parma or Parma Ham is prosciutto from the Parma region of Italy. It is regarded as the best of the Italian hams and made according to strict regulations and supervision.

Canned ham can contain scraps and pieces of meat pressed and formed to fit in the can and may contain up to ten percent water or broth. Canned ham labeled "shelf stable" can be stored at room temperature for three years. The Hormel Company sold the first canned ham in 1926.

'Corning' is the word for curing with salt. Pack a fresh ham (with or without the skin) with kosher or pickling salt, wrap it with plastic wrap, refrigerate it, and turn it occasionally for one week. Rinse off the salt then roast or simmer it. Corned ham is popular in Maryland and the Carolinas. In southern Maryland, corned ham is stabbed all over with a knife and the slits are filled with a mix of cabbage, kale, collards, onions and herbs to make Stuffed Ham.

The original bologna is Mortadella, a very large smoked sausage from Bologna, Italy that dates back to the fifteenth century. It is studded with cubes of pork fat, peppercorns, and green olives. The original recipe included myrtle (*mortella* in Italian, hence the name).

Liverwurst is a spicy cooked sausage that is made with a mixture of ground liver and pork and seasoned with a range of spices and onions. It comes in many flavors that vary by region and can be sliceable or spreadable.

Sausage is seasoned ground pork often enclosed in a casing that can come from a variety of cuts of pork. Sausage may be fresh, smoked or cured. Different sausage varieties contain different ingredient combinations. Summer sausage is a mildly seasoned smoked, semi-dry sausage. Pepperoni is a dry sausage that is characteristically firm, spicy, and bright red in color. Salami is a general classification for dry sausage, sometimes highly seasoned, with a characteristic fermented flavor. Dry sausage is a style of pork sausage seasoned with fennel or anise as the primary seasoning.

In the United States, the most common varieties of Italian sausage are hot, mild, and sweet. Hot sausage has hot red pepper flakes added to the spice mix. In Italy, there are a wide variety of sausages, many of which are different from the product commonly known as Italian sausage in the United States. Banger is British slang for sausage – if it isn't pricked before cooking it will burst with a bang. Mexican and Spanish Chorizo is smoked, highly spiced, and similar to a large frankfurter in size. It is also a term that denotes any type of Spanish style sausage.

Polish Kielbasa, also known as Polish sausage, is coarsely ground lean pork with beef added and highly seasoned with garlic. French and Cajun Andouille sausage is heavily spiced and smoked. German Bratwurst is a pork (or pork and veal) mixture that is highly seasoned, made in links, and available both fresh and fully cooked. Its unique flavor is derived from pepper, sage, and nutmeg. Sheboygan, Wisconsin is the Bratwurst Capital of the World. German Knackwurst, also called Garlic Sausage, is similar in ingredients to frankfurters and bologna, with additional garlic added for stronger flavor. Although fully cooked, it is usually served warmed. Vienna sausage is a smaller version of a frankfurter but softer in texture. It is also a term applied to small sausages packed in cans of water.

In 1893, eating sausages at baseball parks became popular. This tradition is believed to have been started by a St. Louis bar owner, a German immigrant who also owned the St. Louis Browns major league baseball team. Also in 1893, at the Colombian Exposition in Chicago, visitors consumed large quantities of sausages sold by vendors because the people liked that they were inexpensive and easy to eat.

Germany is credited with originating the frankfurter in 1487. The city of Frankfurt, Germany celebrated the 500th birthday of the hot dog in 1987. Wien (Vienna), Austria believes that the term 'wiener' (named after the city) proves they are the birthplace of the hot dog. German immigrants brought sausages to America, as well as dachshund dogs (hot dogs). The name 'dachshund sausage' most likely began as a joke about the similarity to the small, long, thin German dog. Eventually it became known as dachshund dog. How the term 'hot dog' came about is debatable. One theory is that the name was coined in 1901 at the New York Polo Grounds where vendors were selling hot dogs from portable hot water tanks. They walked through the crowd shouting, "Get your dachshund sausages while they're red hot!" A sports cartoonist who was present that day drew a picture of barking dachshund sausages in warm rolls and labeled them' hot dogs.' Another theory is that the word 'hot dog' began appearing in the 1890s in college magazines. At Yale in the fall of 1894, dog wagons sold hot dogs at the dorms. The name was in reference to German dachshund sausages. Here is another possibility: A popular term of approval in the late nineteenth century was ' hot.' When it was paired with a joking reference to the meat scraps that thrifty butchers added to sausage casings, people began calling the item a hot dog.

Before the Federal Meat Inspection Act of 1906, mothers warned their children never to eat hot dogs but New Yorkers bought them anyway, from vendors at parks, on boardwalks, and on the street. Nathan Handwerker made Nathan's® Famous hot dogs synonymous with Coney Island in 1915. Today, hot dogs are made from specially selected meat trimmings of beef and/or pork. Poultry hot dogs are made from poultry trimmings. Kosher hot dogs do not contain pork.

The words frankfurter, wiener, and hot dog are used interchangeably. Hot dogs range in size from big dinner frankfurters to small cocktail size. They can be skinless or with natural casings. As to who was first to serve the hot dog in a roll is questionable. It may have been a German immigrant who sold them, along with rolls and sauerkraut, from a push cart in New York City during the 1860s. Or, it may have been a German baker who opened the first Coney Island hot dog stand in 1871.

Hot dog toppings differ radically throughout the United States. Chicago hot dogs are layered with yellow mustard, dark green relish, chopped raw onion, pickle spear, peppers and tomato slices, and topped with a dash of celery salt and served in a poppy seed bun. Kansas City serves their hot dogs with sauerkraut and melted Swiss cheese on a sesame seed bun. The Texas dog has chili, cheese and jalapenos. The Rockie Dog, served at Coors Field in Colorado, is a foot-long dog with grilled peppers, sauerkraut and onions. The West Virginia dog is topped with chili, mustard and coleslaw, and served in a steamed bun. The Michigan Coney Island dog is topped with chili sauce, mustard, and onion. Cincinnati style tops their hot dog with chili and a heaping mound of grated cheddar cheese on top. The Philadelphia dog is an all-beef hot dog with a fish cake inside the bun, and often topped with a sweet vinegary slaw and spicy mustard.

California offers a bacon-wrapped hot dog with grilled onions and peppers. In Alaska, the hot dog is commonly called a Reindeer hot dog or sausage (it is made from caribou, not reindeer meat) and is served in a steamed bun with grilled onions that are sometimes sautéed in Coca-Cola®. The Southwestern Sonoran dog is a grilled bacon-wrapped hot dog with pinto beans, grilled onions, green peppers, chopped tomatoes, relish, salsa, mayonnaise, mustard and shredded cheese. In Cleveland, the Polish Boy is a kielbasa or hot dog served in a bun covered with a layer of French fries, a layer of sweet southern style barbecue sauce or hot sauce, and a layer of coleslaw. In Washington, D.C. the half-smoke is a half pork, half beef sausage hot dog with extra spice, topped with chili, onions, and mustard. At Fenway Park in Boston, the hot dog is boiled and grilled and served in a New England style bun with mustard and relish. New England dogs may also be topped with Boston baked beans. In New York, your hot dog will come served with steamed onions and deli-style yellow mustard.

President Franklin D. Roosevelt served hot dogs to King George VI of England during his 1939 visit to the United States. Hot dogs are the number one ballpark food. According to one legend, baseball great Babe Ruth ate twelve hot dogs and drank eight bottles of soda between doubleheader games. The National Hot Dog and Sausage Council offers a full guide for how to eat a hot dog. Here are a few guidelines: Don't put hot dog toppings between the hot dog and the bun – dress the dog, not the bun. Condiments should be applied in the following order: wet condiments like mustard and chili are applied first, followed by chunky condiments like relish, onions and sauerkraut, followed by shredded cheese, followed by spices like celery salt or pepper. Sesame seed, poppy seed, and plain buns are acceptable but never put a hot dog on a sun-dried tomato bun. Utensils should never be used when eating a hot dog on a bun – eat it with your hands. Don't bring wine to a hot dog barbecue; beer, soda, lemonade and iced tea are preferable.

Charcuterie is a word that reflects a French culinary art from the fifteenth century. It is the appetizer course featuring a platter of cooked and dry-cured meats, sausages, and smooth pâtés accompanied by baguettes, mustards, pickles, and other savories. Here are some guidelines for assembling a charcuterie platter:
- Select foods with a variety of textures, such as firm sausages, pâté and mousse, one or two semi-firm cheeses and at least one soft cheese that are complementary in flavor, and crusty baguettes, artisan breads or crackers.
- Have several flavors like smoky, spicy, and salty cured meats, smooth flavors of soft and semi-firm cheeses (not smoky-flavored varieties), and the acidity from pickles.
- Make it attractive by using several colors on the platter by adding green olives or pickles to the dark cured meats and the pale hues from cheese.
- Vary the shapes on the platter. Fold paper thin meat into a small triangle or roll them, slice some of the cheeses into wedges or rectangular strips, and add crackers that are rectangles, hexagons, or squares.

NOTE: Sodium nitrite, a particular type of salt, is a good preservative because it inhibits the growth of *Clostridium botulinum*, a deadly pathogen. It also gives cured meats their characteristic reddish-pink color and adds to their taste and texture. According to several health-related websites, about five percent of nitrite intake comes from cured meats but ninety-five percent comes from drinking water and vegetables such as lettuce, spinach, celery, and carrots. These things contain *nitrates*, some of which are converted by our digestive system to nitrites. In the stomach, nitrite can create nitric oxide, important in healing wounds and burns, controlling blood pressure, and boosting immunity. Physicians prescribe nitrates for angina and chest pain. Research done in the 1970s that indicated sodium nitrite could cause cancer in laboratory animals was later disproved. The World Health Organization published a survey of dozens of research papers that stated the data provided no evidence for an association between exposure of humans to nitrite and nitrate and the risk of cancer. The Food and Drug Administration (FDA) and the U.S. Department of Agriculture (USDA) set a maximum amount of nitrites allowed in food. The meat industry has significantly reduced the amount of nitrates and nitrites added to meats.

POULTRY

Poultry is divided into a number of different categories and classes. The four most common are domestic land fowl, domestic water fowl, game birds, and other poultry. The most common variety of domestic land fowl is the chicken, which has been bred into several varieties both for its meat and its eggs. The turkey is another domestic land fowl and other types include the small Guinea fowl, domesticated pheasant, and Rhea (a flightless bird that is often mistaken for an ostrich). Domestic water fowl includes the waterborne birds. Duck is one of the most common varieties and goose is another. During medieval times, hardier fowls like the partridge were more popular than chicken. Many game birds are wild versions of their domestic counterparts such as wild turkey, wild duck, wild goose and wild pheasant, and have a more bitter flavor. There are a few varieties of poultry that do not fall into these three categories such as doves and pigeons (also referred to as squabs). Other larger birds such as the ostrich and emu are also included in this category. Wild birds vary in their body type and usage. The Muscovy duck, from Brazil, is the only breed of duck not originating from the Mallard. The controversial product *Foie gras*, made from goose liver, dates back over four thousand years in Egypt.

Chickens have been domesticated for at least four thousand years but no one is exactly sure where the first chickens originated. They may have come from areas of South and Southeast Asia, southern China, Thailand, Burma or India. The Egyptians built brick incubators that held up to ten thousand chicks at a time. Eggs hung in Egyptian temples to ensure a bountiful river flow. The ancient Romans used the chicken to foretell the future, especially during wartime. Roman armies brought chickens with them and observed their behavior before battle; a good appetite meant victory was likely. The Romans were the first to make an omelet and to stuff the birds for cooking. Chickens may have been brought to the Polynesian islands from Southeast Asia at least three thousand years ago. Some archaeologists believe that chickens were first introduced to the New World by Polynesians who reached the Pacific coast of South America long before Columbus.

Todays domesticated chickens are descendants of the red jungle fowl of India and Southeast Asia. Most of the birds raised in the United States are from the Cornish, a British breed, and the White Rock, a breed developed in New England. Many different breeds of chickens have been developed for different purposes. There are three general categories: laying breeds (known for their egg-laying capacity), meat-producing breeds (broad breasted and larger than the laying breeds), and dual-purpose breeds (large and hardy, they are used for meat and eggs). Depending on how it is prepared, chicken is very low in fat and calories while also being high in protein. It is rich in niacin, a vitamin that is essential for cancer protection and brain health, and may have protective effects against Alzheimer's disease and dementia. The vitamin B6 in chicken keeps the heart healthy and selenium helps to keep thyroid function normal. Gainesville, Georgia is the Chicken Capital of the World.

Chickens have a great memory. They are able to recognize and remember more than one hundred different faces of people or animals. When an object is taken away from them and hidden, they are able to comprehend that it still exists – not many animals have the ability to do this (and neither do young human children). Chickens have full-color vision, are able to solve complex problems, understand cause and effect, pass on knowledge, and demonstrate self-control. They enjoy digging a shallow pit in the dirt and rolling around in the dirt. Dust baths help chickens maintain proper feather insulation and ward off parasites. Chickens like to run, jump, play, and sunbathe.

> Colonel Harland Sanders made the first batch of Kentucky Fried Chicken® at Sanders Cafe in Corbin, Kentucky in 1957. The recipe has changed over the years.

The rooster's wattle is used to bring attention to him when dancing for the hens. In the Bible, the rooster fulfilled the prophecy that Peter would deny Jesus before the cock crowed. In the ninth century, Pope Nicholas I decreed that a figure of a rooster should be placed atop every church as a reminder of that incident. Many churches still have cockerel-shaped weather vanes. The Old English Game was developed for cockfighting purposes by the Romans in the fifth century AD. Cockfighting was later banned for cruelty reasons. The Ancient Romans also discovered that castrating roosters caused them to fatten on their own, creating what we now call the capon.

The Aztecs domesticated turkeys. They used them for food and religious sacrifices, and the feathers for decoration. Henry VIII was the first English king to enjoy turkey. A male turkey is called a tom and a female turkey is a hen. Tom turkeys gobble and hen turkeys make a clicking noise. Domesticated turkeys cannot fly but wild turkeys can fly for short distances. Turkeys are social animals and enjoy the company of other creatures, including humans. They like having their feathers stroked. A turkey can easily be taught to eat out of one's hand and will come when called. When Neil Armstrong and Edwin 'Buzz' Aldrin sat down to eat their first meal on the moon, their foil food packets contained roasted turkey and all the trimmings. June is National Turkey Lovers' Month.

Turkey is a very rich source of protein, niacin, vitamin B6 and the amino acid tryptothan, which produces serotonin, a neurotransmitter that helps improve your mood. Tryptothan plays an important role in strengthening the immune system. Turkey also contains zinc and vitamin B12 and has less cholesterol than chicken, pork or beef.

Caution: Purines, a naturally occurring substances commonly found in plants, animals and humans, is contained in turkey. Some people are susceptible to problems related to an excessive intake of purines that can lead to excess accumulation of uric acid in the body, resulting in the formation of kidney stones and may lead to gout.

Many aromas and flavors are only soluble in fat and using fat in your cooking releases these flavors. Fat stops food from sticking to the pan and uniformly conducts heat to the food's surface, helping it to brown evenly. Animal fats are an important cooking ingredient because their low polyunsaturated fatty acid content makes them stable when heated and slower to oxidize. When cooking meats, cook beef in beef fat and poultry in poultry fat to reinforce the flavor. Beef fat, tallow (a rendered form of beef or mutton fat), or suet (see page 224) has a subtle beef flavor that is ideal for deep-frying and sautéing. It also adds richness to savory pie pastry. Suet has a milder flavor that can also be used in sweet preparations. Poultry fats are better for shallow frying. They can be used for pastry making but must be well chilled because of their lower saturated fat content. Pork fat is the most neutral flavored fat.

Vegetable fat is any fat or oil that has a plant origin rather than an animal origin. Trans fats are vegetable fats that have been treated so they act more like animal fats (like lard). They last a lot longer than animal fats. Lard is good for deep and shallow frying because it gives a crisp texture and doesn't impart a flavor of its own (it also makes a very flaky pastry).

Fats have many important functions in the body. They provide energy, build cells and protect organs, help absorb vitamins from foods, and produce hormones that help the body work properly. Some fats lower bad cholesterol. Unsaturated fats are the healthy ones. They are liquid at room temperature. There is a natural trans-fat called CLA (conjugated linoleic acid) that is beneficial in protecting us against cancer, heart disease, and weight gain.

Saturated fats, or man-made trans fats created when liquid fat is made solid by hydrogenation, are bad for our health because our bodies cannot process these fats. Highly polyunsaturated fats can suppress the immune system. Saturated fat can be found in foods like red meat, skin-on chicken and other poultry, pork, whole-milk dairy products, butter, eggs, and palm and coconut oils.

NOTE: Some studies have found no evidence that saturated fats directly contribute to heart disease. The American Heart association recommends that we get no more than five or six percent of our daily calories from saturated fat.

EGGS

Over four hundred million hens are used a year for eggs. Hens begin to lay eggs when they are about sixteen to twenty weeks of age. They'll lay at least twenty dozen eggs the first year. At fourteen months, they usually begin to molt (they drop their old feathers and grow new ones) and no eggs are laid during this period. After molting, hens will lay larger but fewer eggs per year (about sixteen to eighteen dozen). A healthy hen will lay eggs for several years. A mother hen talks to her chicks when they are still in the egg and the chicks chirp back to her and to each other through their shells. A mother hen turns her eggs about fifty times a day. If the temperature is correct, a chicken egg will hatch in twenty-one days (twenty-eight for turkeys and ducks).

The breed of hen determines the color of the egg shell. Breeds with white feathers lay white eggs. Breeds with red feathers lay brown eggs. Dual purpose chickens lay large brown-shelled eggs. The Aracauna chicken, native to South America, lays green eggs. Ameraracauna, an American breed of domestic chicken developed in the 1970s, lays blue ones. Some Easter Eggers lay pink and green eggs. Other breeds lay speckled eggs.

The type of food a chicken eats largely determines the color of the egg yolk. A white cornmeal diet will produce egg yolks that are almost colorless. Occasionally, a hen will produce double-yolked eggs. A chicken's feed also affects the nutritional quality of its eggs. Egg white makes up about sixty percent of an egg's weight and more than half of an egg's protein. The only source of protein higher in quality than eggs is a mother's breast milk. Egg yolks are one of the few foods that naturally contain vitamin D. They are an excellent source of B vitamins and also contain several minerals, including calcium and phosphorus.

Eggs may be labeled in different ways. Free-range means the chicken laying the eggs is not caged (but it does not necessarily mean that the chicken roams outdoors – the chicken has access to open space at some point each day). Vegetarian-fed ensures no animal by-products are fed to the chickens laying the eggs. Organic means the chicken's feed is organic.

China produces more eggs than any other country. Eggs will age more in one day at room temperature than in one week in the refrigerator. Eggshells have more than seventeen thousand pores and can absorb other food odors in the refrigerator. Store eggs in the carton, on the middle or bottom shelf of the refrigerator to help keep them fresh, not in the door. You can see how old an egg is by filling a bowl with water and dropping the egg in. If it sinks to the bottom it is fresh; if it floats, it's not fresh. Once cracked open, if the white of the egg is cloudy, it is fresh. Chickens are not the only birds that lay edible eggs. The duck, turkey, emu, goose, ostrich, and quail all lay eggs. One ostrich egg can weigh three to six pounds and make an omelet for ten people. It would take at least forty-five minutes to hard boil an ostrich egg.

When hard-boiling an egg, it is better to use a not-so-fresh egg because, in fresh eggs, the white sticks closely to the shell, making it more difficult to remove once boiled. Overcooking and using water with a lot of iron will produce a greenish-colored yolk (it is safe to eat). For perfect hard-boiled eggs, place eggs in a two-to-three-quart pot full of cold water. Heat eggs to a rolling boil then remove from heat and let stand, covered, for twelve minutes. Drain the eggs and place them in the refrigerator.

MILK

Around 10,000 B.C. societies changed from nomadic tribes to those who settled in communities. With this came domesticated animals and soon people began to use by-products, such as milk. The remains of dairy cattle have been found in various sites in Turkey from around 6500 B.C. but they may have been domesticated much earlier. Archaeological evidence found that cows were being milked in Great Britain at least six thousand years ago. In ancient Egypt, milk and other dairy products were reserved for royalty, priests and the very wealthy. The ancient Greeks and Romans referred to barbarians as 'milk drinkers.' In the late thirteenth century, Marco Polo discovered the nomadic Tartars boiling mare's milk, skimming the cream from the top, and then exposing it to the hot sun until it dried (the first powdered milk). When they wanted to use it, they added water to it and, while riding their horse, the mixture would be shaken, producing a thick porridge for dinner. By the fourteenth century, cow's milk became more popular than sheep's milk. European dairy cows were brought to North America in the early 1600s. California produces the most milk of any U.S. state.

Louis Pasteur, a French microbiologist, conducted the first pasteurization tests in 1862. Pasteurization is the process of heating raw milk at a high enough temperature for a sufficient length of time to make it bacteriologically safe and increase its keeping quality. He revolutionized the safety of milk and the ability to store and distribute milk beyond the dairy farm. Commercial pasteurization machines were introduced in 1895. In 1948, Michigan became the first state to require statewide pasteurization of milk. Most milk sold in the United States is pasteurized. Pasteurization has little effect on milk's nutritive value. Homogenization is the mechanical process of incorporating the natural fat globules into the liquids in milk to keep them blended.

Other than the fat content, all types of milk contain sixteen essential nutrients: vitamins A, B6, B12 and D, calcium, folate, magnesium, niacin, pantothenic acid, phosphorous, potassium, protein, riboflavin, selenium, thiamine, and zinc. Whole milk contains at least 3.25 percent milk fat, which is lighter than cream but has more body than low fat milk. When a portion of the milk's fat is removed it becomes partly skimmed milk (one percent or two percent) depending on the quantity removed. Skim milk has only about 0.1 percent fat and contains more calcium than whole milk. Lactose-Free milk is regular milk that has been processed to break down the lactose (sugar) in milk. Organic milk is from cows that are fed organically grown crops. Regular and organic milk are equally safe and nutritious. Chocolate milk contains no more sugar than unsweetened apple juice and only a very small amount of caffeine found naturally in cocoa.

Milk was first sold in glass bottles in 1879. In the 1930s, milk cans were replaced with large on-farm storage tanks and plastic-coated paper milk cartons were invented. This allowed for wider distribution of fresh milk. Plastic milk bottles were introduced in 1967.

Gail Borden developed a method to make condensed milk in 1853. About sixty percent of water is evaporated from milk to create evaporated milk. The high temperature needed to sterilize the milk causes a browning to occur, giving this milk a slightly darker color. It takes just over two pounds of whole milk to make one pound of condensed milk. Unlike sweetened condensed milk, evaporated milk contains no sugar. Thick sweetened condensed milk is made by condensing milk to one third of its original volume and then adding sugar. To make powdered milk, partly evaporated milk is heated and dried instantly. There are instant and regular forms and once the package is opened, it should be used within one month.

Sterilized milk that has been heat-treated at an ultra-high temperature, cooled, and then poured into a sterilized package without air contact will keep, unopened, for several months at room temperature. Once opened, it must be refrigerated and used within three days. Buttermilk was originally the low-fat liquid remaining after churning cream into butter. Today, it is made by adding lactic acid-producing bacteria to pasteurized milk with nonfat dry milk solids under controlled conditions. Almond milk is a natural source of calcium and vitamin E but is low in protein and missing vitamin B. Coconut milk has a good amount of phosphorous, potassium, and fiber but is very high in calories and lower in calcium than cow's milk. Goat's milk has more calcium than cow's milk and more tryptophan, an essential amino acid that helps the body process protein. Hemp milk is made from hemp plant seeds (it does not contain the psycho active ingredient found in marijuana). Hemp milk has more calcium and phosphorous than cow's milk and the same amount of protein. It doesn't contain saturated fat but does contain fiber. Oat milk is made from ground-up oat groats. It is free of saturated fats but is higher in carbohydrates than cow's milk and lower in protein. Rice milk contains no saturated fats but only has one gram of protein (cow's milk has eight). It also has twice as many carbohydrates as cow's milk. Soy milk is rich in protein and contains no saturated fat. It is low in calcium but some types have added calcium and vitamin D. **Caution: Soy protein can interfere with mineral absorption, including iron.**

You can add milk to many of the foods you prepare to increase your intake of calcium and other nutrients. When you make soup, reduce the amount of water or broth and add some milk at the end of cooking. Replace water with fresh milk when making bread dough and other baked goods. Use powdered milk as one of the dry ingredients in pancakes, muffins, and cookies. You can also add powdered milk to meat loaf and meatballs. Make a specialty coffee house drink at home by whipping cold milk then warming it in the microwave, and topping your coffee or hot chocolate with it.

According to Julie Hynson: "I am married to a dairy farmer, Allen, and I see firsthand that it takes a lot of effort, time (thirteen-hour days, seven days a week) and physical work, and creates dirty clothes (which I don't really mind). When people ask me what I do on the farm, I usually reply, "I supply the health insurance!" Allen's dad started the dairy farm in the mid-1930s, which, to me, would have been a leap of faith. There probably won't be a Century Farm in the future as none of his grandchildren or great-grandchildren are interested in continuing it. Allen sells his milk to a co-op that pays him by the pound – there are 8.6 pounds of milk in a gallon (no wonder those jugs are so heavy!). Yet milk is sold by quart, gallon, etc. I have noticed that the milk industry is trying to make it easier to buy single-servings of milk and you can now find them in round-bottom containers so they fit in the drink holder in your car or stroller. They used to be square or rectangular (think school cafeteria). Cows have approximately the same time span for pregnancy as people (about two hundred eighty days). I could never understand why, knowing this,

Allen breeds cows so that they are born the week of the Christmas holidays! (Can't you adjust this a week or two, Allen?) My frustration with dairy farming is that Allen and I never have time to do anything together. Weddings, funerals, birthdays and other celebrations, eating at a restaurant, school conferences, errands needing Allen, or getting stranded with a dead car battery all revolve around the farm schedule. It is a guarantee that if we plan a three-hour day trip away from the farm something will go wrong. So we miss a bunch of social opportunities, although I frequently go alone. It is nice to live rural where we can go outside to actually see the stars, let the dog out without a leash, hang the clothes on the clothesline, and keep the grandson's vintage Tonka truck under a tree without worrying about the neighbors' opinions. Allen and his brother have a partnership. From our early marriage, Allen said that as long as he was a dairy farmer I wouldn't have to entertain or invite the boss to dinner!"

YOGURT

Yogurt is one of the oldest and most popular fermented foods and can be found in almost every region that uses milk. No one knows for sure how long yogurt has been in existence. The discovery of yogurt was probably accidental. Early man may have tried to store milk in the intestines of animals, in a warm climate, and the enzymes that were present in the intestines may have started the initial fermentation process. Yogurt spread from Central Asia to the Middle East and Europe, and throughout the world. It is mentioned in many ancient texts, including the Bible (*Genesis 18:8*). Genghis Khan and his armies lived on yogurt. In the sixteenth century, a Turkish doctor saved the life of King Francis I, who had been suffering from some type of intestinal illness, by treating him with yogurt made from goat's milk. This brought a new surge in the popularity of yogurt as a health food.

Around 1900, scientists started studying and isolating the bacteria that made yogurt, and its health benefits. It was determined that the bacteria in cultured milk products like yogurt helped to reduce the amount of bad bacteria in the gut. Probiotic yogurt has additional bacteria that are useful in preventing and treating many intestinal conditions. It contains substances like inulin, in addition to live probiotic cultures. These ingredients help the body to keep the probiotic bacteria alive so they can reproduce in the intestine. Enriched yogurts contain added vitamins, minerals, fatty acids and other healthy ingredients such as fiber, calcium, and omega-3 fatty acids.

The word 'yogurt' comes from Turkey and refers to a tart, thick milk. When fresh milk is left in a container with friendly bacteria, the milk thickens and develops a slightly sour taste. The lactic acid produced by the fermentation process also acts as a preservative. The bacteria used to make yogurt are known as yogurt cultures. FDA regulations require that all yogurts be made with active cultures. Yogurt labeled "Contains active yogurt cultures" has the live and active bacteria thought to provide yogurt with its many healthful properties. Yogurt labeled "Heat-treated" has been heated after culturing, thereby killing the beneficial live and active yogurt cultures.

There are three types of yogurt: regular, low fat and nonfat, and three main styles of yogurt, as well as many minor varieties. Balkan style yogurt is poured into containers and allowed to ferment in the containers without stirring. It is very thick and often used in traditional Middle Eastern recipes. Swiss style yogurt is made in a large batch fermented together and cooled before adding to containers. It is thinner than Balkan yogurt and is often flavored or sweetened, and may have fruit added. Greek yogurt, also called Mediterranean style yogurt, is made by straining the water from milk prior to fermenting, or straining off the whey after fermenting. It is very thick and has a higher protein content than other yogurts. Both Balkan and Greek style yogurts are made with high milk-fat content. Swiss style yogurt can be made from either whole, low fat, or non-fat milk. Fruit on the bottom is a type of Swiss style yogurt – the fruit is not mixed prior to packaging.

The first industrialized production of yogurt is attributed to Isaac Carasso in 1919 in Spain. His company, Danone, was named for his son, Daniel. In the 1940s, Daniel Carasso and Juan Metzger took over a small yogurt factory in New York. That company is now called Dannon. Fruit was first added to commercially produced yogurt in 1946 by Dannon. It was not until the health food craze of the 1950s and 1960s that yogurt really gained a huge popularity in the United States. Kefir is a yogurt drink made with traditional cultures. It also has yeast that adds an extra tang to the flavor and has additional health benefits.

Frozen yogurt, unless made with live cultures, is not a true yogurt. Most frozen yogurt uses heat-treated yogurt which kills the live and active cultures. Or the cultures may be added to the mix along with acidifiers, skipping the fermentation step. In order to qualify as true frozen yogurt, it must be a product made by fermenting pasteurized milk using traditional yogurt cultures, until the proper acidity is reached. Then, according to a manufacturer's recipe, the yogurt is mixed with a pasteurized ice cream mix of milk, cream and sugar, plus stabilizers. It can then be blended with fruit or other ingredients and then frozen. The freezing process does not kill any significant amount of the cultures. When consumed, it provides all the benefits of cultures in a refrigerated yogurt product. To ensure that the frozen yogurt you eat contains yogurt produced by traditional fermentation and has a significant amount of live and active cultures, look for a *Live & Active Cultures* seal.

The word 'dairy' is from the Middle English word *dey* (meaning 'a female servant'). In Europe, milking, making cream, butter, and cheese was always done by women.

BUTTER

There is a recorded use of butter from four thousand years ago in northern Asia. Not only was it eaten, but also used as an illumination oil, for medicinal purposes, and as skin coating to insulate people from the harsh winter cold. Conquest and colonization brought butter to southern regions but it could not be stored as easily in the warm climates. The people in southern Asia were the first to clarify butter in order to keep the fat from spoiling. The earliest known process of making butter is derived from the Arabs and Syrians who used a vessel made from goatskin for a churn. The churn was then suspended from the tent poles and swung until butter formed. Before the turn of the twentieth century, people in western United States placed cream in a bag, strapped it to the saddle of a horse, and rode the horse for a few miles so the churning process made butter.

In Hindu culture, the cow is sacred and represents the soul, and butter is the only animal fat that Hindus will eat. It was also a sacred offering, a food fit for the gods. The Bible references butter in the Old Testament (*Judges 5:25 -"She brought forth butter in a lordly dish"*). The word 'butter' comes from *bou-tyron*, Greek for cow cheese (the Greeks preferred olive oil to butter). Until the eighteenth century, people from Mediterranean regions believed that butter was a cause of leprosy. Butter has been colored yellow since the fourteenth century (it was colored with marigold flowers).

Making butter was mostly done in the home but as communities expanded many families purchased butter from local farmers. As early as 1791, populations became more congested and cities sprang up, and the farm production of dairy butter began to expand. It was sold as pats, balls, rolls and prints. It takes about twenty-one pounds of milk to make one pound of butter. Refrigeration was not common and, in 1806, enormous blocks of Arctic ice were towed to destinations all over the Atlantic world. In 1851, the first refrigerated rail car, cooled by natural ice, transported butter. The compressed-gas cooler, perfected in Australia in the 1870s for brewing, replaced the expensive ice. The first creameries in the United States began operating around 1860 in New York State.

The definition and standards for butter in the U.S. were first set by congress in 1886. Current standards have not been changed since 1923. The quality of butter is based on its body, texture, flavor, and appearance. The U.S. Department of Agriculture assigns quality grades to butter: Grade AA is the highest possible grade; Grade A butter is almost as good; and Grade B butter is used only for cooking or manufacturing. Whipped butter is made by whipping nitrogen gas into the butter. In the second half of the twentieth century, butter was blamed for a host of health problems but butter's negative reputation was undeserved and recent studies show how important butter is to a healthy diet. It supplies our bodies with vitamins and minerals, boosts our immune system, helps hormone production, and supports our bones, organs, and our brain. Butter substitutes and manmade trans fats are the things that pose threats to our health.

Butter tips:

- Don't defrost frozen butter in a microwave, cut it into chunks and leave it out until it's cold but malleable. If butter is too hard, it won't aerate properly.
- When creaming butter, it should be at a consistency that's spreadable. Whip the butter for three minutes on low speed, not high. Unsalted butter has less liquid than salted butter and is more likely to aerate properly when creamed.
- The salt content of regular butter varies by manufacturer so using unsalted butter can control how much salt is in baked goods. If you use salted butter, reduce the amount of salt in the recipe by one-fourth teaspoon per one-half cup of butter.
- Don't use your fingers to cut butter into flour (it can cause the butter to melt). Use a food processor, or use a cheese grater to shred the butter and then two knives to combine the butter and flour.
- There are different varieties of butter that sometimes produce different results in baking. The higher the fat content, the less water the butter contains, making pastries flakier. American butter has a fat content of at least eighty percent; some other butters can have up to eighty-five percent fat.
- Butter, unlike shortening, contains water but doesn't contain hydrogenated fat. Shortening is more stable at warmer temperatures and it causes the gluten in flour to expand less.
- The type of butter can influence the flavor of sauces. The cream used in most commercially produced butter in the U.S. has a uniform and indistinct flavor. Artisanal or farmhouse butters have a distinct individual taste that come from both the cows' diets and the microbial strains found in each.
- It is easier to mix in herbs, spices, cheese, wine reductions, and stocks when butter is at room temperature. The result is called 'worked butter' or 'compound butter.' It can be used to spread on bread or to place over meats, vegetables, and other foods. Compound butter can be stored in the freezer for up to three months.

Ghee is a dairy product that is considered a staple ingredient in Southern Asian cooking, particularly Indian cuisine. It is made from butter that has been further cooked to remove all milk solids as well as moisture. Other names are 'drawn butter' and 'clarified butter.' Making clarified butter involves slowly heating unsalted butter and letting it boil until the water vaporizes. Once the bubbling stops, look for signs of clarification: white, and then brown specks at the bottom of the pan. There will be three layers: whey protein, liquid fat, and casein particles. Remove the top layer (whey protein), or strain the contents of the pan through a triple layer of cheesecloth or a coffee filter. What remains is the clarified butter. Clarified butter is used for frying at high heat because the components that cause butter to scorch (protein and casein) have been removed. Regular butter can be used for frying at medium heat.

Margarine was developed in 1869 by a French chemist. Napoleon III offered a prize for a butter substitute for his army and navy, because butter spoiled easily. Margarine received a U.S. patent in 1873. Margarine is about eighty percent fat and twenty percent water and solids. It is flavored, colored, and fortified with vitamin A and sometimes D to match butter's nutritional content. During World War I, coconut oil was mostly used as the fat in margarine. In the 1930s, cottonseed was used and in the 1950s it was soy. Today, soy and corn oils predominate. During the second World War, there were quotas on butter so margarine production increased. In the latter part of the 1900s, when butter was considered bad for our health, margarine consumption surpassed butter (almost three times more margarine was eaten than butter).

CHEESE

Cheese production can be dated back to 8000 B.C. when sheep where first domesticated. The remains of cheese at least four thousand years old have been found in Egyptian tombs. The art of cheese-making is referred to in ancient Greek mythology. The word 'cheese' comes from the Latin word *caseus* which means 'to ferment.' According to legend, cheese was made accidentally by an Arabian merchant who put milk into a pouch made from a sheep's stomach. The rennet (an extract from the stomach of certain animals) in the lining of the pouch, combined with the heat of the sun, caused the milk to separate into curd and whey. He drank the whey and ate the curd (cheese). Cheese soon made its way to the Roman Empire. By the time of Julius Caesar, hundreds of varieties of cheese were being produced and traded. Italy became the cheese-making center of Europe during the tenth century. During the Middle Ages, cheese was made and improved by the monks in the monasteries of Europe. The Pilgrims brought cheese with them on the Mayflower in 1620. Making cheese was a very effective way to preserve perishable milk.

Women were the local farmstead cheese producers, They would skim off the cream to make butter and then use the rest of the milk for making cheese. The demand for cheese increased and the industry gradually moved westward to the rich farmlands of Wisconsin. In 1831, Wisconsin's first farmstead cheese factory was opened. A group of Swiss immigrants settled in Wisconsin in 1845 and started manufacturing foreign cheese in America. The first industrial cheese factory in the United States was built in New York in 1851. Wisconsin's first factory was a Limburger plant that opened in 1868. By 1880, there were almost four thousand dairy factories nationwide. Processed cheese also experienced a surge in consumer demand.

"Dessert without cheese is like a beauty with only one eye"
Jean Anthelme Brillat-Savarin
French lawyer and politician
1755-1826

The United States produces more than thirty percent of the world's cheese. More than one third of the milk produced in the U.S. each year is used to manufacture cheese. Wisconsin is the largest producer of cheese in the U.S. and makes over six hundred varieties. They are also first in specialty cheese production. In 1914, the first Cheese Days were held in Wisconsin to honor the cheese-making industry. Wisconsin has more licensed cheesemakers than any other state.

Cheese, mainly composed of fat and protein, the proportions of which depend on the type of cheese, is categorized by the type of milk used to make it: cow, buffalo, goat, sheep, horse, or camels. It is also categorized by the butterfat content. The higher the butterfat content, the creamier the cheese. Low-fat cheese has about twenty percent butterfat, regular cheese has forty-five percent, and cream cheeses have between sixty percent and seventy-five percent. Hard cheeses and soft-ripening cheeses are also high in butterfat. Cheese is very high in saturated fat but provides a fair amount of monounsaturated fat. It also contains small amounts of carbohydrates and is a concentrated source of vitamins and minerals including calcium, zinc, riboflavin, and vitamins A and K2. Moderate consumption of dairy products, like cheese, is effective against osteoporosis and is beneficial for heart health. Certain cheeses, such as aged Cheddar, Swiss, Blue, Monterey Jack, Brie, Gouda, and processed American cheese, have been shown to help prevent tooth decay.

Fresh cheeses do not require aging; they have a mild flavor. Semisoft cheeses are aged from a few days to a few months; they have a mild flavor and melt quickly when heated. Soft-ripened cheeses have white rinds and creamy interiors that get softer as they age. Hard cheeses are aged for years; they have a crystalline texture and a longer shelf life than soft cheeses. Blue cheeses are aged with a mold injected into them to give them their color; they can be creamy, crumbly, or hard. During the manufacturing process, the particular bacteria that produces the flavor and texture of Swiss cheese also produces carbon dioxide gas as a by-product. These bubbles of gas produce the holes. The USDA regulates the size of the holes in domestically produced Swiss cheese.

Many of the popular cheeses we eat today, such as Cheddar, Swiss, Parmesan and Gouda, appeared within the last five hundred years. Almost ninety percent of all cheese sold in the U.S. is classified as a Cheddar type cheese. Cream cheese is one of the oldest American packaged foods. Pasteurized Process Cheese is a blend of fresh and aged natural cheese that has been melted, pasteurized, and mixed with an emulsifier and coloring.

It was once believed that eating cheese before bed could cause nightmares. The terms 'Big Wheel' and 'Big Cheese' originally referred to those who were wealthy enough to purchase a whole wheel of cheese. Carrot juice and marigold petals were used to color cheeses. Cheddar, Cheshire (the oldest cheddar type), and Leicester cheeses have been colored with annatto seed for over two hundred years. A seller of cheese is known as a cheesemonger. Cheese tastes best at room temperature so take it out of the refrigerator at least an hour before serving.

An entire cup of milk is used to produce one slice of cheese. Lactose, also called milk sugar, is the main carbohydrate found in milk products. Some people are unable to fully digest lactose; this is known as lactose intolerance. Fresh cheeses, such as cottage cheese and cream cheese, usually contain more lactose than well ripened, aged cheese. People with lactose intolerance can often eat aged cheese in moderate amounts without problems.

Vegan cheese is completely free of milk and animal-based enzymes. Most are made primarily from nuts, usually cashews or almonds. Others are made from dairy-free milks or tofu. Oils, emulsifiers, and thickeners are also used to produce firmer types. The main difference between real cheese and vegan cheese is the consolidated protein (curd). Real cheese goes through stages where the proteins physically bond to each other; vegan cheese doesn't experience any modification in proteins and may not have the same flavor that comes from milk-based cheese. Vegan cheese doesn't necessarily mean healthy – like some cheeses, varieties of vegan cheese can be highly processed. It is healthier if you make it yourself. There are numerous cooked vegan and raw vegan cheese recipes available online.

According to Stephanie Van Coops, "I love eating vegan! I first considered changing my diet because I have always had high cholesterol, even as a child. Over the years I tried other ways to reduce it but I had not learned the solution. I first became a vegetarian after giving up meat for Lent. It agreed with me and was easy so I stayed vegetarian even after Easter rolled around. The following year I attempted to go vegan but realized I was eating too many processed vegan foods. I needed to learn to cook vegan and not just eat vegan. Once I learned all of the foods that were available to me, eating vegan became easier and I was able to eat a more whole foods diet and cut out processed foods. As a result, my health has improved greatly and my cholesterol is finally normal and healthy. I believe there is a misconception that being vegan puts limits on your diet. When you stop looking at what you can't have and begin focusing on all the wonderful foods available to you, you find new dishes and food favorites that you never would have explored otherwise. The past six years I've learned so much."

> Animal welfare groups seek to ensure the humane treatment of animals. Since 1951, the Animal Welfare Institute has been dedicated to reducing animal suffering caused by people in the laboratory, on the farm, in commerce, at home, and in the wild.

CHAPTER 5

Gone Fishing

There are two categories of water-borne animals: fish and shellfish. Fish are vertebrates with fins and gills. They are separated into freshwater and saltwater fish. Freshwater fish have hundreds of tiny, light bones. Saltwater fish have thicker, fewer bones. Fish are also categorized as flatfish or roundfish. Flatfish are flat, oval-shaped and swim along the bottom of the sea or ocean. They have both eyes on the top of their body. Roundfish have round or oval bodies with eyes on opposite sides of the head. The Latin word *piscis* became the Germanic word *fisch* which became the Old English word *fisc* which became today's word, fish. The term 'fish' is used when referring to one species of fish; fishes refers to more than one species. There are more than thirty thousand species of fish that we know of and more are being discovered all the time. There are more than two thousand types of catfish alone.

Shellfish are divided into two categories: mollusks and crustaceans. Mollusks cover their soft bodies with a shell or they've developed beyond the need for a shell. There are three classes of mollusks: gastropods (like snails and conch) have one shell, bivalves (like the clam and oyster) have two shells hinged together by a muscle, and cephalopods (like squid and octopus) have no external shells. Crustaceans have a tough shell-like exoskeleton, usually jointed with pairs of legs on each segment. This group includes lobster, crab, shrimp and crayfish.

One of man's earliest tools was a gorge – a piece of wood, bone, or stone an inch or so in length, covered with some kind of bait. With the coming of the use of metals, a hook was made. The oldest fishhook ever found dates to forty-two thousand years ago. A Chinese account from the fourth century B.C. refers to fishing with a silk line and a bamboo rod, with cooked rice as bait. The oldest known painting of a fisherman using a rod, line, and nets is from Egypt and dates to around 2000 B.C. References to fishing are also found in ancient Greek, Assyrian, Roman and Jewish writings. Fishing (catching freshwater or saltwater fish with rod, line, and hook) originated as a means of providing food for survival but sport fishing, also called angling, is old as well. Sport fishing is distinguished from commercial fishing. More than ninety percent of all fish caught are caught in the northern hemisphere. Most of America's catch of salmon, crab, halibut and herring come from Alaska. The largest private industry employer in Alaska is the seafood industry. About half of the world fish production is farmed. China farms more freshwater fish than any other country, dating as far back as thirty-five hundred years ago.

Protect fish and ocean animals by making good decisions when purchasing seafood. Ask if it is sustainable seafood and help shape the demand for, and supply of fish that's been caught or farmed in environmentally responsible ways.

Fish contains high-quality protein, iodine, and various vitamins and minerals. Fish and fish products are the best dietary sources of vitamin D. The fatty types of fish, like salmon, trout, sardines, tuna and mackerel, are considered the healthiest because they are higher in fat-based nutrients. Fatty fish are also much higher in omega-3 fatty acids, essential for growth and development and linked to reduced risk of many diseases. Omega-3 fatty acids can also ease the symptoms of rheumatoid arthritis and are beneficial against depression. People who eat fish regularly seem to have a lower risk of heart attacks and strokes, and have more grey matter (the major functional tissue in your brain containing the neurons that process information and store memories). Other health benefits include lowering the risk of developing macular degeneration (a leading cause of vision impairment and blindness) and reducing the risk of Type 1 diabetes and other autoimmune diseases. Some studies show that children who eat more fish have a lower risk of developing asthma. **Caution: Children, pregnant women and women who are nursing should limit their seafood consumption to twelve ounces of low-mercury seafood per week.**

ABALONE

Abalone are large edible marine gastropods having an ear-shaped shell with a row of holes along the outer edge. They are prized not only for their flesh but also for their beautiful shells that are lined with iridescent mother-of-pearl. They eat kelp and can be found in kelp beds but are difficult to pry from the rocks they cling to. The taste of abalone is similar to scallops when tenderized before cooking. Abalone is highly regarded in Asian cultures for its health benefits and is believed to promote healthy eyes, alleviate colds, reduce fluid retention and improve circulation.

ACADIAN REDFISH

Acadian Redfish, also known as Ocean Perch, is called Redfish in New England and Canada. Acadian Redfish can weigh up to five pounds but tends to be three pounds or less. The flesh is firm and white but turns opaque white when cooked. The meat requires careful handling because it tends to spoil more quickly than other fish. Redfish is growing in popularity because of its versatility and ability to be served whole.

AMBERJACK

There are many types of Amberjack, native to tropical marine waters. They average forty to fifty pounds but smaller ones weighing fifteen pounds or less are the best to eat. They have dense flesh and a light flavor that holds up well to a variety of cooking methods. The Amberjack is a colorful fish with lavender and golden tints and an amber band from the eye to the tail. The back is blue or olive green and the side and belly are silvery-white. Some may have an amber, pinkish cast to their body. They are voracious predators that forage over reefs and wrecks in small groups.

ANCHOVIE

There are over one hundred and forty species of anchovies found in the Atlantic, Indian and Pacific Oceans, and in the Black Sea and the Mediterranean Sea. Tiny salt water fish no more than six inches long, they are green-colored as a fresh fish but change to a greyish-black color when cured. They contain a lot of small bones that are edible when cooked and are usually sold packed in oil in a can, as a paste in jars or tubes, or as a sauce. Anchovies packed fresh in oil and wine vinegar retain more of their white silvery color. White anchovies are fresher in age, more perishable and may not last long after being purchased. Their salty flavor is so strong that only a small amount of anchovy is needed to add flavor to sauces, salad dressings, pasta and pizza. Anchovies contain essential fatty acids, protein, and other nutrients. They are the fish with the least mercury that are safe to consume.

ANGLERFISH

There are more than two hundred species of Anglerfish. Dark gray to dark brown in color, they have huge heads and enormous crescent-shaped mouths filled with sharp, translucent teeth. They are bony fish, less than a foot in length but some can reach up to three feet. The only edible part is the tail, a low-fat meat similar in taste to lobster. The name 'angler' comes from the wormlike filament that grows on its head (only on females) by which it lures prey. A young, smaller male latches onto a female with his sharp teeth and eventually fuses with the female, connecting to her skin and bloodstream and losing his eyes and all his internal organs except the testes. A female will carry six or more males on her body. The deep-sea Anglerfish lives in the lightless bottom of the sea. Frogfish, a stocky Anglerfish with a plump, often brightly colored body, can jet propel itself or use its pelvic fins to walk across the sea floor, inflating like a pufferfish when threatened.

All fish have a skeleton of either bone or cartilage. The bony fish are so numerous they make up half of all vertebrates. Some bony fish fossils date back four hundred million years.

ARCTIC CHAR

There are both freshwater and saltwater Char that live in the icy waters of North America and Europe. It is also farm-raised for commercial use. Its flavor is a cross between trout and salmon and it is a good substitute for farm-raised salmon because it has a more delicate texture and mild flavor. Its high fat content makes it well-suited for broiling and smoking. Char is a good source of protein and is high in two kinds of omega-3 fatty acids.

BARNACLES

Barnacles look like empty mollusk shells but they are actually small, grayish-white crustaceans that are related to crabs and shrimp. They grow by adding calcium carbonate to the edges of their shell plates. The interior grows by shedding its exoskeleton (the way blue crabs and other crustaceans molt). They vary in size from less than half an inch to one inch in diameter and they have a flat base and an opening at the top that has two valves that open and close like trap doors. The feathery appendages emerge to collect and sweep in tiny food particles such as plankton. Barnacles live on rocks, pilings, boat hulls and other hard surfaces, and are sensitive to very cold or dry weather. The Acorn Barnacle and Gooseneck Barnacle are popular in Spanish, Portuguese and Moroccan coastal cuisines. Once steamed, the flavor is similar to other crustaceans.

BARRACUDA

The Barracuda, a saltwater ray-finned fish known for its large size, is found in tropical and subtropical oceans worldwide. The Great Barracuda that can grow to one hundred pounds or more isn't eaten because its flesh is often toxic. The Pacific, or California Barracuda is the only one marketed in the United States. It ranges from five to ten pounds. Properly handled, it poses no health threat and is good grilled or smoked.

BLACKFISH

The Blackfish, also known as Chub, is a species of freshwater fish in the Carp family. It is a lean, meaty fish with excellent flavor but contains tiny bones. It is often smoked whole which gives the skin a shiny golden color. The skin is not edible.

BLENNY

The Blenny is covered with a mucous membrane instead of scales. Only four to six inches in length, it is found in fresh and salt water. With a mild taste, it is good for frying. Recipes for this fish date back to Medieval times.

BASS

Bass is the common name shared by members of over two hundred different species of marine, brackish, and freshwater fish. Largemouth Bass and smallmouth bass are the most popular game fish in North America. About half of Striped Bass sold in markets is farmed and referred to as Hybrid Striped bass, with a milder flavor than wild bass. Its firm pink flesh has a sweet smell and the skin is edible. Striped Bass under ten pounds tend to have more tender flesh. Black Sea Bass can be found from Florida to Rhode Island and are sold as live or fresh, never frozen. The flesh is firm and lean, with a mild flavor. White Sea Bass isn't actually seabass, it's a type of Croaker known for its large size and good flavor. The European Sea Bass is a round saltwater fish found in the eastern Atlantic Ocean, the Mediterranean and Black Sea. It is now also fished off the coasts of Argentina, South Africa, Australia, and other waters in the southern latitudes. It has a rich oily flavor that is in high demand and bass farming has made it available throughout the year. The European Sea Bass can be broiled, baked, fried or steamed. The meat will appear opaque when properly cooked.

BLUEFISH

Found in the Atlantic Ocean and Gulf Coast, the Bluefish ranges from three to five pounds and can weigh as much as twenty-five pounds. It is long, forty to forty-five inches in length, with a greenish-blue body and a forked tail. Its large mouth has strong jaws and sharp teeth and it is very aggressive – it will kill another fish just for the sake of killing it. Bluefish eats squid and small schooling fish. It is best baked or broiled.

BRILL

Brill is a European saltwater flatfish that can be found in deep offshore waters in the North Atlantic, Baltic Sea and Mediterranean. It has a brown slender body covered with lighter and darker colored flecks. Like other flatfish, it has the ability to match its color to its surroundings. Brill can be broiled, fried, baked, grilled or poached.

BUFFALO FISH

Buffalo Fish, also known as Ictiobus, is a bottom-feeding species found mostly in the Mississippi River or its tributaries. It is also found in Canada, Mexico and Guatemala. It has a humped back and a network of small bones throughout. The Big Mouth Buffalo is the largest of the buffalo fish and can reach a length of more than four feet and weigh up to sixty-five pounds. Buffalo fish can be baked, poached, sautéed or grilled.

CARP

Carp is a very large group of freshwater fish from Asia and is extensively farmed in Asia, Europe, and the Middle East. In the Middle Ages, monks raised carp in ponds to provide food for fast days when they could not eat meat. Carp have long been an important food fish to humans but demand has declined in North America, partly due to a preference for trout and salmon. Several species, such as goldfish and koi, are popular ornamental fish.

CATFISH

The long feelers hanging down from around the mouth of the Catfish look like cat whiskers, hence the name. Most are freshwater but there is a saltwater one found on the Atlantic and Gulf coasts. The majority are farmed in ponds. Channel Catfish farming started in Arkansas in the 1960s and grew to the Mississippi Delta were most of the catfish farms and processing plants are today. Belzoni, Mississippi is known as the Catfish Capital of the World. Channel Catfish have a more mild-tasting and sweet flavor than the catfish caught in lakes and rivers. Catfish is sold both fresh and frozen and can be prepared in a variety of ways, including soups and stews.

CLAM

There are two main varieties of clams: hard-shell and soft-shell. Their names are based on their size and region. When buying hard-shell clams, they must be live with tightly closed shells. A bushel definition varies among suppliers so purchase them by the piece or by the pound. Hard-shell clams have a mild flavor that is sweet and briny. Steaming and baking are the most common ways of cooking. Native Americans used parts of the shell to make wampum (beads for barter).

There are two species of hard-shell clams called Littlenecks. On the East Coast, Littleneck is named after Little Neck Bay on Long Island. Pacific Littlenecks are found on the West Coast. Both measure less than two inches across and are usually eaten on the half-shell. The small, sweet Butter clam is native to the protected bays and estuaries of the Pacific Northwest. The Cherrystone Clam is medium-size. The Pismo clam, considered the best of the Pacific hard-shell class, is one of the largest types of clams found along the California Coast and can grow up to seven inches. A Mahogany clam is a marketing name for a small ocean quahog that is harvested off New England close to shore. Surf clams, dredged off the mid-Atlantic and New England coasts, are used in chowders and breaded strips. The Venus clam is farmed in remote bays along the West Coast of Mexico's Baja Peninsula. The Manila clam was introduced from Asia in the 1930s and is the largest clam resource on the West Coast.

Cockles are very similar to clams and can be eaten either raw or cooked. The Rock Cockle, found from the Pacific Northwest to San Francisco, is the best known and most widely used for food.

The soft-shell clam actually has a thin and brittle shell instead of a soft shell. It can't completely close its shell because of a long, rubbery foot that extends out of the shell. The most common East Coast soft-shell is the Steamer Clam, known as Steamers. The most famous West Coast soft-shells are the Razor Clam that resemble a folded straight razor, and the Geoduck clam with a shell about six inches long and a foot that can reach outwards up to one-and-a-half feet.

COD

Cod, from the North Pacific and Atlantic Oceans, is the name of a family of sixty species of fish that range from one and a half pounds to one hundred pounds. It is sometimes referred to as the Chicken of the Sea because of its white flaky meat and mild taste. Atlantic Cod has a lean meat and firmer texture, with a mild flavor and large white flakes when cooked. The Pacific Cod is lean and flaky with a mild taste, but is not as firm as Atlantic Cod because of a higher moisture content. Two thirds of all Pacific Cod are from Alaska and most of that is trawl-caught (pulling a fishing net through the water behind one or more boats). The quality of this fish can vary depending on how well it was handled at sea. Cod has been an important commodity in Europe for over a thousand years. Dried, salted cod was used on long voyages from Europe to the New World.

The most common cod names are Scrod, Icelandic, and Lingcod (which is a greenling, not a cod). Scrod is a term used for a young codfish, under two and one-half pounds. Icelandic is for fish caught in Icelandic waters. Lingcods, only found on the west coast of North America, are predators that can grow to over eighty pounds. They have a large mouth with eighteen teeth and their flesh is white with a mild flavor. Lingcod have been harvested for centuries by the indigenous coastal people of Alaska. Cusk, a small North Atlantic saltwater fish in the Ling family, is mainly found in New England. It is similar in nutritional value to cod and haddock and can be prepared the same as cod.

The cod family also includes Haddock, Hake, Hoki and Pollock. Haddock's thin connective tissue layer differentiates it from cod. It is one of the most popular fish used in British fish and chips. Smoked haddock is called *finnan haddie*. Hake is found in the Atlantic and northern Pacific Oceans. Hoki is a type of fish in the hake family, found off the coasts of New Zealand and Australia. Pollock differs from other codfish because its lower jaw extends beyond the upper jaw. It has a mild flavor and firm texture with a nice flake. It can be found in the waters from California to Alaska as well in the waters of Russia, China, and Japan. In the United States, Pollock is caught by large factory trawlers that process the fish at sea, either making surimi or frozen block products. Surimi is the main ingredient in Imitation crab.

NOTE: Don't confuse Alaskan Pollock with the two pollocks from the Atlantic. Atlantic Pollock is larger and has a higher oil content than Alaskan Pollock, which is a different species. Alaskan Pollock averages three pounds in size.

CHILEAN SEA BASS

The Chilean Sea Bass is not a bass, it's a cod. It is a big fish that can weigh one hundred pounds, although the average is closer to twenty pounds. First commercially harvested in Chilean waters, it is mostly found in arctic regions. Prior to 1977, it was called the Patagonian or Antarctic Toothfish.

CONCH

Most conch (pronounced conk) are found in warm waters and are popular in Florida, the Caribbean, Southern Europe, and China. Conch is often used in chowders, eaten raw in salads, or sautéed after being tenderized. It is the second best known edible snail (the first is escargot).

CORAL

Coral, the eggs of a crustacean (roe), gets its name from the coral-red color it turns when cooked. It is often eaten directly from a lobster or crab.

NOTE: Roe is the eggs of a fish, from Coral to rare Caspian sturgeon caviars like beluga.

CRAB

Crab is any one of a large variety of crustaceans that have a shell and five pair of legs (the first pair have pincers). They are found in cold and warm water as well as fresh and salt water. The oldest crab industry in the United States is the Blue Crab industry of the Chesapeake Bay area, dating back to the early 1600s. The Blue Crab is from the Atlantic seaboard and Gulf coast. America has more varieties of crabs than anywhere else in the world. The major crabs from the Pacific are the Dungeness, the King, and the Snow crab.

In order for a crab to grow larger, it must periodically shed its old shell. The new shell is soft, and for a few days it is a Soft-shell Crab. The Blue Crab is the most commonly eaten soft-shell crab in the U.S. The tinges of blue on the dark shell are what give it its name. It is a very small crab, averaging only four to six 6 inches across. Males grow larger than females and the claws on the male are blue, while a female's are orange-tipped. The tiny soft-shell Oyster Crab, also known as Popcorn Crab, is less than one inch wide. It is a parasite that lives inside oysters. It can be quick fried and added to various dishes for a crunchy texture.

The Stone Crab, from Florida, has an oval shell. Only one claw is harvested and then it is released to grow a new one, which can take one to two years. Female Stone Crabs are not allowed to be de-clawed.

The Dungeness Crab, first commercially harvested in the town of Dungeness, Washington can be found from Alaska to Mexico. It can range from one to four pounds and is one of the most flavorful of all crabs.

The Snow Crab, also known as the Queen Crab or Spider Crab, is harvested off Canada's North Atlantic coasts. The meat is mild and sweet and usually served cool in salads or added to a variety of dishes.

The King Crab is the largest member of the Spider Crab family (legs on spider crabs are jointed backwards). It can grow up to six feet across. It is found around Alaska's and Japan's northern Pacific waters but most of the king crab sold in the U.S. comes from Russia. Only male King Crabs, which are much larger than females, are fished. The Red King Crab can weigh up to twenty pounds. The Blue King Crab, with dark coloring on the tip of its legs, is almost as large as the Red King Crab. The Brown King Crab, also known as Golden King Crab, is smaller.

Backfin is a blend of broken pieces of jumbo lump and special crab meat. It is often used in crab cakes, dips, salads and casseroles, and for stuffing fish, chicken, vegetables or seafood.

CRAYFISH

Crayfish, any of the more than five hundred species of crustaceans that resemble tiny lobsters, are also known as crawfish, crawdads, freshwater lobsters, or mudbugs. Most are fresh water species (a few are salt water) that grow to three to six inches in length and weigh from two to eight ounces. More than half of them can be found in North America, particularly in Kentucky and Louisiana in the Mississippi Basin. The tail meat is the only edible part. Battered and fried, they are known as Cajun popcorn. Breaux Bridge, Louisiana is the Crawfish Capital of the World.

CUTTLEFISH

Cuttlefish resemble a large squid and can reach up to sixteen inches in length. They have ten tentacles, eight of which have suction cups on their inner surface. Two longer arms can launch out to capture prey. Cuttlefish can be prepared like squid and octopus, and are popular in Japanese, Indian, and Mediterranean cuisines.

DOGFISH

Dogfish, also called Huss, is the name for several species of small sharks found in the northeast Atlantic Ocean, the Pacific Ocean, and the Mediterranean Sea. The most well-known are the Spiny Dogfish and the Smooth Dogfish. The names refer to the size and shape of the fish, and the young are called pups. It is a white fish with a lot of flavor, partly due to its diet which includes crustaceans. Dogfish is a popular fish sold in Fish & Chip shops.

DRUM

Drum, spiny-finned fish, are found in both the Atlantic and Pacific oceans. One type can be found in mid-North American freshwater. The Drum can weigh up to thirty pounds but usually average only one pound. A subclass of Drum is the Croaker, named for the deep croaking noise it makes, mostly during breeding season.

EEL

The Eel is a snake-like fish that range in length from four inches to ten feet. The different species live in fresh and saltwater throughout much of the world. It is popular in many cuisines, particularly Japanese, Chinese, and in Europe where it is sometimes smoked or jellied. The thick, tough skin, once used as leather, must be removed before cooking. According to legend, in parts of the Philippines, eels are the souls of the dead. In Europe, it is thought that rubbing your skin with eel oil will cause you to see fairies.

FLOUNDER

Flounder is any one of several species of large flatfish. It is often sold as Filet of Sole in the United States. Alaska has the largest Flounder resource in the world. Flounder is low in fat with a delicate flavor and can be prepared sautéed, baked, broiled, poached, or steamed. The color of a raw Flounder fillet ranges from tan to pinkish to snow white but they all turn pure white when cooked. As a Flounder becomes a bottom dweller, one of its eyes moves over to the other side, causing either a right-eyed or left-eyed flatfish. Most of the Flounder harvested for commercial use will be right eyed, except for Fluke (also called Summer Flounder). Fluke is considered a good source of B vitamins and niacin. It has edible skin and flaky white meat. Yellowtail Flounder are caught on the Atlantic coast. They are a lean, flaky fish with a mild sweet taste and firm texture. The best way to cook Flounder is with wine, sauces, and other liquids to help keep them from drying out.

FLYINGFISH

The Flyingfish is found in most tropical waters but especially in the Caribbean. The name comes from its ability to soar through the air for great distances. It is a small fish with a firm texture and mild flavor.

Gefilte fish is made of ground, deboned White Fish that has been formed into fish balls or patties. The consistency can vary from chunky to smooth, or jellied like the type sold in jars.

GROUPER

Grouper is the largest of the Sea Bass family. It is usually found in the tropical and subtropical waters of the Atlantic and Gulf of Mexico. There are more than one hundred species that grow from nine inches to nine feet. The Spotted Jewfish can weigh up to six hundred pounds. Grouper has a mild flavor. The lean, firm meat should be skinned before cooking. Grouper is considered a good source of vitamins B6 and B12, phosphorus, potassium, and selenium. Red Grouper is the most common type. It is not as firm and has a milder, sweeter flavor than the Black or Gag types. Gag Fish are marketed as Black Grouper. They are very similar in taste and texture. Both of these fish have a high oil and moisture content which makes them suitable to cook many different ways.

HALIBUT

Halibut, a species of Flounder, is a saltwater fish found in the Northern Pacific and Atlantic oceans. Alaskan Halibut or Pacific Halibut are the largest flatfish as well as one of the largest fish species in the sea. They can grow up to eight feet in length and can weigh over six hundred pounds, but most will be from ten to two hundred pounds. The California type is usually between four to twelve pounds and commonly filleted because it is not large enough to cut into steaks. The mild and sweet tasting flavor of California Halibut resembles Summer Flounder.

Classified as White Fish, Halibut is low-fat with a mild flavor. Halibut cheeks are a delicacy, with a texture similar to crab. The size of the cheeks can range from a few ounces to over a pound. Frozen Halibut cooks faster than fresh halibut but has a reputation for being dry.

NOTE: Over-fishing in the Atlantic has put Halibut on the endangered list.

HERRING

Herring is a saltwater and freshwater fish with over one hundred varieties. Most swim in large schools in the cold waters of the North Atlantic and Pacific oceans, the Baltic Sea, and the Mediterranean, as well as the Mississippi River and the Finger Lakes. They are small, usually less than one pound, with no scales and a silvery skin tinged with blue-green tones. The Shad variety can grow to three to five pounds and its eggs become Shad roe.

Young Herring are frequently packaged as sardines (although the only true sardine comes from the Mediterranean). They are a high-fat fish often salted and smoked (kippers), and also pickled. Atlantic Herring has a high oil content and a soft, fine texture when cooked fresh. It is also sold cured with smoke, salt, or other spices. Herring are highly perishable so most are sold canned and frozen as whole fish.

JOHN DORY

John Dory is native to Europe and rarely exported to the United States. It has a flat, curved body and an unusual-looking head that is large and spiny. It has a mild flavor and can be pan fried, baked, broiled or grilled.

LANGOUSTINE

Langoustines, found in both the Atlantic Ocean and the Mediterranean Sea, are pinkish-orange saltwater crustaceans that look like very small lobsters. They can grow up to nine inches long and have two claws but the tail is the only part that is eaten. Some restaurants call very large shrimp Langoustine, but it is not a shrimp.

LIMPET

Limpets are gastropods that can be found clinging to rocks. They are mainly found in coastal areas. The meat can be eaten raw or lightly sautéed.

LOBSTER

There are two major varieties of lobsters: those with claws and those without claws. The most common with claws is the Maine Lobster, also called the American Lobster. About ninety percent of the United States lobster supply is caught off the coast of Maine. The Chicken Lobster, weighing about a pound, is the smallest lobster allowed to be sold in the U.S. It takes four to six Chicken Lobsters to make one pound of meat. The meatiest part of the lobster is the tail. Whole lobsters are best steamed, boiled, or broiled.

The main difference between the American whole lobster and the clawless lobster, known as Spiny or Rock Lobster, is that the Spiny does not have any front claws. There are around forty species of clawless lobster found throughout the world. The clawless lobster, ranging from one to five pounds, supplies most of the lobster tails served in restaurants. The tail is about thirty three percent of their body weight.

There are two types of lobster tails: warm-water tails and cold-water tails. Warm-water tails mainly come from Brazil, Florida, Cuba, Nicaragua, or the Caribbean. Cold-water tails come from Australia, New Zealand, or South Africa and are harder to find locally unless you have a good fish market, a high-end grocer, or buy online. Cold-water tails are tender and have a whiter meat, and may be much sweeter than warm water types. They also shrink less when cooked. Most lobster tails that are sold will be the warm-water type due to the less expensive price. Frozen tails are readily available but read the label if buying a packaged product – tails can be soaked in sodium tripoyphosphate which helps preserve the frozen tail longer in storage. Don't buy thawed lobster tails.

MACKEREL

Mackerel are saltwater fish found in the Atlantic Ocean and off both the North American and European coasts. There are sixty species and they are classified as an oily fish with pale and firm flesh. They have a strong savory taste. The Albacore, Bonito, Tuna, and King Mackerel, also called Kingfish (Pacific Kingfish is also called Wahoo) can be smoked, salted, or canned. Mackerel is a good source of omega-3 fatty acids, selenium, niacin, vitamin B6, and vitamin B12.

MAHI-MAHI

Mahi-Mahi is a dolphinfish (but not the mammal dolphin). It was marketed under its Hawaiian name to avoid confusion. It is found in the tropical and sub-tropical waters around the world. Mahi-mahi can reach up to fifty pounds but averages five pounds. Its diet includes squid, shrimp and crab, and it sometimes pursues flying fish by leaping out of the water. It is a sweet-flavored fish, low in saturated fat and a good source of vitamins B12 and B6, phosphorus, potassium, niacin, and selenium. It is usually frozen at sea when caught. Mahi-mahi can be grilled with the skin on or off.

MARLIN

There are about ten species of Marlin native to the tropical and temperate waters of the Atlantic, Pacific, and Indian Oceans. Marlin has an elongated body and a spear-like snout, and is among the fastest fish in the ocean. The Marlin is the fish that is featured in Ernest Hemingway's 1952 novel, *The Old Man and the Sea*. The Blue Marlin is the largest of the Atlantic Marlins and one of the biggest fish in the world. Females are significantly larger than males and can reach fourteen feet in length and weigh almost two thousand pounds, but average sizes range eleven feet and two hundred to four hundred pounds. Its meat is considered a delicacy, particularly in Japan, where it is served raw as sashimi.

The Black Marlin is found in tropical and subtropical areas of the Indian and Pacific Oceans. It is a mid-sized fish with a rounded and forked snout and rigid pectoral fins. White Marlin's most noticeable feature is the dorsal fin. White Marlin fishing is very popular but there are restrictions in place to limit the size of fish that can be taken. Ocean City, Maryland is known as the White Marlin Capital of the World. Researchers have identified White Marlin fossils dating back fifteen million years. The Striped Marlin is a smaller type found in tropical to temperate Indo-Pacific oceans.

MONKFISH

Monkfish, sometimes called Anglerfish, can be found in the Atlantic Ocean, Mediterranean Sea, and other northern European waters. Just above the mouth is a spike-like apparatus used to entice prey by waving it back and forth. It is a large fish but the boneless tail is the only part that has any meat. Monkfish have a mild taste and texture similar to lobster.

MULLET

There are over one hundred species of Mullet. It is a round-bodied saltwater fish found throughout the world in coastal temperate and tropical waters. Some species can also be in fresh water. Freshwater mullet is delicate with mild, white flesh. The two most commercially harvested species of mullet fish in Florida are the Striped Mullet and White Mullet. The Striped Mullet is commonly called a Black Mullet, Gray Mullet, or Jumping Mullet and the White Mullet is called a Silver Mullet. Although classified as White Fish, the flesh is actually oily. It is the only fish that has a gizzard (like a chicken) that is used to grind up and digest plant material. Its average weight is two to three pounds but it can reach six pounds. Mullet swim in large schools and are commonly seen jumping out of the water. The firm, light meat has a moderate flavor. Their roe is considered a delicacy.

MUSSEL

There are about seventeen species of edible mussels that are harvested or cultivated worldwide. They have been used as a food source for more than twenty thousand years and cultivated for almost eight hundred years in Europe. During elections in ancient Greece, votes were cast by scratching the names of candidates inside mussel shells. Mussels have thin, oblong shells ranging in size from one and one half to six inches long. Their color can be blue, green, or yellow-brown. Blue Mussels, found along the Atlantic and Pacific coasts, are the most widely consumed mussel in North America. Mediterranean mussels are most common in Europe but are now grown on the Pacific coast of North America. Cooked mussels are used in bouillabaisse and paella. Canned or smoked mussels are also available. Mussels feed by filtering up to eighteen gallons of water per day so their flavor is influenced by the minerals in the water.

OCTOPUS

Octopus are cephalopods. Most octopi don't grow more than two feet, which includes their tentacles. They are predators that eat other mollusks. Their body and tentacles are edible and the meat is flavorful but rubbery. They are popular in Japanese and Mediterranean cuisines and can be eaten raw or prepared in a variety of ways. Smoked and canned octopus is also available. The black ink can be used to color and flavor pastas and other dishes.

NOTE: Cephalopods have advanced beyond the need for an external shell. They all share two major characteristics: tentacles attached to the head and ink sacs. The sacs are used to evade predators.

ORANGE ROUGHY

The Orange Roughy fish was first discovered in the deep cold waters of New Zealand and Australia, where it was known as a Slimehead. The name changed to improve marketing. Uncooked, it has pearly white meat, with the skin side sometimes showing an orange to brown color. The flavor is moist, mild and delicate. Its moderate oil content helps it to retain moisture when cooking in a variety of ways.

OYSTER

Oysters are a bivalve mollusk found around the world in natural and cultivated beds. There are three species harvested in the United States, each named for the place they are found: the Pacific, Eastern (or Atlantic), and the Olympia. There are various market names for the same species, such as the Bluepoint named after a town on Long Island in New York. Oysters are filter feeders – they syphon up to twenty-five gallons of water a day through their system so their flavor is influenced by the trace minerals in the water. Oysters are a good source of vitamins A, B1, B2, B3, C and D, as well as iron and calcium. They can be eaten raw on the half-shell, cooked, batter-fried, or added to special dishes. They are also canned, frozen, and smoked. *"Don't eat oysters in a month spelled without an R"* is an old rule of thumb that warned against eating them in the hot summer months when spoilage could cause food poisoning. Refrigeration now makes them available year-round.

Oysters have been cultivated for at least two thousand years. The Chinese cultivated them in ponds. The ancient Romans imported them from all over the Empire, sending slaves to gather them from the English Channel. Aphrodite, the Greek goddess of love and beauty, emerged from the sea on an oyster shell – some people think this is why they are known as an aphrodisiac. Colonists in America found an abundance of oysters along the coastlines and in the bays. Before the nineteenth century, oysters were inexpensive and the working classes were able to eat them. As the demand for them increased, foreign varieties were introduced which brought disease, and they became a rare delicacy. The city of Crisfield, Maryland is built on a foundation of oyster shells. Virginia is known as the Oyster Capital of the east coast. The world's only oyster museum is located in Chincoteague Island, Virginia.

PERCH

Many species of freshwater gamefish resemble Perch but to be considered a true Perch the fish must be of the family Percidae. There are more than six hundred species of Perch. Its white and flaky meat is flavorful and low in fats and rich in phosphorous, manganese, selenium and vitamin B12. It also contains omega-3 fatty acids but is high in cholesterol.

Freshwater Nile Perch is found in the lakes and rivers of central Africa. Commercial sizes range from six to fourteen pounds but can reach up to three hundred pounds and six feet in length. It has a mild flavor and a moist, medium-firm texture.

PLAICE

Plaice is a saltwater flatfish found in the North Pacific and North Atlantic, and from the Barents Sea (located off the northern coasts of Norway and Russia) to the Mediterranean. Plaice can grow to twenty-eight inches and have a mild flavor. They can be filleted, battered and fried, and also make a good substitute in Sole recipes.

POMPANO

Pompano is a saltwater fish found off the South Atlantic and Gulf states. Florida Pompano are common in inshore and nearshore waters, especially along sandy beaches, along oyster banks, and over grass beds. They are also found in turbid water and may be in water as deep as one hundred and thirty feet. Pompano has a mild flavor and many consider it to be America's finest fish. The Pacific Pompano is a variety of Butterfish.

PRAWN

The term 'prawn' is used to refer to a variety of shellfish that are members of the lobster family, such as Italian Scampi, Spanish Langostino, and Florida Lobsterette. They are shaped like small Maine lobsters, six to eight inches long. Prawn can also describe any large shrimp, called jumbo shrimp or colossal shrimp. It also refers to freshwater prawn that look like elongated lobsters with long spindly legs – they are different from shrimp that live in salt water.

PUFFERFISH

Pufferfish is a delicacy in the Philippines and Japan (it is the only food not permitted to be served to the Emperor of Japan). It is one of the most poisonous vertebrate in the world (the first is the Golden Poison Frog). One fish contains a poison sac so toxic it is enough to kill thirty people. About one hundred people die every year of pufferfish poisoning. Fishermen must wear thick gloves to avoid poisoning from the skin or by getting bitten when removing the fish from the hook. Only qualified chefs trained in removing the sac may prepare it.

Jellyfish is popular mainly in Chinese cuisines. Rarely found fresh, they are almost always dried and salted or in long strands resembling cellophane noodles.

ROCKFISH

There are seventy species of Rockfish. Some are named after their physical characteristics but most are named after the color of their skin, such as copper, olive, red, green, blue, and brown. Those that live deeper in the water are much brighter in color. Common market names include Pacific Red Snapper, Rock Cod, and Pacific Ocean Perch. The Alaskan Rockfish is an ocean fish with a delicate, nutty flavor. Rockfish fillets can be either red-fleshed or brown-fleshed. Red is the more desirable of the two categories due to a longer shelf life and less oil content. The lean delicate meat has a sweet, nutty flavor with a medium to firm texture. The Chilipepper Rockfish, that lives in deep water, is one of the most important commercial species of the Rockfish family. Other types include Pygmy, Shortbelly, Yelloweye, Quillback, Longspine, Vermillion, and Canary.

SABLEFISH

Also known as Butterfish or Black Cod (although it doesn't belong to the Cod family), the Sablefish is a deep-sea fish that can be found in the waters from central Baja California to Japan and the Bering Sea. Most Sablefish are trap-caught to eliminate unnecessary bycatch. It has pearly white flesh that flakes into large chunks when prepared, with a buttery taste and texture. Its high fat content makes it ideal for smoking.

SAND DAB

Sand Dab, a flatfish, inhabits the waters from Alaska to Central America. Commercial fishing is restricted to the Pacific coast. Sand Dabs have a delicate, sweet flavor and are usually pan-fried or grilled with the bone – the scales don't have to be removed.

SARDINE

Sardines, found in the Mediterranean, are small young saltwater fish with soft edible bones. They are related to herring and were named after the island of Sardinia. Fresh sardines must be chilled immediately and eaten as soon as possible. Most sardines are canned. Older sardine fish, larger than four inches, are called Pilchards. There are other small, young saltwater fish found that are called sardines, such as the Pacific and Atlantic Herring, Blueback Herring and Sprat, but they are not true sardines.

SEA BREAM

Sea Bream, found mainly in the Mediterranean Sea, is a round fish that grows to two feet in length. It has a slightly sweet flavor.

Salmon is both a saltwater and freshwater fish –it is born in fresh water and migrates to the ocean, then returns to fresh water to reproduce. Wild salmon gets its coloring from eating tiny shellfish. Most of the salmon supply is farmed and Atlantic salmon account for more than ninety-five percent of farmed salmon. The majority of these farms are located in Australia, Canada, Chile, Norway, Russia, and the U.K. Often, Atlantic salmon takes on the name of the country where it was farmed, such as Norwegian Salmon. It takes about three years to raise an Atlantic salmon to ten pounds. The flavor is milder than wild salmon and the flesh coloration ranges from a deep orange to a pinkish-orange, depending on the type of feed used in the different farms.

Coho Salmon has a rich, reddish-orange meat and has been called one of the best tasting salmon. It costs less than King and Sockeye Salmon but its quality is high. Coho are a medium fatty salmon that have nearly two times the oil content of Pink and Chum salmon, but less than Sockeye or King. Chum, the meatiest of the wild salmon, has a mild taste, is low in sodium, and is a good source of omega-3 fatty acids, niacin, vitamin B12, and selenium. Chum is sometimes sold as Coho because they are similar in size.

King Salmon (or Chinook), is the largest, weighing from five to forty pounds but can exceed one hundred ponds. Sockeye Salmon can weigh up to fifteen pounds and has the reddest flesh of any salmon species. It has a high oil content and the highest level of omega-3 essential fatty acids. The further sockeye are caught from their birthplace, the higher the quality. Pink Salmon is the smallest wild Pacific salmon. Its flesh is pale pink, is softer than most salmon, and has a small flake. It contains a relatively low amount of oil and has a mild-flavor. Pink Salmon is mostly sold frozen or canned.

Season and grill salmon fillets or steaks.

SCALLOP

A scallop is a mollusk that propels itself along the bottom of the ocean by opening and closing its shell. There are hundreds of species of scallop around the world but the three most popular in the United States are the North Atlantic, the Bay, and imported scallops. North Atlantic sea scallops are harvested from Nova Scotia to Virginia. They are the largest scallops sold in the U.S. Bay scallops live in bays and estuaries from New England to the Gulf of Mexico and are smaller and sweeter, and more expensive. There is also a tiny Calico scallop that is caught off the coast of Florida. Other Bay Scallops are imported from Peru, Mexico, Canada, China and Japan. The part eaten in the U.S. is the disc-shaped muscle that connect a scallop's tissue to its shell, used to open and close the shell. Live scallops are eaten whole, like clams or oysters. Many frozen scallops come from China where they are farm raised. When buying frozen scallops, avoid any that list tripolyphosphate on the label.

SEA URCHIN

The sea urchin has a hard shell that is covered by prickly spines and can grow up to ten inches in diameter. Its mouth is underneath because it is constantly grazing as it moves. It is harvested mostly for its eggs and is considered a delicacy in Japan, Korea, and other Asian countries. The name 'sea urchin' comes from the Old English name for spiny hedgehog.

SHAD

Shad is the largest member of the Herring family. It is born in freshwater and migrates to saltwater to mature, then returns to freshwater to spawn. It has a slight oiliness and mild flavor and is hard to fillet because of its many bones. It can be steamed or baked at a low temperature for six hours, until the bones disintegrate.

SKATE

Skate, a large saltwater flatfish, is part of the Ray family and is related to the shark. There are over two hundred species found worldwide. The fins, or wings, are boneless and are the only edible part of the fish. The meat has a mild, sweet flavor.

SMELT

Smelt are found on the northern east coast of the United States as well as in many lakes and ponds in New Hampshire, Maine, and various Canadian lakes. They spawn in fresh water but live in saltwater. Smelt are small fish (seven to nine inches longs and no more than six ounces) that are similar in appearance to sardines and anchovies. They are full of healthy nutrients and low in mercury.

SHRIMP

There are hundreds of species of shrimp found worldwide. They can live in freshwater, saltwater, brackish water* or a combination of habitats. Most are divided into warm-water (large shrimp) or cold-water (small shrimp). Warm-water shrimp come from tropical waters in southern parts of the world and cold-water shrimp come from colder northern waters. Larger cold-water shrimp have a sweeter flavor than smaller sizes. Size also varies by region. Names include Colossal Shrimp, Jumbo Shrimp, Extra-large Shrimp, Large Shrimp, Medium Shrimp, Small Shrimp, and Popcorn Shrimp. Large typically means about forty shrimp per cooked pound, Medium has about fifty, and Small has about sixty. In the United States, Colossal and Jumbo Shrimp are called Prawns. Shrimp is low in saturated fat and a very good source of selenium and vitamin B12.

Gulf Pink Shrimp are tender and mild with sweet-tasting flesh in their tails. Key West Pinks are easy to distinguish as they have a bright pink color when raw. Pacific Pink Shrimp, also known as Ocean Shrimp, are smaller than northern shrimp. Almost all Pacific Pink Shrimp are cooked and peeled and sold fresh or frozen. Alaskan Prawn, also known as Spot Shrimp, are mostly frozen aboard the boat and sold frozen raw, whole, or raw shell-on tails. These shrimp have a sweet flavor, particularly the largest ones, and are expensive.

Shrimp are crustaceans like lobster and crab that belong to the arthropod category: they have their skeleton on the outside instead of the inside. The exoskeleton is rich in nutrients and commonly consumed in most other countries but not in the United States. Shrimp account for about thirty percent of all seafood consumed in the U.S. They are sold peeled, unpeeled, veined, deveined, and with head on or head off. Deveining a shrimp is not done for health safety, but for cosmetic reasons. There are various shrimp products, such as breaded or stuffed shrimp, shrimp spread, dried shrimp, and shrimp paste.

*Brackish water, also called briny water, is water that falls in between freshwater and saltwater.

SNAIL

Snails have been eaten as food since ancient Roman times, or before. Apicius, the author of the oldest surviving cookbook (First century B.C.), has a recipe for snails in his cookbook. Conch is the second best known edible snail, the first being Escargot from Burgundy, France. Escargot is a generic term for edible snails. The most common preparation is boiling or steaming, and the snails are often served in the shell on a special plate that has small depressions for each shell. They are served with a variety of sauces – garlic and butter is the most common. Snails can be collected in the wild or farmed.

SNAPPER

Snapper, a Whitefish, is mainly a saltwater fish but some live in estuaries. Red Snapper, one of the best-known varieties, is found in the waters from North Carolina to Florida and the coastal waters of Louisiana and Texas. Red Snapper sold on the West Coast may be Rockfish, which has a very different texture and flavor. Snapper eat shrimp, which is what gives them their red coloring. The common market size is four to six pounds although some can be as large as thirty-five pounds. When used for sushi, Red Snapper is known as *Tai* (although several other species are also marketed as *Tai*). There are many other species of Snapper that can be cooked different ways. Imported Snapper comes from Mexico.

SNOOK

Snook are found from central Florida south, usually in coastal and brackish waters, and are also on reefs and around pilings near shore. The most abundant of the twelve Snook species is the Common Snook, which changes from male to female after maturation. The skin must be removed before cooking. Three U.S. Navy submarines have been named for this species.

SOLE

Most Sole are saltwater flatfish but some types live in fresh water. They can grow to twenty-eight inches in length. They have a mild buttery flavor. The true Dover Sole, named for the English fishing port and fished in the eastern North Atlantic off Europe, is highly valued and priced. The Dover Sole fished off the West Coast of Alaska is a Flounder and sells for a lot less. It has a delicate taste and firm-texture although it is not as mild as English Dover Sole. Yellowfin Sole has a firm, delicate texture with small flakes when cooked, with a mild, sweet flavor.

NOTE: Flatfish quality can vary. Look for Dover Sole that has uniform color and lacks bruises. Don't purchase these fish whole since soft-fleshed fish may not be detected until after they've been filleted.

SQUID

Also called Calamari, Squid is a mollusk with an internal shell called a pen. Market squid have eight arms and two tentacles and can grow from two to ten inches long. There are almost one hundred species of squid. The Japanese Flying Squid and the Argentine Shortfin Squid account for over half the world harvest. Squid is popular in Asian and Mediterranean cuisines, although fried Calamari is a popular appetizer in the United States. A squid's ink, used to color or flavor foods, is a milky and purple iridescent coloring that can change depending on environmental factors. Frozen squid will have a reddish tinge, and poor-quality squid will smell like iodine or ammonia.

STURGEON

Sturgeon matures in saltwater but migrates to fresh water to spawn. It can weigh up to sixty pounds although some specimens grow much larger. The roe from a sturgeon is considered the true caviar and is more important than its meat.

SUSHI

Sushi originated in Southeast Asia in the fourth century B.C. as a method for preserving fish. The fermentation of the rice prevented the fish from spoiling. Sushi actually means 'vinegared rice' and does not need to contain raw fish at all. It is a rice dish which may include vegetables, cooked fish, raw fish, poultry or other proteins.

SWORDFISH

Swordfish, a large elongated round saltwater fish, can reach fourteen feet in length and over one thousand pounds but most are between fifty to two hundred pounds. It can be found in all tropical to temperate oceans including the Atlantic and Pacific oceans, and is only fished at night. The United States is a major market for Swordfish but American fishermen only catch about five percent (Japan and Taiwan are leading producers). Swordfish meat is firm and flavorful and ideal for grilling and broiling. Quality can vary greatly because swordfish boats will be at sea for different lengths of time. Bright white or pink Swordfish meat with a bright red bloodline denotes freshness. Avoid swordfish meat that is gray with brown bloodlines. Swordfish is a good source of selenium, niacin, vitamin B12, and zinc.

TILAPIA

Tilapia has been farmed for at least forty-five hundred years and is now farmed in dozens of countries. In the United States, Tilapia consumption is higher than Trout. It is a white fish with a mild, bland flavor – it tastes like the water where it was raised. According to legend, Tilapia is the fish Jesus served the multitudes, and its nickname is St. Peter's fish.

TILEFISH

Tilefish are small, slender bottom-dwelling fish found in warm sandy areas, especially near coral reefs. They resemble the Sea Bass family in appearance. There are six species found along the Atlantic coast of the United States. Two species, the Golden Tilefish and the Blueline Tilefish, are plentiful near Florida. The Golden is the most colorful. Tilefish is low in fat and has a firm but tender white meat with a delicate sweet flavor, similar to lobster or crab. The Blueline is similar in taste.

The Tripletail, or Atlantic Tripletail, is a warm-water marine fish found across the tropics. Rounded fins and tail fin give the Tripletail fish its name. It averages about nineteen to twenty inches in length. It will often lie just below the surface of the water, floating with one side exposed, possible waiting for its dinner to swim by, but there is no scientific evaluation of why it behaves this way. The flesh of the Tripletail is firm and white, and considered by many to be equal to or superior to Red Snapper or Grouper.

TROUT

Trout, a member of the Salmon family, is the name given to a number of round bodied freshwater fish mostly found in cool streams and lakes. They are born in freshwater but migrate to the sea and return to freshwater to spawn. There are many types, including Speckled, Steelhead, Silver, and Rainbow. Rainbow Trout have been farmed throughout the world for hundreds of years. Small trout farms can be found in almost every state but Idaho produces eighty percent in the United States. Farmed trout take ten to twelve months to grow to a pound or two but in the wild, Rainbow Trout can reach fifty pounds. Trout have a delicate meat with a mild flavor. They are eaten fresh or smoked. Claudius Aelian, an ancient Roman author and teacher, wrote about trout fishing in Macedonia with artificial flies and hooks.

NOTE: Sea Trout, also known as Weakfish, is a round saltwater fish with a mild, sweet flavor that can be broiled, baked, or fried.

TUNA

Tuna is a round saltwater fish that is more popular canned than fresh. It can be found in tropical and subtropical oceans worldwide. Popular species include Albacore and Yellowfin. Albacore tuna is commonly eighty pounds and can reach two hundred pounds. It has a mild flavor and contains more omega-3 fatty acids than other tunas. It is the only tuna that can be called White in the United States (and it is the most expensive canned tuna). The Hawaiian name for the Yellowfin tuna is *Ahi* (meaning 'fire'). When these tuna feed at night the bright yellow dorsal fin and the yellow strip down its side resemble flashes of fire. It is one of the largest tunas and can weigh up to four hundred pounds. It has a similar texture to beef, with a mild flavor that is more flavorful than Albacore, and is often eaten raw as sushi. Canned Yellowfin tuna is marketed as light tuna and is slightly darker than Albacore.

Skipjack is the species most commonly used in canned tuna and mainly sold as chunk light tuna. It is also available fresh and frozen. Skipjack gets its name because it seems to skip out of the water. Other types of tuna include Blackfin, the smallest species (weighing no more than forty-six pounds), Northern Bluefin, the most rare tuna and used only in sushi and sashimi (weighing over one thousand pounds), Pacific Bluefin (weighing up to twelve hundred pounds), and Southern Bluefin (weighing over eight hundred pounds).

TURBOT

Turbot, a diamond-shaped flatfish, is a saltwater fish found in the Mediterranean, Baltic Sea, Black Sea, and the North Atlantic. It is also farmed in Spain, Chile, and China. It can grow to forty pounds in the wild. Turbot has a delicate flavor and bright white meat. It is considered to be the King of all flatfish. Special Turbot kettles were designed so that cooks in upper class households could cook large, whole fish.

WHELK

Whelk, also known as Scungilli, is related to the Conch. It is popular in Italian and Chinese cuisines. Naturally tough, it must be cooked for a long time or tenderized before cooking. Smooth Conch inhabit tropical waters and are vegan. Knobbed Whelk live in cooler waters and are carnivorous.

Fantastic Fish Facts

- Most fish reproduce by laying eggs but some fish give birth to live babies, called pups.
- A female Sunfish can lay three hundred million eggs each year and each egg is smaller than the period at the end of a sentence.
- Some fish can raise their body temperature which helps them hunt for prey in cold water.
- Fish do not have vocal chords; they use a variety of low-pitched sounds to convey messages to each other such as moans, grunts, hisses, whistles, creaks, shrieks and wails. They also rattle their bones and gnash their teeth and use other parts of their bodies to make noise.
- Fish form schools containing millions of fish. The fish in the middle of a school control the school; the fish on the outside are guided by those in the middle. Special hairs in their pores sense changes in water pressure from the movements of other fish or predators.
- There are some species of fish that enjoy swimming backwards. This is more of a preference than something it naturally does.
- Sharks and Rays do not have swim bladders and have to swim all the time, even when they are sleeping, or they will sink to the bottom of the ocean.
- Many fish can shoot their mouths forward like a spring to catch startled prey because their jaw is not attached to their skull.
- Electric Eels and Electric Rays have enough electricity to kill a horse.
- Fish have sleep-like periods but they do not share the same changes in brain waves as humans do when they sleep.
- Most fish have taste buds all over their body.
- Saltwater fish need to drink more water than freshwater fish.
- Many fish use colors to camouflage themselves.

- The Batfish plays dead when in danger. It floats motionless on its side, making it look like a dead leaf floating on the surface of the water.
- Sharks are the only fish that have eyelids.
- Anableps, four-eyed fish, can see above and below water at the same time.
- Fish can see you peering at them in a fish tank.
- Most fish can see in color.
- A Seahorse can move each of its eyes separately. One eye can look forward while the other looks backward.
- Seahorses can change their color to match their environment.
- Seahorses are the only fish that swim upright.
- Female Seahorses lay their eggs inside a pouch on the male's belly. When the babies are ready to hatch, the male holds onto a piece of seaweed with his tail and rocks back and forth until the babies pop out of his pouch.
- The Seahorse is the slowest moving fish.
- The fastest moving fish is the Sailfish.
- The biggest fish in the world is the giant Whale Shark that can grow to nearly sixty feet and can weigh over twenty-five tons.
- The world's smallest fish are the freshwater Pygmy and Luzon Gobies of the Philippines, the saltwater Marshal Islands Goby, and the tiny Rice Fish from Thailand. They all reach a maximum length of about the size of a grain of rice.
- The brownish colored Stone Fish looks like a stone on the ocean floors. Its sting can cause shock, paralysis, and even death if not treated within a few hours.
- The Mudskipper spends most of its time out of water and can walk on its fins. It carries a portable water supply in its gill chambers when it leaves the water. It can also breathe through the pores of its wet skin.
- A Lungfish has both gills and a lung and can live out of water for several years. It secretes a mucus cocoon and burrows itself under the dirt. It takes in air with its lung through a built-in breathing tube that leads to the surface.
- Fish would suffocate if they tried to chew because chewing would interfere with water passing over their gills.
- A fish can drown in water. They need oxygen and if there isn't enough oxygen in the water they will suffocate.
- A fish turns over when it dies because its heaviest part, the keel on top that keeps it from capsizing, sinks.
- Flying fish can reach heights up to nineteen feet and can glide about one hundred and sixty feet but have been known to glide more than six hundred feet.
- Salmon, after journeying across the ocean, can find the river where they were born.
- An Atlantic Hagfish can make enough slime in one minute to fill a bucket.

- The Cuttlefish is a mollusk, not a fish. It can rapidly change the texture of its skin, often used to communicate during mating rituals, and it also helps the cuttlefish hide from predators. If hiding doesn't work, the cuttlefish can quickly jet away, leaving behind a cloud of foul tasting black ink in the face of its attacker.
- While traveling over water, tornadoes can pick up fish and carry them over land, where the fish rain down. This phenomenon was described as far back as the first century A.D. by a Roman writer.
- Most brands of lipstick contain fish scales.
- The Greek word for fish, *Ichthys*, is an acronym for "Jesus Christ, God's Son, Savior." It was used to mark early Christian tombs and meeting places.

A Jellyfish is not a fish. It is ninety-five percent water, has no brain, and eats and defecates out of the same opening. Most species have tentacles loaded with stinging cells. The toxicity to humans varies – some stings are mildly irritating and others are potentially deadly within minutes. The Box Jellyfish's venom immediately affects the heart and nervous system, leading to death. The Lion's Mane Jellyfish is the largest species and can weigh up to a quarter ton. Its sting is painful and can be potentially fatal. The sting from a Sea Nettle can be extremely painful and form a rash on the skin but is not generally dangerous. The small, transparent Umbrella Jellyfish looks like a miniature umbrella. Its mouth has four frilly lips and when food is snared, the mouth swings over to lick the meal off the tentacles.

Moon Jellyfish are translucent white but may take on a pink, purple or orange hue depending on their last meal. Their four stomachs can be seen through their transparent bodies. The Upside-Down Jellyfish rests upside-down on the sea floor and rarely swims. It looks like a flower. When disturbed, it releases strings of mucous containing stinging cells. It is commonly found in mangrove swamps and sea grass beds, two habitats threatened by coastal development. The Portuguese Man o' War is a whole colony of organisms working together, not a single jellyfish. In severe cases, the sting causes intense pain followed by fever, shock, and impaired heart and lung function leading to possible death.

Sea Walnuts are not true jellyfish, they belong to a group known as Comb Jellies. Their name comes from rows of paddle-like hairs called combs that refract visible light into a pulsing rainbow. Comb Jellies have no stinging cells – they use sticky mucous to catch their prey.

The Anemone is closely related to jellyfish and coral. It paralyzes and captures its prey after it comes in contact with its stinging tentacles. Once immobilized, the anemone pulls the prey into its mouth (located in the middle of the tentacles). When digestion is complete, it excretes waste through the same opening.

CHAPTER 6

My Favorite Carbs

BREAD

Bread is a staple food in many of the world's cultures. It is made from flour or meal mixed with other dry ingredients and water. Beer and other liquids may be used in specialty recipes. There is usually a leavening agent to make the bread rise. Leavening is the process of adding gas to a dough to produce a lighter, airier, more easily chewed bread. There are two types of leavening agents: chemical agents and yeast. Chemical agents like baking powder and baking soda are used to produce quick breads and soda breads. Baking soda requires an acidic ingredient (like buttermilk) to create the chemical reaction that produces gas. Yeast is a natural leavening agent. It ferments carbohydrates in the flour, producing carbon dioxide.

Yeasts are single celled fungi used for thousands of years in fermentation and leavening processes. Ancient Egyptians are credited for discovering yeast's leavening power. To make dough, they mixed a type of flour made from ground nuts, salt, water and leaven, and were able to make over fifty types of a raised and coarse bread. They varied the shape and used flavorings like poppy seed and sesame. Over the centuries, yeast was eventually cultivated and there are now more than six hundred species and thousands of different strains. The first commercial compressed yeast was manufactured by German bakers in 1825. In 1866, Charles Fleischmann and his brother Maximilian founded the first yeast factory in the United States. Most commercial bakers leaven their dough with yeast made from a pure culture to produce uniform results. The commercial yeast used for leavening bread is also used for brewing beer, whiskey, and other alcoholic beverages.

Many artisan bakers produce their own yeast by keeping a starter culture that can last for years. A starter is a small amount of uncooked leavened dough retained from a previous batch, used to start the new batch of dough. The yeast or bacteria in the old dough starts the fermentation of the carbohydrates in the fresh batch of dough. Wild yeast is required to make authentic sourdough. There are many varieties of wild yeast, each with its own flavor characteristics.

Eggs provide added leavening when mixed into a recipe, along with yellow color and softness to sweet breads. An egg wash gives a glossy sheen and deeper color to the bread (mix an egg with water or milk and brush it on the outside of the bread prior to baking).

Humans were grinding seeds to make dough at least twenty thousand years ago. Ground seeds were mixed with water and cooked on flat hot stones in a fire. The first grinding stone was invented in Egypt in 8000 B.C. Ancient Egyptians used bread as a form of currency and it was also placed in tombs for the afterlife. They used moldy bread to disinfect cuts. The oldest baker's oven in the world was from Babylon in 4000 B.C. Large commercial bakeries were developed in Rome in the second century B.C. to meet the demands of increasing bread consumption. Bread was important in Roman culture and religion. Color was one of the main tests for quality, and Ancient Greeks and Romans liked their bread white. In Western Europe in the 1500s, the type of bread eaten by individuals depended on their income and status. The upper and middle classes preferred white bread. The poor, for whom bread represented three-quarters of their budget, ate black or brown bread made from bran, oats, rye, or barley. Workers got the burnt bottom of the loaf, the family got the middle, and guests got the top, or the upper crust. Napoleon's soldiers found it easier to carry their bread in an elongated shape – they stored it down their trousers for ease when moving about on the battlefield, and the baguette was born. Napoleon is also credited with the name given to a loaf of dark rye bread when he demanded "Pain pour Nicole" which meant 'bread for Nicole,' his horse. To Germanic ears the request sounded like pumpernickel, the name we use today.

In 1890, women baking at home produced more than eighty percent of the bread eaten in the United States. By the late 1920s, most bread was baked in commercial bakeries by men. Otto Frederick Rohwedder worked for many years on developing a bread slicer and by 1928 he designed a slicer that would also wrap the bread. Sliced bread was introduced under the Wonder Bread label in 1930. Toasters also became popular. In 1943, the U.S. Secretary of Agriculture banned the sale of sliced bread and the manufacture of metal bread slicing machines for the duration of World War II. Sliced bread went stale faster, causing Americans to use more wheat, needed to feed soldiers. Bread slicing machines also needed metal parts for repairs and metal was needed for manufacturing ships, tanks, guns and other equipment for the war effort. Comedian Red Skelton is credited with saying the phrase "the best thing since sliced bread" for the first time in a 1952 interview when he advised not to worry about television because it's the greatest thing since sliced bread.

The English word 'bread' is related to brood (Dutch), brot (German), bröd (Swedish) and brød (Danish and Norwegian). The Latin term is crustum. The use of the word 'dough' in English as slang for money dates back to 1851. A family of four could live ten years off the bread produced by one acre of wheat. Murphy's Law dictates that buttered bread will always land buttered-side down. One bread superstition is to put a piece of bread in a baby's cradle to keep away disease. Another superstition says it is bad luck to turn a loaf of bread upside down or cut an unbaked loaf. An Australian specialty for children's birthday parties is sliced white bread spread with butter and covered with sprinkles. According to some customs, whoever eats the last piece of bread has to kiss the cook. In Britain, it's a tradition to leave a piece of bread, a piece of coal, and a silver coin outside a door on New Year's Day to bring you food, warmth, and riches in the year ahead. Scandinavian traditions hold that if a boy and girl eat from the same loaf, they are bound to fall in love. In Russia, bread (and salt) are symbols of welcome. Bread is a metaphor for the resurrection of Christ, and several cultures have a celebratory Easter bread—often a rich, sweet yeast style baked with eggs, fruits and nuts. "Breaking bread" is a universal sign of peace.

Most bread products are high in carbohydrates. Sweet breads, like banana bread, can be high in calories, sugars and fats. Bread products made with enriched flour are high in iron, thiamin, riboflavin, niacin and folate. Refined bread products made with unenriched flour do not contain substantial amounts of these nutrients. Many types of bread contain heart-healthy nuts or seeds that are high in unsaturated fats. Products that have walnuts and flaxseed provide omega-3 fatty acids, and those containing dried fruit are high in potassium and dietary fiber. Celiac disease is a genetically-linked autoimmune disorder caused by the small intestine reacting to gluten. A gluten-free diet excludes gluten from sources including bread.

Typical leavened bread is kneaded, shaped into loaves and baked. Middle Eastern and African breads tend to be unleavened flatbreads. Flatbreads are the simplest breads, requiring no leavening. They can be very thin, like a tortilla, or slightly thicker, like focaccia. Pizza is a flatbread made in a variety of diameters as a base for an assortment of toppings. Most pizza is wheat-based, although whole-wheat and semolina varieties can be found. Pita is a thick flatbread with a pocket used to hold other ingredients. It is also used for dips like hummus, and to wrap gyros. Roti, the word for bread in Hindi, Urdu and many languages of India and Pakistan, is a flatbread similar to a tortilla. Each region of India has its own version of roti, with varying names. A tortilla is thin, unleavened flatbread, dating to prehistoric times. Originally made from finely ground maize (corn), it is also made from wheat flour.

White bread is made from refined, bleached wheat flour. To make white flour, the bran that contains fiber, protein, and trace minerals is removed as well as the germ, which contains B vitamins along with a percentage of the grain's fat (this increases the flour's shelf life). What's left is the endosperm which is ground into flour and has a slightly yellowish color. The flour is then bleached using chemicals to give it a pure white hue. Since many of the nutrients are destroyed in this process it is then enriched. In the United States, white flour must be enriched with folic acid, iron, niacin, riboflavin and thiamin to compensate for the loss of these nutrients during the milling process. Enriched white flour has a higher gluten content than All-purpose flour, with a medium amount of gluten. All-purpose flour is not suitable for bread machines. Cottage bread is a white loaf made from two round pieces of dough and is often dusted with flour before baking. Farmhouse bread is a white loaf baked in a special tin and cut lengthwise along the top.

Whole wheat flour has more fiber and protein, and fewer calories than white flour and unbleached All-purpose flour. Wheat bread contains at least ninety percent wheat flour. These breads are light brown in color. Until recent times, brown bread was cheaper to make than refined white bread and was considered inferior.

Whole grain products contain all three parts of the grain kernel and are more nutritious. A whole grain loaf can be made in any size and shape from one or more whole grains: corn, flaxseed, hemp, oats, rye, spelt, and whole wheat.

NOTE: Although breads labeled multigrain are made from two or more grains, they may contain a variety of refined grains that are not whole grains. Read the label. Multigrain is not the same as whole grain.

Sour bread has a sour flavor caused by either a natural leaven fermentation, such as sourdough, or through the addition of souring agents like sour salt, vinegar or yogurt. Not all sour bread is sourdough bread, which must be leavened by a sourdough culture of wild yeast and lactobacilli. It has a mildly sour taste. Cowboy cooks took their sourdough starter to bed with them to keep the cold night air from stopping the crucial fermenting process.

Rye bread contains at least ninety percent rye flour, which is higher in fiber and denser than wheat bread, and stronger in flavor. It is made with a sourdough starter. There are light and dark rye breads, depending on the flour, and added ingredients such as molasses for flavor or caramel for color. Artisan loaves can include spices like anise, coriander and fennel. A marble rye is a dense loaf that twists pumpernickel rye dough with traditional rye creating a swirl loaf. Jewish rye is a mix of wheat and rye flours. Often, caraway seeds are included for extra flavor.

Pumpernickel is a dark, dense rye bread made from crushed or ground rye grains. It can be dark brown to almost black. A longer baking time causes the dark color. Like most rye breads, it is made with a sourdough starter. There are different types of pumpernickel, such as German Westphalian pumpernickel with a profound rye flavor, and American Jewish-style pumpernickel which has a milder flavor.

French bread is a generic term that applies to a variety of different-shaped loaves that have a crusty exterior and a chewy inside. They are typically made from wheat flour, water, yeast and salt. A Boule is a round, crusty loaf (*boule* is the French word for ball or round). Brioche is an enriched bread noted for its high butter and egg content.

A Croissant is a crescent-shaped roll made of puff pastry that layers yeast dough with butter (this is known as laminating). The earliest French reference is in 1853. The croissant is descendant of the Austrian kipfel, a crescent roll that was later made with puff pastry by the French. A chocolate croissant (*pain au chocolat*) is baked with a piece of dark chocolate in the center. In the early 1970s, croissants began to be used as a sandwich, filled with savories like ham and cheese.

A Baguette is a long, narrow loaf. The name means 'small rod' in French. Sandwich-sized baguettes are called demi-baguettes. Parisienne, or flute, is a long loaf, wider than a baguette.

NOTE: The baguette was developed in Vienna, Austria and not in France. In the mid-nineteenth century, the first steam ovens made it possible to bake a crisp crust with a chewy white interior.

A Bolillo, often baked in a stone oven, is a Mexican roll inspired by the baguette. It is six inches long and wider than a baguette, and used for tortas and molletes (Mexican sandwiches).

Italian bread is similar to French bread but the loaves are shorter and plumper. Ciabatta bread is a wheat loaf that is broad and flattish and should be somewhat collapsed in the middle. It has a crisp crust dusted with flour and a porous interior. Some are seasoned with marjoram or rosemary. It is a popular sandwich bread used for panini.

Foccacia is a flat, thick snack bread. Olive oil is brushed over the dough prior to baking to retain moisture. It can be topped with fresh herbs and other ingredients.

Crostini, thin slices of lightly-toasted bread, are small toasts or large croutons used for paté, as a base for canapé toppings, or as a bread with soups and salads. Slices of garlic bread are referred to as crostini.

Challah is a braided, sweetened egg bread that is part of the celebration of the Jewish Sabbath. The word refers to a tithe of bread that was given to the priests who had no income.

Cuban bread, used to make an authentic Cuban sandwich, is a white bread similar to long French and Italian loaves but made with lard or vegetable shortening.

Quick Bread is a light, airy bread made with baking powder or baking soda. It doesn't have to be kneaded because it is made without yeast, and it doesn't need time to rise before baking. Types of quick bread are biscuits, cornbread, popovers, soda breads, sweet breads like Portuguese Sweet Bread (a lightly sweet round loaf made with milk, sugar and/or honey), and muffins. Muffins are quick breads but the sugar and butter content of many types put them into the non-iced cake category. Coffeecakes, pancakes, and waffles are also quick breads.

A fruit bread is a cake-like quick bread made in a loaf pan. It contains small pieces of dried fruit, such as cranberry or raisin, or it may blend the fruit into the dough, as with banana bread and pumpkin bread.

There are many types of cornbread, made from cornmeal. The earliest type is a skillet bread (also known as hoecake) made from cornmeal, egg and buttermilk, fried in fat, then baked in the oven. The result is a cake-like bread with a crunchy crust. Corn pone is a cornbread made of thick cornmeal dough that is baked or fried. Johnnycakes are batter-based, skillet-fried cornbread similar to pancakes.

A biscuit is a small, individually-portioned bread made with baking powder or baking soda as a leavening agent. It is very soft and without a traditional crust. Buttermilk biscuits and cheese biscuits are two popular varieties. Sweet biscuits can be served with butter and jam, or split and served with berries and whipped cream as a shortcake. In the United Kingdom, 'biscuit' is the term for cookie. In the United States, tea biscuits are cookies.

The popover, an egg batter cooked in custard cups or muffin tins to produce a very light, hollow roll) is an Americanization of Yorkshire Pudding. The name comes from the fact that the batter swells or pops over the top of the cup while baking. Popovers need to be eaten hot or they become rubbery.

English muffins, an American invention made by an English immigrant, are fork-split yeast roll related to the crumpet. They were originally made by cooking dough in a circular form on a cast-iron griddle. English muffins are the base for Eggs Benedict.

Crumpets, like English muffins, are small round griddle cakes with a spongy texture full of nooks and crannies. They're always made with milk and baking soda (not yeast) and are cooked only on one side. They are served whole (not split) with jam and butter on top.

Irish Soda Bread, often containing raisins, is a quick bread made with baking soda instead of yeast. Baking soda reacted better with the soft wheat grown in Ireland's climate. Soda bread dates back to approximately 1840 when bicarbonate of soda was introduced to Ireland.

Monkey bread, also called pull-apart bread, is a specialty bread that is rolled into small balls, dipped in butter, and baked in a tube pan. The individual balls adhere together but are pulled apart when eaten. First Lady Nancy Reagan served Monkey Bread at the White House.

Peasant bread is generally a large, round rustic loaf with a thick crust and a hearty, flavorful interior. Rural peasants often made this type of simple bread with whole grains, baked in open fireplaces or large brick community ovens.

A plait is a braided shape, usually plaited with three strands of white dough, sometimes enriched with eggs or milk.

Potato replaces a major portion of the wheat flour in potato bread. It developed in Ireland as a way to use leftover mashed potatoes.

A wrap is a flatbread, generally a tortilla, used to make a sandwich. The filling is rolled up in the middle.

A bagel is the only bread product that is boiled before it is baked. Jewish Austrian immigrants brought the beugel (bagel) with them. The first bagel bakeries were founded in New York City in the 1920s. Bagels have been used to symbolize the continuous cycle of life. Prepackaged bagels first became available in grocery stores in the 1950s. Frozen bagels were introduced in 1960.

The bialy was developed in Bialystok, Poland. It is a large, flat, chewy yeast roll, up to six inches in diameter. Unlike the bagel that is boiled before baking and has a hole in the middle, a bialy has a depression that is filled with chopped onions and poppy seeds prior to baking. A bialy is most often eaten as is or spread with butter.

A bread bowl is a scooped-out round loaf of bread made from any type of bread. Rye, sourdough and wheat are common types. Rolls, like ciabatta rolls, are used for individual bowls.

Hot Cross Buns are a sweet yeast bun made with raisins or currants. The top is decorated with a cross made by knife cuts in the dough or by using icing. The cross symbolizes Christ's crucifixion and the buns are traditionally eaten on Good Friday, although they are believed to predate Christianity – the cross symbolized the four quarters of the moon. The first recorded use of the word 'hot cross bun' appeared in 1733.

Kalache is a kettlebell-shaped or ring-shaped yeast bread.

Tandor bread is a type of bread baked in a clay oven that is called a tandor.

Tiger bread, from the Netherlands, is a rice paste bread made with sesame oil. A pattern is baked into the top, made by painting rice paste onto the surface prior to baking. The paste dries and cracks during the baking process creating a two-color effect similar to a tiger's markings.

Texas toast, an untoasted white bread, is sliced at double the typical thickness of most sliced breads. It is useful for foods with barbecue sauce or for extra thick French toast.

Slices of bread dipped in a mixture of beaten eggs and milk, and pan-fried in butter (or on a griddle) is French Toast. It is often garnished with confectioner's sugar, syrup, jam or fresh fruit.

The Belgian waffle is a type of waffle popular in North America but not common in Belgium. It is larger than a standard American waffle, has a lighter batter, larger squares, and a higher grid pattern that forms deep pockets.

A pancake is a thin, flat, round quick bread (some use a yeast raised or fermented batter) that is cooked on a hot griddle or frying pan. It is flipped partway through to cook the other side.

A crepe' is a very thin pancake that contains either a sweet or savory filling.

Milk toast is a breakfast food consisting of toasted bread in warm milk, with sugar and butter. Other ingredients may also be added. In the New England area, milk toast refers to toast that has been dipped in a milk-based white sauce.

Crouton has two meanings. The first is a small cube of re-baked bread, often seasoned, that is added to salads, soups and other dishes for flavor and texture. The word derives from the French word croûte, for crust. The second is a small slice of toasted bread (like crostini) used as a base for canapés, for spreads and dips, and as a bread accompaniment to soups and salads.

The bread stick originated in Italy. Strips of bread were baked so they became very dry and crisp and could be stored for longer periods. Typical bread sticks (*grissini*) are plain, slender and long, but there are many other lengths and flavors.

Bread crumbs are small pieces of dry bread used for breading, poultry stuffing, and topping casseroles. They can be homemade from bread that is several days old or has been dried in the oven. Italian-style breadcrumbs are generally larger than regular bread crumbs. Panko, or Japanese breadcrumbs, are made from bread without crusts and are crisper and lighter in texture.

Bread stuffing is typically made from day-old bread or breadcrumbs, mixed with fat and vegetables like onion, celery and mushrooms, or chestnuts. In some areas, stuffing is referred to as dressing (a term coined in Victorian England). Some stuffing is not bread-based, such as forcemeat – a mixture of finely ground raw meat, fish or poultry that is highly spiced and bound with butter and eggs, and may include other ingredients. Stuffing is cooked in the body cavity of birds, fish, and cuts of meat. Vegetables can also be stuffed, although bell peppers, cabbage, grape leaves, tomatoes, and other vegetables tend to be stuffed with rice and/or meat.

Bread Pudding was originally a way to use stale bread. Cubes or slices of bread are drenched with a mixture of milk, eggs, sugar, vanilla and spices and baked plain, or with fruits or nuts added. It can be served hot or cold, with or without whipped cream or a sauce, such as hard sauce or custard sauce.

Spoon bread, more of a soufflé than bread, is a Southern specialty originating in Virginia. It is made with cornmeal rather than wheat flour and is baked in a casserole or soufflé dish. It rises like a soufflé but is heavier, like a pudding. It must be served immediately and eaten with a spoon. It can be made with a variety of savory flavors.

A Pullman loaf, also known as a sandwich loaf, is a white or whole wheat bread baked in a long, narrow, lidded pan. The lid creates a flat top, as opposed to a curved top crust. The shape of the loaf made it easier to store aboard railway dining cars which may account for its name. Sweet loaf breads, such as banana bread, are sometimes called sweet Pullmans.

The Club sandwich, also called a clubhouse sandwich, was created around 1894 at a private gambling club in Saratoga Springs, New York. It originally consisted of sliced cooked poultry, fried bacon, lettuce, tomato and mayonnaise between two slices of bread, often toasted. Modern versions have two layers separated by an additional slice of bread. It is cut into quarters or halves and held together by toothpicks.

 In the United States, depending on the area, a sandwich on a long narrow roll became known as a grinder, hero, hoagie, poor boy, torpedo, or submarine. Ingredients also varied regionally. With the rise of the luncheonette in the 1920s, hot sandwiches were served. Today, sandwiches are made with all types of breads as well as bagels, croissants, and wraps.

"A crust eaten in peace is better than a banquet partaken in anxiety."
Aesop   620-564 B.C.   Ancient Greek storyteller

The word 'sandwich' originated in the eighteenth century. As the story goes, the fourth Earl of Sandwich (1718-1792) asked for meat between two slices of bread to be served to him at his club so he could remain at the gaming table without leaving for supper. He may have been inspired by visits to the Mediterranean where he observed Greeks and Turks stuffing pita bread with meats and other fillings. The sandwich became a popular late-night meal at society balls. During the nineteenth century, leftovers from lunch (the main meal of the day) were often made into sandwiches. They were common fare at taverns and train stations. When a Victorian cookbook recommended that the crusts be removed from the bread, sandwiches began to be served at Tea.

NOTE: Afternoon Tea is a British food tradition of sitting down at 4:00 p.m. for a treat of tea, small sandwiches, scones and cake, served in the parlor or garden to fill in the gap between lunch and a late dinner. High Tea was served after the work day ended and consisted of heartier foods and tea. People sat on high back chairs at their dining table (hence the name).

CRACKER

The cracker is an American invention, first made in 1792. Its long shelf life was popular with sailors who called it hardtack or sea biscuits. The name 'cracker' came from the crackling noise made when a batch of baking biscuits burned. At first, crackers were sold in soda cracker barrels from local producers. At the beginning of the twentieth century, Adolphus Green (one of the founders of the National Biscuit Company, later renamed Nabisco) replaced the barrel with whole crackers in triple-wrapped packages. Crackers are made of flour, water and salt (but no leavening). Some have seasonings added. There are many types such as cheese crackers, oyster crackers, saltines, and matzoh. Holes in crackers are there for a purpose: if the holes are too close together, the crackers will turn out flat and tough; if they are too far apart, the upper layer of the cracker will separate.

Crispbread, also called flatbread, is a small, crisp bread-like product that originated during medieval times. It was made to preserve the wheat crop over the long cold winters. Originally made with rye flour, salt and water, today there are varieties made from all major grains. Crispbread is available in large, decorative rounds or cracker-size portions. Crispbread is not the same as soft flatbreads like pitas and tortillas.

Melba toast is dry, crisp, thinly sliced toast. Famed chef Auguste Escoffier created it for a friend's wife, Marie Ritz, when she commented that she could never find thin enough toast. He originally called it 'Toast Marie' but renamed it Melba toast when he was working at London's Savoy Hotel in 1897. The Australian opera singer, Dame Nellie Melba, was staying there and ate it regularly. (Peach Melba is another food that was named after the opera star.)

Zwieback, from Germany, is a crisp, sweetened bread made with eggs and baked twice. It is sliced before it is baked a second time, which produces crisp, brittle slices that resemble Melba toast.

Chinese noodles, made with wheat flour and water, are the oldest form of noodles. Made from unleavened dough, rolled flat, and cut into a variety of shapes, they are usually cooked in boiling water. They can also be stir-fried and are often served with sauce or in a soup. October sixth is National Noodle Day.

In Asia, noodle dishes are symbolic of happiness, health, friendship, and commitment. Many Asian cultures encourage you to slurp your noodles. The Chinese word for noodles is *mien*. Chinese noodles vary widely according to ingredients, shape or width, the region of production, and manner of preparation. The most common types are wheat flour noodles, rice noodles, and cellophane noodles. Rice noodles, made from rice flour, sometimes have other ingredients, like tapioca or corn starch, added to increase the chewy texture. Noodles made from brown rice flour are an alternative to those made with wheat flour, for people who have a wheat or gluten allergy. Cellophane noodles, also called glass noodles, are made from water and a starch such as mung bean, yam, potato, or cassava. They are round and come in various thicknesses. Cellophane noodles should not be confused with Rice Vermicelli made from rice – it is white in color, not clear after cooking.

Lamian is a type of Chinese noodle made by twisting, stretching and folding the dough into strands. The length and thickness of the strands depends on the number of times the dough is folded. Misua is a very thin variety of salted Chinese noodles made from wheat flour. Oil noodles, or cooked noodles, are also made of wheat flour. Shrimp roe noodles have tiny black spots on strips of the noodles from salty shrimp roe. Yi mein is a variety of flat egg noodle made from wheat flour. It has a golden yellow color and chewy texture, due to the carbonated soda water used in making the dough. It is then fried and dried into flat patty-like dried bricks. Wonton is a Cantonese word for dumpling, usually served in a hot broth. Its chewiness comes from the addition of egg in the dough.

There are two main kinds of Chow Mein noodles: steamed (with a softer texture) and crispy. Crispy Chow Mein uses fried, flat noodles; soft Chow Mein uses long, rounded noodles. Crispy Chow Mein is usually topped with a thick brown sauce; steamed Chow Mein is mixed with soy sauce before being served. The term 'Chow Mein' is different on the east and west coasts of the United States. On the west coast, it is always the steamed style; the crispy style is simply called Hong Kong style. On the east coast, it is always the crispy style; the steamed style is a separate dish called Lo Mein. Lo Mein, meaning 'stirred noodles' in Cantonese, is made with wheat flour noodles. It is usually stirred with a sauce made from soy sauce and other seasonings, and vegetables and meat or fish can added. In some parts of the U.S., Chow Mein may be served as Chop Suey with crunchy fried noodles.

Fideos (Mexican spaghetti) are thin noodles. Sopa de Fideo is a Mexican noodle soup made with fideos simmered in a tomato-based broth.

There are many varieties of Ramen noodles, such as wavy, straight, thin and thick, and just as many types of broth. Although they originated in China, Ramen became popular in Japan in the late 1800s. Nearly every region in Japan has its own variation. Udon noodles, the thickest type of Japanese noodle, are made from wheat flour, salt, and water. They are most commonly served in soup broth. Soba noodles are traditionally eaten on New Year's Eve as a symbol of longevity. They are made from buckwheat flour and have a nutty flavor and slightly chewy texture.

The German and Austraian Schupfnudel, also called Fingernudel (finger noodle), is a type of dumpling or thick noodle similar to gnocchi. It is made from rye or wheat flour and egg (and sometimes potato). Spatzele, meaning 'little sparrow,' is German egg pasta that is either round in shape, or completely irregular.

Couscous, similar to rice in shape, color and texture, is a North African dish of small steamed balls of semolina, usually served with a stew spooned on top. It is also widely used in Middle Eastern countries.

PASTA

The word 'pasta' comes from the Italian word for paste. Pasta in Italy can be traced back to the fourth century B.C. Utensils used for pasta making and a picture in an Etruscan tomb show people making something that looks like pasta. At least ten years before Marco Polo's trip to China, Romans were eating some form of pasta. Southern Italians claim it was introduced to Sicily by the Arabs. The Pope laid out standards for the quality of pasta in the thirteenth century. Italians eat more pasta per year than anyone else but in the past, dry pasta was a luxury item in Italy – the semolina had to be kneaded for a long time, resulting in high labor costs. Thanks to the industrial revolution, a mechanical process allowed for large scale production of dry past and it became more affordable.

Thomas Jefferson may have been the one to introduce pasta to the colonies when he returned to America after serving as ambassador to France. He had eaten and enjoyed it when he visited Italy. He brought a pasta making machine back with him in 1789 but it was not until later in the nineteenth century that pasta became popular in the United States. The first commercial pasta plant in the U.S. was founded in Brooklyn, New York in 1848. Americans are the only people who use a fork with a spoon to twirl and eat spaghetti; most other countries twirl the fork against the plate. October is National Pasta Month.

Most pasta is made using wheat flour and high-quality pasta is made from durum wheat. It can be made in different shapes and colors. Squid ink colors black pasta, spinach colors green, saffron colors yellow, and tomatoes color red. Uncooked dry pasta can be kept for up to a year.

Meatballs were invented in America, not Italy.

Pasta has many health benefits as it contains various nutrients and minerals. It is a good source of B vitamins, iron and niacin, is very low in sodium, and is cholesterol free. Pasta is an excellent source of complex carbohydrates. These carbohydrates cause your body to produce a chemical called serotonin which helps you to relax.

Flat pasta is best with cream sauces. Tomato sauces are better for pasta shapes. 'Gravy' is a term sometimes used by Italians for a tomato sauce that is simmered for a long time. Simmering sauce on low heat burns off excess water and allows the flavors of the spices to blend into the sauce.

A few Italian pasta sauces are:

Acciughe - anchovies flavored with garlic, oil and parsley
Aglio e olio - garlic, olive oil and parsley
Alfredo - butter, cream and freshly grated cheese
Amatricana - fresh tomatoes, chopped bacon, onion and garlic
Bolognese (also called Ragu) - meat sauce
Burro - butter and grated Parmesan cheese
Cacciatore - meat and vegetable sauce
Frutti di mare - seafood sauce
Funghi e piselli - mushrooms, bacon and fresh green peas
Marinara - fresh tomatoes, olive oil, garlic and basil
Noci - pounded walnuts and pine nuts with oil, garlic and chopped parsley
Pesto - oil, grated cheese, pine nuts, basil and garlic pounded into a paste
Pomidoro - tomato sauce
Romana - meat and chicken sauce with chopped mushrooms
Tartufata - truffle sauce flavored with Marsala or white wine and garlic
Umbria - pounded anchovies, oil and garlic flavored with tomatoes and truffles
Vongole - clam sauce with onions, tomatoes, olive oil and garlic

Pasta is best cooked al dente (firm but tender). There are more than five hundred different pasta shapes worldwide. Types of Italian pasta include (their meaning is in parenthesis):

Acini di pepe (peppercorn) – bead-like pasta
Agnolotti (angel) – semicircular stuffable pockets
Alfabeto (alphabet) – pasta shaped as letters of the alphabet
Anelli (ring) – small rings of pasta; Anellini is a smaller version
Biciclette (bicycle) – bicycle-shaped pasta
Barbina (little beards) – thin strands often coiled into nests
Bigoli – thick tubes, often made of buckwheat or whole wheat flour
Bucatini (hole) –a thick spaghetti-like pasta with a hole running through the center

Cacavelle – large, stuffable bowl-like pasta

Calamarata (squid-like) – wide ring-shaped pasta

Campanelle (little bell) – flattened bell-shaped pasta with a frilly edge on one end

Cannelloni (large reeds) – large tube, stuffable pasta

Cappelletti (little caps) – square of dough, filled with minced meat, and closed to form a triangle

Capellini – angel Hair pasta

Capunti – short convex ovals resembling an open empty pea pod

Casarecce (homemade) – short lengths rolled into an S-shape

Caramelle (candy) – a stuffed pasta resembling double twist candies

Castellane (castle dweller) – shell pasta coiled into a conical shape.

Cavatappi (corkscrew) – corkscrew-shaped

Cavatelli (to hollow) – short, solid lengths

Cencioni (large rags) – petal shaped, slightly curved with rough convex side

Chifferi – short and wide

Conchiglie (shell) – seashell shaped; Conchigliett are smaller; Conchiglioni are larger & stuffable

Corallini (little coral) – small short tubes of pasta

Cresti di galli (cock's comb) – short, curved and ruffled

Croxetti (little crosses) – flat coin-shaped discs stamped with coats of arms

Ditalini (small thimbles) – short tubes; Ditali is a larger version

Fagottini (little cloth bundle) – a bundle, or purse, of stuffable pasta

Farfalle (butterfly) – bow tie or butterfly shaped; Farfalline are smaller; Farfalloni are larger

Fedelini (little faithful ones) – very thin spaghetti

Fettuccini (little slices) – a wide ribbon of pasta; Fettucce is a wider version of fettuccini

Fettucele – a narrower version of Fettuccini

Fiorentine (Florentine) – grooved cut tubes

Fiori (flower) – shaped like a flower

Foglie d'ulivo (olive leaf) – shaped like an olive leaf

Funghini (little mushroom) – small mushroom-shaped pasta

Fusilli (long rifles) – long, thick, corkscrew-shaped pasta that may be solid or hollow

Fusilli Bucati – long coiled tubes that are hollow

Garganelli – egg pasta in a square shape rolled into a tube

Gemelli (twins) – single s-shaped strand of pasta twisted in a loose spiral

Gigle (lily) – cone or flower shaped

Gnocchi – dumplings made from potatoes or bread crumbs (not wheat)

Gramigna (weed) – short curled lengths of pasta

Grattoni (grain) – large granular, irregular shaped pasta; Grattini are a smaller version

Lanterne (lantern) – curved ridges

Lasagna (cooking pot) – very wide pasta that often has fluted edges

Lasagnette – a narrower version of lasagna

Linguine (little tongues) – flattened spaghetti

Linguettine – a narrower version of linguini

Lumaconi (large snail) – large snailshell-shaped pieces of pasta

Lumache – a smaller version of Lumaconi

Macaroni (food made from barley) – thin tubes of pasta

Mafalde – short rectangular ribbons

Malfaldine – long ribbons with ruffled sides

Maltagliati (badly cut) – flat roughly cut triangles

Manicotti – large stuffable ridged tubes

Mezzani – short curved tube

Mezzi bombardoni –a wide short tube

Mezzelune (half moons) – semicircular stuffable pockets

Midolline – flat teardrop shaped pasta (larger than Orzo)

Mostaccioli (mustache-like) – similar to penne but without ridges

Occhi di lupo (ribbed wolf eyes) – large, penne-shaped stuffable pasta

Occhi di pernice (partridge eyes) – very small rings

Orecchiette (little ears) – bowl-shaped or ear-shaped pasta

Orzo (barley) – rice shaped pasta

Risi (little rice) – a smaller version of Orzo

Paccheri (slap) – large tube pasta

Pappardelle – thick flat ribbon

Pastina (little pasta) – small spheres

Penne (quill pen) – medium length tubes with ridges, cut diagonally at both ends

Penne Rigate – it has ridged sides

Penne Zita – a wider version of Penne

Pennette – a short thin version of Penne

Pipe – similar to Lumaconi but has lines running the length of it

Pizzoccheri – a flat ribbon pasta made with mostly buckwheat flour

Quadrefiore (square flower) – square with rippled edges

Quadrettini (little square) – small flat squares of pasta

Radiatori (radiator) – shaped like old-fashioned radiators

Ravioli (little turnip) – large square of stuffable pasta

Rigatoni (large lined ones) – medium to large tube with square-cut ends, sometimes curved

Rigatoncini – a smaller version of Rigatoni

Tortiglioni – similar to Rigatoni but narrower

Tuffoli – ridged Rigatoni

Ricciolini (little curl) – short wide pasta with a ninety-degree twist

Rotelle (little wheel) – wagon wheel-shaped pasta

Rotini – related to fusilli, but has a tighter corkscrew

Sacchettini (little sack) – small square of pasta brought around the stuffing and twisted;

Sachettoni – a larger version of Sacchettini

Seme di melone (melon seed) – small seed-shaped pasta

Sorprese (surprise) – bell shaped pasta with a crease on one side and a ruffled edge;

Sorprese Lisce – a larger version of Sorprese

Spaghetti (little strings) – a long, thin, cylindrical pasta

Spaghettini a- small little twines

Spaghettono – spaghetti that is extra thick or extra long

Spirali – a tube which spirals round

Spiralini – more tightly coiled

Stelle (star) – small star-shaped pasta

Stelline – a smaller version of Stelle

Stringozzi (shoestring) – similar to shoelaces

Stortini (Little crooked one) – smaller version of elbow macaroni

Strozzapreti (priest choker) – rolled across their width

Tagliatelle (to cut) – a ribbon, narrower than fettuccini

Torchio (winepress) – torch shaped

Tortellini (little pies) – ring-shaped, stuffable pasta

Tortelloni – a larger version of Tortellini

Trenne – Penne shaped as a triangle

Trenette – a smaller version of Trenne

Tripolini - small bow tie-shaped pasta with rounded edges

Trofie – thin twisted pasta

Vermicellli (worms) – think pasta that is thicker than spaghetti

Ziti (bridegroom) – long, narrow tubes smaller than Rigatoni but larger than Mezzani

Ziti Rigati – it has lines or ridges on the pasta's surface

"Life is a combination of magic and pasta."
Federico Fellini
Italian film director and screenwriter
1920-1993

CHAPTER 7

Save Room for Dessert

CAKE

The word 'cake' comes from Middle English word kake, which may have originated from the old Norse word kaka. It is also related to the German word for cake, kuchen. The Spanish word for cake is pastel (pastry), and in Italian it is torta (tart). The meaning of cake has changed over time. In ancient Rome, eggs and butter were often added to basic bread dough to give it a consistency that later would be called cake-like, and honey was used as a sweetener. In the Middle Ages in Scotland and parts of Wales and northern England, cake was a thick, hard flat biscuit made from oatmeal and baked on both sides. From the seventeenth to the nineteenth centuries, Scotland was humorously known as the Land of Cakes. The pagan festival of Hogmanay was also known as Cake Day, from the custom of calling on people at home on New Year's Day and sharing cake. Poundcake originated in the first half of the eighteenth century, so named because the original recipe consisted of one pound each of butter, sugar, flour, and eggs. In the nineteenth century, the French word for cake, gâteau, was often used to refer to a savory dish that included meat.

The famous saying, "Let them eat cake" was attributed to Marie Antoinette (1755-1793) upon learning that her people had no bread but an earlier version, "Why don't they eat pastry?" is attributed to Marie Thérèse (1638-1683). The proverb, "You can't have your cake and eat it too" first appeared in the sixteenth century. The term, "A piece of cake" (to mean something that is easy to do) was coined in the twentieth century and is possibly related to the cakewalk dance, a competition in graceful walking with cake awarded as a prize. Some examples of cake being made for superstitious reasons are: A burial cake was kept close to the head of the deceased person and a viewer had to have a piece of the cake in one's mouth when looking at the body. A soul cake is made on All Souls' Day in various parts of England and kept for good luck. In seventeenth century England, people believed that putting a fruit cake under your pillow would make you dream about the person you would marry. A taste of the cake before a wedding means loss of the husband's love but a piece of cake kept after the wedding ensures his fidelity.

Cakes are the most common dessert at ceremonial occasions. The first birthday cake, dating back to ancient Rome, was originally a cake given as an offering on a person's birthday. The Western tradition of adding lit candles to the top of a birthday cake originated in Germany in the eighteenth century. Wedding cakes also began in the Roman Empire. Originally, they were piles of sweet bread that the bride and groom would kiss over. France introduced a tower of profiteroles (cream puffs) decorated with strands of spun sugar. In England, a bride cake was a small cake that the bride ate a piece of when she entered her new home. She then threw the rest of the cake over her head ensuring she and her husband would never lack for anything. The groom threw the plate over his head – if it broke, their future happiness was assured. The wedding cake was originally cut and distributed to guests by only the bride to ensure fertility but eventually, as the number of guests increased, the groom began to help. Tiered cakes originated after 1870. Queen Victoria popularized the white wedding cake, symbolizing purity and virginity. Using white icing also meant that only the finest refined sugar had been used, a display of the family's wealth. An 1872 cook book published in Boston contained one of the first layer cake recipes – multiple stacked sheets of cake held together by frosting or another type of filling.

ICING

Covering cakes with powdered sugar was introduced in the seventeenth century. The first icing (frosting) was a boiled composition of sugar, egg whites and flavorings. It was applied to the cake then hardened in the oven. Buttercream is a common topping for cakes. It is made by creaming butter (or lard) with powdered sugar and colorings, and flavorings may be added. Using a pastry bag, icing can be formed into decorative shapes like flowers. The simplest icing is a glacé icing containing powdered sugar and water. It can be flavored and colored as desired.

A glaze is applied to baked goods with a brush or by dripping. Ganache is a type of chocolate glaze: hot cream is poured over chopped chocolate and blended until smooth. The ratio of cream to chocolate is determined by its purpose. Butter is added to create a shiny appearance and flavorings may also be added. Ganache can also be a whipped frosting, sauce, or filling for pastries. In the 1960s, an Australian baker created a sweet mixture with glycerin that was dough-like in appearance and texture and could be rolled out like pastry and placed over a cake, completely covering it. Rolled fondant became the new fashionable frosting for covering special occasion cakes. When frosting is used between layers of cake it is called filling.

FOOD COLORING

Food coloring is added to foods to impart color. It comes in many forms – powder, gel, paste, and liquid (the most common form for home use). Certain colors are associated with certain flavors and adding food coloring can enhance natural variations in color in some foods, increasing the taste perception. Food coloring may also make food more attractive. Coloring mist and edible ink designs may be used on top of icing. Edible ink printing uses food colorings to create images on thin, edible paper made of starches and sugars. Food coloring is also used in a variety of non-food applications, such as cosmetics and pharmaceuticals.

There are many variations of cake depending on the flavorings added, fillings, icings, decorations, and the shape of the pan used in baking. A Bundt® cake is baked in a pan with fluted or grooved sides and a cylindrical hole through the center of the cake for more even heat distribution. Nordic Ware trademarked the pan style with the Bundt® name so similar pans sold are labeled tube pans.

Butter cakes, also called creamed cakes, are made with fat such as butter, margarine or vegetable shortening and produce a finely textured and moist cake. Sponge cake and chiffon cake are often referred to as foam cakes. They do not contain fat and have more eggs than butter cakes. Sponge cake has a firm consistency but is well aerated. Battenburg cake, invented in the nineteenth century, is a light sponge cake with jam added to create a check pattern when cut. It is covered with marzipan. A jellyroll, also called Swiss Roll although it originated elsewhere in Europe in the nineteenth century, is another type of sponge cake that is filled with whipped cream, jam or icing, and then rolled. Rum cake is usually made from a sponge cake that can absorb the added rum. In many parts of the Caribbean, rum cake contains dried fruit that has been soaked in rum for months before being added to batter. Italian cassata cake consists of sponge cake moistened with fruit syrup or rum, and filled with dried fruit or a sweetened ricotta cream filling with chocolate chips (similar to cannoli filling). It can be covered with whipped cream or, more traditionally, with marzipan. In India, cassata refers to a layered ice cream sponge cake topped with chopped nuts.

A Tres Leches cake (Spanish for 'three milk cake') is a sponge cake soaked in evaporated milk, condensed milk, and heavy cream. Recipes for soaked-cake desserts were seen in Mexico as early as the nineteenth century and were based on Medieval European cakes like the British trifle and tiramisu from Italy. A trifle contains layers of sponge cake (sometimes soaked in sherry), fruit and custard, topped with whipped cream. Some recipes include a fruit-flavored jelly. A Creole Trifle, also known as a Russian Cake, consists of pieces of a variety of cakes moistened with red wine or rum and a sweet syrup or fruit juice, then chilled. Tiramisu, meaning 'lift me up' in Italian, is a coffee-flavored dessert made with lady's fingers and layered with a whipped mixture of eggs, sugar and mascarpone cheese flavored with cocoa. Angel food cake, a type of sponge cake with a light and fluffy texture, originated in the United States. It got its name because it was said to resemble the food of the angels.

A chiffon cake, a combination of both batter and foam type cakes, uses vegetable oil instead of butter or shortening. The eggs are separated and the whites are beaten before being folded into the batter, creating a light texture. It can be baked in a tube pan or layered with fillings.

Coffee cake is a term used to refer to a cake that is intended to be eaten with coffee or tea. It may also refer to a sponge cake flavored with coffee. Babka, from Poland, is a brioche-like yeast cake traditionally baked for major holidays like Easter and Christmas. It is glazed with icing and decorated with almonds or candied fruit. A Jewish version, made from a doubled and twisted length of dough, is baked in a high loaf pan and contains cinnamon or chocolate.

Cheesecake contains eggs, sugar, and a mixture of soft, fresh cheese like cream cheese and ricotta. It often has a crust made from crushed graham crackers and may be topped with fruit or whipped cream. Most cheesecakes are baked in a springform pan. New York-style cheesecake was made famous by Lindy's deli on Broadway in the heart of Manhattan's theater district. In the United States, French-style cheesecake refers to a version made with uncooked batter, using a binder of gelatin or whipped topping instead of eggs.

Fruitcake originated in ancient Egypt and was considered an essential food for the afterlife. It has just enough cake batter to hold it together, which results in a very dense, moist, heavy cake. It may contain candied fruit, dried fruit, fruit rind, nuts, spices, and sometimes liquor. Claxton, Georgia, is known as the Fruitcake Capital of the World.

Carrot cake has carrots mixed into the batter which soften as it bakes. The most popular icing on this cake in the United States is a sweet cream cheese frosting. In Europe, you may find it covered with icing sugar and lemon juice or Kirsch (cherry liqueur). Carrots, which contain more sugar than any other vegetable besides the sugar beet, have been used in sweet cakes since the middle ages when sweeteners were scarce and expensive.

A Depression Cake was commonly made during the Great Depression because it used little or no milk, sugar, butter or eggs (ingredients that were scarce or expensive). Shortening was substituted for butter, water was used instead of milk, and baking powder took the place of eggs. It was also known as a War Cake because it didn't use ingredients that were being conserved for use by the military.

Chopped fruits (pineapple is the most popular) and a butter and sugar topping are placed on the bottom of a cake pan before the batter is poured in, creating a decorative topping when inverted after baking. This is called an upside-down cake.

There are many types of Spice cake but the most common flavorings used are cinnamon, cloves, nutmeg, ginger and allspice. A maple spice cake, an American version, adds maple syrup.

King Cake is associated in a number of countries with the Epiphany.* The cake is eaten from the Eve of the Epiphany (also known as Twelfth Night**), throughout Mardi Gras until Shrove Tuesday (also known as Fat Tuesday – the day before Ash Wednesday, the start of Lent). The cake originated three hundred years ago as a dry bread dough with sugar on top. A bean, representing the infant Jesus, was baked inside. Today, some King Cakes are made of a sweet brioche dough in the shape of a hollow circle with a glazed topping sprinkled with purple, gold, and green colored sugar. Others are made of puff pastry filled with a variety of fillings such as apple or chocolate. They all have a small figure hidden inside, such as a plastic baby. The person who gets the piece of cake with the figure has various privileges.

*The visit of the three Magi to the Christ Child is celebrated in the Catholic Church on January sixth.

** The Twelve Days of Christmas are counted from Christmas Eve until this night.

An ice cream cake has layers of cake and ice cream although some types do not contain cake. Victorian era versions, called bombes, consisted of ice cream and fruit in decorative molds that were sometimes lined with cake or biscuits. The ice cream in Baked Alaska is placed in a pie dish lined with slices of sponge cake and topped with meringue. It is then placed in an extremely hot oven only long enough to caramelize the meringue. The meringue acts as insulation and the short cooking time prevents the ice cream from melting. In 1974, Jacqueline Halliday Diaz invented a baking pan that forms a hollow in the cake that can be filled with ice cream.

NOTE: Renaissance-era desserts composed of cream and sponge cake were called trifles. Early recipes for ice cream cakes were based on the same creams used for trifles. By the nineteenth century, the ice cream cake had several definitions in the United States.

In 1879, when Rodolphe Lindt developed conching, a process for making smoother chocolate, baking with chocolate became easier and versions of the chocolate cake became popular. Devil's Food cake, invented in the United States in the early twentieth century, has more chocolate than regular chocolate cake, making it darker. German chocolate cake, filled and topped with coconut-pecan frosting, was created in the United States, not Germany. Samuel German, a chocolate maker, developed a formula for dark baking chocolate that was used in the recipe. Black Forest cake (Schwarzwälder Kirschtorte) is a German dessert consisting of several layers of chocolate cake filled with whipped cream and cherries and topped with whipped cream, marachino cherries and chocolate shavings. The cake is not named after the Black Forest region in Germany but rather from the specialty liquor of that region called Kirschwasser. German law mandates that Kirschwasser must be added to the cake. A Chocolate Overload cake is a chocolate cake with chocolate chips, fudge icing, and chocolate shavings.

Red Velvet cake is chocolate cake with a red color, from either food coloring or beets. When foods were rationed during World War II, bakers used boiled beet juices to enhance the color of their cakes. The cake is topped with cream cheese or buttercream frosting, or a light and fluffy French-style butter roux icing (also called ermine icing). Flourless chocolate cake is popular for gluten-free diets. One type is the Chocolate Decadence cake, a molten chocolate cake, or lava cake, with a liquid chocolate center. It was created mostly as a single-serving dessert. Chocolate Blackout Cake is a chocolate layer cake with a chocolate pudding filling, and frosting that is covered with some of the cake crumbs. It was developed in Brooklyn, New York during World War II and named for the wartime blackouts (city lights were turned off and windows were covered with black material. These drills were performed by the Civilian Defense Corps).

Other flavors of chocolate cake include chocolate cream, fudge, white chocolate, raspberry, peanut butter, marshmallow, coconut, and even zucchini. Turtle cake has caramel and pecans added. Chocolate cake balls, originally created from the crumbs of leftover cake or stale cake, are made by blending crumbled chocolate cake with chocolate frosting and shaping them into small balls. They are then dipped in a coating of melted chocolate.

The Chocolate soufflé, a tall puffed-up pastry dusted with powdered sugar, is a popular chocolate cake dessert. It often consists of a thick egg yolk-based sauce or puree that is lightened by stiffly beaten egg whites (add a pinch of salt). Don't open the oven door while it is baking.

Boston Cream Pie is a cake, not a pie. It has two layers of sponge cake with a custard filling and only the top is covered with chocolate, not the sides. The first Boston cream pie, then called Parker House Chocolate Cream Pie, was created at the Parker House Hotel in Boston in 1856. The first printed use of the word 'Boston Cream Pie' was in an 1878 cookbook. The similar Washington Pie is also a two-layer cake filled with pastry cream and topped with a chocolate glaze, although the original version was filled with jam and topped with confectioner's sugar.

A Yule Log, traditionally served at Christmas time, is made of sponge cake and frosted to look like a small log. A fork is dragged through the chocolate icing to produce a bark-like texture. One end of the cake is cut off and set on top, to resemble a branch. It is sprinkled with powdered sugar to resemble snow. The original yule log recipe dates back to the nineteenth century.

A Torte is a multilayered cake filled with whipped cream, buttercream, mousse, jam or fruit and is glazed when cooled. The most well-known is the Austrian Linzer Torte, with a lattice design on top of the pastry. Tortes are commonly baked in a spring form pan.

A cupcake was called by that name because it was cake made from ingredients measured by the cupful and often baked in individual pottery cups. The earliest mention of a 'cup cake' was in a 1796 cookbook. The spelling later changed to cupcake. Today, there are more than five hundred types of cupcakes consisting of a wide variety of ingredients and frostings.

Cake in a mug uses a mug as the cooking vessel and is baked in a microwave. Vegetable oil is mixed with flour and other ingredients and as the oil heats, it creates air pockets in the mixture which allow the cake to rise quickly.

Sweet leavened bread dates back to Roman times but the first mention of Panettone, a tall dome-shaped yeast bread filled with candied fruits and raisins associated with Christmas, is from the eighteenth century. Some modern versions add chocolate. Its name means 'large loaf' in Italian. One legend tells of a young chef named Toni who accidentally burned the dessert he was making on Christmas Eve for a grand dinner party. Desperate, he mixed bread dough and butter with raisins and candied fruit and baked another dessert. Dinner guests enjoyed it and called it *Pan del Toni* (Tony's bread), which evolved to Panettone.

Streusel, a crumb topping prepared with butter, flour and sugar, is baked on muffins, pies, cakes, and crumbles. Some recipes add spices and chopped nuts. Streusel originated in Germany.

Scones are quick breads similar to biscuits. They are baked both in the traditional wedge form or in round, square, and diamond shapes. Some recipes produce a hard, dry texture but cream scones, that use heavy cream in the recipe, produce a moister scone. Their origin is not known but the first known print reference is from a Scottish poet in 1513. The name may have come from the Gaelic word sgonn which referred to a shapeless mass or large mouthful. Scone is pronounced 'skahn' (rhymes with gone) in Scotland and Northern England, and 'skoan' (rhymes with own) in the south of England and the United States. Originally, scones were made with oats shaped into a large round, scored into four or six triangles and griddle-baked over an open fire. They are related to the ancient Welsh tradition of cooking small round yeast cakes on bakestones, and later on griddles. Traditional English scones may include raisins or currants but are often plain and served with jam, preserves, lemon curd or honey, and clotted cream. American scones have a higher ratio of fat-to-flour than British scones and may contain dried fruits, nuts, orange rind, and chocolate morsels.

NOTE: Clotted Cream is a thick cooked cream product that originated in the counties of Devon and Cornwall in Southwest England. It is an excellent source of calcium, folic acid, magnesium, phosphorus, riboflavin, vitamins A, B12 and D, and zinc. Devon cream is the same product with slightly less butterfat.

DONUT

Donuts, also spelled doughnuts, are a type of fried dough that can be either cake-like or yeast-risen. They come in a variety of shapes and some are filled with a sweet filling like custard or fruit preserves. Donuts may be glazed or frosted, or dusted with powdered sugar. They may also be embellish with sprinkles or other edible adornments. The hole in a ring donut has been attributed to a young Dutch baker's apprentice who, in 1847, removed the uncooked center from a fried doughnut, resulting in a ring donut. However, archaeologists found petrified fried cakes with holes in them in prehistoric Native American ruins in the southwestern United States.

In the early 1900s, a military doctor began handing out donuts to the wounded soldiers he was helping and eventually the Salvation Army helped with this program. The first Donut Day, honoring the female volunteers who served donuts to soldiers during World War I, was in 1938. Throughout World War II, the Red Cross distributed donuts to soldiers and the women volunteers were known as Doughnut Dollies. National Donut Day is the first Friday in June.

Every culture has their version of a doughnut and many countries have the jelly donut. A *Berliner Pfannkuchen*, or simply called a Berliner, is a German donut with a jam filling topped with powdered sugar or conventional sugar. The similar Austrian *Faschingskrapfen* (little carnival cake) is popular on Saint Joseph's Day. In Lithuania, *Spurgos* are donuts filled with jam and coated in sugar. *Sufganiyah*, a traditional Hebrew dessert, is filled with jelly or chocolate, dolce de leche, or custard. *Krofne* are round donuts filled with jelly, chocolate, Nutella®, or cinnamon and as a sign of good luck and prosperity, they are served on New Year's Day in Croatia and Slovenia.

Fried dumplings, often containing currants, raisins or candied fruit, are called *olykoeks* (oil spheres) in the Netherlands and *Smoutenbollen* (lard ball) in Belgium. In Japan, the *An-doughnut* is fried dough with a red bean-paste. *Kuih keria* are sugar-coated, fried, sweet-potato donuts in Malaysia. Armenian doughnuts are referred to as *chickies.* In Brazil, donuts are referred to as *sonho* (dream). In India, *Balushahi* is fried dough soaked in sugar syrup and sometimes flavored with spices. Little balls of fried dough with syrup, honey, or chocolate sauce are called *Lokma* in Turkey and *Loukoumades* in Greece. They can be either crispy and shaped like the number eight or a larger, softer one shaped like an 0.

Zeppole are a fried Italian pastry that are served warm and dusted with confectioners' sugar or cinnamon-sugar. They can also be filled with a sweetend ricotta cheese or custard (similar to a cream puff). This is known as *Sfinge di San Giuseppe* (St. Joseph puffs). French *Pets de nonnes* (Nun's puffs) are lightly dusted fritters that come with or without a cream filling. In Canada, a Beaver Tail is hand stretched to resemble a beaver's tail, fried, then topped with things like cinnamon sugar, chocolate hazelnut spread, or apple pie filling. *Zooloobiya* is an Iranian fritter that comes in various shapes and sizes and is coated in a sticky sweet syrup. Russian *Ponchik* are deep-fried sphere-shaped pieces of dough with a sweet or savory filling. Ring-shaped fried rice dough called *Sel Roti* are eaten during celebrations in Nepal. *Donat kentang* is an Indonesian ring-shaped donut made from flour and mashed potatoes and coated in powdered sugar or icing sugar.

Portuguese *Malasadas* are deep fried dough covered in sugar. They are also popular in Hawaii. *Smultring*, small unglazed fried donuts flavored with cardamom, are Norwegian donuts. The *Beignet*, popular in New Orleans, is a square piece of dough, fried and covered with powdered sugar. In Nigeria, crispy little sticks made of fried dough are called *Chin-Chin. Pa Thong Ko* is another stick-shaped piece of fried dough from Thailand. Spanish *Churros* are fried until they become crunchy then sprinkled with sugar. The shape is usually long and straight but may also be curled or twisted. They are ridged because they're piped from a syringe-like tool with a star-shaped nozzle.

In Viet Nam, *Bánh rán* is a fried rice dough ball filled with mung bean paste often scented with jasmine, and covered in sesame seeds. Peruvian *Picarones* are made from fried squash and sweet potato dough, soaked and served in a sugary syrup. *Paczi* (little package) are semi-flattened round donuts, often containing a sweet filling, that are popular in Poland. Romanian *Gogoşi* are donut holes filled with jam, chocolate syrup or cheese. *Koeksister*, from South Africa, are deep fried dough balls with cinnamon, ginger, dried tangerine, aniseed, and sugar syrup. They are dipped in coconut when cooled. South American *Buñuelos* are thinly rolled balls of yeast dough, often soaked in anis (licorice flavoring) and filled with sweet or savory fillings. They are known as a sign of good luck and fortune. In Argentina, *Bolas de fraile* (monk's balls) are fried balls of dough filled with dulce de leche (caramelized sugar in milk).

A pie is a baked dish, usually made of pastry dough and filled with various sweet or savory ingredients. The first pies were predominately meat pies. The ancient Romans made a plain pastry of flour, oil and water to cover meats and fowls to keep in the juices, but the covering was not meant to be eaten. In Europe, pies became a staple of traveling and working people. Regional variations were based on what was grown locally and what meats were available. Recipes for Dutch Apple Pie go back to the Middle Ages. In 1644, Oliver Cromwell banned the eating of pie in England – it was thought to be a pagan form of pleasure. The ban was lifted in 1660. Pie came to the American colonies with the first English settlers. Colonists cooked their pies in long narrow pans called coffins. The crust was there to hold in the filling during baking but was not eaten. The term 'crust' was first used during the American Revolution.

Pies come in a variety of sizes and flavors. A single-crust, or bottom crust pie, has filling placed on top of the pastry. A top-crust pie has the filling in the bottom of the dish and is covered with pastry before baking. In a two-crust pie, the filling is completely enclosed in a pastry shell. Shortcrust pastry is often used for baked pie crusts and cream pies may have a graham cracker crust. In rural homes in the nineteenth century, apple and other fruit pies were often a common item served for breakfast on farms. It was considered a good hearty beginning for a hard day's work. Yale College served apple pie at every supper for more than one hundred years.

A betty, baked pudding made with layers of spiced sweetened fruit and buttered bread crumbs, dates back to Colonial America. The cobbler, a deep-dish fruit pie, got its name from the biscuit dough crust on top that looks cobbled. It originated in the United States in the mid-nineteenth century. Throwing a cream pie in a person's face has been a part of film comedy since 1909. Pie has become a big part of American culture throughout the years and apple pie is considered America's favorite dessert. People will often say that someone or something is "As American as apple pie."

Pot pies have a flaky crust and bottom, with a filling of meat, gravy, and mixed vegetables. Quiche has an open-faced pastry crust with a savory custard filling containing cheese, meat, vegetables, or a combination.

PASTRY

The ancient Egyptians made the first crude pastries out of grain meal flavored with honey, fruits, and spices. Pastries became a culinary art form in the Middle East and were first brought to Europe in the seventh century. The most innovative recipes were created during the Renaissance (a period in European history from the fourteenth to the seventeenth century). Puff pastry originated in 1645 in France when an apprentice pastry chef created a special loaf of bread for his ailing father who could only eat water, flour, and butter. Classic puff pastry is a wheat dough spread with butter or other solid fat and repeatedly rolled out and folded to create a soft, buttery, flaky bread. It uses steam to rise.

Baklava is a Greek pastry made of layers of filo dough (paper-thin sheets of unleavened flour dough). It is filled with chopped nuts and sweetened with syrup or honey.

The Bear Claw, which originated in the United States during the mid-1920s, is made with sweet yeast dough shaped in a semicircle with slices along the curved edge. It is filled with almond paste and as the dough rises, the sections separate so it looks like a bear's claws.

The cannoli has a tube-shaped shell of fried pastry dough, with a sweet creamy filling containing ricotta cheese. It may have tiny pieces of dried fruit or chocolate chips added. Some bakers dip one end in melted chocolate that hardens.

Cinnamon rolls are made of rolled sheets of sweet yeast dough with a mixture of cinnamon and sugar sprinkled over a thin coat of butter. The dough is then rolled, cut into individual portions, and baked or deep fried. They are often topped with icing or glaze.

A cream horn is made with flaky or puff pastry and filled with whipped cream. The horn shape is made by winding overlapping pastry strips around a conical mold.

The cronut is a croissant-donut pastry attributed to New York City.

A cruller is fried dough that has been twisted or braided and topped with powdered sugar or cinnamon sugar. A French cruller is a fluted, ring-shaped donut with a light airy texture.

Danish is yeast dough rolled into flattened layers. Thin slices of butter are placed between the layers. Some are topped with chocolate, glaze, nuts, jam, or custard. They may be formed into a variety of shapes like circles, figure-eights, or spirals. There is also a sweet cheese danish.

An éclair is an oblong pastry made with a light pastry dough called choux. It is filled with pastry cream, custard, or whipped cream and topped with chocolate icing.

A fig roll is an ancient Egyptian pastry filled with fig paste (the forerunner of the Fig Newton®).

Fritters are fried small cakes. Apple fritters are very popular but there are also savory fritters made with things like corn.

Central European Kolache have puffy pillows of dough topped with fruit. Several cities hold annual Kolache Festival celebrations.

Kolacz, from Poland, has a light and flaky dough made from cream cheese, butter, and flour. It is filled with a variety of sweet and savory fillings such as apricot, raspberry, prune, sweet cheese, poppy seeds, or a nut mixture.

The Scandinavian Kringle is a variety of sweet, salty, or filled pretzel. Roman Catholic monks brought it to Denmark in the thirteenth century.

Ladyfingers, small sponge cakes shaped like fingers, originated in the fifteenth century. They may be soaked in a sugary syrup or liqueur and used in trifles, tiramisu, and a variety of other desserts.

A Macaron is a French confection with ganache, buttercream, or jam sandwiched between two very small meringue-like cookies.

Macaroon is the American word for a flourless, egg-white-based cookie made with coconut.

Meringue is made from egg whites and sugar. Lemon, vinegar, or cream of tartar may also be added as well as vanilla, almond, or coconut flavoring. The mixture is whipped until stiff peaks form and then baked until just the tips are a golden brown. Meringue cookies are light and airy and fat free. They come in a variety of colors and some contain miniature chocolate chips. Meringue is also used as a topping for lemon meringue pie.

The Napoleon originated in France and is made up of three layers of puff pastry with pastry cream between them. The top is glazed with icing or fondant.

Pastaciotti, an Italian pastry with a flaky crust and sweet creamy filling, looks like a small handheld pie. Fillings may include ricotta cheese, or vanilla or chocolate pudding.

A Petit four is a very tiny cake. Its name is French for 'small filled.' It was traditionally made in a smaller oven next to the main oven because it had a lower temperature than the larger oven used for baking bread and roasting meats. The icing is spread over the top and sides.

Rugelach is a small crescent-rolled Jewish pastry. The crescent is shaped by rolling a triangle of dough around a filling such as nuts, fruit, or chocolate.

Sfogliatelle are shell-shaped filled pastries native to Italy. The name means 'many leaves or layers' and the texture resembles leaves stacked on each other. Some types of filling include orange-flavored ricotta, almond paste, or candied peel of citron.

The oldest recipe for Strudel, a layered filo pastry with a sweet filling, dates back to 1696. The best-known strudel is apple, a traditional Viennese pastry. There are also savory varieties.

A Tart is a baked dish consisting of a filling over a shortcrust pastry base with an open top not covered with pastry. The filling may be sweet or savory but most are fruit-based, sometimes with custard added. Tartlet refers to a miniature tart.

Stollen, first mentioned in Germany in 1474, is a bread containing dried fruit or chopped candied fruit and covered with powdered sugar or icing. It is traditionally eaten during the Christmas season in Germany.

A soufflé, a baked egg-based dish, originated in the early eighteenth century in France. It can be sweet or savory. Sweet soufflés are often dusted with powdered sugar. The word 'soufflé' is from the French word souffler, meaning 'to breathe or to puff.'

A turnover is made by placing a filling on a piece of dough, folding the dough over, sealing it, and baking it. It can be sweet or savory. Sweet turnovers have a fruit filling and are made with puff pastry. Savory types include the Italian Calzone, an oven-baked folded pizza that originated in Naples; a Pasty from the United Kingdom that has a meat and vegetable filling; and an Empanada, a Spanish or Latin American turnover filled with a variety of savory ingredients and baked or fried. Empanadas may also have a sweet fruit filling.

SNACK CAKE

McKee Foods Corporation is the maker of the Little Debbie Snacks and Drake's cakes. Little Debbie Snacks, named after the four-year-old granddaughter of the company's founder, include Swiss Cake Roll® (a rolled cream-filled chocolate-covered cake), Oatmeal Creme Pie® (also chocolate chip, raisin, and fudge flavors), Marshmallow Pies® (also banana and jelly flavors), Nutty Bar® (four cookie wafers sandwiched together in a peanut butter mixture and covered in chocolate), Cosmic Brownie® (thick fudgy layer of chocolate with small, candy coated pieces on top), and Zebra Cake® (frosted cream-filled cake with white and chocolate stripes). The Drake's brand distributes items such as Ring Dings®(chocolate cake and frosting filled with cream), Yodels® (frosted, cylindrical-shaped cream-filled chocolate cakes.), Devil Dogs®, and coffee cake.

Tastykake, established in 1914, is the brand name for a line of snack foods that include cupcakes, Krimpet® (shaped sponge cake with butterscotch icing or jelly filling), Cookie Bars, Kandy Kake® (chocolate-enrobed cakes with filling), Kandy Bar Kakes® (with actual candy bar flavors), Dreamies® (sponge cake with cream filling), and individual pies.

The first Hostess Brands Inc. product was the Hostess Cup Cake®, introduced in 1919. They also offer donettes, mini muffins, honey buns, cinnamon rolls, mini coffee cakes, single-serve fruit pies with a sugary glaze, Ding Dongs® (small, round, cream-filled chocolate cake whose name was given to coincide with a television ad campaign featuring a ringing bell), HoHo® (frosted, cream-filled chocolate cakes first created in 1920), and Sno Ball® (a cream-filled chocolate cake covered with pink marshmallow frosting and coconut flakes). Hostess produces the Twinkie®, invented in 1930 by an Illinois baker. It is a small yellow sponge cake filled with vanilla-flavored cream that originally held banana cream. During World War II, bananas were rationed and the company switched to vanilla cream. A deep-fried Twinkie® involves freezing the cake, dipping it into batter, and deep-frying it. Zingers® are similar to Twinkies® but in devils' food, vanilla, and raspberry flavors.

Many products have carried Dolley Madison's name and image, including the Dolly Madison brand of pre-packaged snack cakes named for her in 1937 (but spelled without the 'e'). Now owned by Hostess Brands, Dolley Madison was best known for its long association with characters from the *Peanuts®* comic strip by Charles M. Schulz. Charlie Brown and his friends appeared on Dolley Madison packages and in TV commercials in the 1960s through the 1980s. The bakery was one of the sponsors of the *Peanuts®* animated specials telecast on TV.

The Sara Lee Corporation produces a frozen line of pound cakes, cheesecakes, pies, coffee cakes, carrot cake, and banana cake. Charlie Lubin named his new line of cheesecakes after his eight-year-old daughter, Sara Lee. She has appeared in television advertisements throughout the years, sharing with viewers that her father told her the product had to be perfect because he was naming it after her.

Pop Tarts® were introduced in 1964. They come in many flavors and various one-time, seasonal, and limited-edition flavors. Most varieties are frosted but they are designed to be warmed inside a toaster.

Toaster Strudel® is a frozen pastry that is heated in a toaster, and then spread with icing. There are several flavors.

The Moon Pie, originally developed as a snack sold to Appalachian coal miners in 1917, is made with a marshmallow sandwiched between two graham crackers, and dipped in chocolate. There is a Moon Pie Festival in June each year in Tennessee.

The Whoopie Pie has two soft cookie-like cakes with a sweet, fluffy white filling. It originated with the Amish in Lancaster County, Pennsylvania. There is an annual Whoopie Pie Festival in Maine.

Granola bars (rolled oats with honey, nuts and puffed rice) can help lower cholesterol, regulate digestion, aid in weight loss, improve heart health, increase energy, promote proper organ function, increase cognitive activity, and build stronger bones. Stanley Mason invented the granola bar. He is also responsible for products like the disposable diaper, the squeezable ketchup bottle, heated pizza boxes, heatproof plastic microwave cookware, and dental floss dispensers.

Nutrition bars are a great source of protein, healthy fats, and wholesome ingredients if you choose the right ones. Some are loaded with processed ingredients, unnatural sugars, and unnecessary fillers so read the list of ingredients on the package. Look for: less than five grams of fat, three to five grams of fiber, fifteen or more grams of protein, and the amount of carbohydrates and calories. A lot of people feel they are doing something good for their body by eating a protein bar or other type of nutrition bar but there are ingredients in foods that are missing in these bars. Most nutritionists emphasize that for a quick snack, you may be better off eating an apple or a banana.

Cookies originated in Rome around the third century B.C. They were called bis coctum (meaning 'twice baked'). Bis coctum is also the origin of the word 'biscuit' that later became known as a cookie or cracker. The Roman cookie was not sweet. Sugar was added by the Dutch and they called it koekje (little cake). The Dutch took them to America in the eighteenth century and the word became 'cookie.' Cookies come in a variety of shapes, flavors, and textures (soft, chewy, crispy). A few unusual flavors are chili chocolate chip, maple bourbon bacon, olive oil raisin, and Greek yogurt and lemon. Christmas cookies date back to Medieval Europe.

To make molded cookies, the dough is formed by hand into shapes such as crescents, wreaths, candy canes, or balls (ball are sometimes flattened with the bottom of a glass). Rolled cookies are made using a rolling pin. Chilled dough is rolled out and cut into shapes by using a knife, pastry wheel, or cookie cutter. Pressed cookies are made by pressing the dough through a cookie press or pastry tube to form different shapes. For drop cookies, balls of dough are dropped from a spoon onto a cookie sheet. Refrigerator, or ice box cookies, are prepared by shaping the dough into long rolls and then refrigerating them. Once cold, the dough can be sliced and baked.

Bar cookies were developed in the United States during the late nineteenth century. The brownie is a flat, baked dessert square that comes in a variety of forms and can be either cake-like or fudge-like. Often, other ingredients are added such as chocolate chips and nuts. It is thought that the brownie came about when the pastry chef at the Palmer House Hotel in Chicago made a small cake-like confection that could be included in boxed lunches at the World's Columbian Exposition (the World's Fair held in Chicago in 1893). His creation included walnuts and an apricot glaze. The first-known printed use of the word 'brownie' appeared in an 1896 cookbook. A Blondie is a variation that is made without melted chocolate in the batter. It may contain nuts and white or butterscotch chips.

Presbyterian minister Sylvester Graham invented graham crackers in 1829. The first commercial cookie in the United States was the Animal Cracker, introduced in 1902. The carrying string on the box was designed so it could be hung on a Christmas Tree. Over time, there have been thirty-seven different animals in a box of animal crackers. The current crackers are tiger, cougar, camel, rhinoceros, kangaroo, hippopotamus, bison, lion, hyena, zebra, elephant, sheep, bear, gorilla, monkey, seal, and giraffe. The Oreo® was developed and introduced by Nabisco in 1912. The original chocolate chip cookie, the Toll House Cookie, was invented by Ruth Graves Wakefield in the 1930s. She and her husband owned the Toll House Inn in Massachusetts and Ruth cooked for her guests. One day she had to substitute chopped semi-sweet chocolate for baker's chocolate in a cookie recipe. When she removed the cookies from the oven she noticed that the semi-sweet chocolate didn't melt into the dough as the baker's chocolate had. Today, chocolate chip cookies are the most popular homemade cookie. The Great American Cookie Company is the originator of the cookie cake. December fourth is National Cookie Day.

The first known recipe for gingerbread came from Greece in 2400 B.C. Gingerbread, flavored with ginger, cloves, nutmeg or cinnamon and sweetened with honey, sugar or molasses, can either be soft like cake or more like a cookie. During the fifteenth century, gingerbread became a gift of love and respect. Cutting gingerbread into shapes exists in many countries. The shapes change with the seasons and are often covered with glaze. Elaborately decorated gingerbread cookies became synonymous with all things elegant, and gold leaf was often used as an embellishment. The gingerbread man cookie, especially popular during the Christmas season, was first served to foreign dignitaries by Queen Elizabeth I of England. It was dunked in port wine. In Germany, the soft form is called lebkuchen. In Norway and Sweden, pepperkaker decorated with glaze and candy aren't only eaten, they are also used as window decorations. Switzerland fills their gingerbread, known as biber, with marzipan and decorates them with engraving or icing. A traditional Polish gingerbread that has been produced since the Middle Ages is called piernik toruński. Russian gingerbread, called pryaniki (the Russian word for pepper), has an embossed ornament or text on the front side. In Bulgaria, medehka is a large, round, flat gingerbread cookie with a thin layer of chocolate.

Fortune cookies were invented in 1916 by George Jung, a Los Angeles noodle maker. They had a thank you note inside but over time they were made with a fortune inside. The largest manufacturer of fortune cookies is Wonton Food Inc., headquartered in Brooklyn, New York. They make over four million fortune cookies per day and have a data base of over fifteen thousand fortunes. Fortune cookies are baked as flat circles. After they are removed from the oven, the paper fortunes are folded inside while the cookies are still warm and flexible. As the fortune cookies cool, they harden into shape. July twentieth is National Fortune Cookie Day.

In the early 1900s, Girl Scouts in different parts of the country baked their own simple sugar cookies and sold them to raise money for their activities. The first commercially baked Girl Scout cookies took place in 1934 and today there are two official Girl Scout Cookie bakers. Girl Scouts sell almost two hundred million packages of cookies each year, including a gluten-free variety. In 2014, they began the Digital Cookie® platform – selling cookies on line. Thin Mints® are the top-selling flavor in the United States. In 2016, Girl Scouts took the stage at the Academy Awards to sell cookies to Hollywood's A-list.

Tinsmiths first made cookie cutters by hand in the 1700s. They were introduced to American colonists by the Dutch and Germans. The American National Cookie Cutter Historical Museum is located in Joplin, Missouri. The Cookie Cutters Collectors Club is a nonprofit organization founded in 1972. National Cookie Cutter Week is celebrated each year during the first week in December. American cookie jars first appeared in the 1930s. Depression-era housewives stopped buying bakery-made foods and began baking at home to save money. They needed a place to store cookies that would keep them fresh. Many people collect cookie jars as a hobby.

Unagi Pie are Japanese cookies made with crushed eel bones and eel extract.

Culinary historians believe that the first actual cookies were used as little test cakes. Bakers would bake a tiny bit of cake batter in the oven to test oven temperature. Cookies grew increasingly popular over time and the idea of the cookie spread around the world. Every country has their own name for the cookie. In Spain they are called galletas, while in Germany they are called kels *or keks*. In Australia and England they are called biscuits. Italy calls their cookies names such as biscotti or ameretti. Hundreds of thousands of cookie recipes and variations exist, including those for gluten-free cookies and no-bake cookies. A few favorite no bake cookie recipes include Rice Krispie Treats®, coconut date balls, rum balls, and peanut butter balls.

Cookie Tips

Use butter unless a recipe calls for margarine. Butter has a lower melting point and spreads more than shortening. Margarine should contain at least eighty percent vegetable oil – less than that and it will have a high water content which can result in cookies that spread excessively, stick to the pan, or don't brown well.

To get cookies to hold their shape, chill the dough before baking according to the chilling time given in a recipe. If you need to speed up the chilling process, wrap the dough and place it in the freezer. Twenty minutes of freezer time is equal to one hour in the refrigerator. Keep the dough chilled in between baking batches of cookies. Always chill cookies made with margarine in the freezer.

Place parchment paper on a cookie sheet before adding the dough. Slide the baked cookies off the paper onto the cooling rack, then slide the next prepared parchment paper onto the baking sheet. Cool cookie sheets in between batches by running tepid water over the back of them.

A cookie sheet should not have high sides (they hamper the even flow of heat). Dark non-stick surfaces cause the bottoms of cookies to brown too quickly. Use light sheets or double insulated cookie sheets.

Soft cookies should be stored in a container with a tight lid. Add a slice of apple to keep them from drying out. Crisp cookies should be stored in a container with a loose lid, like a cookie jar. If there is a lot of humidity, add a piece of bread to the container to absorb the moisture.

For thinner cookies, use room-temperature ingredients or let dough stand at room temperature. For thicker, puffier cookies, decrease the amount of fat and use shortening instead of butter and allow the dough sit in the refrigerator for up to thirty-six hours before baking it.

For less crumbly cookies, use higher protein flour and cut the sugar and fat by a few tablespoons.

For cookies with more color, substitute 1 to 2 tablespoons of light corn syrup for sugar. For paler cookies, use cake flour or bleached all-purpose flour.

Ancient Roman cooks recognized the binding properties of eggs. They created egg-based dishes that were either savory (meats and vegetables) or sweet (flavored with honey, nuts, and spices). Custard, a cooked mixture of milk or cream and egg yolk, dates to the Middle ages. It was eaten alone or used as fillings for pies, tarts, and pastry. An Italian cookbook published in 1475 stated that custard-type dishes were considered health food. In 1847, an English chemist introduced custard powder as an alternative to egg thickeners. Custard powder consists mainly of cornstarch and sugar, and hot milk is added to make a sauce. By the turn of the twentieth century there were many recipes for cornstarch puddings, especially if fresh eggs were not available.

Most sweet custards add sugar and vanilla and are cooked in a double boiler, steamed, or baked in a water bath. Custard can vary in consistency from a thin sauce to a thick cream. When flour or cornstarch is added, the result is called a pastry cream or confectioner's custard, used as a filling for cakes and pastries such as cream puffs and éclairs. Crème anglaise, French for 'English custard,' is a rich, pourable custard sauce that can be served hot or cold over cake, fruit or other dessert. Crème anglaise collee is custard thickened with gelatin. In Europe, custard is also known as *blancmange* and is thickened with starch. American pudding is a sweetened milk mixture thickened with cornstarch, then cooked. It has no eggs in it. When a recipe is exceptionally smooth and light, it is often called 'silk' pudding for its silky texture. Custard bases may also be used for savory items like quiche.

Crème caramel, or flan, is a light egg custard that is baked in a caramel-lined mold in a water bath. After the custard is baked, it is chilled and then turned out of the mold.

Crème brulee' is a sweet baked custard made with cream instead of milk. It is topped with a layer of caramelized brown sugar. The name is French but it most likely originated in England.

Creamy puddings are mostly served chilled but a few may be served warm. Instant pudding does not require boiling and can be prepared more quickly. The earliest print reference for chocolate pudding is 1730. Americans had very few bananas until after the Civil War but a few bunches made their way from the West Indies to American ports. They were considered rare, perishable treats. Faster steam ships and new trading firms brought more affordable bananas from the Caribbean and Central America to the U.S. Imports surged to over sixteen million by the turn of the twentieth century. In addition to peeling and eating them, cooks started incorporating bananas into a variety of dishes and desserts, like banana pudding.

Tapioca is made by processing the root of yuca plant. There are many forms of processed tapioca: flakes, seeds, and pearls. Traditionally, it was considered a healthy food because this form of starch is easy to digest. In the nineteenth century in the United States, tapioca pudding was often prescribed for the young, old and infirmed. Minute brand tapioca was introduced in 1894.

A mousse has air bubbles that give it a light and airy texture. It can range from light and fluffy to creamy and thick, depending on how it is prepared. It may be sweet or savory. Sweet mousses are made with whipped egg whites or whipped cream and a flavoring like chocolate, coffee, caramel, puréed fruits, or herbs and spices are added. It is served as a dessert or used as a cake filling. Savory mousse may be flavored with herbs, fish, or liver (similar to pate').

Zabaglione is an Italian dessert, or sometimes a beverage, consisting of egg yolks, sugar, and a sweet wine (typically Marsala) whisked together over heat until it froths. The creamy dessert is usually served in a champagne glass with strawberries, blueberries, peaches or other fruit. A Neapolitan variation uses egg whites and whipped cream to make a richer but lighter dessert.

Bakewell tart was always known as a pudding until the twentieth century. There were two main kinds. One was filled with a sweet egg custard over a layer of candied fruit on a pastry shell. A second version was made without eggs, butter or milk – the filling was ground almonds and sugar made into a liquid paste and flavored with spices.

Charlotte is a molded custard that can be eaten cold or hot. For a cold charlotte, the mold is lined with sponge cake, ladyfingers, biscuits or bread and filled with layers of fruit and custard or mouse or Bavarian cream (whipped cream that has been fortified with gelatin). The dessert is chilled thoroughly and unmolded before serving. The original charlotte is said to have been named for Queen Charlotte, wife of King George III of England (1738-1820). *Charlotte Russe,* decorated elaborately with whipped-cream rosettes, was created for the Russian Czar Alexander. *Charlotte aux Pommes* (Apple Charlotte) is a hot charlotte that uses a buttered-bread or brioche shell filled with sweetened apples sautéed with apple brandy, baked and served hot with fruit sauce.

Rice pudding is an ancient dish that can trace its roots to the grain pottages* made in the Middle East. It was associated with good nutrition and easy digestion and was first mentioned in medical texts rather than cookbooks. Medieval rice pottages (an early version of rice pudding) were made of rice boiled until soft, then mixed with almond milk or cow's milk, sweetened, and sometimes colored. Recipes for baked rice puddings began to appear in the early seventeenth century.

*A pottage is a medieval term for porridge, a semi-liquid cooked dish of oatmeal, barley, rye, or wheat. Early American versions were made with maize. The world comes from the French *potage* meaning 'something cooked in a pot.' Pottages were eaten by poor families as a complete meal. Wealthy people used them to accompany the meat dish. Pease porridge descends from pease pottage, an ancient dish of boiled legumes. Hasty pudding, a type of porridge made from cereal grains and milk and sweetened with brown sugar or syrup, is a quickly prepared dish that dates back to the late 1500s.

The Christmas Pudding, sometimes called figgy pudding or plum pudding, is a cake-like dish served at the Christmas meal in Great Britain. It consists of a steamed pudding made with dried fruit, spices, candied peel, eggs, suet and breadcrumbs. Many people make the pudding at least four weeks before Christmas and hang it in a cloth in a dry place until the holiday meal. It is decorated with a sprig of holly and served with brandy poured over it, which is then lit. According to tradition, the person who makes the pudding, and even each member of the household, should make a wish while stirring the batter. Sometimes a coin is added to the batter and the person who finds it has prosperity in the new year.

Plum pudding dates back to the Middle Ages where it was known as mince pie. The ingredients were partridge, pheasant, poultry and rabbit, and it was boiled in animal stomach lining along with root vegetables. Dried fruits like raisins and prunes were introduced in the 1500s as they became accessible and more affordable. (In 1660, 'plum' was used to mean a dried grape or raisin used for puddings and cakes.) Eventually, the animal stomach was replaced by a pudding cloth, which in turn was replaced by the pudding basin and it was no longer boiled, but steamed. The meat was phased out over time but suet remained.

NOTE: There is also a Plum Pudding that contains plums encased in a pie shell and then steamed. It is made at any time of the year and is not a holiday dish.

In Victorian times, a pudding was most often served as a sweet dish but savory recipes also existed. Roly-poly pudding is a suet* pudding made in a roll shape. Spotted dick is a loaf-shaped suet-based pudding that descended from Roly-poly pudding. Spotted alludes to the visual effect created by the raisins or sultanas. It is often served with custard.

*Suet comes from the fat that grows around the kidneys in cows and sheep. It is easy to purchase from grocery stores in the United Kingdom but in North America, if you find any in a store, most likely it has been partially hydrogenated. Substitutes for suet are lard, shortening, butter, bacon fat, and vegetable suet. Canadian grocery stores sell bags of frozen suet.

There are other foods that are called pudding: black pudding or blood pudding (sausage), bread pudding (stale bread baked in a custard sauce), steamed pudding (cake-like), and batter puddings made from meat fat that dripped into the pan during roasting, named Yorkshire Pudding in 1737. Today, Yorkshire pudding is made from a batter of eggs, flour, and milk or water (it looks like a popover). It is often served with a beef roast and gravy.

Ambrosia (its name is a reference to the food of the gods in Greek mythology) may have first appeared in a cookbook in the Southern United States in 1867. Early recipes called for a combination of sliced oranges, grated coconut, and sugar layered in a glass bowl. In the 1880s, recipes started popping up that included sliced pineapple along with the oranges. A few recipes added a little sherry or Madeira to the layers of fruit and some were served with whipped cream. Twentieth century cooks began incorporating more modern and sweeter components like marshmallow. Around World War I, Stephen F. Whitman & Son of Philadelphia introduced Marshmallow Whip, a jarred marshmallow product for use in preparing desserts. Individual recipes for ambrosia were developed and some included a package of orange flavored gelatin and evaporated milk. Other creamy binders that are used are sour cream, heavy cream, whipped cream, yogurt, or frozen whipped topping. One recipe includes a can of fruit cocktail, bananas, miniature marshmallows, canned crushed pineapple and grated coconut, baked until the coconut is browned.

DESSERT SAUCES

Dessert sauces are spooned, drizzled, or poured over ice cream, fruit, and certain cakes. Some chefs also use it for plate decoration. The sauces may be cooked or uncooked, and served cold or hot (like hot fudge). A hard sauce has the addition of alcohol. Dessert sauces are made with a variety of items like chocolate, caramel, yogurt, or assorted fruits. Evaporated milk, semi-sweet chocolate chips and a dash of vanilla extract make a creamy chocolate sauce. Combining unsweetened cocoa powder with granulated sugar and light corn syrup, and a dash of vanilla extract, makes a chocolate syrup. Granulated sugar, sweetened condensed milk, butter and a dash of vanilla extract creates a caramel sauce. Lemon curd is a spreadable sweet sauce that is smooth and buttery and spread on scones or used as filling for cookies, tarts and pies.

GELATIN

Gelatin has been used since the time of the ancient Egyptians. Peter Cooper obtained the first American patent for the manufacture of gelatin in 1845. In 1895, a cough syrup manufacturer purchased the patent and developed a packaged gelatin dessert. His wife named it Jell-O®. The original flavors were orange, lemon, strawberry, and raspberry. Fruits that sink in Jell-O® are seedless grapes, fruit cocktail, and peaches and pears in heavy syrup. Fresh fruits that float are bananas, citrus sections, sliced peaches, diced apples, and fruit in light syrup.

Gelatin is found in soft caramels, marshmallows, chocolate coated mallows, licorice, and many other sweet items. It gives candy elasticity, chewy consistency, and a longer shelf life. Edible gelatin is also the basic ingredient in gummi candy. Hans Riegel, the owner of the German candy company Haribo, invented gummi bears and gummi candy during the 1920s. In 1981, another German gummi candy manufacturer, Trolli, made the first gummi worm.

CANDY

Man has always craved something sweet to eat. Cavemen ate honey combs and honey. As far back as 1500 B.C. the ancient Egyptians rolled fruits, nuts and spices in honey. Around the same time, Greeks used honey to make candied fruits and flowers. The Aztecs used the cocoa bean to make a bitter chocolate drink that was sweetened with sugar fifteen hundred years later. The manufacturing of sugar began during the Middle Ages but it was so expensive that only the rich could afford candy made from sugar. The price of manufacturing sugar was much lower by the seventeenth century when hard candy became popular. The first candy came to America in the early eighteenth century from Britain and France. Rock candy, made from crystallized sugar, was the simplest form of candy but it was only attainable by wealthy colonists because only a few of the early colonists were proficient in sugar work. Before the Industrial Revolution (the period from about 1760 to sometime between 1820 and 1840), candy was considered a form of medicine to calm the digestive system or cool a sore throat. Technological advances and the availability of sugar made candy more attainable for all people. Children bought penny candy – a penny per piece even though much of it was sold in bulk by the pound. By the 1850s, there were hundreds of confectionery factories in the United States.

Marshmallow candy originated in ancient Egypt. It was a honey candy flavored and thickened with marsh mallow plant sap. In the nineteenth century, juice from the marsh mallow plant's roots was extracted and cooked with egg whites and sugar, then whipped into a foam that hardened. This was used as a medicinal candy to soothe children's sore throats. Eventually, gelatin replaced the sap in the modern recipes. Today, marshmallows are made from sugar, corn syrup, and gelatin. In 1953, the Just Born candy company bought the Rodda Candy Company, which produced a handmade candy marshmallow chick. A year later, a machine was invented that could mass-produce marshmallow chicks, trademarked as Peeps®. In the 1960s, seasonally shaped Peeps® were also produced. They were only made in pink, white, and yellow colors until 1995 when lavender was introduced. In 1998, blue Peeps® were produced for Easter. In 1999, they created vanilla flavored Peeps® and a year later strawberry flavor was added. Today, there are also different shapes and colors used for various holidays, chocolate Peeps®, and Peeps Minis®.

Caramel is a sweet brown product made by heating a variety of sugars. Different types of candies and desserts are made with caramel and it is also used as a filling or topping. Soft, dense, and chewy caramel candy is made by boiling a mixture of milk or cream, sugar, butter, and vanilla. Sugar Daddy®, invented in 1925, is a candy bar on a stick that is a small block of semi-hard caramel. A bite-sized caramel flavored jelly bean candy is called Sugar Babies®. Caramel apples are made by dipping or rolling apples on a stick in hot caramel and allowing them to cool. They are called candy apples, taffy apples, or toffee apples when additional ingredients like crushed peanuts are applied.

Taffy is made by stretching or pulling a sticky mass of boiled sugar (corn syrup), butter, glycerin, flavorings, and coloring until tiny air bubbles are produced. It is then rolled, cut into small pieces, and wrapped in wax paper to keep it soft. Salt water taffy, created at the New Jersey shore, does not contain salt water. Mary Jane®, originally made in 1914 by Charles Miller, is a peanut butter and molasses flavored taffy-like candy with peanut butter in the center. It was named after Miller's favorite aunt, Mary Jane, and the candy has used the same little girl illustration on the wrappers since its inception. Bit-O-Honey® first appeared in 1924. It consists of six pieces of a honey-flavored taffy with almond bits and is available in a large bar and small, bite-sized pieces. Now And Later® bite-sized squares of taffy come in nineteen different fruit flavors. When they were introduced in 1962 the company encouraged consumers to "enjoy a piece now and save a few for later." Laffy Taffy® has the flavor of the taffy printed on each label. Each piece of taffy is individually wrapped and inside each wrapper is a joke (hence the name). The jokes have been written and sent in by children since 1970. The Abba Zaba® bar is a thick, chewy taffy bar with a peanut butter center.

Marzipan, or almond paste, is made from sugar or honey and ground almonds. It is used in candy (often shaped like small fruits), as a pastry filling, or rolled into thin sheets for icing cakes. In Holland and Belgium, marzipan figures are given as presents to children during Saint Nicholas Eve. In Germany, it is common to give marzipan in the shape of bread or small potatoes during Christmastime. In Denmark and Norway, marzipan pigs are eaten for Christmas and marzipan eggs for Easter.

Licorice comes from the root of the Glycyrrhiza glabra plant. It is fifty times sweeter than sugar and is known for its antiviral, antibacterial, anti-inflammatory, antioxidant, and antidepressant properties. Greece, Egypt, and Asian nations have been using licorice root for flavoring and medicinal purposes for centuries. Licorice was discovered in King Tut's tomb. Alexander the Great and Roman Emperor Caesar endorsed the health benefits of licorice and Napoleon's warriors used it to quench their thirst during battle. **Caution: Licorice Root may raise blood pressure levels when used in large quantities on a regular basis.**

Modern licorice candy dates from seventeenth century Holland. In the United States, anise seed is substituted for licorice flavoring in candy. Cherry Twizzlers® licorice candy is made by one of the oldest confectionery firms in the U.S., established in 1845. In 1914, the American Licorice Company's first product was Black Licorice Twists® and in the 1950s they began producing Raspberry Vines (people called them red licorice because of their similarities to the original black licorice twists and the name was later changed to Red Vines®). Crows®, popular since the 1890s, are a black licorice-flavored gum drop. Good and Plenty® are brightly colored, candy-coated, licorice candy. Spain is the largest producer of licorice. Most of the licorice used as a flavoring is used to flavor tobacco. April twelfth is National Licorice Day.

Chewy nougat, used in a variety of candy bars and chocolates, is made with sugar or honey, whipped egg whites, roasted nuts and sometimes chopped candied fruit. There are three types of nougat. White is the most common and dates back to fifteenth century Italy. Torrone® is a popular white nougat candy. Brown nougat has a firmer, crunchier texture. The Viennese, or German nougat, is a chocolate and nut praline. Theodor Tobler and his cousin Emil Baumann invented a Swiss milk chocolate, honey and nougat infused candy bar called Toblerone® in 1908.

There are different types of pralines. French pralines are a combination of almonds and caramelized sugar. American pralines are softer and creamier and combine syrup and nuts with milk or cream. Belgian pralines consist of a chocolate shell with a softer, sometimes liquid, filling. A praline cookie is a chocolate biscuit containing ground nuts.

Toffee is made by caramelizing sugar with butter, and sometimes flour. Nuts or raisins may be added. In 1928, Heath Bar®, the first chocolate-covered toffee bar, appeared. It was originally only offered for home delivery since they were sold by a dairy salesman.

Brittle is flat broken pieces of hard sugar candy embedded with nuts. It has many variations around the world. One legend tells of a woman in the southern United States who was making taffy in 1890 but added the wrong ingredient, resulting in the first batch of peanut brittle.

Mint leaves have been used in medicine and cooking since ancient times. Mint candy has mint flavoring or real mint oil that can be peppermint (the oldest and most popular flavor of mint-flavored confectionery), spearmint, or wintergreen. In addition to breath freshening, mints that contain actual peppermint oil or extract can help with digestion. Soft mints, like dinner mints and butter mints, are soft candies often containing a higher butter content. Hard mints using peppermint oils were popular in Victorian England. Altoids® were created in 1780 in London. In 1932, Peppermint Mentos® were developed in the Netherlands and new flavors were added in 1973. Tic Tacs® were first produced in 1969. Ice Breakers® are a sugar-free brand of gum and disc-shaped mint candy first made in 1996.

Cotton candy, also called spun sugar, dates back to the late 1890s. It was originally called Fairy Floss and early machines were hand cranked. It is made entirely of sugar with flavoring and food coloring added. The 1904 St. Louis World's Fair introduced Americans to cotton candy, along with waffle ice cream cones, peanut butter, and iced tea.

Hard candy is made from a sugar-based syrup that is boiled. Coloring and flavoring are added and then it is poured into a tray to cool until it can be folded, rolled, or molded into the shapes desired. There are also sugar-free versions.

The butterscotch disk was discovered in Scotland in the early 1800s. Today's varieties are artificially flavored and individually wrapped.

In the early 1930's, the Ferrara Pan Candy Company created Red Hots® - small hot cinnamon flavored candies that are sometimes called cinnamon imperials. The name "cinnamon imperials" is a generic name used by the candy industry to indicate a piece of cinnamon hard candy. Several candy companies, like Brach's, produce cinnamon hard candy discs.

The Atomic Fireball®, a type of jawbreaker, is a round, cinnamon-flavored hard candy invented in 1954. The outer layers are bright red and the interior layers are white.

Jawbreakers, or Gobstoppers®, are a type of hard candy with a number of layers and each layer dissolves very slowly so it lasts a long time. They are too hard to bite which helps them last long.

Life Savers® were created in 1912 by Clarance Crane, a candy maker from Ohio. The mints looked like miniature life preservers so he called them Life Savers. They were the first candy in the United States to be wrapped in tinfoil to keep them fresh. Known as a candy that would not melt in the summertime, they originally came in one flavor, Pep-O-Mint. By 1921, they came in three fruit flavors, each packaged in their own separate rolls. The classic Five-Flavor roll was introduced in 1935 and contained pineapple, lime, orange, cherry, and lemon. In 2003, three of the flavors were replaced in the U.S. Today, the rolls contain pineapple, cherry, raspberry, watermelon, and orange.

NOTE: All hard sugar-based candies emit some light when you bite them. Crystalline sugars are crushed, forcing some electrons out of their atomic fields. The free electrons bump into nitrogen molecules in the air and when they collide, the electrons impart energy to the nitrogen molecules causing them to vibrate. In this excited state, and in order to get rid of the excess energy, the nitrogen molecules emit a small amount of visible light. Wintergreen oil emits a longer wavelength, specifically as blue light. When you bite into a Wint-O-Green Life Saver®, a greater amount of visible light can be seen.

PEZ® candy were created by Eduard Haas III in 1927 in Vienna, Austria as a mint for smokers (they did not come with a character head on a dispenser). The word 'pez' was created using the first, middle and last letter in the German word for peppermint, pfefferminz. Manufacture began in the United States in 1952 when they were marketed in the familiar plastic dispensers as a children's candy. The most popular dispenser is Santa Claus.

In 1949, Smarties® candy roll wafers were introduced as a candy that wouldn't melt in the heat. They come in six assorted colors and flavors: white (orange-cream), yellow (pineapple), pink (cherry), green (strawberry), purple (grape), and orange (orange).

Skittles® were first made commercially in 1974 in Britain and were introduced in North America in 1979. Domestic production of Skittles® began in the United States in 1982.

Lemonheads®, introduced in 1962, are a round, lemon-flavored candy consisting of a sweet coating, soft sour shell, and a hard candy core. They also come in a chewy variety. Other flavors include Appleheads® and Grapeheads®.

Bottle Caps® disc candy provides a sweet soda sensation. They come in cherry, root beer, cola, orange, and grape flavors.

Lollipops were first made in New Haven, Connecticut in 1908. They were named after the inventor's favorite race horse, Lolly Pop. Samuel Born invented a lollipop making machine in San Francisco in 1916. The machine mechanically inserted sticks into lollipops. In 1931, Tootsie Roll Pops® were introduced and were considered the first novelty candy because they combined two candies in one (a chewy chocolate center). In 1979, Frank Richards invented the Ring Pop®.

Sweethearts Conversation Hearts®, popular for Valentine's Day, are little heart-shaped sugar wafer candies with romantic sayings written on them. Examples include: Be Mine, Be True, The One I Love, Love Me, Kiss Me, and Sweet Talk. The heart sayings are always being updated to include more modern expressions like Email Me, Tweet Me, U Rock, and LOL. Invented in 1847 and still manufactured by the New England Confectionery Company (NECCO) – the oldest continuously operating candy company in the United States – about eight billion Sweethearts Conversation Hearts® are sold every year. The inspiration for the candy hearts goes back to a mid-1600s homemade candy called cockle (a shell-shaped candy made of sugar and flour). A motto was written on a slip of colored paper, rolled up, and baked inside each cockle.

NECCO also makes Necco Wafers®. Each roll contains eight flavors: lemon, lime, orange, chocolate, clove (purple), cinnamon (white), wintergreen (pink), and licorice (black). In 1928, Admiral Richard Byrd brought over two tons of Necco Wafers® with him on his legendary expedition to Antartica.

The original Charms Co. offering was the Charms Squares®, hard square candies in an assortment of fruit flavors.

Candy Buttons have three flavors on a strip of paper eleven and one half inches long – lemon, lime, and cherry.

In 1983, Angelo Fraggos invented Nerds®, tiny crunchy colorful sweet and sour hard candies. Originally, they came in cherry/orange or strawberry/grape flavors in a two-toned box with separated flavor compartments. Today, they come in various other flavors such as Sour-Lightning

Lemon/Amped Apple, Wildberry/ Peach, or Wild Cherry/ Watermelon. Some people believe the candy was named after a reference in the Dr. Seuss Book, *If I Ran the Zoo*, where a 'nerd' is mentioned as one of the creatures the narrator collected for his zoo.

The first Valentine's Day boxed candy was created by Richard Cadbury in 1868 when he decorated a candy box with a painting of his daughter and her kitten.

Stick candy, a long, cylindrical variety of hard candy, has been around since 1837. It has at least two different colors swirled together in a spiral pattern and is often sold as old-fashioned candy.

The Original Salem Black Jack® black strap molasses stick candy is made by hand just the way they were back in the 1800s, using the original recipe.

Candy cigarettes were introduced in the early 1930s when smoking wasn't seen as a health hazard. In the 1950, reports on the dangers of smoking were released and by the 1970s the word 'cigarette' disappeared from most candy cigarette packaging – it was labeled 'candy sticks.'

Jolly Rancher® candy was created in 1949 in Colorado. Jolly Rancher is also the name of the original company that produced them, named to suggest a hospitable western company. Flavors include apple, cherry, blue raspberry, watermelon, mountain berry, lemon, wild strawberry, strawberry, strawberry-watermelon, strawberry-banana, fruit punch, raspberry lemonade, peach, banana, orange-tangerine, pineapple, and banana-pineapple.

Jujube candy originally contained juice from the Chinese date, cultivated in China for over four thousand years. In the nineteenth century and early twentieth centuries, jujube candy often contained cough medication. Jujubes® are small, chewy candies in assorted fruit flavors of cherry, lemon, lime, orange, and grape. Jujyfruits® are another fruit-flavored candy with shapes like asparagus, tomato, grapes, banana, pineapple, raspberry and pea pods. The shape has nothing to do with the flavor; the candy's color cues the taste.

The term 'gum drop' first appeared in print in 1860 but the gumdrop, a soft gelatin-based candy, may have been created in 1801. Brightly colored and often coated in granulated sugar, gumdrops come in fruit and spice flavors. February fifteenth is National Gumdrop Day. Dots®, a popular gumdrop, were created in 1945. The original flavors are still found in boxes today – cherry, strawberry, lemon, lime, and orange. Tropical Dots®, Yogurt Dots®, and Sour Dots® also exist. More than four billion Dots® are produced every year.

Mike & Ike's® are an oblong-shaped fruit-flavored chewy candy first sold in 1940. Hot Tamales®, a chewy, spicy cinnamon-flavored candy similar in appearance, were introduced in 1950.

In 1960, Starburst Fruit Chews® were introduced and were later fortified with Vitamin C.

Chuckles® are soft jelly candies covered in sugar. The original five colors are red, orange, yellow, green and black. There is also a mini variety and seasonal selections.

Air Heads® chewy candy were created in 1986. Hundreds of children were asked to try it and helped give it its name.

Wine gums are chewy, firm gumdrop-like candies without a sugar coating. Different varieties contain various sweeteners, flavorings, and colorings.

The Swedish Fish® is a type of wine gum. A Swedish confectionery developed them specifically for the United States and Canada in the 1950s. The word 'Swedish' is branded into their side.

Jellybeans are most likely descended from the Middle Eastern confection known as Turkish Delight, a jelly-like confection coated with powdered sugar. The method for making the sugar shell coating on a jellybean was developed in seventeenth century France and is known as panning. The first advertisement for jelly beans was in the Chicago Daily News in 1905. Jellybeans became associated with Easter in the 1930's. Over sixteen billion jellybeans are made in the United States each year for Easter. The mini jellybean was developed in 1965. Its center was also flavored with natural flavoring, not just the outer shell. In 1976, a similar jelly bean that used natural purees was created, named Jelly Belly®. The first flavors were Very Cherry, Tangerine, Lemon, Green Apple, Grape, Licorice, Root Beer, and Cream Soda. They were sold as separate flavors instead of a variety in one bag. By the 1980s, many more flavors had been developed. Jelly Belly® was the first jellybean in space, on the space shuttle Challenger in 1983. President Reagan gave jars of Jelly Belly® jelly beans to visiting dignitaries.

The Boston Baked Bean® is a sugar-coated peanut developed in the early 1930s.

PayDay® is a candy bar consisting of salted peanuts rolled in caramel surrounding a firm nougat-like center. It was first introduced in 1932 by Frank Martoccio and is currently produced by the Hershey Company.

Big Hunk® is a candy bar made of honey-sweetened nougat filled with whole roasted peanuts. Some people eat it after it's been refrigerated (smack it and break it into small pieces), or microwave it for five to ten seconds and enjoy it soft and chewy.

Squirrel Nut Zippers® (vanilla, caramel and nut taffy) were named after an illegal drink during Prohibition. During the 1990's, a retro swing band named themselves "Squirrel Nut Zippers" and gave out the candy during their performances.

Candy-coated almonds, known as Jordan Almonds, are often given out in small tulle bags as a wedding favor. In many cultures, the almond represents life and love – fresh almonds have a bittersweet taste which is said to represent life and the candy coating is added so the newlyweds' life will be more sweet than bitter. There are five almonds in each bag, signifying five wishes for the new couple: health, wealth, happiness, children, and long life. White candy-coating is the color most often used at weddings but they also come in different colors.

Fun Dip® has been on the market in the United States since the 1950s and was originally called Lik-M-Aid. It consists of a pouch of powdered candy and a hard candy stick, called a Lik-a-Stix®, that you lick and dip into the pouch. It comes in flavors like Grape Yumptious Dip, Cherry Yum Diddly Dip, and RazzApple Magic Dip.

Pixy Stix® is a sweet and sour colored powdered candy packaged in a wrapper that looks like a paper drinking stray.

SweeTarts® were created in 1962 using the same basic recipe as the Pixy Stix® (parents wanted a less messy candy). Flavors include cherry, grape, lemon, lime, and orange.

The original version of candy corn hasn't changed since it was first made in 1880. An estimated thirty-five million pounds of candy are sold each year.

In the United States, the custom of trick-or-treating on Halloween began in the 1930s and early 1940s. Children were given homemade cookies and pieces of cake, fruit, nuts, coins, and toys. In the 1950s, candy manufacturers began promoting their products and candy became an affordable, convenient offering to trick-or-treaters. But it wasn't until the 1970s that wrapped, factory-made candy was viewed as the only acceptable thing to hand out. The first individually-wrapped penny candy sold in the United States was the Tootsie Roll®. The candy was invented by Leo Hirshfield, an Austrian immigrant living in New York City. He started his candy business in 1896 and named the candy after his daughter, whose nickname was Tootsie.

Looking for nostalgic candy from your childhood? There are many on-line candy companies that offer a wide selection, including the candy necklace and candy bracelet, wax candy bottles, sticks, mustaches and lips, Cow Tales® (sticks of caramel with a cream center) and Slo Poke® caramel candy. You'll also find candy drops like Claey's Old Fashioned Sugared Hard Candies®, made in the United States since 1919, Zotz® hard candy with the fizzy sour center, Reeds Candy Rolls® in butterscotch, root beer, and cinnamon flavors, and Razzles® -- "first it's candy - then it's gum!"

CHEWING GUM

As far back as the Ancient Greeks and Mayans, people have been chewing various gums, resins and latex secretions of natural plants (like chicle) to freshen their breath. Native Americans chewed the resin from spruce trees. Chewing gum releases flavor slowly over time and some of today's chewing gums help to keep teeth clean and breath fresh. The first commercial packaged chewing gum, named State of Maine Spruce Gum, was introduced in 1850. W.F. Semple patented chewing gum in 1869. Black Jack Gum® was the first to be sold in sticks in the United States. Chicklets® are a candy-coated gum created in 1906. In 1928, Walter Diemer came up with Double Bubble®, a new gum recipe that was less sticky and stretched more easily. His bubble gum was successful and sold over a million and a half dollars the first year. Bazooka® bubble gum, in its distinctive red-white-and-blue packaging, was sold at the end of World War II and in 1953 the company began wrapping a small comic strip around the gum (the gum was discontinued in 2012). Big League Chew® bubble gum is made to look like a pouch of tobacco that some big league baseball players chew. Flavors include Wild Pitch Watermelon, Swingin- Sour Apple, Ground Ball Grape, and Outta' Here original flavor. **Caution: Don't swallow chewing gum as it can stay in your system for a very long time.**

Ribbon candy, a type of hard candy, is most often for sale around the Christmas holiday season. It acquires its shape by first being fashioned as warm sugar into a flat strip, then folded back and forth over itself to form a hardened ribboned stick. The sugar is often colored and the candy has a glossy sheen.

The first candy cane was made by hand over three hundred and fifty years ago. Originally, it was only white. A candy cane turned upside down resembles the letter J, which many believe represents Jesus, and the candy's white color represents his purity. Candy canes were first mentioned in association with Christmas in 1874 and they were first hung on Christmas trees in 1882. Red and white striped candy canes were first made around 1900. A machine that could automatically make candy canes was invented in 1921. Today, around two billion candy canes are sold in the month before Christmas. Peppermint is the traditional flavor but candy canes also come in a variety of other colors and flavors, including chocolate. They are also used as a stirrer for hot chocolate or crushed for toppings on desserts. Candy canes do not have any fat or cholesterol. December 26 is National Candy Cane Day.

CHRISTMAS TRIVIA

In the Middle Ages, Christmas celebrations were a lot like today's Mardi Gras parties.

Gingerbread houses originated in Germany during the sixteenth century and became associated with Christmas tradition.

The first eggnog made in the United States was consumed in Captain John Smith's 1607 Jamestown settlement.

The celebration of Christmas was banned in Boston from 1659 to 1681 because the pilgrims believed that it was a decadent celebration. Anyone showing Christmas spirit was fined.

Poinsettia plants are named after Joel R. Poinsett, an American minister to Mexico, who brought the red-and-green plant from Mexico to the United States in 1828.

Christmas wasn't declared a federal holiday in the U.S. until 1870. Americans changed it from a raucous holiday into a family-centered day of peace. Old World customs were reintroduced.

The Salvation Army has had Santa Claus-clad donation collectors since the 1890s.

The Rockefeller Center Christmas tree lighting tradition began in 1931.

In 1939, Robert L. May, a copywriter, wrote a poem about Rudolph, "the most famous reindeer of all," to lure customers into the Montgomery Ward department store.

Archaeologists found evidence of cacao (cocoa) at a site in Honduras, dating from about 1100 B.C. Mayans were drinking chocolate around 400 A.D. They mixed cocoa with water, chili peppers, cornmeal, and other ingredients to make a spicy, not sweet, chocolate drink (sugar was not available to them). Cacao seeds were used for ceremonial purposes and as a means of payment. By 1400 A.D., the Aztecs associated cacao with the goddess of fertility and often used chocolate beverages as sacred offerings. The word 'chocolate' originates in Mexico's Aztec cuisine, possibly derived from the Nahuatl word xocolatl (pronounced o'kolatil), meaning 'bitter water.' When Cortez explored Mexico in 1518, he noted the cacao usage by Montezuma's court. The Spaniards called it chocolatl and developed an intense liking for it. They believed it was good for the stomach. Cortez returned to Spain, bringing cocoa with him, and there soon became a high demand for this new drink. Cocoa was given as a dowry when members of the Spanish Royal Family married other European aristocrats. Eventually, Europeans added sugar and milk to counteract the natural bitterness. The Industrial Revolution, in the 1800s, made mass production of chocolate bars and related products possible, and people began consuming chocolate worldwide. Chocolate was taken into space as part of the diet of U.S. astronauts.

Here are a few interesting dates in the history of chocolate:

1657 - The first chocolate house, similar to a modern coffee shop, opened in London.

1764 - Chocolate was made for the first time in the United States.

1780 - The first machine-made chocolate was produced in Barcelona, Spain.

1828 - The cocoa press was invented, improving the quality of the beverage by squeezing out part of the cocoa butter. Drinking chocolate became smoother and more pleasing to the taste.

1847 - Joseph Fry made the first chocolate for eating, followed in 1849 by the Cadbury brothers. In the 1850s, cultivation of the cocoa bean was introduced to Western Africa, which became a dominant cocoa region in the world within one hundred years.

1867 - Daniel Peter discovered how to combine milk and cocoa powder. He was assisted in removing the water content from the milk to prevent mildewing by his neighbor, a baby food manufacturer named Henri Nestlé. Milk chocolate was introduced in 1875.

1879 - Rudolf Lindt invented conching, the process of stirring liquid chocolate to make it smooth.

1900 - The first wrapped chocolate bar was produced.

1913 - Jules Sechaud of Switzerland introduced the process for filling chocolates.

1938 - The U.S. government recognized chocolate's role in the Allied Armed Forces. It allocated valuable shipping space for the importation of cocoa beans. The U.S. Army D-rations included three, four-ounce chocolate bars. 1946 - A refrigerated display case was developed to prevent chocolate from melting, and extended the selling season through the summer months.

The Whitman's Samplers® box of chocolates debuted in 1912. It was the first box of chocolates to include an index. During 1942 through 1945, to help maintain wartime morale, women at the Whitman's Candy Company slipped notes to soldiers in boxes of Whitman's Chocolate Samplers® that were shipped to the troops. The notes resulted in a few marriages.

Goo Goo Clusters® were introduced in 1913. They are the first candy bar to combine milk chocolate, marshmallow, caramel, and peanuts.

The Turtle®, a chocolate covered caramel and nut candy that resembles a real turtle, was introduced in 1916.

In 1922, the Fox Cross Candy Company created the Charleston Chew®, inspired by the swinging Charleston dance.

The Baby Ruth® candy bar, named for President Grover Cleveland's daughter, was introduced by Curtiss Candy Co. in 1923.

Chocolate-covered peanuts, also known as Goobers® (the earliest and one of the most popular brands of the product), were introduced in the United States in 1925.

Milk Duds® were first sold in 1926.

Raisinets® are chocolate-covered raisins and were introduced in 1927. Supposedly, they are the number one selling candy in United States history.

The 5th Avenue® candy bar was introduced in 1936.

The Kit Kat® bar, first sold in England in 1935 as a Rowntree's Chocolate Crisp, was renamed in 1937 as the Kit Kat Chocolate Crisp. The name was derived from a London literary and political group, the Kit-Cat Club, established in the late seventeenth century. In the United States, it is distributed by Hershey's but made by Nestle.

In 1949, Junior Mints® were introduced. They were named after a radio show called Junior Miss that starred child actress Shirley Temple.

Other chocolate mint candies include York Peppermint Patties®, After 8 Thin Mints®, and Andes Crème de Menthe®, originally called Andy's Candies after the founder, Andrew Kanelos, who soon realized that men were hesitant to give candy to their wives or girlfriends with another man's name on the box so he changed the name to Andes.

Recipes for wedding cakes using tiny white candy balls date back to the eighteenth century. At some point in time they were added to a dark chocolate drop. Nonpareils are dark chocolate discs that are sprinkled with tiny white candy balls. The name is derived from the French words non parei, meaning 'without equal.' Sno Caps® are a smaller version.

In 1920, Williamson Candy Co. introduced the Oh Henry!® bar. There is no definitive explanation as to the exact origin of the name. Some say it was originally named after a boy who frequented the Williamson company and others say it is an homage to the American author, O. Henry. Another theory is that the candy bar was invented by Tom Henry who ran the Peerless candy factory. In 1919, he made the Tom Henry candy bar and sold the candy to Williamson Candy Company in 1920, where they later changed the name to Oh Henry!® Nestle acquired the U.S. rights to the brand in 1984.

In the 1700s in France, a confection called griottes was made by enclosing long stalked sour griotte cherries with a little kirsch (a clear, colorless fruit brandy) in chocolate. Many confectioners make chocolate-covered cherries (also called cherry cordials) but the three most popular are Cella's, Queen Anne's, and Brach's. Cella's, the oldest brand, began making them in 1864 but didn't begin large-scale production until 1929. The Brock Candy Company began making them in the 1930s. Their chocolate-covered cherries helped keep the company afloat during the Great Depression. Queen Anne's began making chocolate-covered cherries in 1948.

Many families celebrate Hanukkah, the Jewish festival of lights, with gelt -- chocolate coins covered in gold and silver foil. What began as an end-of-the-year tip for itinerant workers became chocolate by the end of the nineteenth century. The custom switched from giving tips to giving a little gift to children.

In 1923 in Minnesota, Frank Mars launched the Milky Way® bar, designed to taste like malted milk. It is one of the first candies with a nougat center. In 1930, he introduced the Snickers® bar, named after the Mars' family beloved horse. The 3 Musketeers® bar came along in 1932. When first introduced, a package contained three small, separate nougat bars: one chocolate, one vanilla, one strawberry. Rising costs and wartime restrictions phased out the vanilla and strawberry pieces in 1945. Frank's son, Forrest Mars, relocated to England where he created the MARS Candy Bar® in the early 1930s (later renamed Snickers Almond Crunch® in the late 1990s).

Forrest also invented the recipe for M&Ms® chocolate candies. During the Spanish Civil War (1936-1939) he observed soldiers eating pieces of chocolate covered with a hard sugary coating. The coating prevented the candy from melting in the hot sun. Forest Mars anticipated that World War II would produce a cocoa shortage, so he partnered with Bruce Murrie, son of a Hershey executive. M&Ms® were introduced in 1941 as a snack for U.S. soldiers serving in World War II. They were originally packaged in cardboard tubes but in 1948 the packaging changed from a tube to a brown plastic pouch. M&Ms® are named after the two partners who created them, Mars and Murrie. The letter "m" is printed on each candy with vegetable dye. In 1954, "M&Ms Peanut Chocolate Candies®" were introduced. That same year, the M&Ms® brand characters and the famous slogan, "The milk chocolate melts in your mouth, not in your hand," were both trademarked.

Sixlets,® small round candy-coated, chocolate-flavored candy made in Canada, come in a variety of colors, with each color having a slightly different taste than the next. They are often sold in thin cellophane packages in a tube-like formation and have existed since the 1960s.

In 1894, Milton Hershey began the Hershey Chocolate Company and produced Hershey chocolate caramels, breakfast cocoa, sweet chocolate and baking chocolate. He later sold his caramel business and concentrated on chocolate-making. Hershey was a pioneer in the mass-production of milk chocolate and turned what previously had been a luxury item into something affordable. In the early 1900s, he built an entire town around his chocolate factory in Pennsylvania. The town is called Hershey. Until 1970, Hershey did not advertise because the company was so well known.

The first Hershey's Milk Chocolate Bar® was produced in 1900 and Hershey's Kisses® made their debut in 1907. In 1925, Hershey introduced the first Milk Chocolate Bar with Peanuts, called Mr. Goodbar®. The Krackel® candy bar, that originally combined almonds and crisped rice, was introduced in 1938. In 1943, due to wartime food rationing, it was changed to an all rice formula.

Hershey introduced the Symphony Bar® in 1989. In 1990, Hershey sent over one hundred thousand heat-resistant candy bars to soldiers in the Gulf War. The heat-resistant formula is identical to what they sent to soldiers in WWII. Miniature Hershey's Kisses® as well as white chocolate kisses called Hugs® were introduced in 1993.

The Hershey Chocolate Company has made or currently owns many famous chocolate candies including Cadbury Creme Eggs®, Hershey's Cookies 'n' Creme® candy bar, Hershey's Nuggets®, Reese's Crunchy Cookie Cups®, Reese's NutRageous® candy bar, York Peppermint Patties®, and Almond Joy®. Mounds® made its debut in 1923 (it was invented by Peter Paul Halijian but sells under the name Peter Paul Mounds since Halijian is difficult to pronounce). Malted Milk Balls are another of their products. They debuted in 1949 as Giants but the name was later changed to Whoppers®.

Rolo®, a small cone-shaped chocolate with a caramel center, was first manufactured in England in 1937 and has been produced in the U.S. by Hershey since 1969. Twix® caramel cookie candy bar was introduced in 1979. In 1992, the Dove® chocolate bar was introduced in dark chocolate and milk chocolate. The Heath® bar, made of toffee and milk chocolate since 1914, has been manufactured by Hershey since 1996.

In 1917, Harry Burnett Reese was employed as a dairyman for the Hershey chocolate company and later worked at its factory. He began making candies in his basement and in the mid-1920s, he built a factory of his own and produced an assortment of candies. Reese's Peanut Butter Cups®, made with Hershey's chocolate, were first marketed in 1928 and in 1963, Hershey acquired the H.B Reese Candy Company. Reese's Pieces® were introduced in 1978.

Henri Nestlé's infant cereal company opened in 1867 and merged in 1905 with the Anglo-Swiss Condensed Milk Company. Nestlé manufactured milk products but, in 1925, chocolate became a large part of their business. Nestlé USA, Inc. makes Butterfinger®, a candy bar created in 1923 in Chicago. They manufacture the Nestle Crunch® bar that debuted in the late 1930s. Nestlé Chunky® was also introduced in the 1930s. It is a candy bar known for its trapezoidal shape and consists of milk chocolate, raisins and roasted peanuts. The original bar was a one-piece section, not sectionalized. The 100 Grand Bar® was created in 1966. In the early 1990s, two Boston DJs talked for weeks about giving away one hundred Grand until finally revealing to the winner that the prize was actually just the candy bar, not money. The winner filed a lawsuit. In 2005, the same prank was pulled by a different radio station. That winner also sued.

Nestlé USA, Inc. owns the Willy Wonka Candy Factory and produces Wonka Chocolate and an assortment of non-chocolate items like Runts® and Sprees®. Runts® are small hard candies in the shape, color, and flavor of fruit. Spree® is another hard candy with a colorful fruit-flavored shell, available in rolls or thin cardboard tubes. There is also a chewy variety. Nestlé manufactures other types of chocolate candy such as *Aero®*, with a unique bubbly texture. The Cailler brand, one of Switzerland's oldest, best-known and best-loved chocolate brands, is also part of Nestlé. A key secret behind Cailler chocolate is the blending of fine milk from the region with top quality cocoa. Orion is another much-loved chocolate brand that came into existence in 1896 in Prague and was acquired by Nestlé in 1991.

In addition to candy bars, Nestlé is also known for several beverages, including Nesquik® chocolate milk, Nestea® iced tea, Pure Life® bottled water, Carnation® condensed milk, Boost® nutrition shakes and Nescafé® coffee. During World War II, Nescafé® became a staple drink among American servicemen in Europe and Asia.

In 1824, John Cadbury opened a shop in England where he sold tea, coffee, and drinking chocolate. In 1831 he opened a chocolate and cocoa factory with his brother. Joseph Fry, a competitor of Cadbury's, began experimenting with making moldable chocolate bars in 1847, which sparked Cadbury's experimentation in moldable chocolate. In 1875 he created the first chocolate egg filled with sugary treats. The two companies merged by 1919 and in 1923 they created the very first chocolate eggs filled with cream. However, the Cadbury Creme Egg® we know today wasn't invented until 1963 under the name Fry's Creme Eggs. The name changed in 1971. Eggs have long been associated with Easter as a symbol of new life and Jesus' resurrection. Easter is the second best-selling candy holiday in America, after Halloween.

World's Finest Chocolate company is known for chocolate bars commonly sold by schools and social service organizations as part of fundraisers. Many other chocolate companies, and individual chocolatiers, produce chocolate bars, truffles, pralines, filled chocolates, molded chocolate figures and shapes, toffee, and fudge.

The Ferrero' Family was the first Italian manufacturer after World War II to open production sites and offices abroad in the confectionary sector. They are known for Nutella®, launched in 1964, and a line of Kinder Chocolate® (individually wrapped small milk chocolate bars with a creamy filling), Kinder Surprise® (the taste of Kinder chocolate with a surprise and toy in every egg), and Bueno® (a creamy hazelnut, white, dark or milk chocolate, and crispy wafer candy bar). Two other popular confections they make are Ferrero Rocher® and Raffaello®. Rocher® begins with a whole hazelnut surrounded by hazelnut filling and a crisp wafer shell, covered with chocolate and roasted pieces. Raffaello® is a combination of a crunchy almond, smooth cream, and a crispy wafer shell covered with coconut flakes.

In 1852, Domenico Ghirardelli opened a chocolate shop in San Francisco. When the great San Francisco earthquake and fire of 1906 destroyed much of the city, the Ghirardelli plant was not damaged. In 1923, the now-famous Ghirardelli illuminated light bulb sign was created, a welcome sight to ships passing through the Golden Gate Strait. A Ghirardelli Soda Fountain & Chocolate Shop opened in Downtown Disney (now Disney Springs) in Orlando, Florida in 1997 and in 1998, Lindt & Sprungli acquired the Ghirardelli Chocolate Company.

In 1856, confectioner David Sprüngli-Schwarz and his son, Rudolf, opened a small confectionery shop in Zurich. They used a new recipe from Italy to make chocolate in solid form. Around that same time, Rodolphe Lindt developed a conche technique (the process of stirring liquid chocolate to make it smooth) which contributed significantly to the worldwide reputation of Swiss chocolate. The men joined together in 1899, creating the Lindt & Sprüngli Chocolate Company. Lindt's Master Chocolatiers created the iconic Lindor® recipe (a chocolate shell enrobes a smooth filling). In 1989, they introduced Lindt Excellence®, a gourmet chocolate bar. Today, their chocolate is sold in over eighty countries with eight production sites in Europe and the U.S.

Mary See developed her own homemade candy recipes. She made them in her son's bungalow, in a black and white kitchen. When her son, Charles, opened the first See's candy shop in Los Angeles in 1921, he chose the now-iconic checkerboard theme inspired by that kitchen. Mary used only the finest and freshest ingredients, continued by See's Candies today. There are now over two hundred black-and-white shops across the U.S. and a thriving on-line business.

Russell Stover and his wife began Mrs. Stover's Bungalow Candies in 1924. They operated out of the kitchen in their bungalow, making boxed chocolates. In 1925, the couple opened a candy factory in Denver and another in Kansas City. During the 1940s, the name of the company changed to Russell Stover Candies. By 1954, the company was producing eleven million pounds of candy annually and selling its products through forty Russell Stover shops and about 2,000 department stores. The Swiss chocolate-maker Lindt bought Russell Stover Candies in 2014.

Chocolate manufacturers currently use forty percent of the world's almonds
and twenty percent of the world's peanuts.

Bean-to-Bar chocolate companies process cocoa beans into a product in-house rather than melting chocolate from another manufacturer. Forrest Mars Sr. created Ethel M Chocolates in his mother's honor. Using her timeless recipes that date back to 1910, his vision of sharing fresh-crafted, small-batch, premium chocolates was born. Today, Ethel M Chocolates, located just outside of Las Vegas, is still made in small batches for peak freshness, and they pack every box by hand.

Here is a partial list of other Bean-to-Bar companies.

In the United States:	In Switzerland:
Amano Artisan Chocolate	Villars
Askinosie	Lindt
Blommer Chocolate Company	Barry Callebaut
Guittard	Frey
Mast Brothers	
Mindo Chocolate Makers	In Italy:
Scharffen Bergen	Amedei
Taza Chocolate	Venchi
In France:	In Norway:
Bonnat Chocolates	Freia

Fudge is a type of confectionery made of sugar, butter, and milk. It is heated to the soft-ball stage and then beaten while it cools to acquires a smooth, creamy consistency. Fruits, nuts, caramel, cocoa, and flavorings are often added. No one knows who made the first batch of fudge but American folklore has it that fudge was invented in the United States in the early 1880s. A bungled, or 'fudged' attempt at making a batch of caramels resulted in an entirely new type of candy – fudge. Dictionaries from as early as 1811 denote the word 'fudge' as meaning nonsense and later define it as "to fabricate or contrive in a careless or blundering manner; to bungle" (hence the name). The first known sale of fudge, at a Baltimore grocery store in 1886, was for forty cents a pound. Penuche is a fudge-like candy made from brown sugar, butter and milk, using no flavorings except vanilla.

Studies have found that ingesting chocolate stimulates the release of endorphins
that make us feel good. And chocolate can stimulate the body's production of serotonin,
acting as a natural anti-depressant.

The origins of ice cream can be traced back to at least the fourth century B.C. The ancient Persians poured various concentrated fruit juices and sugar or honey over bowls filled with snow collected from the mountains and stored in underground chambers where it remained solid even in the hottest months. The Roman emperor Nero had ice, brought from the mountains, combined with fruit toppings. Eventually, milk ices evolved. China had a method of combining heated, fermented milk, flour and camphor and chilling it. Some historians believe that in the thirteenth century, Marco Polo brought a recipe for a frozen dessert to Europe from his journey to the Far East.

The first ice cream, made from milk or cream, is thought to have been made in Italy in the seventeenth century. French-style ice cream descended from medieval egg custards and creams. Although frozen desserts were common in regal circles, it wasn't until 1670 when the Cafe Procope in Paris served iced creams and sherbets to the common people. *De'Sorbetti*, the first book entirely dedicated to the art of making frozen confections, was published in Naples in 1775. The first ice cream parlor in America opened in New York in 1770 but ice cream was a rare and exotic dessert enjoyed mostly by those of status and wealth. George Washington, Thomas Jefferson, and Dolly Madison served ice cream.

A major breakthrough in ice cream technology came about when the method of using ice mixed with salt to lower and control the temperature of ice cream ingredients during its making was discovered. The invention of the wooden bucket freezer with rotary paddles also improved ice cream's manufacture. Nancy Johnson is credited with inventing the ice cream maker in 1843 and her patented design is still used today. Ice cream became accessible and affordable to more people. Immigrants at Ellis Island were served ice cream as part of their first meal in America.

From the Latin word gelare (to freeze), gelato is typically made with egg custard, sugar, and flavorings. It has less butter fat and less sugar than ice cream and is frozen in small batches so it is less aerated and denser. Tortoni, a famous Italian ice cream maker in the early nineteenth century, created many layered ice cream cakes. The term 'Neapolitan' is used to refer to any molded dessert that is made with three layers, but Neapolitan Ice Cream (a block of ice cream composed of layers of chocolate, vanilla, and strawberry) originated in the United States in the late nineteenth century.

NOTE: Italian water ice, also known as sorbetto, and the English word 'sherbet' come from the sweet fruit syrups that were diluted with ice water. Sometimes spelled 'sherbert,' the correct spelling is sherbet and the pronunciation is sher-bit (sounds like hermit). In the United States, sherbet may sometimes be referred to as sorbet. Sherbets contain milk or another fat making it similar to ice cream. Sorbets are generally fruit-based but can also be made with any ingredient, like chocolate. In fine restaurants in the mid-nineteenth century, formal dinner menus offered sorbet in the middle of the meal to cleanse the palate.

Milk Shakes were introduced at soda fountains in the mid-1800s. When the term first appeared in print in 1885, a milk shake meant a sturdy, healthful eggnog type drink that may have contained whiskey. Warm or cold cream-based drinks, combined with coffee, tea, or alcoholic beverages like ale, have long been associated with good health and healing. By the 1900s, the milkshake, made with chocolate, strawberry or vanilla syrups, was considered a wholesome drink. A malted is made with malted milk powder, invented in 1887 in Wisconsin. Made from dried milk, malted barley, and wheat flour, it was promoted as a drink for invalids and children. By 1891, there were more soda fountains than bars in New York. By the 1930s, a malt shop was a soda fountain not attached to a pharmacy.

The original ice cream soda was made from syrup combined with cream and cold soda water or cream mixed with flavored syrup. In Philadelphia in 1874, Robert Green is credited with serving it with ice cream instead of cream. Frank Wisner, owner of a soda fountain as well as a mining company in Colorado, combined root beer and ice cream in 1893. He was gazing at the dark Cow Mountain and its snow-capped peak inspired him to float a scoop of vanilla ice cream in his root beer. He called the sweet creation Black Cow Mountain, later shortened to Black Cow. Since then, the term has been used to describe an ice-cream soda made with a scoop of vanilla ice cream, chocolate syrup, and root beer. A Purple Cow, made with grape juice and ice cream, surfaced in the 1940s. In the 1920s, the egg cream was invented at a soda fountain in Brooklyn. Made from chocolate syrup, milk, and seltzer, it has never contained eggs or cream.

Layered, molded ice cream treats with fruits, syrups and liqueurs were popular in Europe and America. The original parfait (the French word for perfect) was a nineteenth century frozen coffee-flavored French ice dessert made in a tall and thin ice cream mold. It was removed from the mold and served on decorated plates. Parfait, as is currently known in the United States, is a multi-layered ice cream treat presented in a tall and thick parfait glass. A sundae is most often served in a wide-mouth glass. No one is sure about the originator of the ice cream sundae. It may have been soda fountain owner Ed Berners of Wisconsin who served a customer, at his request, a dish of ice cream topped with the syrup used for sodas in 1881. A competing soda fountain owner decided to only serve the dish on Sundays. When it was a big hit, he served it daily and changed the name to ice cream sundae. Another story has drugstore owner Chester Platt inventing the sundae in 1893. He served a dish of vanilla ice cream with cherry syrup and a candied cherry to the Reverend John Scott on a Sunday. The reverend named the dish after the day. The most expensive ice cream sundae is served at Serendipity restaurant in New York City. It's called the Grand Opulence Sundae and costs fifteen hundred dollars. The banana split was invented in 1904 at Strickler's Drug Store in Pennsylvania.

The term 'Philadelphia ice cream' – used since the early nineteenth century – meant a specifically American style of rich ice cream. The basic ingredients are cream, sugar, and vanilla. Fruits and other flavors can be added. After the great exposition of 1876, Philadelphia became known for the excellence of its ice cream.

At the end of the nineteenth century, Italo Marchiony began serving ice cream in edible cups on the streets of New York City, but Ernest Hamwi is credited with creating the first true conical-shaped edible ice cream cone during the 1904 Saint Louis World's Fair (there were over fifty ice cream and waffle vendors at the event, many of whom claimed to take credit for the popular creation). Hamwi had a booth and sold waffles next to an ice cream vendor who ran out of bowls. To help out, he rolled a waffle to hold the ice cream. In 1910, Hamwi founded the Missouri Cone Company and called his container the ice cream cone. Lebanese immigrant Abe Doumar, who was also at the 1904 World's Fair, built one of the first machines in the United States for making ice cream cones. Charles Menches of St. Louis started filling pastry cones with TWO scoops of ice cream. He was at the World's Fair in 1904 too. Today, the world's largest ice cream cone company, the Joy Cone Company, produces almost two billion cones per year.

"In serving ice cream, it is suggested that a china or silver cup be used. Wafers, mints, and other tidbits are very nice to serve along with the ice cream. A small glass of ice water should always be served with each order." — Soda Fountain Publications, New York 1925

It takes three gallons of milk to make a gallon of ice cream. Air is an important ingredient because it keeps the ice cream from freezing solid. Vanilla is the number one flavor in the United States. Of the vanilla beans used in the ice cream industry, eighty percent are grown in Madagascar. The top five ice cream consuming countries (per capita, gallons per year) are New Zealand, The United States, Australia, Finland, and Sweden. California produces the most ice cream in the U.S. Brain freeze occurs when ice cream touches the roof of your mouth – blood vessel spasms are triggered by the intense cold from the ice cream, resulting in a headache. To avoid this, eat ice cream slowly. At one time it was against the law to serve ice cream on cherry pie in Kansas. Le Mars, Iowa is known as the Ice Cream Capital of the World.

The U.S. Army delivered pints of ice cream to soldiers in foxholes during WW II. In the early days of television, mashed potatoes were used to simulate ice cream on cooking shows because real ice cream melted under the heat from the lighting. Five percent of ice cream eaters share their ice cream with their pet. Baskin Robbins made "Beatle Nut" ice cream for the rock band's first visit to America. Haagen Daz ice cream originated in the U.S. The creator thought Denmark had a good marketing image. The first Ben and Jerry's store opened in an old gas station. Farmers in Vermont used to feed leftovers provided by Ben and Jerry's to their hogs (the hogs didn't care for Mint Oreo® Cookie flavor). Their ice cream was included in the supplies on the space shuttle.

The world's first soft-serve ice cream machine was in an Olympia, Washington Dairy Queen. Dippin' Dots®, created by microbiologist Curt Jones in 1988, are tiny beads of ice cream, frozen yogurt, sherbet or flavored ice that are flash frozen. In 1984, president Ronald Reagan proclaimed July as national ice cream month in the U.S. July twenty-first is National Ice Cream Day.

There are hundreds of flavors of ice cream. Bacon ice cream, made by mixing bacon bits with custard and freezing it, started out as a gag for April Fool's Day. The bacon bits are candied in syrup before being added. Japanese ice cream flavors include fish, octopus, crab, eggplant, rice, bean, whale, and oyster. Brown bread ice cream, a popular dish in New England and Canada, was created in Nova Scotia in 1919. Supposedly, a chef ran out of fresh fruit when she was making ice cream for the restaurant where she worked so she added some cereal instead. People liked the flavor and it was soon being mass-produced and sold throughout the entire area. Heavenly Hash ice cream has candy, chopped nuts, and marshmallows (the name first appeared in print in the U.S. in the late 1800s). Chocolate syrup is the world's most popular ice cream topping. The phrase 'a la mode,' referring to topping pie or other baked goods with ice cream, became popular in early twentieth century America (the term originally referred to a popular way of preparing beef).

Victorian-era chefs crafted fancy molded ice cream with or without cakes. They also made small frozen cream-filled sandwich cakes. Ice cream sandwiches, as we know them today, fall into the category of novelties. They were novel, or new, because they were pre-made. Prior to this time, ice cream was scooped fresh by street vendors, soda jerks, and restauranteurs. Freeze-dried Space Bar ice cream sandwiches were invented in 1989 by U.S. scientists connected with the Smithsonian Institution.

Ice cream bars and popsicles were introduced in the 1920s although frozen fruit treats and juice bars existed in the late 1800s (snow cones can be traced back to the ices made long ago from real snow mixed with fruit and honey). In 1905, an eleven-year-old boy named Frank Epperson left a cup filled with soda powder, water, and a stirring stick on his porch overnight. The mixture froze, and Frank accidentally created the popsicle. Epperson was the first to mass market this product. The twin popsicle was invented during the Great Depression so two people could share one for a nickel. The Good Humor Bar® was created by ice cream parlor owner Harry Burt in the 1920s. To keep the messy chocolate coating from getting all over his customer's hands, he put his new treat on a stick.

NOTE: According to food historians, frozen fruit treats were cheaply priced items hawked by street vendors in cities and at resorts and fairs in the late 1800s. People who made a living selling icy treats from carts were known as hokey pokey men. The term 'hokey pokey' (as it relates to food) is traced to Italian street vendors who sold inexpensive goods. O che poco, meaning 'how little,' related to the low price of the goods. It held great appeal to children and working-class people. The British interpretation of hokey pokey refers to slices cut from bricks of ice cream. The brick was layered with three different flavors of ice cream, and each crosswise slice revealed all three. Whole bricks were sold to ice cream shops and street vendors who sold a piece for two pennies (children could buy half a slice for half the price).

"We dare not trust our wit for making our house pleasant to our friend so we buy ice cream."
Ralph Waldo Emerson   1803-1882
American poet

Popcorn was discovered at least four thousand years ago. It was an important food for the Aztec Indians, who also used it as a decoration for ceremonial headdresses and necklaces, and as ornamentation on statues of their gods. Some Native American tribes popped corn right on the cob. They speared the corn cob with a stick and held it near the fire, and the kernels would pop and stay attached to the cob. Popcorn was very popular in the late 1800s – street vendors, pushing steam or gas-powered poppers, followed crowds through fairs, parks, and expositions. The first mobile popcorn machine was introduced at the Chicago World's Fair in 1893.

Because of its low cost, popcorn was ideal for food, Christmas decorations, and gift-giving. In the late nineteenth and early twentieth centuries, popcorn balls were one of the most popular confections and often given as gifts. Popcorn was also a popular breakfast food during this time. It is a whole-grain that is easily digested, adds fiber to the diet, is low in fat and calories, and is gluten-free.

Popcorn was first sold at movie theatres in 1912 even though the owners thought it would be a distraction from the film. Popcorn sales in theatres increased throughout the Great Depression because of its low cost for both patron and owner. During World War II, Americans ate three times more popcorn than usual because sugar was scarce to make candy. During the early 1950s, when television became popular and attendance at movie theaters dropped, so did popcorn consumption until the public began eating popcorn at home.

Microwave popcorn was available for the marketplace in the early 1980s. Most microwave ovens have a popcorn button.

NOTE: Percy Spencer discovered how to mass-produce magnetrons that were being used to generate microwaves for use in World War II. He developed the microwave oven in 1946 and popcorn was key to many of his experiments.

Popcorn is a type of flint corn but has a thicker hull. It pops because water is stored in a small circle of soft starch in each kernel. As the kernel is heated, the water heats, the droplets of moisture turn to steam and the steam builds up pressure until the kernel finally explodes to many times its original volume. There is no such thing as hull-less popcorn. All popcorn needs a hull in order to pop but some varieties have been bred so the hull shatters upon popping.

Most popcorn comes in two basic shapes when it is popped: snowflake, used in movie theaters and ballparks because it looks and pops bigger, and mushroom, used for candy confections because it doesn't crumble.

Nebraska produces more popcorn than any other state in the U.S. – about two hundred and fifty million pounds each year. Popcorn tins feature a variety of flavored popcorn. The traditional tin contains caramel corn, butter popcorn, and cheddar cheese flavored popcorn. National Popcorn Day is January nineteenth.

Kettle corn is popcorn cooked in oil with both sugar and salt. It originated with the colonists in Pennsylvania and was often made for special occasions, holidays, and at fairs.

Caramel corn was introduced in the 1870s. It is made by heating a sugar solution, or sometimes molasses, until the sugar caramelizes and turns to a golden-brown color and is then drizzled over the popcorn or mixed all together. Caramel corn is often sold as is or with different types of nuts mixed in, such as peanuts, almonds, pecans, and cashews. In the 1930s and 1940s, caramel corn shops were typically located near streetcars and bus lines. People walking by would smell the delectable aroma and stop to buy some. By the 1950s, caramel corn became popular at county fairs.

A German immigrant, Frederick William Rueckheim, sold popcorn from a cart in Chicago in 1872 (he also helped clean up after the famous Chicago fire). Rueckheim, together with brother Louis, invented popcorn candy, a snack consisting of molasses-flavored caramel-coated popcorn and peanuts. The original name was Candied Popcorn and Peanuts, later changed to Cracker Jack®. It was first mass-produced and sold at the Chicago World's Fair in 1893. (The Ferris Wheel, Aunt Jemima® pancakes, and the ice cream cone were also introduced at that event.) "Crackerjack" was a slang expression at that time that meant "something very pleasing or excellent" so that is likely the origin of the name. The wax-sealed, moisture-proof box was introduced in 1899 and a toy surprise was added in each package in 1912. Cracker Jack®'s mascots, Sailor Jack and his dog Bingo, were introduced in 1916. The sailor boy was modeled after Frederick Rueckheim's grandson, Robert, and the dog was based on a real-life dog named Russell. The song "Take Me Out to the Ball Game," written in 1908 by Norworth and Von Tilzer, references Cracker Jack® in the lyrics.

Fiddle Faddle® is made with popped corn, roasted peanuts, and creamy caramel or butter toffee. Poppycock® is another brand of candied popcorn. The original mixture consists of clusters of popcorn, almonds and pecans covered in a candy glaze. Other combinations include cashews, pecans, and chocolate. Poppycock® may have been invented by Howard Vair in the 1950s who wanted a snack to take along on road trips. (The word 'poppycock' means nonsense or rubbish and is American in origin. It was first heard around 1852).

Chicago Mix ™ is caramel corn and cheese popcorn combined in one bag, creating a sweet and salty snack combination. There is much debate (and even some law suits) on who originated it.

"The laziest man I ever met put popcorn in his pancakes so they would turn over by themselves."

W.C. Fields   1880-1946

American comedian, actor, and writer

PRETZEL

Early pretzels were of the soft variety. In A.D. 610, an Italian monk rolled out ropes of dough, twisted them to resemble hands crossed on the chest in prayer, and baked them. He called his snack pretiola (Latin for 'little reward') and gave them to his students. Parents who tasted their children's classroom treat referred to it as brachiola, (little arms). They made their way to Germany where they were called bretzels. Medieval street vendors carried pretzels on a stick and sold them door-to-door. In the sixteenth century in Austria, pretzels adorned Christmas trees and on Easter morning they were hidden, along with hard-boiled eggs. Catholics once considered soft pretzels the official food of Lent and it was a tradition to eat pretzels on Good Friday in Germany. The pretzel has long been considered a good-luck symbol. German children wore them around their necks on New Year's Day. The phrase "tying the knot" came from Swiss wedding ceremonies – newlyweds traditionally made a wish and broke a pretzel.

Soft pretzels were brought to the United States in the 1700s with German immigrants (later known as the Pennsylvania Dutch. The word 'Dutch' does not refer to Dutch people but to the German settlers known as *Deutsch* in their language. Soft pretzels have been a mainstay of New York City's street life for more than one hundred and fifty years. Originally sold from baskets or piled high on sticks, they cost only a penny as late as the 1920s. As a snack or appetizer, soft pretzels are often served with mustard or liquid cheese for dipping.

In 1861, Julius Sturgis opened the first commercial pretzel bakery in Pennsylvania. It was the first factory to develop hard pretzels. In an air-tight environment, hard pretzels last longer than the soft type and can be sold in stores far away from the bakery and kept on shelves much longer. Until the 1930s, all pretzels were handmade. The first automated pretzel machine was introduced in 1935 and enabled large pretzel bakeries to make five tons a day. Today, about eighty percent of pretzels made in America are made in Pennsylvania. Hard pretzels are not only covered in salt they are also sold dipped in chocolate or sweet yogurt. At one time, pretzels were considered disreputable because they were so closely associated with beer drinking and saloon life. Prohibition changed the pretzel's association with beer.

CHIPS

A corn chip, usually in the shape of a small noodle or scoop, is a snack food made from cornmeal fried in oil or baked. It is thick, rigid, crunchy, heavily dusted with salt, and has the aroma and flavor of roasted corn. Around 1832 in Southwest Texas, C.E. Doolin deep fried some *masa* (a type of flour used to make tamales, tortillas, and other Mexican dishes) and invented the Frito corn chip (frito is Spanish for fried). Fritos Corn Chips® were first marketed in 1961. The Frito Pie, also known as the Walking Taco or the Texas Straw Hat depending on where you live, has chili and other nacho and taco toppings dumped into an open bag of Fritos Corn Chips® and is eaten with a fork. January twentyninth is National Corn Chip Day.

Potato chips are the number one snack food in the United States. The first recipe for potato chips, called fried shavings, appeared in an 1824 cookbook. But, according to legend, in 1853, Native American Chef George Crum invented potato chips at Moon's Lake House in Saratoga Springs, New York. A picky customer complained about the thickness of his French fries so Crum sliced some potatoes paper thin, creating the first potato chips. An average potato chip is .04 to .08 of an inch thick. It takes about ten thousand pounds of potatoes to make twenty-five hundred pounds of chips. Potato chips were first sold in bulk out of wooden barrels or scooped from behind glass counters in small shops.

Laura Scudder made the first potato chip bag at the company she opened in California in 1926. The bag was originally made of waxed paper that was hand-ironed into grease-resistant packets. Air is left inside a potato chip bag to add cushioning, to prevent breakage. Nitrogen is also pumped into the bag to keep the chips fresher before opening. During World War II, potato chips were considered a nonessential food and production halted but people protested and the decision was reversed. Manufacturers introduced the ruffled chip (four times thicker than a standard chip) because consumers wanted a chip that wouldn't break when dipped in dip. Chip manufacturers began seasoning potato chips in the 1950s. Pringles®, made from dried potatoes instead of fresh ones, appeared in 1968. Traditional chip makers battled with the company that produced them for almost ten years. Finally, Pringles® became known as potato crisps. The first flavor was salt and vinegar. March fourteenth is National Potato Chip Day.

SunChips® are rippled, multigrain chips launched in 1991. Flavors include Original, Harvest Cheddar, French Onion, Sweet and Spicy BBQ, and Garden Salsa. In 2008, compostable packaging made of plant-based material was introduced but was discontinued in 2010 because consumers complained the bag created excessive noise. In 2011, a new, quieter biodegradable bag was released but current bags are not labeled as compostable.

Cheez-It® is a small square cheese-flavored cracker introduced in 1921. There are different flavor-types.

Cheetos® (formerly called Chee-tos until 1998) is a brand of cheese-flavored puffed cornmeal snack invented in 1948. There are twenty-one different flavor-types in North America and many others sold in other countries to match regional taste and cultural preferences .

Cheez Doodles® are a cheese-flavored cheese puff that debuted in the 1950s. There are different flavor-types.

Cheese straws are a popular snack in southern United States. The most common type is made with butter, flour, salt, cheddar cheese and cayenne pepper, using a cookie press. Different types of cheese and spices are also used.

Most tortilla chips are triangular shaped because they are cut from a round tortilla. Blue Corn tortillas (blue corn is a special variety of maize) have less starch and twenty percent more protein than white corn tortillas. In Mexico, tortilla chips are called *tostados* (toasted chips). In the late 1940s, Rebecca Webb Carranza, president of a tortilla factory in Los Angeles, fried misshapen tortillas that the machine sometimes produced and served them to her family at a party. They loved them and she began selling them to the public for ten cents a bag. Eventually, her company produced only "Tort Chips," as they were then called. February 24 is National Tortilla Chip Day.

While on vacation with his family at Disneyland in California, Archibald West, who worked in marketing at the Frito-Lay company, discovered toasted chips at a restaurant. They were leftover tortillas that the chef seasoned with his own special blend of spices and toasted. At first the idea didn't go over well with West's bosses but he created a prototype in 1966 which eventually became the Doritos® we know today.

Nachos, chips topped with shredded cheese, salsa, sour cream and a variety of other things, were created by Ignacia Anaya in 1943 in Mexico. He was without a chef when a group of guests arrived at his restaurant so he began cutting up tortillas and topped them with cheese and jalapeño peppers. Supposedly, 'Nacho' was Ignacia's nickname.

Beer Nuts® is a U.S. brand of snack food of peanuts with a sweet and salty glaze. They do not contain beer but are often served with beer.

CornNuts®, made of roasted or deep-fried corn kernels, were introduced to the U.S. in 1936 by Albert Holloway. He sold them to tavern owners to be given away free. He called them Olin's Brown Jug Toasted Corn, and later renamed them CornNuts®.

Chex Mix® includes Chex® breakfast cereal and a variety of other ingredients such as chips, hard breadsticks, pretzels, nuts, and crackers. The pre-packaged product was introduced in 1985 although recipes for homemade Chex Mix® appeared on boxes of Chex® cereal in 1952.

Funyuns® are an onion-flavored corn snack introduced in the U.S. in 1969 by Frito-Lay®. There are different flavor-types.

A puffed rice cake is a flat hard food made with puffed rice. It is mostly round in shape and comes in assorted flavors and sizes. Riceworks® is a line of gluten-free whole-grain brown rice crisps launched in 2005. They come in a variety of flavors. Quaker® also makes a line of rice cakes.

Rice Krispies Treats® were invented in 1939 by Malitta Jensen and Mildred Day as a fund raiser for Camp Fire Girls. Traditionally made at home using Kellogg's Rice Krispies®, butter, and melted marshmallows, Kellogg's began to market the treats in 1995. Over the years, people have come up with many different flavored Rice Krispies Treats®, such as chocolate, pumpkin spice, S'mores, strawberry, salted caramel, peanut butter, and peppermint.

Dried fruits, which date back to the fourth millennium B.C. in Mesopotamia, have a sweet taste and a long shelf life. Sweetened, dried slices of bananas are called banana chips. Apple chips are dehydrated, or microwave vacuum-drying may be used. They are usually sweetened with powdered sugar and cinnamon. There are also various vegetable chips.

Joray Fruit Rolls® are an apricot-based fruit snack produced in the 1970s by Joseph Shalhoub & Son, Inc. in New York City. They come in ten flavors.

Fruit Roll Ups®, introduced in 1983 by General Mills, are a flat, fruit-flavored snack rolled up within itself.

Fruit by the Foot®, initially called 'A Yard of Fruit,' is a fruit snack introduced in the United States in 1991 by General Mills. It is about three feet long and rolled up within itself. In the early 1990s, it came with stickers that children put on their lunch boxes.

Fruit Gushers® are hexagonal fruit snacks with thick, sweet liquid centers. They were introduced in 1991 by General Mills and originally came in Gushin' Grape and Strawberry Splash. They now come in a variety of flavors.

Sunkist Fruit Gems®, originally known as 'Sunkist Fun Fruits' when they were introduced in 1987, were manufactured with fruit from Sunkist Growers. They were small and soft and came in cherry, grape, orange, and strawberry flavors, and were available in assorted shapes. They are now produced by the Ben Myerson Candy Company and General Mills.

Trail mix dates back to the 1910s. It is a combination of granola, dried fruit, and nuts. Sometimes chocolate is added. Trail mix was developed to be taken on hikes because it is lightweight, easy to store, and nutritious.

Energy bars are supplemental bars containing cereals and other high energy foods. The majority of their food energy is from carbohydrates.

Meal replacement bars are used to replace the variety of nutrients in a meal.

Protein bars contain a high proportion of protein and are usually lower in carbohydrates, vitamins and minerals, and may contain high levels of sugar.

Jerky is lean meat that has been trimmed of fat, cut into strips, and dried, dehydrated, or smoked with low heat to prevent spoilage. It is usually marinated in a seasoned spice rub or liquid. Many jerky products are very high in sugar. Slim Jim®, created in 1929, is an American brand of jerky snacks. The original version is different from the one known today.

CHAPTER 8

Raise Your Glass

BEER

Beer was the first alcoholic beverage known to civilization. Beer jugs dating to the Neolithic period are evidence that early people intentionally made fermented beverages. The Babylonians made more than a dozen different varieties of beer from various grains and honey as far back as 4000 B.C. It was the accepted practice in Babylon that for a month after a wedding, the bride's father supplied his new son-in-law with all the beer he could drink. Because their calendar was lunar based, this period was called the honey month, which we know today as the honeymoon. The oldest known code of laws is the Code of Hammurabi from ancient Babylonia, around 1750 B.C. One of the things it regulated was the practices of drinking houses. It called for the death penalty for proprietors found guilty of watering down beer – they were to be drowned in a river. The Egyptians believed that the god of agriculture, Osiris, taught humans how to make beer. In ancient Greece and Rome, they drank *hydromel* (mead) made by fermenting honey and water, and sometimes spices and fruit were added. Often, yeast was added to speed up fermentation.

In sixteenth century Europe, beer and wine were the staple drinks at all meals including breakfast (even for children). Water was not a common beverage and drunkenness was very seldom punished. In pubs in old England, when customers got unruly, the bartender would tell them to "mind their pints and quarts and settle down" (ale is ordered by pints and quarts). That's where we get the phrase 'Mind your P's and Q's.' Pub frequenters had a whistle baked into the rim or handle of their ceramic cups and when they needed a refill they used the whistle to call the bartender. "Wet your whistle" is the phrase inspired by this practice.

Beer is made by fermentation caused by bacteria feeding on yeast cells and then defecating. The commercial yeast used for leavening bread is also used for brewing beer, whiskey, and other alcoholic beverages. Almost half of the United States crop of barley is used for brewing beer. Lager beer is the dominant beer style throughout the brewing world today. Different fermentation methods give ale a stronger hop flavor and higher alcoholic content than lager. Before the seventeenth century, ale referred to beer brewed without the addition of hops. Today, ale may refer to beer made with unroasted malt or with milder or quickly fermented hops. Nog is an English word for strong ale. Eggnog was originally made with ale and sweetened milk.

252

Molson Companies Ltd. in Montreal, Quebec is the oldest brewery in North America, founded in 1786. Beer was first sold in bottles in 1869 in England. It was the first legal alcoholic beverage to be sold when prohibition was repealed. In 1935, Krueger Brewing became the first brewery to sell beer in cans. Beer in bottles and cans outsold draught beer for the first time in 1940. The aluminum beer can was introduced in 1959 by Coors. Canned beer outsold bottled beer for the first time in 1969. Anheuser-Busch brewery in St. Louis, Missouri is the largest beer producing plant in the U.S. Wisconsin is known as the Beer Capital of the United States. The Czech Republic has the largest beer consumption per capita in the world. In a Czech beer house, the bartender will refill your glass every time you empty it, until you place your coaster on top of your glass, signaling that you have had enough.

Ginger Beer is made with fermented ginger, sometimes with lemon peel, lemon juice or citric acid added. It is made in both nonalcoholic and mildly alcoholic versions. Ginger Beer has a much stronger ginger flavor than Ginger Ale.

The earliest icehouses existed in Mesopotamia about four thousand years ago.
The wealthy cooled their wines with ice.

WINE

Archaeologists found grape seeds (pips) dating from 8000 B.C. in Turkey, Syria, Lebanon, and Jordan – evidence of wine-making. The standard wine container of the ancient world was the *amphora,* a clay vase with two handles that could be carried by two people. It was invented by the Canaanites, who introduced it into Egypt before the fifteenth century B.C. In the Old Testament, only the Book of Jonah has no reference to the vine or wine. In ancient Egypt, the ability to store wine until maturity was considered alchemy and was the privilege of only the pharaohs. When Tutankhamen's tomb was opened in 1922, the wine jars buried with him were labeled with the year, the name of the winemaker, and comments such as "very good wine." In ancient Greece, a dinner host would take the first sip of wine to assure guests the wine was not poisoned, hence the phrase "drinking to one's health." Plato (427-437 B.C.) wanted the minimum drinking age to be eighteen, and then wine in moderation until age thirty-one. When a man reached forty he could drink as much wine as he wanted to cure the crabbedness of old age. Hippocrates (460-375 B.C.), the father of medicine, included wine in many of his recorded remedies.

Wineskins were a common way to transport wine in the ancient world. Animal skins were cleaned and tanned and turned inside out so that the hairy side was in contact with the wine. Toasting began in ancient Rome when they started dropping a piece of toasted bread into each wineglass to temper excessive acidity. The Romans discovered that mixing lead with wine helped preserve wine and gave it a sweet taste (they didn't know about lead poisoning). They also added other items like fermented fish sauce, garlic, onion root, and absinthe because they felt the seasoning was more important than the primary flavor of wine. Early Roman women were forbidden to drink wine. A husband who found his wife drinking was at liberty to kill or divorce her. Around 1000 A.D., the Vikings called America 'Vinland' (wine-land) for the many native grape vines they found there. In the Middle Ages, the most innovative winemakers were monastic orders, such as the Benedictines. They understood that the combination of soil type, climate, degree of slope, and exposure to the sun is what makes each wine unique. A crop of newly planted grape vines takes four to five years to grow before it can be harvested.

From 1920 to 1933, alcohol sales were banned by the eighteenth amendment to the U.S. Constitution. The prohibitionists, known as the Drys, fought to remove any mention of wine from textbooks and other literature. They also sought to prove that Biblical praises of wine were for unfermented grape juice. During these Prohibition years, wine growers added large labels on their grape juice that stated, "Warning: Will Ferment and turn into wine" and then gave detailed instructions of what not to do so the grape juice wouldn't accidentally turn into wine.

California is the fourth-largest wine producer in the world, after France, Italy, and Spain. More than ninety percent of U.S. wine production is in California. Every type and origin of grape produces a different quality and flavor of wine. European wines are named after their geographic locations and non-European wines are named after different grape varieties. The wine fermentation process occurs naturally but temperature, container size, and material used during fermentation contribute to wine quality and taste. After fermentation, the wine needs to mature to reach its peak level of quality. Some wines may not be bottled the same year the grapes are picked. A vintage wine is a product of a single year's harvest. A non-vintage wine is a blend of wines from two or more years. Most wines are ready to drink and don't have to be aged – only a rare few will last longer than ten years. The smell of young wine is called an aroma. A more mature wine has a subtle bouquet.

Darker shades of wine usually come from warm climates, and lighter colors, like white wines, come from cooler climates. Red wines are red because fermentation extracts color from the grape skins. White wines are not fermented with the skins. Red wines tend to lose color with age but white wines gain color, becoming golden and eventually brown-yellow. Eiswein, invented by the Germans, is wine that is made from frozen grapes. The sediment found at the bottom of a bottle of red wine is tannin (the skins, pips, and stalks of grapes) and is an excellent antioxidant. There is increasing scientific evidence that moderate, regular wine drinking can reduce the risk of heart disease, Alzheimer's disease, stroke, and gum disease.

Most wine is served in a glass that has a gently curved rim at the top to help contain the aroma. Thinner glass is best. Wine glasses should always be held by the stem and not the bowl because the heat of the hand will raise the temperature of the wine. Wine testers swirl their glass to encourage the wine to release all of its aromas. Women have a better sense of smell than men and tend to be better wine testers. A 'dumb' wine refers to the lack of odor in a wine, although it may develop a pleasing odor in the future. A 'numb' wine has no odor and no potential of developing a pleasing odor in the future. When tasting wine, hold the wine in your mouth for a moment or two and then spit it out. A really good wine will have a long aftertaste. Store wine bottles on their side to keep the wine in contact with the cork so the cork won't dry and shrink, letting in air. Wine with an artificial cork may be stored vertically. Contrary to popular belief, smelling the cork reveals little about the wine. Look for mold, drying, cracking, or breaks in the cork, as well as the date and other identifying information on the label. Oenophobia is the fear of wine.

The method of making bubbles in a bottle was invented by Frere Jean Oudart (1654 - 1742). French monks were the first to bottle a sparkling form of wine called Champagne, named after the Champagne region of France. Sparkling wine made outside that region cannot be called champagne. The Benedictine monk, Dom Pierre Perignon (1639-1715), founded many principles and processes in the production of champagne that are still used today. The pressure in a bottle of champagne is about three times that of a car tire. Champagne bottles are made of thicker glass to prevent them from exploding from the inside pressure.

"Age and glasses of wine should never be counted."
Unknown Author

LIQUOR

Liquor, also called hard liquor in the United States, is created by a distilling process that produces ethanol by a means of fermenting potatoes, grains, fruits or vegetables. The distillation process raises the alcohol strength from anywhere between forty and ninety-five percent. Liquor does not include other alcoholic beverages such as wine, beer, and hard cider that are not distilled and are lower in alcohol content. The origin of the word 'spirit' in reference to alcohol comes from Middle Eastern alchemists involved in medical elixirs. The vapors given off and collected during some of their alchemical processes were described as being 'the spirit' of the original object. When processes similar to distillation were carried out by accident, alcohol was produced and the result was known as a 'spirit.' The fear of alcohol is called methyphobia.

The Dutch word *busen* means to drink excessively. Their word for drinking vessel is buise. The first reference to the word 'booze' appeared around the fourteenth century but it was spelled bouse. The name changed to 'booze' in the seventeenth century. The first published book about distilling, from the 1500s, treats alcohol like medicine (most liquor produced during the Middle Ages was used for medicinal purposes). By the 1600s, a travelogue mentions recreationally drinking aqua vitae, an early nickname for liquor. During the seventeenth and eighteenth centuries, liquor spread with trade, exploration and colonization. The term 'hooch' used to be popular slang for liquor and it referred to any illegal liquor during 1920s Prohibition. The origin of the word' hooch' comes from the Hoochinoo Indians of Alaska who distilled alcohol using metal coils in the nineteenth century.

Liquor may be served with water or a simple mixer such as club soda, tonic water, juice or other soft drink. Alcoholic beverages may also be blended with crushed ice, cream or ice cream. When liquor is served "neat" it is at room temperature without any additional ingredients. When served "on the rocks" it has ice cubes. When served "up" it is shaken or stirred with ice, then strained. A shooter, or shot, is usually drunk quickly rather than being sipped. A cocktail is any beverage that contains three or more ingredients, and at least one of those ingredients is alcohol. When a cocktail contains only a distilled spirit and a mixer, it is called a highball. Contrary to what most people believe, when using beer, wine or other alcoholic beverages in recipes, a lot of alcohol still remains after cooking. Alcohol consumption has short-term psychological and physiological effects, depending on the concentrations of alcohol in the body. Driving under the influence (DUI) of alcohol increases the risk of a car accident. There are many varieties of liquor, but Rum, Vodka, Gin, Tequila, Whiskey and Scotch are the main types.

Rum got its beginnings in the Caribbean when it was discovered that molasses, a by-product of sugar processing, could be fermented into alcohol. Later, distillation of these alcoholic by-products concentrated the alcohol and removed impurities, producing the first true rums. The clear liquid is aged in barrels to obtain its darker color and variations in taste. Rum can also be flavored with spices, caramel, coconut, and citrus.

Vodka may have originated in Russia during the ninth century when it was used for medicinal purposes (the Russian word for water is voda). Vodka was made from potatoes but today it is mostly made from barley, wheat, corn, and sorghum. It is not aged, and due to distillation and filtering processes, most vodkas lack any flavor. Many brands have developed flavored varieties of vodka that include fruit, citrus, spice, almond, and vanilla. Vodka was used as an ingredient in early European formulations of gunpowder.

Gin, invented by a Dutch physician as a treatment for medical problems such as kidney disease, lumbago, gallstones and gout, was originally known as *jenever* (juniper) – it is processed like vodka but infused with juniper berries to produce a dry flavor. Gin is also often flavored with orange peel, anise, licorice, cinnamon, and coriander. By the end of the seventeenth century, gin had become popular in Britain. The English military living in India mixed tonic water with gin – the quinine in the tonic water was effective in fighting malaria. Sloe Gin isn't gin, it's a liqueur made with blackthorn bush berries.

Prior to the sixteenth century, the Aztecs fermented a beverage from the agave plant that they called octli. Spanish conquistadors, at or near the Mexican town of Tequila, began producing an agave beverage when they ran out of brandy. The new beverage, known today as Tequila, was the first North American distilled spirit. Tequila is made clear or colored depending on how long it is aged in oak barrels. The clear type is bottled immediately after distillation while the darker type is normally aged a minimum of three years.

Whiskey has its roots in Scotland and Ireland. During the thirteenth to fourteenth centuries, the habitants distilled barley mash. Unlike vodka, whiskey is aged and there are variations in how the variety of whiskies are produced.

Scotch Whiskey, often called scotch, must be made in Scotland. It is produced from grains that have been smoked in special peat moss smokers. Scotch whiskey must be aged at least three years in oak casks (usually previously used for making bourbon or sherry) and normally distilled at least twice.

Irish Whiskey is made in Ireland and there are two types: Single Malt and Blended. Single Malt is made of pure barley; Blended is a combination of single malt and grain whiskey that has been produced using other grains such as corn or wheat. Blended whiskey has a lighter taste but Single Malt is considered the purer form and is more expensive.

Bourbon Whiskey, named for Bourbon County, Kentucky where it was first made in the late eighteenth century, contains at least fifty-one percent corn. It must be aged in charred oak barrels for at least two years. All Bourbon Whiskey must be made in the United States. Canadian Whiskey is very similar to the blended styles of American and Irish Whiskies. It must be made in Canada and is aged for at least three years in wooden barrels. Canadian whiskey is known for being very smooth.

Liqueurs, made from distilled spirits that are flavored with a variety of items, are sweet and often syrupy in consistency. Most have a lower alcohol content than liquor. Liqueurs were made in Italy as early as the thirteenth century and were often prepared by monks. A cream liqueur contains dairy cream. Layered drinks are made by floating different-colored liqueurs in separate layers. Each liqueur is poured slowly into a glass (over the back of a spoon or down a glass rod) so the liquids remain unmixed, creating a striped effect. In the United States, liqueurs may also be known as cordials.

Brandy is a strong alcoholic spirit distilled from grapes or other fermented fruit such as apples or apricots. It is possible that an unknown Dutch trader invented brandy in the sixteenth century by boiling wine to remove the water as a way to save cargo space. A few sources credit the Chinese. Schnapps is a term for a family of alcoholic beverages, including distilled fruit brandies, herbal or flavored liqueurs, and infusions.

In Colonial times, apple cider was the alcoholic drink of choice. Johnny Chapman, also known as Johnny Appleseed, was indirectly responsible for spreading the cider. The difference between apple juice and apple cider is that apple juice is the juice of the fruit only, and apple cider is the whole apple, which gives it a deeper color. Apple juice is pasteurized but apple cider is not. Fermented apple juice (which is alcoholic) is called hard cider in the U.S.

When first made, distilled spirits are clear – they get their colors and hues from the aging process in oak barrels. Moonshiners skip the aging process to reduce risk of arrest so the color of the product remains clear. 'White lightning' is a name for illegally distilled spirits.

Modern glass packaging and brand names began to emerge around the middle of the nineteenth century. The term 'brand name' came from American distillers. They branded their names and logos on kegs before shipping them. There are now lesser-known brands of liquor with terms like 'artisan' and 'craft' on the label. This is known as craft distilling which began in the United States in the latter part of the twentieth century, after the popularity of microbrewing beer.

Using a celery stick to garnish a Bloody Mary originated in the 1960s at Chicago's Ambassador East Hotel. An unnamed celebrity got a Bloody Mary without a swizzle stick so he grabbed a stalk of celery from the relish tray to stir his drink.

The Daiquiri cocktail originated around 1900. It got its name from the village and iron mines of Daiquiri near Santiago, Cuba.

A martini becomes a Gibson simply by adding a miniature onion to it.

George Washington, Benjamin Franklin, and Thomas Jefferson made some of their own alcoholic beverages.

Paul Revere supposedly had two drinks of rum before taking his famous ride.

Each member of the American Colonial Army received a daily ration of four ounces of either rum or whiskey.

The taxation of whiskey in 1794 caused the Whiskey Rebellion, the first test of federal power over states and individuals in the U.S.

When President Lincoln was told that General Grant drank whiskey while leading his troops, he wanted to find out the name of the brand so he could give it to his other generals.

Bathtub gin was common during Prohibition. It was mixed in bottles or jugs that were too tall to be filled with water from the kitchen faucet so they were commonly filled in a bathtub. Prohibitionists (temperance supporters) strongly opposed drinking alcohol but the medicines they used contained forty percent alcohol.

Food slows down the absorption rate of alcohol so you will not feel the effects as quickly as you would on an empty stomach. Fatty foods break down slower than other foods.

The body uses eight ounces of water to metabolize one ounce of alcohol. Effects of dehydration may include dry mouth, hangovers, headaches, and queasy stomachs.

Food sensitivities may increase if you consume alcohol at the same time.

"My rule of life prescribed, as an absolutely sacred rite, smoking cigars and also the drinking of alcohol before, after and if need be during all meals and in the intervals between them."

Winston Churchill 1874-1965
Former Prime Minister of the U.K.

SOFT DRINKS

The first marketed non-carbonated soft drinks appeared in the seventeenth century and were made from water and lemon juice sweetened with honey. Scientists later discovered that carbon dioxide was in the bubbles in natural mineral water and in 1767, Englishmen Joseph Priestly discovered a method of infusing water with carbon dioxide, thus inventing the first man-made carbonated water. Around 1783, German-Swiss jeweler Jacob Schweppe was the first large-scale producer of aerated water. Soda, originally known as tonic water because it was used for medicinal reasons, was created in the 1800s when flavoring was added to seltzer water. It was called a soft drink to differentiate it from alcoholic hard drinks. Carbonated beverages did not achieve great popularity in the United States until 1832 when John Mathews invented an apparatus for making carbonated water and then sold them to soda fountain owners. Soft drink creation and soda fountain manufacturing were handled primarily by local pharmacists because of their experience with chemistry and medicine. Early American pharmacies with soda fountains became a popular part of culture. The word 'soda' is derived from the sodium salts within the water.

Customers wanted to have the new beverage at home as well as at a soda fountain so a soft drink bottling industry grew from consumer demand. In 1835, the first bottled soda water was produced in the United States. In 1899, the first patent was issued for a glass-blowing machine for the automatic production of glass bottles. Earlier glass bottles had all been hand-blown. During the 1920s, the first Hom-Paks were invented (a six-pack beverage-carrying carton made from cardboard). Automatic vending machines also began to appear in the 1920s, dispensing sodas into cups. Aluminum cans were first used in soda vending machines in 1965. Plastic bottles were introduced in 1970. The Coca-Cola® Freestyle beverage dispenser is the newest type of soda fountain innovation. It serves over one hundred different beverages including traditional sodas, flavored waters, carbonated or non-carbonated beverages, and energy drinks.

NOTE: Some people believe that you can reduce the spray from a shaken can of soda by tapping on the lid, but that does nothing – it's just something to do while waiting for the soda to settle.

Regular soda, with sugar, has ninety percent water; diet soda has ninety-nine percent. The first official diet soft drink was introduced in 1952. Research indicates that drinking cocktails made with diet soda verses regular soda can get a person eighteen percent drunker. The body views the sugar in regular soda as food and slows the absorption of alcohol into the bloodstream.

The first soda pop made in the United States was Vernor's Ginger Ale, created in Michigan in 1866. James Vernor sold it in his drug store for thirty years before opening a factory to produce it on a larger scale.

Moxie, a brand of carbonated beverage that was among the first mass-produced soft drinks in the U.S., was created in 1884 by Dr. Augustin Thompson, a homeopathic physician. He wanted to make a cure-all which did not contain harmful ingredients like cocaine and alcohol. Moxie bottle wagons were used to dispense Moxie at fairs and amusement parks. It was promoted as a health and vigor beverage until 1909 (the likeness of Teddy Roosevelt, an exponent of the strenuous life, was used in advertising). By then, the word 'moxie' had become a synonym for vim, vigor, stamina, and guts.

Dr. Pepper® was invented in Waco, Texas in 1885 by Charles Alderton. He named it after the father of a girl he had loved when he lived in Virginia. Dr. Pepper® contains twenty-three ingredients and the exact formula is kept secret.

In 1886, Dr. John Pemberton, a pharmacist, created a cola beverage called Coca-Cola Elixir and Syrup. The two main ingredients were from the coca plant and the caffeine-rich kola nut. Pemberton's partner and bookkeeper, Frank M. Robinson, is credited with naming the beverage Coca-Cola® and designing the trademarked script still used today. The first bottle with a trademark design was sold in 1894 (the soda was previously only sold as a fountain drink). Until 1905, it was marketed as a tonic. Coca-Cola®, also known as Coke®, was the first product to appear on the cover of Time magazine in May, 1950. Coca-Cola® cans appeared in 1955. Coke® was the first soft drink in space, taken on the Space Shuttle Challenger in specially designed cans. Sprite was created in 1961 by Coca-Cola Co.

NOTE: Extracts from the coca leaf contain cocaine, which in its concentrated, synthesized form is a stimulant with possible addictive properties. When Coca-Cola® was invented, cocaine was thought to be good for one's health. The coca leaf has been chewed and brewed for tea for centuries in the Andean region. Cocaine was removed from the soft drink in 1903 and replaced with a decocainized coca extract.

Pepsi-Cola® was created in the late 1800s by Caleb D. Bradham, a North Carolina pharmacist. Originally called Brad's Drink, he renamed it Pepsi-Cola® in 1898. The name refers to the marketing claim that it cured peptic ulcers.

Pharmacist Claud Hatcher invented R.C. Cola (Royal Crown) in 1905 in the basement of his family's grocery business.

Referring to a carbonated soft drink as a coke, even if it's not Coca-Cola®, is common in the southern United States. It is called 'soda' on the northeastern coast and 'pop' in the Midwestern states. Caramel coloring makes most brown soft drinks brown.

Root beer entered the marketplace in 1876. ICB Root Beer was developed in 1919 as an alternative to alcoholic beverages during Prohibition. Mug® Root Beer was bought by Pepsi in 1986. Barq's®, a unit of Coca-Cola Co., is the only major root beer that contains caffeine. A&W Root Beer is named for its founders, Allen and Wright.

Shasta Beverages, that began in California in 1889 producing bottled mineral water, manufactures Shasta Soda®, a value-priced soft drink line with a wide variety of soda flavors. In the 1950s, they introduced the packaging of soft drinks in cans, the introduction of low calorie soft drinks, and the distribution of cans and bottles directly to grocers through wholesale channels, which became industry standards.

Canada Dry, known for its ginger ale, also produces other soft drinks and mixers. The word 'dry' in its name refers to not being sweet. During Prohibition, its flavor helped mask the taste of homemade liquor and it became very popular. Although it originated in Canada in 1904, it is now produced in many countries, including the United States.

Russian immigrant bakers created Faygo® soda in 1907 and delivered their product door-to-door. Faygo® invented a purification system to extend shelf life, twist-off caps, and calling soda 'pop.'

7-Up® was originally called Bib-Label Lithiated Lemon-Lime Soda when it was invented in 1929 by C. L. Grigg. Until 1948, it contained lithium (a mood stabilizing drug used to treat depression). It was marketed as the un-cola in 1967. The term 'un-cola' expanded over time to mean all lighter colored drinks and many others that are not caramelized.

Squirt® is a caffeine-free citrus-flavored carbonated soft drink created in 1938 in Arizona. In 1983, Diet Squirt® was the first soft drink in the U.S. to be sweetened with aspartame. Ruby Red Squirt® contains caffeine. In 2008, Squirt Citrus Power® was introduced. It is also caffeinated and contains other ingredients similar to an energy drink.

Mountain Dew®, slang for moonshine, was invented by the Hartman brothers in Tennessee in the 1940s. It was used as a mixer for whiskey.

Fanta®, a Coca-Cola Co. product, was first made in Essen, Germany during World War II. It was not available in United States during that time. Today, Brazil is the top consumer of Fanta®.

Crush®, currently owned by the Dr. Pepper Snapple Group, was invented by a California chemist. It was originally marketed as an orange soda but today, there are additional flavors such as grape, strawberry, and cherry.

> Soda is universal and there are many exotic soda flavors worldwide. Yogurt, green tea, octopus, wasabi, and eel are a few soda flavors offered in Japan.

Dr. Brown's soda has been around since the 1960s. They have a soda with celery flavor, extracted from the celery seed. All of Dr. Brown's sodas are kosher.

Fresca®, made by Coca-Cola Co., has been marketed in the United States as a calorie-free, lime and grapefruit-flavored soft drink since 1966. President Lyndon B. Johnson loved it and had a soda fountain containing Fresca® installed in the Oval Office.

Mello Yello®, produced by Coca-Cola Co., is a highly-caffeinated citrus-flavored soft drink introduced in 1979. It was featured in the 1990 movie, *Days of Thunder*, starring Tom Cruise. His character drove a Mello Yello®-sponsored car to victory in the Daytona 500 race.

Jones Soda was launched in Vancouver, British Columbia in 1995. Customer-submitted photos adorn their retro glass bottles. Soda flavors include traditional favorites like Root Beer as well as unique ones like Blue Bubblegum, Fufu Berry, Bacon, and Turkey and Gravy. Entertaining quotes can be found under their bottle caps, and the caps can be redeemed for prizes.

LaCroix is a soda beverage distributed by the Sundance Beverage Company. It comes in twenty flavors and all are free of sweeteners, sodium, and calories.

Beverages charged with carbon dioxide under pressure are carbonated. SodaStream® is a device that carbonates water by adding carbon dioxide from a pressurized cylinder to create soda water to drink at home. Different flavors are created by adding one of more than one hundred types of concentrated fruit-flavored syrups and flavorings.

Ben Weiss founded Bai in 2009 in Princeton, New Jersey. Bai Bubbles® carbonated beverages are flavor infused with antioxidants. They are only five calories and one gram of sugar, with no artificial sweeteners.

Omar Knedlik, owner of a Dairy Queen in Kansas, invented the first frozen carbonated drink machine in the late 1950s. When his soda fountain broke down, he put the sodas in a freezer to stay cool which caused them to become slushy. His customers liked them so he created a machine to make a slushed ice drink from carbonated beverages. Knedlik hired artist Ruth E. Taylor to create a name for his invention, the ICEE®. She designed the original logo that is still used today.

A Slurpee® is a frozen carbonated beverage sold at 7-Eleven convenience stores. The store chain has celebrated Free Slurpee Day on July 11 (7/11) since 2002. 2016 marked the fiftieth anniversary of the Slurpee® – there was even a birthday cake flavor to mark the occasion.

NOTE: There are also non-carbonated slush machines that don't require a pressure chamber and a carbon dioxide source.

Snow cones, an icy treat drizzled with sweet flavoring, are served in a cone-shaped wax paper cup. They are made by crushing ordinary ice. The most common flavor options are cherry, grape and blue raspberry. Shaved ice, shaved from a block of ice, is a fine and fluffy ice mimicking real snow. The flat shaving surface allows for a fluffier texture. The syrup, poured on top, comes in a variety of flavors, and toppings are sometimes added, such as sour spray on the fruity flavors and sweet cream on the less acidic flavors.

In 1927, Edwin E. Perkins invented Kool-Aid®, a powdered soft drink. The original flavors were cherry, grape, root beer, orange, lemon, raspberry, and strawberry (tropical punch came later). Hastings, Nebraska holds a Kool-Aid® Days festival each year in August.

Crystal Light®, a low-calorie powdered beverage mix produced by Kraft Foods, was originally marketed in 1982. It was first packaged in multi-serve canisters. Single-serve "On The Go" packets were introduced in 2004. There are twenty-four flavors available in naturally and artificially sweetened varieties.

Hawaiian Punch® contains seven natural fruits, including pineapple and papaya.

Yoo-Hoo® originated in New Jersey in 1926 and is currently manufactured by the Dr. Pepper Snapple Group. It is neither a soda or a milk drink; it is a non-carbonated chocolate soft drink that won't spoil in the heat. Yogi Berra, a famous baseball player, helped inventor Natale Olivieri promote Yoo-Hoo® chocolate drink in the 1950s.

In 1948, Nestlé launched a mix for chocolate-flavored milk called Nestle Quik. The name was changed to the worldwide brand Nesquik® in 1999. Nesquik® Banana Powder was introduced 1954 and Nesquik® Strawberry Powder was introduced prior to 1960. Nesquik® Vanilla Powder was introduced in 1979 but was discontinued in 2006. Nesquik® syrup products were introduced in 1981. Ready-to-Drink Nesquik® Chocolate Milk was introduced in 1983 and a fat-free version was introduced in 1998. Nestlé® introduced Nesquik® Magic Straws in 2008.

Ovaltine is a milk-flavoring powder product made with malt extract. Some flavors also have cocoa. It was developed in Switzerland where it is known by its original name, Ovomaltine (from *ovum*, Latin for egg, and *malt,* its main ingredient). The U.S. children's radio series *Little Orphan Annie* (1931–1940) and the *Captain Midnight* TV series (1954–1956) were sponsored by Ovaltine, but it is currently not advertised on American television.

Swiss Miss® is a cocoa powder sold by ConAgra Foods. In the 1950s, the company sold its original hot cocoa product as an onboard beverage to airline passengers. Once the drink became popular, it sold in grocery stores. Swiss Miss® is available in regular and no sugar added, with or without small marshmallows.

Instant breakfast drinks typically refer to food products that are manufactured in a powdered form, generally prepared with the addition of milk. They may contain protein, vitamins and minerals, and sugar. Carnation Instant Breakfast (Breakfast Essentials®) was introduced in 1964.

One hundred percent fruit juice contains naturally occurring fructose (the sugar from the fruit). Juice drinks may contain added sugar in the form of high fructose corn syrup. Canned juices are usually an enriched product since the heat used in the processing destroys most of the vitamins. If the fruit juice is labeled cold-pressed, it is a higher quality product with most of its vitamin content intact. Fruit juices help to maintain a proper acid-base balance in the stomach but may irritate ulcers. When serving fruit juice, lemonade or punch, make ice cubes from the drinks to keep the drinks from becoming watered down.

Tropicana Products, Inc., founded in 1947 in Bradenton, Florida makes fruit-based beverages and specializes in orange juice. In 1954, its founder, Anthony Rossi, developed flash pasteurization, a process that rapidly raised the temperature of juice for a short time to preserve its fresh taste.

Minute Maid was the first company to market frozen orange juice concentrate. It also produces lemonade and several soft drinks, including Hi-C® created in 1946. The original flavor was orange.

The eight juices in V-8 Juice® are tomato, spinach, celery, carrot, beet, lettuce, watercress, and parsley juice.

Mott's, founded in 1842 in New York, primarily produces apple juice and apple sauce. Their products were exhibited at the Chicago World's Fair in 1893.

An Arnold Palmer, named after the professional golfer, is half ice tea and half lemonade.

A Shirley Temple is made with ginger-ale and Grenadine (cherry syrup) and often topped with a cherry. It was named for the actress, who tried it and found it too sweet. A Kiddie Kocktail uses Sprite® or 7-Up® and a splash of Grenadine.

Gatorade®, the original sports drink, was created in 1967 by the University of Florida for their football team, the Gators.

Energy drinks have the effects that caffeine and sugar provide. U.S. dietary guidelines suggest that moderate caffeine intake may not only be safe, but also healthy. Red Bull®, created in 1987, is one of the most popular energy drinks worldwide. Powerade® was introduced in 1988. Monster Energy® drink, introduced in 2002, is known for supporting many extreme sports events. The Monster Energy® drink logo is a large green M on a field of black. The M looks like the claws of a monster ripping through the can. 5-Hour Energy shot was launched in 2003. It contains caffeine but no sugar. **Caution: Children under the age of twelve, nursing or pregnant women, and people with a sensitivity to caffeine should avoid energy drinks.**

Minerals like calcium and magnesium occur naturally in water but can be removed during the osmosis process used by the most popular purified bottled waters. Although minerals can be added back to the water, the amounts tend to be lower than those in tap water. Bottled water may have an expiration date but water itself doesn't expire. If bottled water is kept unopened, it will remain safe for drinking indefinitely. However, if the bottle is exposed to direct sunlight or heat, which can break down the plastic, the taste may diminish over time. If you are storing water for an emergency, periodically use that water and replace it with new bottles. An opened bottle of water should be used within two weeks. Plastic water bottles should be recycled but the plastic isn't usually used to make more plastic water bottles. It is used for other applications, such as carpets and clothing. Some plastic can't be recycled at all.

Bottled spring water may outperform tap water for these minerals. Spring water is water that has risen from aquifers beneath the surface and absorbed minerals along the way (the amount and type of minerals varies depending on the source of the water). When Perrier® production began, the owner of the spring, Sir John Harmsworth, was inspired to shape the bottles after Indian clubs that he used for exercising. Mineral water must contain a specific amount of minerals.

Distilled water has been processed through distillation to have the impurities removed. The distillation process removes the minerals that can lead to build-up in machinery, which is why distilled water is often used for industrial purposes. There is no reliable science supporting the claim that drinking distilled water is harmful.

Seltzer water was named for Niederselters, a town in Germany famous for its mineral springs. It originally referred to a naturally effervescent mineral water but today, seltzer is known as artificially carbonated club soda or soda water.

Tonic water contains quinine, an antimalarial drug derived from the bark of the South American cinchona tree. Tonic water was originally prescribed as a medicine. Some people are extremely sensitive to quinine's toxic effects but the FDA (Food and Drug Administration) hasn't banned quinine from tonic water. The low dose of quinine found in a glass or two of tonic water isn't enough to trigger health issues in most people. Some people believe it helps relieve leg cramps. Because of the quinine in tonic water, it glows under an ultraviolet light.

There are many types of flavored waters available. They contain an array of additional ingredients including natural and artificial flavors, sugar, sweeteners, vitamins, minerals, and antioxidants. A few brands contain water and only natural enhancements.

Spa water in Belgium was bottled for export in 1583.
A Boston spa offered bottled water for sale in 1767.

Why is drinking water important to our health?

Water supports our metabolism.
Water helps prevent headaches.
Water improves our energy.
Water provides us with pure hydration.
Water helps our digestive system.
Water allows our bodies to naturally flush out toxins.
Water helps prevent muscle cramps.
Water supports our immune system.
Water helps us generally feel well.

TEA

Tea, a very popular beverage throughout the world, dates back over four thousand years. Legend says that in 2737 B.C. the Chinese Emperor, Shen Nung, discovered tea when a tea leaf accidently fell into his bowl of hot water. In Ancient China, tea was used as a form of currency. Afternoon tea, or Low tea, began in the 1800s by the seventh Duchess of Bedford. She served tea and sweets as a snack before the later dinner. Low tea, served at low tables in a sitting room, is usually served between three and six o'clock in the afternoon. The later it is served, the more substantial the food. High Tea was created during the Victorian era and is served at high dining tables at dinner time. English tea gardens were the first public place where women were allowed to mix with men, without scandal.

It takes between three and five years before a newly planted tea bush is ready for harvest. The higher the altitude, the longer it takes to reach maturity. Once mature, the bush will yield tea for fifty years or more. There are over three thousand varieties of tea but only four major types: black green, white, and oolong. They are all from the leaves of the Camellia senensis plant but how the leaves are treated makes the different types of tea. Black tea is made from leaves that are fermented and then heated. Green tea leaves are not fermented; they are steamed and then heated. Oolong teas can be brewed up to three times. Flavored teas are made of real tea with various added essences. Herbal teas are tea-like drinks that are infusions from roots, leaves, flowers, seeds, and fruits of other plants. They are not from the Camellia senensis plant.

An unknown Chinese inventor invented the tea shredder, a small device that shredded tea leaves in preparation for drinking. In tea ceremonies, the teapot should be warmed first and tea leaves should always remain in the pot. Hot water should be added to the pot while drinking the tea, until the flavor fades. The tea egg and tea ball are perforated metal containers filled with loose leaves that are dropped into boiling water. A chain was attached to the ball to aid retrieval. The first tea bags, made from hand-sewn silk muslin bags, appeared commercially around 1908. A machine was soon invented to replace the hand sewing of tea bags.

Thomas Lipton incorporated the Lipton Tea Company in 1915. Lipton Tea® patented a novel four-sided tea bag in 1952 called the flo-thru tea bag. Tea absorbs moisture so store loose tea or tea leaves in a sealed container. Loose leaves in an air-tight container will remain fresh for up to two years and tea bags for six months. Lemon and milk should not be used in the same cup of tea as lemon will curdle the milk.

For centuries, tea was used only as medicine. It took almost three thousand years for it to become an enjoyable beverage. Today, tea leaves and other parts of the plant are also used in dietary supplements and other health products, and cosmetics. There are thousands of different types of tea containing catechins, a type of antioxidant that can reduce the risk of heart disease, stroke, diabetes, and certain types of cancer (catechins are also found in dark chocolate). One cup of white tea contains as high a concentration of antioxidants as ten cups of apple juice. Some people believe regularly drinking green tea is helpful when trying to lose weight – the oxidants in the tea help reduce fat digestion. Catechins in tea can also protect the skin from harmful UV rays and wet tea bags can take away the sting of sun burn. Putting wet teabags over your eyes for twenty minutes reduces puffy eyes. Tea contains between one-third and one-half as much caffeine as coffee. Hot drinks do not raise body temperature.

A recipe for iced tea dates back to 1877 in Virginia. It was served at the St. Louis World's Fair in 1904 because it was so warm that hot tea wasn't selling. An ice tea spoon is thin with a very long handle and is used for stirring sugar or other sweeteners into cold tea, traditionally served in a tall glass. Sweet tea, popular in southern states in the United States, is made from black tea and is served very cold or with ice. Before World War II, sweet tea was made from green tea but the war caused most sources of green tea to be unavailable to the U.S. India, controlled by the British, produced black tea that the U.S. could obtain. Supposedly, the U.S. is the only nation in the world that consumes more iced tea than hot tea. Many health food and specialty stores carry iced tea made of whole leaf tea without additives. Iced tea is sometimes made by steeping tea leaves for at least one hour in the sun, called Sun Tea. An alternative is brewing the tea in the refrigerator overnight to prevent the growth of harmful bacteria. Powdered or frozen iced tea is a common preparation at home due to its ease of use.

Companies like AriZona Iced Tea, Nestle, and Brisk offer a variety of ice teas. Ice-Tea® is the brand name of a carbonated variety of iced tea marketed by Lipton since 1978. They also market a number of other non-carbonated iced teas under the Ice Tea® brand. Snapple® was founded in 1972 in New York by two brothers and a health food store owner. They spent fifteen years experimenting with different types of apple sodas and seltzer water before they came up with Snapple® tea, named after a carbonated apple soda that was part of the original beverage line. Snapple® comes in assorted flavors.

"You can never get a cup of tea large enough or a book long enough to suit me."
C.S. Lewis   1898-1963   Writer

Coffee is the second largest traded commodity in the world (oil is the largest). Sixty-five countries along the equator grow coffee, called the coffee belt. Brazil is the largest coffee producer in the world today (they issued a coffee scented postage stamp in 2001). Coffee grown in the United States is only grown in Hawaii. Coffee represents about seventy-five percent of all the caffeine consumed in the U.S. There are two types of coffee plants: Arabica and Robusta. Robusta coffee beans have twice as much caffeine as Arabica beans. It takes five years for a coffee tree to reach full maturity and the trees can live up to one hundred years. Coffee beans start out as red berries. The largest coffee beans are found in Nicaragua. Coffee grown at an altitude above five thousand feet is known as Hard Bean. The English word 'coffee' originated from the Arabic word kaweh, meaning 'strength or vigor.'

According to legend, Ethiopian shepherds first realized the caffeine effects of coffee when they noticed their goats jumping around after eating coffee berries. In the fourteenth century, the Arabs began to cultivate coffee plants. They flavored their coffee with spices during the brewing process. Sixteenth-century Muslim rulers banned coffee because of its unusual stimulating effects. The first coffee house in Europe opened in Venice in 1645. The custom of tipping waiters "to insure promptness" (tip) originated in early European Coffee Houses. In 1675, Charles II of England issued a proclamation banning Coffee Houses. He believed they were places where people met to plot against him. In the same century, Pope Clement VIII banned coffee, stating it was the "Devils Tool" but changed his mind once he had a cup. Dorothy Jones of Boston, the first American coffee trader, was granted a license to sell coffee in 1670. The first coffee house in America opened in Boston in 1676. Both the American Revolution and the French Revolution were plotted in coffee houses. During the American Civil War, soldiers were given coffee beans as a primary ration. Cowboy Coffee originated from Cowboys using their dirty socks as coffee filters out on the trail.

Adding sugar to coffee is believed to have started in 1715 in the court of King Louis XIV. Frederick the Great (1712-1786), King of Prussia, had his coffee made with champagne and mustard. Citrus has been added to coffee for several hundred years. The drip pot was invented by a Frenchman around 1800 and the coffee percolator was invented in 1865. In 1822, the first espresso machine was made in France. The modern-day, high pressure espresso machine was created in 1946. The first pump-driven espresso machine was produced in 1960. Instant coffee was created in Chicago by a Japanese American chemist in 1901. In 1938, Nescafe® freeze-dried coffee was invented. It was the first food to be freeze-dried. Melitta Bentz, a housewife from Germany, invented the first coffee filter, patented in 1908. Her company also patented the filter bag in 1937 and vacuum packing in 1962. The first web cam was used for coffee in 1991: Cambridge University scientists placed a camera on a coffee pot in their work place, streaming the footage live on the web so they would be able to see if the pot was empty or not.

Manual espresso making is considered a skilled task. A latte is a shot of espresso with steamed milk and foamed milk, but a cappuccino is equal parts espresso, steamed milk and foamed milk. The word 'cappuccino' comes from the resemblance of the drink to the clothing of the Capuchin monks. A Café Cubano is an espresso shot sweetened with demerara sugar as it is being brewed (demerara is unrefined sugar with a light yellow color and large grain). A Mocha has equal parts espresso and chocolate, with half steamed milk. A Half-caf is made with half parts caffeinated and decaffeinated beans. A Breve is made with steamed half-and-half cream. Cafe au lait is brewed coffee over espresso with scalded milk. A doppio is a double shot of espresso. An Americano is a shot of espresso with twice that amount of water.

Standard American roasted beans, or breakfast roast, is a medium-light roast and produces coffee that isn't strong or dark. Medium-dark roasted beans, such as a Viennese roast, produce a darker, richer coffee. Dark-roasted coffee beans, usually called French or Italian roast, are used for making espresso. Dark roasted coffees have less caffeine than medium roasts; the longer a coffee is roasted, the more caffeine burns off during the process. Roasted coffee beans start to lose small amounts of flavor within two weeks. Ground coffee begins to lose its flavor in one hour. Brewed coffee and espresso begins to lose flavor within minutes. Coffee beans are flavored after they are roasted. Java and Mocha beans are named after their ports of origin. Kopi Luwak is collected from the feces of Asian Palm civets after they've ingested coffee beans – it costs well over one hundred dollars per pound. The most expensive coffee in the world is called Black Ivory coffee, made from elephant dung. It costs fifty dollars a cup.

The body naturally produces cortisol, a hormone that helps you feel alert and awake. It is released when you first wake up so wait till later, between 9:30 a.m. and 11:30 a.m., to have a cup of coffee (your caffeine isn't wasted during a time when cortisol is at its highest). A single cup of coffee contains vitamins B2 and B5, manganese, magnesium, potassium, and niacin. It has a lot of antioxidants that help the body fight free radicals. As a result, coffee drinkers are at a lower risk of diseases such as Parkinson's Disease, Type II Diabetes, and Heart Disease (as long as you don't have unhealthy habits like smoking or drinking alcohol heavily). The caffeine in coffee can increase metabolism, helping with weight loss. It only takes ten minutes to feel the effects of caffeine after you take a sip. Espresso coffee has one third of the caffeine of a cup of regular coffee.

Mazagran, a cold, sweetened coffee beverage that originated in Algeria around 1840, is the original iced coffee. Iced coffee was popularized in the United States in 1920. It is prepared many different ways and variations differ by country. Many coffee retailers use hot-brewed coffee that is chilled, in their iced coffee drinks. Cold brewing is steeping coffee grounds in room-temperature or cold water for an extended period. Cold brew coffee contains up to seventy percent fewer bitter acids than hot-brewed coffee. Frappuccino® is a trademarked brand of Starbucks for a line of frozen coffee beverages consisting of coffee blended with ice and various other ingredients, and often topped with whipped cream. The word 'Frappuccino' is from *frappe*, the New England name for milkshake.

CHAPTER 9

Miscellaneous Trivia

Apicius, a First Century Roman, is the author of the oldest surviving cookbook, *De Re Coquinaria* (On Cookery). Nostradamus, known for his prophecies, also wrote a cookbook that was published in 1555, the same year that his prophecies were published. The first American cookbook was *American Cookery*, from 1796.

The first cooking school in the United States opened in New York in 1876 by Juliet Corson. She believed every woman should understand how to run a kitchen whether or not she did her own cooking, even though she herself knew little about cooking before she started the school. She read cookbooks by the best European authorities and planned, at first, to teach working-class pupils, charging them only what they could afford to pay. Soon, upper-class women arrived for lessons. She later introduced children's classes. Corson published numerous cookbooks over a twelve year period, including pamphlets aimed at helping poor and working-class homemakers prepare satisfying meals for their families at low cost.

The canning process dates back to the late eighteenth century in France. There was a need for a stable source of food for the military and Emperor Napoleon offered a cash prize for a breakthrough in the preservation of food. The Del Monte brand, introduced in 1892, was the first canner to offer a broad line of California processed foods to the entire nation, and the first to advertise nationally. In 1973, they were the first major food processor in the U.S. to include nutrition labels on their products.

Electric can openers were invented almost fifty years after canned foods were introduced.

Aluminum was introduced in metal can making in 1957. More than ninety million aluminum cans are produced every day and only half of them are recycled. The pyramid that crowns the top of the Washington Monument is aluminum.

In 1954, C.A. Swanson & Sons introduced the first TV dinner – roast turkey with stuffing and gravy, sweet potatoes, and peas. It sold for ninety-eight cents and came in an aluminum tray that could be heated in the oven. The idea for the aluminum trays came from the trays used by airlines. Swanson & Sons stopped calling them TV dinners in 1962. The aluminum trays were replaced with plastic, microwavable trays in 1986.

The mortar and pestle is probably the oldest cooking utensil known to man. The mortar is a bowl, and the pestle is the short club used to press or pound the food in the mortar.

Chopsticks originated in China almost four thousand years ago. Using chopsticks instead of knives for eating at the table indicated respect for the scholar over the warrior in Chinese society.

In ancient Rome, vendors sold food ready-to-eat from street stalls.

The non-electric hot plate, made of bronze and filled with embers, was used to heat or cook food at the table in ancient Roman times. Electric hot plates used to cook and warm food are a modern invention.

In the sixteenth century, Spain and Italy were the first countries to adopt the fork for eating rather than just as a serving utensil. During colonial times in America, forks were mainly used in the kitchen to hold meat while cutting it. People used their fingers to eat – forks were only used for eating in restaurants. Spoons were used for soups or stews. Most Americans did not begin using forks until the 1800s. As recently as 1897, British sailors could not use knives and forks to eat because it was considered unmanly.

In the eighteenth century, young Pennsylvania Dutch men gave their sweethearts carved rolling pins as engagement presents.

The toothpick was first used in the United States at the Union Oyster House, the oldest restaurant in Boston that opened in 1826. Ninety percent of the U.S. toothpick supply is produced in Maine.

Gas stoves were first introduced in the 1850s but housewives were afraid that the ranges were too dangerous and might explode.

Dr. John Gorrie of Apalachicola, Florida invented mechanical refrigeration in 1851. In the late nineteenth century, refrigerated railroad cars made vegetables and fruits available to more people for most of the year.

The electric refrigerator was invented by Florence Parpart in 1914. (She also invented an improved street cleaning machine.) Electric refrigerators were first sold in the United States in 1916 and cost nine hundred dollars. In 1949, the first self-defrosting refrigerator was sold.

The Dishwasher was invented by Josephine Cochrane in 1887. She marketed her machine to hotel owners and also opened her own factory.

A British firm introduced an iron wire electric toaster in 1893 that was unreliable and prone to catch fire. The first electric manual toasters (no timer and no pop-up) were patented and sold around 1909. The first automatic pop-up toaster was marketed in 1926.

The first vending machines sold chewing gum in the New York City Subways.

In 1871, Margaret Knight invented a machine that made square bottomed paper bags. She also invented a safety device for cotton mills when she was twelve years old, and that invention is still used today.

Roy J. Plunkett of New Carlisle, Ohio invented Teflon in 1938 but Teflon coated frying pans weren't introduced until 1961.

The first Thanksgiving in North America was held in Virginia in 1619. The first National Thanksgiving Day, proclaimed by President George Washington, was celebrated on November twenty-sixth in 1789, the last Thursday of the month. In 1863, President Abraham Lincoln made Thanksgiving an official annual holiday, celebrated in November. In 1939, President Franklin D. Roosevelt changed it from the last Thursday to the third Thursday. Since 1947, the National Turkey Federation has presented the U. S. President with a live turkey and two dressed turkeys in celebration of Thanksgiving. The annual presentation has become a traditional holiday ritual, signaling the unofficial beginning of the holiday season. After the live bird is pardoned, it is taken to a historical farm to live out the rest of its years. Native Americans never ate turkey. Killing such a timid bird indicated laziness.

In the seventeenth century, farmers in New York City built a wall to keep pigs from roaming. The street running along this wall was named Wall Street.

The Uncle Sam character is modeled after Sam Wilson, a meatpacker from New York. During the War of 1812, the meat he shipped to the government was stamped 'U.S. Beef.' Soldiers began to call this beef Uncle Sam's beef.

In 1921, Sam Gale created a fictional spokeswoman named Betty Crocker so correspondence to housewives could have her signature.

Charles Goodnight devised the first chuck wagon in the 1850s. He fitted an Army wagon with shelves and compartments for storing food, cooking equipment, and eating utensils. It also had room for medical supplies, scissors and a shovel. The cook's duties included acting as doctor, barber, and burying the dead. Cooks were paid double what cowhands earned.

The first railroad dining car was introduced in 1868. It was named Delmonico in honor of the famous restaurant in New York City.

The first food truck was Walter Scott's horse drawn lunch wagon in Providence, Rhode Island. In 1872, he sat inside and customers ordered sandwiches, pie, and other items through open windows in the side.

Chinatown in New York City was filled with restaurants by 1901. People loved the unfamiliar flavors and bargain prices. Home delivery of Chinese takeout didn't begin until 1976.

The word 'delicatessen' is of German origin (delikatessen, meaning delicacies or an abundance of good things to eat). New York's delicatessens date back to the mid-nineteenth century, and were opened by German immigrants who sold the cured meats and salads of their homeland. German Jews, who did not eat these food because they weren't kosher, opened their own delicatessens. Jews arriving later in the century from Russia and Eastern Europe eventually opened their own kosher delicatessens too, that carried both German foods and Eastern European specialties. Today, the term 'deli' can refer to almost any store selling cured meats and sandwiches as well as breads, bagels, smoked fish, and cream cheese.

The first restaurant was opened in 1765 in Paris by a soup maker His was the first establishment to offer a menu with a choice of dishes. The first printed menu in the U.S. was issued in 1836 by New York City's Delmonico's restaurant, established in 1831.

The first restaurant chain in the U.S. was the Harvey House, established by Fred Harvey in 1876 in Kansas to serve railroad travelers.

The first soda fountains, serving floats, sundaes, malteds, egg creams, banana splits, and sodas, opened in New York in the early 1800s. They began to offer light lunches and as the lunch menus expanded, soda fountains became known as luncheonettes, a term that emerged in the 1920s. They offered satisfying hot dishes, larger sandwiches, and fried foods at inexpensive prices

The restaurant industry, with more than two million restaurant servers, is the largest employer in the United States other than the government. Classifications for restaurants are based on menus, methods of food preparation, how the food is served, and pricing.

A Pub (short for public house) is a bar that will often serve food. It is also known as a tavern. A gastropub offers high-quality pub food. The White Horse Tavern in Rhode Island, built in 1673, is the oldest operating tavern in the United States.

Cafeterias serve ready-cooked food at a food-serving counter, without table service. Self service restaurants first appeared in San Francisco during the California gold rush of 1849. The first New York self-service restaurant was in 1898 and by the 1920s there were about one thousand of them. Cafeterias were a place to find an inexpensive but respectable midday meal but after World War II, rising costs made it difficult for cafeterias to maintain their low prices.

The first Automat, Horn and Hardart, was opened by Frank Hardart and Joe Horn in 1912 in New York City. People dropped a nickel in a slot, opened a small window, and pulled out a sandwich, hot dish or dessert, all freshly made. By 1919, every Automat restaurant included a cafeteria. The last one closed in 1991.

Cafés are informal eateries offering hot meals or sandwiches. Coffee shops are similar to cafés but mostly serve hot beverages and have limited food choices, such as pastries and breakfast items.

Buffets offer a selection of food at food stations where patrons help themselves, at a fixed price. The stations may be divided into categories, such as salads and soups, hot entrees, cold entrees, and desserts. The food may be an eclectic mix or a specific type, such as Chinese. Las Vegas is known as the World Capital of Buffets.

A Food court is generally an indoor plaza within a mall or other large venue, offering multiple food vendors and self-serve dining in a common eating area.

A Diner serves a wide selection of mostly American foods, in a casual atmosphere, and is usually open for twenty-four hours a day, seven days a week. The diner came about because many towns banned lunch wagons or placed restrictions on them. Some found a vacant lot, took off the wheels, and hooked up to utilities. New Jersey has more diners than any other state and is sometimes called the Diner Capital of the World.

Casual dining restaurants serve moderately-priced food in a casual atmosphere. They offer table service, unless it's buffet-style. They may be part of a chain of restaurants.

Family-style restaurants are similar to casual dining eateries. Food is brought on platters and the diners serve themselves. They may or may not serve alcoholic beverages.

Fast-food places emphasize fast counter service and use disposable plates and cutlery. Usually they offer a value menu and can be found in most locations throughout the U.S. The oldest fast food restaurant is the White Castle® franchise that opened in 1921.

Fine dining establishments are full-service restaurants with an elegant atmosphere, a trained, formally attired wait staff, aesthetically appealing foods, and sometimes a dress code for patrons. They are often small businesses and single-location operations, though some have multiple locations.

At a Hibachi restaurant, diners sit around a grill (often in multiple, unrelated parties) while the trained chef prepares the food in front of them.

Mongolian barbecue restaurants are similar to a buffet, but once the customer gathers uncooked ingredients in a bowl, those items are handed to a cook who stir-fries the food on a large griddle.

The term 'power lunch' first appeared in 1979 but in the 1830s, Delmonico's restaurant in New York City was the first place for the 'power lunch,' made famous by men in expensive suits who came for the sophisticated cooking, ostentatious decor, and prime location in the business district.

Restaurateur Joe Baum set the standard for high-style New York dining from the 1950s through the 1980s. His grandest creations, famous for their spectacular designs, innovative menus, and towering prices, included the Four Seasons restaurant and a new version of the Rainbow Room (a New York City landmark with world class dining and dancing).

New York's school lunch program began in 1908 to feed undernourished schoolchildren from the city's poor neighborhoods. During the course of the next half century, school lunch became a federal program and an important initiative in child nutrition across the U.S. Some schools offer breakfast as well.

An airport in Amsterdam has a departure lounge that serves pre-flight meals to travelling cattle.

Some sheep farmers use llamas to guard their sheep.

Unusual uses for Coca-Cola®:
- To remove grease stains and smells, pour a can into the wash along with your regular detergent.
- Pour it into a pan with burned-on food, bring it to a boil, and scrub away the crusty stuff.
- Soak a cloth in some and rub it on a copper pot, let it set, then rinse.
- Pour it on a blood stain, let it set, then wash as usual.
- Clean corrosion off battery terminals by wiping them with a cloth soaked in some (it also cleans greasy motors).
- Dip the area of hair with gum in it, let it sit a few minutes, then wipe off the gum.
- Pour some in a spray bottle and use it to clean windows.
- Pour it on eye glasses then rinse clean with water and wipe.
- Pour it around the rim of a toilet bowl to cover the stains, let sit for an hour, then flush the stain away.
- Pour it on a jellyfish sting to lessen the pain.
- Sipping some that has gone flat helps relieve nausea.
- Dab mosquito bites with it to relieve itching, and it also eases the pain of wasp and bee stings.
- Descale a tea or coffee pot by filling it with some and letting it sit overnight.
- Soak rusted items in it and then scrub them clean.
- To remove skunk smell, apply it to the affected skin or fur, wait a few minutes, then rinse well with water.
- For a greener lawn, mix a can with a can of beer, a ½ cup of household ammonia, one cup of mouthwash, and a half cup of dishwashing soap. Pour the solution into a ten-gallon sprayer container for your hose and coat the lawn with the mixture a few times a week.
- It can clean grout and calking, just pour some on the stains.
- Pour it on azaleas or gardenias when you water them to increase the acidity and boost their blooms.
- Add a can to the slow cooker when making pork dishes.
- Pour a can down a garbage disposal, followed by boiling water, to unclog it.
- Drop Mentos® candies into a bottle of Diet Coke® and watch it erupt.

In 1859, George Gilman and George Huntington Hartford invented a new retailing idea. They bought tea from boats at the dock in New York City and sold it directly to the consumer from a store, thereby reducing the price. Soon they were doing the same with coffee, spices, canned goods, and other products. In 1912, Hartford's son eliminated telephone orders, deliveries, credit accounts, and clerks that weighed everything for each customer. In the new store, there was only one clerk, everything was sold for cash, and customers got their own pre-packaged food from the shelves and carried it home themselves. Within five years they had over three thousand stores. The name of the company was originally the Great American Tea Company, which became the Great Atlantic & Pacific Tea Company, named A & P – the first supermarket.

The bar code was invented by Joseph Woodland and Bernard Silver in 1952 but the first bar code scanning equipment wasn't installed in stores until much later. The first item to be scanned using a UPC bar code was a ten-pack of Wrigley's Juicy Fruit Gum®.

Creole refers to the descendants of the aristocratic French and Spanish (and some German & Italian) settlers who established New Orleans in the 1690s. Creole cuisine has a strong European influence as well as Native American, West Indian and African.

Cajuns are descendants of a French colony in East Canada who were exiled by the English in 1755 and made their way to Louisiana. Cajun cuisine is American.

Napoleon's army used rose petals boiled in white wine to treat lead poisoning from bullet wounds.

The phrase "don't upset the apple cart" was first used by Roman playwright Plautus in 255 B.C. in one of his plays.

The Big Apple got its name in the 1920s from the horse racing courses in New York City and its surrounding area. Later that same decade, jazz musicians started to use the term for New York City as a whole and it gradually spread. In the 1970s, New York City used the term extensively in a tourism campaign.

The Cow Chip Throwing Capital of the World is Beaver, Oklahoma. It was established as a tribute to the unique natural fuel source of the town's early settlers, and has taken place since 1969.

Earthworms prepare soil for farming. They pass the top few inches of soil through their guts every year, altering its composition, increasing its capacity to absorb and hold water, and bringing about an increase in nutrients and microorganisms.

A well-treated and well-fed camel can produce ten gallons of milk a day, which is as much as Holstein cows produce.

Au naturel is a French term that refers to food in its natural state (not cooked or altered).

Americans spend four times more on pet food than on baby food.

Ginkgo biloba is the oldest living tree species. It is found in fossils dating back two hundred seventy million years. A single tree can live as long as one thousand years and grow to a height of one hundred and twenty feet. Native to China, the tree is widely cultivated. The largest Gingko farm is in South Carolina.

Pine, spruce, or other evergreen wood should never be used in barbecues because, when burning or smoking, they can add harmful tar and resins to the food. Only hardwoods such as oak, pecan, hickory, maple, cherry, alder, apple or mesquite should be used for smoking and grilling, depending on the type of meat being cooked.

Native Americans treated influenza with a tea made from the bark and twigs of the Canadian Yew tree. The Pacific Yew is being studied today as the source for a drug to treat certain types of cancers. The leaves and seeds of Yew contain poisonous alkaloids so potent, they can cause heart and respiratory failure in an animal so quickly that no symptoms appear, the animal just dies.

There are several edible species of locusts that may be grilled, roasted, boiled, or ground to a paste.

Ants are one of the most popular edible insect species around the world. Harvester ants consume more small seeds than all mammals and birds put together. The first Ant Farm went on sale in 1958.

The first pizza was created in 1889 by a tavern owner in Naples, Italy. It featured red tomatoes, white mozzarella cheese, and green basil (ingredients bearing the colors of the Italian flag) and was named the Margherita Pizza, after Queen Margherita of Italy. Gennaro Lombardi, a Neapolitan immigrant, is known as the founding father of New York pizza – he painted the word 'pizzeria' on his shop's window in 1905. Patsy Lancieri was the first to offer pizza by the slice in 1933 in East Harlem. Chicago's famous deep-dish pizza isn't an Italian export – the Chicago restaurant Pizza Uno first created the dish in 1943. The day of the most pizza sales in the United States is Super Bowl Sunday, followed by New Year's Eve.

The tradition of serving a lemon wedge with fish began during the Middle Ages. People served a slice of lemon with fish because they believed that the juice would dissolve any bones accidentally swallowed.

The first ready-mix food to be sold commercially was Aunt Jemima® pancake flour. It was invented in St. Joseph, Missouri and introduced in 1899.

Spam® stands for Shoulder Pork and Ham.

The dye used to stamp the grade on meat is made from grape skins and is edible.

The first fried dill pickle sold was at the Duchess Drive-In in Atkins, Arkansas in 1963. Atkins has a Pickle Fest every May.

The annual World Grits Festival is held in April in St. George, South Carolina, the Grits Capital of the World.

The BLT sandwich (Bacon, Lettuce and Tomato) became popular after World War II when fresh lettuce and tomatoes were available year-round in grocery stores.

Windom, Kansas, is known as the Covered Dish Capital of the World.

Baseball legend Lou Gehrig was the first athlete to appear on a box of Wheaties® cereal. The first football player on the front of a Wheaties box was Walter Payton.

The world's oldest soup was discovered in China, near the famed terracotta army of Xian, in a vessel found in a tomb dating to 475-221 B.C. The bone soup, cloudy and green from the bronze cooking vessel in which it was sealed, was still in liquid form.

The English word 'soup' comes from the Middle Ages word 'sop,' meaning 'a slice of bread over which roast drippings were poured.' The first canned, ready-to-serve soup in the United States was minestrone, an old family recipe created by Progresso in 1949. The red and white colors of Campbell soup labels come from the colors of the Cornell University football team.

Bouillon cubes, created in 1882 by Swiss flour manufacturer Julius Maggi, are compressed, concentrated cubes of dehydrated meat or vegetable stock. He made them so the poor, who could not afford meat, would have a way to make a more nutritious soup.

Peanut butter was first marketed as a health food. During the 1920s, it became increasingly popular for children's lunches, often mixed with cream, evaporated milk, chili sauce, or other thick liquids that made it easier to spread. When hydrogenated peanut butter became widely available a decade later, most of those combinations faded away.

Sauerkraut was called Liberty Cabbage during World War I. A hamburger was referred to as a Liberty Sandwich and German Measles were Liberty Measles.

The classic French quiche originated in Germany during medieval times. The word 'quiche' is derived from the German word *kuchen* (cake).

John Harvey Kellogg, a surgeon, vegetarian and health food pioneer, developed the first breakfast cereals. In 1884, he applied for a patent for corn flakes. His brother, William K. Kellogg founded the Battle Creek Toasted Corn Flake Co. and in the early days, he signed his name to each box of cereal (the Kellogg's logo used today was derived from the original signature). In 1952, a contest was held to see who would represent their new cereal, Kellogg's Sugar Frosted Flakes of Corn. Tony the Tiger became the sole spokesperson for the cereal.

Peanuts are used in the manufacture of dynamite.

Twenty five percent of all retail establishments in the U.S. are for eating and drinking.

Daniel Gerber, a Michigan food processor, founded the Gerber Baby Foods Company in 1927 when his doctor told him to feed strained peas to his sick child. At first, baby foods were expensive and only available in pharmacies in limited parts of the United States. In 1931, Beech-Nut introduced their strained baby food in glass jars (other companies used tin cans).

French fries originated in Belgium. In England, they are referred to as chips. One of the earliest references of British chips is in Charles Dicken's *Tale of Two Cities* (1859). Though French fries were invented in Europe, potatoes originated in the Americas and were imported. The first occurrence of French fries in America may have been at a diplomatic dinner hosted by Thomas Jefferson. Leaving the potato skin on French fries retains important vitamins that are lost if the skins are peeled away.

Refried beans aren't fried twice, although the name seems like a translation of Spanish frijoles refritos. In Spanish, refritos means well-fried, not refried.

In Los Angeles in 1926, a restaurant owner named Bob Cobb was looking for a way to use leftovers. He threw together avocado, celery, tomato, chives, watercress, hard-boiled eggs, chicken, bacon and Roquefort cheese, and named it after himself, Cobb salad.

Mincemeat was originally a medieval food made of a sweet, spicy mixture of chopped lean meat, (usually beef, or beef tongue), suet and fruit. Over time, the meat content was reduced and today, the mixture contains nuts, dried fruit, beef suet, spices and brandy or rum (but usually no beef).

Henderson William Brand, chef to England's King George IV, created A1 Steak Sauce® in the late 1820s. The king was so pleased with the new sauce he proclaimed it "A number 1." Supposedly it can be used for repairing scratches on wood furniture, shining brown shoes, and polishing tarnish from copper and brass. Some people say it relieves itching from insect bites.

Shrove Tuesday, also known as Pancake Day or Pancake Tuesday, is celebrated world-wide every year. Eating pancakes before Ash Wednesday (the first day of Lent) dates to over a thousand years ago. During Lent, foods such as eggs, flour, fat and sugar were not allowed to be eaten so Shrove Tuesday was the day to use the ingredients. Making pancakes was the best way to finish up these items. In the U.S., Pancake Day is commonly known as Mardi Gras (French for Fat Tuesday). The second side of a pancake takes half the amount of time to cook as the first.

During the Great Depression, there was a need to provide easily made food to millions of economically depressed people in the United States. One company patented a cake-bread mix, establishing the first line of cake in a box. The cake became a mass-produced item rather than a homemade or bakery-made dessert.

Contrary to popular beliefs, chocolate does not cause acne.

Fifty percent of U.S. pizzas are sold with pepperoni on them.

A company in Taiwan makes dinnerware out of wheat, so you can eat your plate!

A hardboiled egg will spin. An uncooked or soft-boiled egg will not.

An egg will float if placed in water in which sugar has been added.

An apple, potato, and onion all taste the same if you eat them while holding your nose

Food can only be tasted if it is mixed with saliva.

Early in the nineteenth century, the most widely published images of the American female form began to change from statuesque to slender. The Gibson Girl, lithe and athletic, exemplified this and by the 1920s the sleek fashions of the flapper era made a narrow figure a must. American women began dieting, a fad that originated in the white middle class but quickly became a mainstay of popular culture. Home lunches included cottage cheese and sales soared from the 1930s until the 1970s. Yogurt sales also increased but the most popular diet lunch for women in the twentieth century was salad.

Jane Cunningham Croly was an experienced editor and widely published journalist when she applied for a ticket to the New York Press Club dinner honoring Charles Dickens in 1868. A woman was not allowed to attend such a prestigious event. A month later, she founded the first organization in America dedicated to raising women's status, Sorosis Women's Club. The club met for lunch at Delmonico's, a venue chosen precisely because, like the city's other leading restaurants, it did not serve women unless they were escorted by men. Sitting down to lunch at Delmonico's was the club's first victory.

In the mid-fifteenth century in England, men wore their hats at the table to keep their long hair out of the food. Guests brought their own knives, and food was eaten with the fingers. Even though forks had been in use in Germany since the fourteenth century, English men and women still ate with their fingers a century later. As late as the sixteenth century, a preacher condemned forks as contrary to the will of God. There were no napkins, and guests were warned not to clean their teeth on the tablecloth. Handkerchiefs were also unknown, and men were requested to use their knife hand to blow their nose, not the hand whose fingers were used for food. Meat was the national food; vegetables were scarce and despised. Heavily spiced foods meant there was a lot of wine and beer consumed. Drunkenness was widespread.

The first napkin was a lump of dough the Spartans called apomagdalie, a mixture cut into small pieces and rolled and kneaded at the table (a custom that later led to using sliced bread to wipe the hands). In ancient Rome, napkins were known as sudaria (Latin for handkerchief) and mappae (a larger cloth spread over the edge of the couch as protection from food taken in a reclining position). Each guest supplied his own mappae and after the meal it was filled with delicacies leftover from the feast (like today's doggy bags).

In the early Middle Ages, hands and mouths were wiped on whatever was available (the back of the hand, clothing, or a piece of bread). Later, the table was laid with three cloths: The first cloth, called a *couch* (from the French word coucher, meaning 'to lie down'), was laid lengthwise before the master's place. A long towel called a surnappe (meaning 'on the cloth') was laid over the couch and indicated a place setting for an honored guest. The third cloth was a communal napkin that hung from the edge of the table. At medieval banquets, the ewerer, the person in charge of ablutions, carried a towel that the lord and his honored guests used to wipe their hands on. To demonstrate that the water for ablutions was not poisoned, the cup bearer kissed the towel on which the lord wiped his hands and draped the towel over the lord's left shoulder for use. The panter carried a portpayne, a napkin folded decoratively to carry the bread and knife used by the lord of the manor. The spoon was wrapped in another napkin.

By the sixteenth century, napkins were an accepted refinement of dining. In Elizabethan times (1558-1603), men knotted their napkins around their necks. This was difficult to do when wearing a stiffly starched ruff (a frilled collar), and led to the saying "making ends meet." When shirts with lace fronts became the style, napkins were tucked into the neck or buttonhole or were attached with a pin.

When the fork was accepted by royalty in the seventeenth century, the size of the napkin was reduced and neatness in dining was emphasized. The French court imposed elaborate codes of etiquette on the aristocracy, such as the person of highest rank in the company should unfold his napkin first. A fabric draped over the left arm of a maitre d' hotel, the man in charge of feasts, was a custom that continued into the eighteenth century. Around 1740, the tablecloth was made with matching napkins. The serviette was a large napkin used at the table. The serviette de collation was a smaller napkin used while standing to eat (similar to today's cocktail napkin). A touaille was a roller towel draped over a tube of wood or used as a communal towel that hung on the wall. In the United States today, a napkin is placed on the left of the plate but in Europe, the napkin is often laid to the right of the spoon.

"If napkins are distributed, yours should be placed on the left shoulder or arm;
goblet and knife go to the right, bread to the left."
Desiderius Erasmus
1466-1536
Dutch Catholic priest & theologian

Classic Diner or Lunch Counter Jargon

Adam and Eve on a raft – two poached eggs on toast

Adam and Eve on a raft and wreck em' – two scrambled eggs on toast

all the way – a burger with lettuce, mayonnaise, onion, and butter.
It may also refer to chocolate cake with chocolate ice cream.

A-pie – apple pie

ant paste – chocolate pudding

axle grease *or* cow paste – butter

baby *or* moo juice – glass of milk

bad breath – onion

bang berries *or* belly busters – baked beans

bank *or* black box – cash register

bark – hot dog with baked beans

battery acid – grapefruit juice

beans to go – coffee

beef on wreck – roast beef sandwich

bees – American cheese

belly chokers *or* sinkers – donuts

belly wash – soup

bib – napkin

birdseed – breakfast cereal

black cow – chocolate milk or milkshake

blond – coffee with cream

blond with sand – coffee with cream and sugar

bloodhounds in the hay – hot dogs with sauerkraut

blowout patches – pancakes

boiled leaves – tea

bowl of fire – chili

burn the British – toasted English muffin

burn one, take it through the garden, and pin a rose on it – put a hamburger on the grill and
add lettuce, tomato, and onion

canned cow – evaporated milk

Cat's eyes – tapioca pudding

CB – cheeseburger

Checkerboard – waffle

Chicago dog – steamed bun with relish

chicken in the hay – egg salad sandwich

city juice *or* Adam's Ale – a glass of water

clean up the kitchen – order of hash

cluck and grunt – eggs and bacon

cold mud – chocolate ice cream

cold spot *or* English winter – ice tea

cowboy with spurs – a western omelet with fries

cow feed *or* rabbit food – salad

cremate a blue bikini, cut – a well done, toasted blueberry muffin cut in four pieces

douse it – cover it in sauce

drag one through Wisconsin – add cheese

draw one in the dark – cup of black coffee

drown one, hold the hail – Coke® with no ice

dry – no condiments

dry stack – pancakes without butter and syrup

echo – repeat the order

eternal twins – ham and eggs

flop two – two fried eggs

Florida tonic – orange juice

fog – mashed potatoes

foreign entanglements – spaghetti

Friday's choice – fish dinner

frog sticks – French fries

full house – a grilled cheese, bacon, and tomato sandwich

Georgia pie – peach pie

give it shoes – take out order

grunt – bacon

heart attack on rack – biscuits and gravy

hockey puck – well-done hamburger

hold the grass – no lettuce

hope – oatmeal

houseboat – banana split

Irish turkey – corned beef and cabbage

java *or* joe – coffee

jerk – ice cream soda

kiss the pan – eggs over easy

looseners – prunes

love apples – tomatoes

lumber – toothpick

MD - Dr. Pepper®

make it cry – add onions

mama on a raft – marmalade on toast

melting snow – melted Swiss cheese

Mike & Ike *or* side arms – salt and pepper shakers

motor oil – syrup

nervous pudding – bowl of Jell-O®

no cow – without milk

on the hoof – cooked rare

on wheels – take out

one on the city – glass of water

paint a bow-wow red – hot dog with ketchup

paint it red – put ketchup on it

pig in a blanket – ham sandwich

pipes – straws

Pope Benedict – eggs Benedict

Popeye – spinach

put a hat on it – add ice cream

quail – goulash

radio (or tuna down) – a tuna fish sandwich on toast

raft – toast

ruff it – add whipped cream

saddle it – well done steak

sand – sugar

sea dust – salt

short stack – order of pancakes

sneeze – pepper

snowball – scoop of vanilla ice cream

sour it – add lemon

splash from the garden – bowl of soup

squeeze it – make it fast

steaming Idaho – baked potato

stretch *or* Atlanta Special – a Coke®

suds – beer

throw it in the mud – add chocolate syrup

top it red – add salsa

top it white – add sour cream

warts – olives

whiskey down – rye toast

yellow paint – mustard

zeppelin – sausage

What Food Each State Is Known For

Alabama	cheese grits
Alaska	salmon
Arizona	Mexican food
Arkansas	cheese dip
California	In-N-Out burger
Colorado	beef enchiladas
Connecticut	New Haven Pizza
Delaware	chicken
Florida	Cuban food
Georgia	peach cobbler
Hawaii	Spam®
Idaho	potatoes
Illinois	meat
Indiana	sugar cream pie
Iowa	corn-on-the-cob
Kansas	bread
Kentucky	fried chicken
Louisiana	crawfish
Maine	lobster
Maryland	crab
Massachusetts	clam chowder
Michigan	cherries
Minnesota	tater tots
Mississippi	biscuits and gravy
Missouri	BBQ
Montana	Rocky Mountain Oysters
Nebraska	Runzas (meat wrapped in a doughy pocket)
Nevada	the buffet
New Hampshire	cider doughnuts
New Jersey	salt water taffy

New Mexico	green chiles
New York	bagels
North Carolina	pork BBQ
North Dakota	bison burger
Ohio	buckeyes (chocolate and peanut butter candy)
Oklahoma	chicken fried steak
Oregon	marionberry pie
Pennsylvania	cheesesteak
Rhode Island	clam cakes
South Carolina	sweet tea
South Dakota	kuchen (sweet doughy pastry filled with fruit and custard)
Tennessee	hot chicken (doused with cayenne)
Texas	Tex-Mex
Utah	Jell-O®
Vermont	maple syrup
Virginia	apples
Washington	Pho (Vietnamese noodle soup)
West Virginia	pepperoni roll
Wisconsin	cheese
Wyoming	beef jerky

CHAPTER 10

National Food Days

National Food Days have been declared by the Federal government, designating a day (or week or month) dedicated to a particular item. The President of the United States has the authority to declare a special day by proclamation. Petitions are introduced by constituents, trade associations, or public relations firms. After the Food Day has been authorized, the petitioner finds ways to promote it to the public

Some state legislatures and governors proclaim special observance days, as do mayors of cities, which is why there can be two National Peanut Butter & Jelly Days. Industries, special interest groups, or non-profit organizations can also declare Food Days to promote their products. Many of these catch on and are celebrated year after year.

There is a food honored for every day of the year in the United States. Here are the National Food Days for each month. You will notice that some days celebrate more than one item and some things are celebrated on more than one day.

National Chocolate Cake Day is celebrated on January twenty-seventh
and National German Cake Day is honored on June eleventh.

JANUARY

1	National Bloody Mary Day
2	National Cream Puff Day
3	National Chocolate-Covered Cherry Day
4	National Spaghetti Day
5	National Whipped Cream Day
6	National Shortbread Day / National Bean Day
7	National Tempura Day
8	National English Toffee Day
9	National Apricot Day
10	National Bittersweet Chocolate Day
11	National Hot Toddy Day / National Milk Day
12	National Marzipan Day / National Curried Chicken Day / National Glazed Donut Day
13	National Peach Melba Day
14	National Hot Pastrami Sandwich Day
15	National Strawberry Ice Cream Day / National Fresh Squeezed Juice Day
16	National Fig Newton Day
17	National Hot Buttered Rum Day
18	National Gourmet Coffee Day / National Peking Duck Day
19	National Popcorn Day
20	National Cheese Lovers Day / National Buttercrunch Day
21	National Granola Bar Day / National New England Clam Chowder Day
22	National Blonde Brownie Day / National Southern Food Day
23	National Pie Day / National Rhubarb Pie Day
24	National Peanut Butter Day / National Lobster Thermidor Day
25	National Irish Coffee Day
26	National Peanut Brittle Day / National Pistachio Day
27	National Chocolate Cake Day
28	National Blueberry Pancake Day
29	National Corn Chip Day
30	National Croissant Day
31	National Hot Chocolate Day / National Brandy Alexander Day

FEBRUARY

1   National Baked Alaska Day / National Dark Chocolate Day / National Cake Pop Day
2   National Tater Tot Day / National Hash Day / National Frozen Yogurt Day
3   National Carrot Cake Day
4   National Homemade Soup Day / National Stuffed Mushroom Day
5   National Chocolate Fondue Day
6   National Frozen Yogurt Day / National Chow Mein Day
7   National Fettuccini Alfredo Day
8   National Potato Lovers Day / National Molasses Bar Day
9   National Bagels & Lox Day / National Pizza Day
10   National Cream Cheese Brownie Day
11   National Peppermint Patty Day
12   National Peanut Butter & Jelly Day / National Plum Pudding Day
13   National Italian Food Day
14   National Cream-Filled Chocolates Day
15   National Gum Drop Day / National Chewing Gum Day
16   National Almond Day
17   National Café Au Lait Day / National Indian Pudding Day / National Cabbage Day
18   National "Drink Wine" Day / National Crab Stuffed Flounder Day
19   National Chocolate Mint Day
20   National Muffin Day / National Cherry Pie Day
21   National Sticky Bun Day / National Biscuits & Gravy Day
22   National Sweet Potato Day / National Margarita Day / National Cherry Pie Day
23   National Banana Bread Day
24   National Tortilla Chip Day
25   National Chocolate-Covered Peanut Day / National Clam Chowder Day
26   National Pistachio Day
27   National Chili Day / National Strawberry Day
28   National Chocolate Soufflé Day
29   LEAP YEAR: National Surf & Turf Day / National Frog Legs Day

MARCH

1	National Peanut Butter Lovers Day / National Fruit Compote Day
2	National Banana Cream Pie day
3	National Cold Cuts Day / National Mulled Wine Day
4	National Pound Cake Day
5	National Cheese Doodle Day
6	National Frozen Food Day / National White Chocolate Cheesecake Day
7	National Cereal Day
8	National Peanut Cluster Day
9	National Crabmeat Day
10	National Ranch Dressing Day / National Blueberry Popover Day
11	National "Eat Your Noodles" Day / National Oatmeal-Nut Waffle Day
12	National Baked Scallops Day
13	National Chicken Noodle Soup Day / National Coconut Torte Day
14	National Potato Chips Day / (Pie) Pi Day (3.14)
15	National Peanut Lovers Day / National Pears Helene Day
16	National Artichoke Day
17	National Corned Beef & Cabbage Day / National Green Beer Day
18	National Sloppy Joe Day / National Oatmeal Cookie Day
19	National Chocolate Caramel Day
20	National Ravioli Day
21	National Crunchy Taco Day / National French Bread Day
22	National Water Day / National Bavarian Crepe Day
23	National Chips & Dip Day / National Melba Toast Day
24	National Cake Pops Day / National Chocolate-Covered Raisin Day
25	National Waffle Day / National Lobster Newburg Day / National Pecan Day
26	National Nougat Day / National Spinach Day
27	National Whiskey Day / National Spanish Paella Day
28	National Black Forest Cake Day / National Something On a Stick Day
29	National Lemon Chiffon Cake Day
30	National Turkey Neck Soup Day
31	National Oysters On the Half Shell Day / National Clams On the Half Shell Day

APRIL

1	National Sour Bread Day
2	National Peanut Butter & Jelly Day
3	National Chocolate Mousse Day
4	National Cordon Bleu Day
5	National Caramel Day / National Dandelion Day / National Raisin & Spice Bar Day
6	National Caramel Popcorn Day / National Tomato Day
7	National Coffee Cake Day / National Beer Day
8	National Empanada Day
9	National Almond Cookie Day
10	National Cinnamon Crescent Day
11	National Cheese Fondue Day
12	National Licorice Day / Grilled Cheese Sandwich Day
13	National Peach Cobbler Day
14	National Pecan Day
15	National Glazed Ham Day
16	National Eggs Benedict Day / National Mushroom Day
17	National Cheeseball Day
18	National Animal Crackers Day
19	National Rice Ball Day / National Garlic Day
20	National Pineapple Upside Down Cake Day
21	National Chocolate-Covered Cashew Day
22	National Jelly Bean Day
23	National Cherry Cheesecake Day
24	National Pigs-in-a-Blanket Day
25	National Zucchini Bread Day
26	National Pretzel Day
27	National Prime Rib Day
28	National Blueberry Pie Day
29	National Shrimp Scampi Day
30	National Oatmeal Cookie Day / National Raisin Day

MAY

1	National Chocolate Parfait Day
2	National Chocolate Mouse Day / National Truffles Day
3	National Raspberry Popover Day / National Raspberry Tart Day / National Chocolate Custard Day
4	National Homebrew Day / National Orange Juice Day / National Candied Orange Peel Day / National Hoagie Day
5	National Enchilada Day / National Chocolate Custard Day
6	National Beverage Day / National Crepes Suzette Day
7	National Leg of Lamb Day
8	National Coconut Cream Pie Day / National Empanada Day
9	National Shrimp Day / Butterscotch Brownie Day
10	National Liver & Onions Day / National Mocha Torte Day
11	National "Eat What You Want" Day
12	National Nutty Fudge Fay
13	National Apple Pie Day / Fruit Cocktail Day / National Hummus Day
14	National Buttermilk Biscuit Day
15	National Chocolate Chip Day
16	National Barbecue Day
17	National Cherry Cobbler Day
18	National Cheese Soufflé Day
19	National Devil's Food Cake Day
20	National Quiche Lorraine Day
21	National Strawberries & Cream Day
22	National Vanilla Pudding Day
23	National Taffy Day
24	National Escargot Day
25	National Brown-Bag-It Day / National Wine Day
26	National Blueberry Cheesecake Day / National Cherry Dessert Day
27	National Grape Popsicle Day
28	National Brisket Day / National Hamburger Day
29	National Biscuit Day
30	National Mint Julep Day
31	National Macaroon Day

JUNE

1	National Hazelnut Cake Day
2	National Rocky Road Day / National Rotisserie Chicken Day
3	National Egg Day / National Chocolate Macaroon Day
4	National Frozen Yogurt Day / National Eggs Benedict Day / National Cheese Day / National Applesauce Day
5	National Ketchup Day
6	National Applesauce Cake Day / National Gingerbread Day
7	National Chocolate Ice Cream Day
8	National Jelly-Filled Doughnut Day
9	National Strawberry-Rhubarb Pie Day
10	National Iced Tea Day / National Black Cow Day (Root Beer Float)
11	National German Chocolate Cake Day
12	National Peanut Butter Cookie Day
13	National Cupcake Lovers Day
14	National Strawberry Shortcake Day
15	National Lobster Day
16	National Fudge Day
17	National Apple Strudel Day / National Fresh Vegetables Day
18	National Cheesemakers Day /National Cherry Tart Day
19	National Martini Day
20	National Vanilla Milkshake Day
21	National Peaches & Cream Day
22	National Chocolate Éclair Day / National Onion Ring Day
23	National Pecan Sandy Day
24	National Praline Day
25	National Catfish Day / National Strawberry Parfait Day
26	National Chocolate Pudding Day
27	National Orange Blossom Day
28	National Tapioca Day
29	National Almond Buttercrunch Day
30	National Mai Tai Day / National Ice Cream Soda Day

JULY

1	National Ginger Snap Day
2	National "Eat Beans" Day
3	National Chocolate Wafer Day
4	National Barbecue Day / National Caesar Salad Day
5	National Apple Turnover Day / National Graham Cracker Day
6	National Fried Chicken Day
7	National Macaroni Day / National Strawberry Sundae Day
8	National Milk Chocolate with Almonds Day
9	National Sugar Cookie Day
10	National Pina Colada Day
11	National Mojito Day / National Blueberry Muffin Day
12	National Pecan Pie Day
13	National French Fry Day / National Franks & Beans Day
14	National Macaroni Day / National Grand Marnier Day
15	National Tapioca Pudding Day / National Gummi Worms Day
16	National Corn Fritter Day / National Spinach Day / National Ice Cream Day
17	National Peach Ice Cream Day
18	National Caviar Day
19	National Daiquiri Day
20	National Ice Cream Sundae Day / National Lollipop Day / National Fortune Cookie Day
21	National Junk Food Day / National Crème Brule Day
22	National Penuche Fudge Day / National Maple Syrup Day
23	National Vanilla Ice Cream Day / National Hot Dog Day
24	National Tequila Day
25	National Hot Fudge Sundae Day
26	National Coffee Milkshake Day / National Bagelfest
27	National Scotch Day
28	National Milk Chocolate Day / National Hamburger Day
29	National Lasagna Day / National Chicken Wing Day
30	National Cheesecake Day
31	National Raspberry Cake Day / National Cotton Candy Day

1	National Raspberry Cream Pie Day
2	National Ice Cream Sandwich Day
3	National Watermelon Day
4	National Chocolate Chip Cookie Day
5	National Waffle Day / National Oyster Day / National Chili Pepper Day
6	National Root Beer Float Day / National IPA Day (craft beer)
7	National Raspberries & Cream Day
8	National Frozen Custard Day / National Zucchini Day
9	National Rice Pudding Day
10	National S'mores Day / National Banana Split Day
11	National Panini Day / National Raspberry Tart Day
12	National Julienne Fries Day
13	National Filet Mignon Day
14	National Creamsicle Day
15	National Lemon Meringue Pie Day
16	National Rum Day / National Bratwurst Day
17	National Vanilla Custard Day
18	National Ice Cream Pie Day / National Soft-Serve Ice Cream Day
19	National Hot & Spicy Food Day / National Potato Day
20	National Lemonade Day / National Bacon Lovers Day / National Chocolate Pecan Pie Day
21	National Sweet Tea Day / National Spumoni Day
22	National Pecan Torte Day / National "Eat a Peach" Day
23	National Sponge Cake Day
24	National Peach Pie Day
25	National Whiskey Sour Day / National Banana Split Day / National Waffle Day
26	National Cherry Popsicle Day
27	National Pots de Crème Day / National Burger Day / National Banana Lovers Day
28	National Cherry Turnover Day
29	National Chop Suey Day / National Lemon Juice Day
30	National Toasted Marshmallow Day
31	National Trail Mix Day

SEPTEMBER

1 National Gyro Day

2 National Grits Day / National Cherry Popover Day

3 National Baby Back Ribs Day / National Welsh Rarebit Day (toasted bread covered in melted cheese and topped with mustard or spices).

4 National Macadamia Nut Day

5 National Cheese Pizza Day

6 National Coffee Ice Cream Day

7 National Beer Lovers Day / National Napoleon Day

8 National Date-Nut Bread Day

9 National "I Love Food" Day / National Steak au Poivre Day

10 National Hot Dog Day

11 National Hot Cross Bun Day

12 National Chocolate Milkshake Day

13 National Peanut Day

14 National Cream-Filled Doughnut Day

15 National Double Cheeseburger Day / National Linguini Day

16 National Guacamole Day / National Cinnamon-Raisin Bread Day / National Peach Pie Day

17 National Apple Dumpling Day / National Monte Cristo Sandwich Day

18 National Cheeseburger Day

19 National Butterscotch Pudding Day

20 National Rum Punch Day / National Punch Day

21 National Pecan Cookie Day

22 National Ice Cream Cone Day

23 National White Chocolate Day

24 National Cherries Jubilee Day

25 National Food Service Workers Day

26 National Key Lime Pie Day / National Pancake Day

27 National Chocolate Milk Day / National Corned Beef Hash Day

28 National Strawberry Cream Pie Day / National "Drink a Beer" Day

29 National Coffee Day / National Mocha Day

30 National Mulled Cider Day

OCTOBER

1	National Pumpkin Spice Day / National Homemade Cookie Day
2	National Fried Scallops Day
3	National Caramel Custard Day / National Soft Taco Day
4	National Taco Day / National Vodka Day
5	National Apple Betty Day (apple crisp)
6	National Noodle Day
7	National Frappe Day
8	National Fluffernutter Day
9	National Moldy Cheese Day / National Dessert Day / National Submarine Sandwich Day (Hoagie, Hero, Grinder)
10	National Angel Food Cake Day
11	National Sausage Pizza Day
12	National Pumpkin Pie Day / National Gumbo Day
13	National Yorkshire Pudding Day / National Peanut Festival / National Pumpkin Festival
14	National Dessert Day / National Chocolate-Covered Insect Day
15	National Mushroom Day / National Red Wine Day / National Chicken Cacciatore Day
16	National Oatmeal Day / National Liqueur Day / National World Food Day
17	National Pasta Day
18	National Chocolate Cupcake Day
19	National Seafood Bisque Day / National Oatmeal Muffin Day
20	National Brandied Fruit Day
21	National Pumpkin Cheesecake Day / National Apple Day
22	National Nut Day (the edible kind!)
23	National Boston Cream Pie Day
24	National Bologna Day
25	National Greasy Foods Day
26	National Mincemeat Day / National Pumpkin Day
27	National Potato Day / National American Beer Day
28	National Chocolate Day
29	National Oatmeal Day / National Pancake Day
30	National Candy Corn Day / National Doughnut Day
31	National Candy Apple Day / National Caramel Apple Day

NOVEMBER

1	National Bison Day / National Vinegar Day / National Fried Clam Day
2	National Deviled Eggs Day
3	National Sandwich Day
4	National Candy Day
5	National Doughnut Day
6	National Nachos Day
7	National Bittersweet Chocolate with Almonds Day
8	National Cappuccino Day
9	National Scrapple Day
10	National Vanilla Cupcake Day
11	National Sundae Day
12	National Pizza with the Works Except Anchovies Day
13	National Indian Pudding Day (corn pudding)
14	National Guacamole Day / National Pickle Appreciation Day
15	National Raisin Bran Cereal Day / National Bundt Cake Day
16	National Fast Food Day
17	National Baklava Day / National Homemade Bread Day
18	National Apple Cider Day / National Vichyssoise Day
19	National Macchiato Day / National Carbonated Beverage with Caffeine Day
20	National Peanut Butter Fudge Day
21	National Cranberry Day / National Gingerbread Cookie Day / National Stuffing Day
22	National Cranberry Relish Day / National Cashew Day
23	National Espresso Day
24	National Sardine Day
25	National Parfait Day / National "Eat with a Friend Day"
26	National Cake Day
27	National Bavarian Cream Pie Day
28	National French Toast Day
29	National Chocolate Day / National Lemon Cream Pie Day
30	National Mousse Day

1	National Pie Day / National Fried Clam Day
2	National Fritters Day
3	National Peppermint Latte Day / National Apple Pie Day
4	National Cookie Day
5	National Comfort Foods Day / National Sacher Torte Day
6	National Gazpacho Day
7	National Cotton Dandy Day
8	National Brownie Day
9	National Pastry Day
10	National Lager Day
11	National "Have a Bagel" Day / National Noodle Ring Day
12	National Gingerbread House Day / National Ambrosia Day / National Cocoa Day
13	National Popcorn String Day
14	National Biscuits & Gravy Day / National Bouillabaisse Day
15	National Cupcake Day
16	National Chocolate-Covered Anything Day
17	National Maple Syrup Day
18	National "I Love Honey" Day
19	National Hard Candy Day / National Oatmeal Muffin Day
20	National Sangria Day
21	National Kiwi Day / National Fried Shrimp Day / National Hamburger Day
22	National Date-Nut Bread Day
23	National Bake Day / National Pfeffernuesse Day (small spice cookies)
24	National Egg Nog Day
25	National Pumpkin Pie Day
26	National Candy Cane Day
27	National Fruitcake Day
28	National Chocolate Candy Day
29	National Pepper Pot Day
30	National Baking Soda Day / National Bicarbonate of Soda Day
31	National Champagne Day

Other books by Nancy Slade

A Guidebook for Chocoholics

Do you know just how many companies will deliver a chocolate fix directly to your home? In *A Guidebook for Chocoholics*, chocolate lover Nancy Slade answers this question and innumerable others, walking the reader through a history of the confection, explaining how it is processed from bean-to-bar, recommending several chocolate shops, cafes, and chocolate events around the world—and supplementing it all with lively anecdotes about her own love of the treat.

Palate Pleasing Places

From authentic Italian to locally sourced and organic, from San Francisco to the Florida Keys, no matter your preference, this delightful book has the restaurant recommendations for you. *Palate Pleasing Places* takes readers on a tour of eateries of every style and persuasion. It begins with the historic, exploring tavern and inns, many of which predate the American Revolution. Others developed their reputations serving suds covertly during Prohibition. The preponderance were founded in modern times but have made names for themselves by boasting unique or interesting menu items, traditions, décor, and ambiance. These restaurants pride themselves for being incomparable in the truest sense of the word, offering patrons a dining experience unlike anything you've ever seen before.

The Cocoa Café – A Story with Chocolate Recipes

Meet Gina Scott, a sixty-four year old retired school teacher who has embarked on a new career as a pastry chef at The Cocoa Café. Gina shows us that life holds many delightful adventures no matter what our age may be. *The Cocoa Café* takes readers on a culinary journey to a fictitious café set in a real place: downtown Tampa, Florida. Some historical and current information has been added to enhance the story. Although the characters are a creation of the author's imagination, the chocolate recipes that are interspersed throughout the book are very much real. Because she didn't want to assemble the recipes in a traditional cookbook style, the author wrote a story that revolves around chocolate treats.

The Cocoa Café 2 – A Year of Chocolate

Gina Scott's adventures as pasty chef continue in the sequel to *The Cocoa Café*. This delightful book includes an entire year of chocolate recipes!

Recipes from The Cocoa Café – Beyond Chocolate

A cookbook that contains a collection of non-chocolate recipes for the foods mentioned in both *The Cocoa Café* books.

Millie, A Chihuahua's Adventures

Little Millie the Chihuahua is busy celebrating her seventh birthday with the other animals in the neighborhood. But that's just the beginning of her adventures. In the year ahead, she'll come face-to-face with a real-life manatee, spend a day at Lake Frilly, and eventually welcome a new member into the home she shares with a nice lady and man. Follow along as Millie plays in the sun, experiences her first Halloween, and gets into trouble … on more than one occasion.

www.ingramcontent.com/pod-product-compliance
Lightning Source LLC
Chambersburg PA
CBHW080717260726
48660CB00010B/3579